TVA Archaeology

TVA Archaeology

Seventy-five Years of Prehistoric Site Research

Edited by Erin E. Pritchard
with Todd M. Ahlman

THE UNIVERSITY OF TENNESSEE PRESS | KNOXVILLE

Frontispiece: Guntersville Basin Survey. Ross Site (28MS134), August 1939.
(Courtesy of the University of Alabama Museums, Tuscaloosa, AL.)

Portions of chapter one were originally published in *TVA Photography:
Thirty Years of Life in the Tennessee Valley* and *TVA Photography, 1963–2008:
Challenges and Changes in the Tennessee Valley* by Patricia Bernard Ezzell, copy-
right 2003 and 2008, respectively, by the University Press of Mississippi. Reprinted by permission of the University Press of Mississippi.

The paper in this book meets the requirements of American National Standards
Institute / National Information Standards Organization specification Z39.48-1992
(Permanence of Paper). It contains 30 percent post-consumer waste and is certified
by the Forest Stewardship Council.

Library of Congress Cataloging-in-Publication Data

TVA archaeology: seventy-five years of prehistoric site research /
edited by Erin E. Pritchard with Todd M. Ahlman. — 1st ed.
   p. cm.
Includes bibliographical references and index.
ISBN-13: 978-1-57233-650-6 (hardcover: alk. paper)
ISBN-10: 1-57233-650-1 (hardcover: alk. paper)
   1. Indians of North America—Tennessee River Valley—Antiquities.
2. Prehistoric peoples—Tennessee River Valley.
3. Antiquities, Prehistoric—Tennessee River Valley.
4. Excavations (Archaeology)—Tennessee River Valley.
5. Historic sites—Conservation and restoration—Tennessee River Valley.
6. Tennessee River Valley—Antiquities.
7. Archaeology—Research—Tennessee River Valley—History—20th century.
8. Archaeology—Research—United States—History—20th century.
9. Tennessee Valley Authority—History. I. Pritchard, Erin E.

E78.T33T89 2009
976.8—dc22
2008032081

Contents

Part I

TVA and the WPA

Part II

Scientific Breakthroughs in Southeastern Archaeology

Part III

History Revisited

Part IV

Current Research Endeavors in the Valley

Part V

TVA and Future Stewardship in the Tennessee River Valley

Illustrations

Figures

Plates

Tables

Preface

THIS VOLUME INCORPORATES a broad spectrum of research conducted the last 75 years that is both directly and indirectly related to the agency. Early on it was clear to the editor that such an assemblage honoring the agency's efforts was much needed. Although the TVA cannot boast a perfect record in archaeological compliance and has seen its fair share of failures, this federal agency made some of the earliest efforts to consider the archaeological record that was being lost by its actions.

As TVA entered its seventy-fifth year of operation, it carried with it a unique history of both innovative change and experimental misfortune. While most archaeological endeavors conducted by government agencies have been directly related to legislation requiring consideration of the effects of its operations on historic properties, TVA has been committed to stewardship efforts beyond those required by law. The agency's support is manifested in its contributions to academic research, publication of archaeological material for both the public and scholar, and proactive efforts to protect and preserve the archaeological resources within its custody.

These efforts, however, cannot be considered heroic, as development on private property along the shorelines of TVA's numerous reservoirs has affected many archeological sites. Although TVA has no purview over many of these actions, it has been forced into this position by its dual role as an agency spurring development for the Tennessee Valley and an agency required to preserve the archaeological record. Criticisms of TVA regarding this development and its failures of the past are certainly based in fact but are not entirely warranted, given the tasks placed on TVA and its cultural resource managers. Though a debate and review of TVA's sometimes-checkered past is needed, it is beyond the scope and intent of this volume. Rather, *TVA Archaeology* is meant to address the past, present, and future research in the valley and TVA's role in this research.

These chapters offer a sampling of those projects that have stood out, those that have defined TVA archaeology, and those that define TVA's current role as a land-managing agency. It was not feasible within the confines of one volume to incorporate all of the many archaeological-related research efforts conducted on behalf or at the behest of the agency. The theme of this volume is the TVA's stewardship, that is, its management of the resources within its domain.

Part 1 focuses on TVA's history. The agency's history correlates with its archaeological efforts as it struggled through world wars, changing politics, and monumental budgets cuts. In the first chapter Pat Bernard Ezzell gives a brief history of the agency and how it has evolved from being part of President Roosevelt's New Deal programs to a nearly corporate power-generating company. Touching on the major events that occurred in the last seventy-five years Bernard-Ezzell provides the reader with an understanding of how major changes in the agency have affected its stewardship role in the valley. As a complementary piece, the second chapter, by Danny E. Olinger and A. Eric Howard, summarizes the history of TVA's direct archaeological efforts. Following the agency from its earliest stages to its last monumental reservoir project, Olinger and Howard outline both positive and negative aspects of TVA's archeological stewardship through the years.

After passage of the National Historic Preservation Act in 1966, TVA's reservoir projects led to several large-scale archaeological efforts that correlated with significant breakthroughs in scientific techniques related to the field. Part 2 focuses on the effects these breakthroughs have had on our understandings of archaeological research in the valley. The next two chapters chronicle two large-scale reservoir projects that occurred in the 1970s. Charles Faulkner examines the archaeological research in the Normandy Reservoir area and Gerald Schroedl the Tellico Reservoir; both document TVA's struggles with the relatively new legislation that required federal agencies to take into account the effects that these new reservoirs would have on archaeological sites. The research on these reservoirs often incorporated the latest research methods (i.e., flotation and archaeomagnetic dating) to interpret the past. Although these projects were scientifically successful in their own right, they also served another role in training a generation of future archaeologists.

In the third chapter in this section, Sarah Sherwood examines the significance of geomorphological investigations in the Tennessee Valley and how this research has changed our understanding of southeastern prehistory. Examples draw from research across the Tennessee River Valley and its tributaries show that geoarchaeological research has helped us to understand how past people utilized their environments. This research is significant because it demonstrates that in one river valley many different forces were acting on the landscape and therefore affecting how people interacted with their respective environments.

Part 3 focuses on the reexamination of data generated by archaeological investigation during the WPA era. Both Sissel Schroeder and Lynne Sullivan in their respective chapters have revisited and reexamined the archaeological collections and sites to two very significant excavation projects from the 1930s. These studies emphasize that the investigations by the WPA crews, made up of local workers directed by trained archaeologists, practiced solid archaeological investigations resulting in data that is useful even more than seventy-five years later. In addition, the cultural material from these investigations can be used to address the questions of concern to today's archaeologists. Schroeder studies the ceramic chronology and occupation of the Jonathan Creek site in western Kentucky and addresses several misconceptions by examining the site's role in a regional context. Sullivan looks at the occupational history of several sites in the Chickamauga basin, particularly examining their reoccupation during the Mississippian period.

Part 4 deals with current research being conducted in the Tennessee Valley. In its first chapter, Jan Simek, Sarah Blankenship, and Alan Cressler discuss two significant archaeological cave-art sites and one pictograph site in the Tennessee Valley, containing some of the most impressive prehistoric art in all of the southeastern United States. For more than ten years, Simek and his numerous coworkers have recorded a variety of art sites throughout the Southeast, and their work has demonstrated how important it is for the TVA to preserve these sites. TVA not only helped fund the research at these sites, but also has taken measures to protect cave-art sites by gating the entrances.

Boyce Driskell notes in the next chapter that Dust Cave in Alabama has been a laboratory for archeological research by numerous students since investigations were undertaken in the 1980s. These efforts have added to our understanding of Late Pleistocene and Early Holocene life in the middle Tennessee River Valley. One of the significant aspects of Driskell's research has been the development of an outreach program that involves volunteers and teachers, exposing nonarchaeologists to archaeology.

The final section, part 5, looks toward the future of TVA. Although the agency continues to change in reaction to competing demands, it maintains a strong commitment to the environment. This reflects the agencies three-fold mission to provide affordable and reliable power, promote sustainable economic development, and act as a steward of the valley's natural resources.

In the first chapter of part 5, Scott Meeks details the importance of cultural resource management (CRM) in the realm of scientific research by analyzing data acquired by TVA-related undertakings. Meeks argues that the collection of archaeological data through CRM projects should maintain a systematic value so that it can be useful in its most simple form. And, in the volume's final chapter, I outline a brief history of stewardship at TVA and discusses its current efforts to manage its resources while maintaining a balance with its mission.

It is hoped that this volume will provide a glimpse of the types of research being conducted on behalf of TVA. It contains only a sampling of the projects that have occurred over the agency's 75-year history. In the Tennessee Valley, a great amount of archaeological investigations were the direct result of cultural resource management, and, as time passes, it is clear that stewardship of archaeological resources is ever more important as development continues to expand in both the Tennessee River Valley and on a national scale. In addition to this volume's effort to highlight these regional endeavors, it also seeks to encourage the archaeological community to partner with agencies and improve the stewardship of these vast archaeological resources.

ERIN E. PRITCHARD

Acknowledgments

THIS VOLUME WAS INSPIRED by my experience as a TVA archaeologist. In my relatively short history at TVA, I have been proud to work alongside a team of professionals so dedicated to the preservation of such an enormous collection of resources. I would like to take this opportunity to acknowledge and thank J. Bennett Graham, Danny E. Olinger, Richard Yarnell, A. Eric Howard, Pat Bernard Ezzell, Tom Maher, Marianne Shuler, and Ted Wells for their commitment to the agency and the resources it manages. Without their support this manuscript would not have been possible. In addition I would like to acknowledge members of our very supportive management team, past and present: Kate Jackson, Bridget Ellis, Buff Crosby, Anda Ray, and Dan Ferry have aided the cultural resources staff and have provided funding for some of the stewardship efforts presented in this volume. Among the many individuals who lent a helping hand, I would especially like to thank Amy D. Wyatt, whose encouragement and support helped me step outside the box and follow my inspiration.

Some of the material in this book resulted from discussions and considerations at the Southeastern Archaeological Conference (SEAC) in Charlotte, North Carolina, in 2003, where TVA sponsored a symposium on current research involving archaeology. Grateful acknowledgment is made for those beginnings, which led me to encourage and assemble this broader perspective of TVA efforts through the years.

Finally, specific thanks and gratitude go to Todd Ahlman who devoted many hours helping me initiate and edit an early version of this volume. His time, effort, and encouragement are deeply appreciated.

PART I
TVA AND THE WPA

1
TVA: Built for the
People of the United States
Patricia Bernard Ezzell

IN 1972 Charles Crawford, director of the Oral History Research Office at Memphis State University (now the University of Memphis), interviewed Thomas M. N. Lewis and Madeline Kneberg Lewis at their home in Winter Haven, Florida, regarding the TVA's early archaeological efforts. Crawford asked T. M. N. Lewis, "Do you know if any agency had ever before been concerned with the preservation of this sort of [archaeological] material, which would be lost as a result of its activity?" Crawford went on to observe: "It seems rather unusual to me that TVA was this concerned with minimizing its impact on the area and possibly losing valuable archaeological resources. I don't know that that had ever been considered before when dams were being built." Lewis replied that the Smithsonian had watched this situation around the country and that universities had field archaeologists, but he did not name another agency with such a program (Kneberg and Kneberg 1972). TVA's early archaeological work, beginning with the Norris basin in 1934, is just one example of the innovative spirit so common in those first heady days of the agency's creation.

For 75 years, the Tennessee Valley Authority (TVA) has demonstrated this innovative spirit as it has become a unique and profound presence in the Tennessee Valley. While most people today associate the agency with their electric bill, TVA is, and always has been, more than just a power company. TVA defines itself as a federal corporation and is proud to be both the nation's largest public power company and a regional economic development agency. Besides operating fossil-fueled plants, nuclear plants, hydropower plants, and producing energy from renewable resources throughout Tennessee and parts of Alabama, Georgia, Kentucky, Mississippi, North Carolina, and Virginia, TVA also manages the Tennessee River—the nation's fifth largest river system—to minimize flood risk, produce power, maintain navigation, provide recreational opportunities, and protect water quality in the 41,000-square-mile watershed (TVA 2006a).

TVA's goals in the twenty-first century are to provide affordable and reliable power, to promote sustainable economic development, and to act as a steward of the valley's natural resources (TVA 2006b). While TVA is very much a modern organization wanting to generate prosperity in the valley and to improve the quality of every life, it is noteworthy that its current goals and values hark back to its original mission: "To improve the navigability and to provide for the flood control of the Tennessee River; to provide for reforestation and the proper use of marginal lands in the Tennessee Valley; to provide for the agricultural and industrial development of said Valley; to provide for the national defense by the creation of a corporation for the operation of Government properties at and near Muscle Shoals in the State of Alabama, and for other purposes" (TVA Act 1933). By working to complete this mission, TVA transformed the Tennessee Valley.

While on the surface just another of FDR's alphabet agencies to stimulate the depressed economy, TVA was actually the result of a variety of national and regional movements and events. The agency can trace its roots back to the progressive era of the late nineteenth century. In the 1890 census the American frontier was declared closed. As the frontier faded into the nation's collective memory, the public began to express concern about the environment. This public awareness of natural resources and their proper use led to the nation's first conservation movement. An early proponent of conservation, Gifford Pinchot contributed the concept of unified resource development. Pinchot, chief forester of the United States, believed that a delicate relationship existed between people and nature. He espoused that the individual resources, such as the rivers and the forests, should not be looked at as separate entities, but rather as one unified resource. Impacts to forests would in turn affect rivers, with repercussions continuing throughout the ecosystem. Pinchot wanted to manage the resources for the good of the people, but not at the expense of the resources. This idea was to become the foundation of the TVA Act (Hargrove and Conkin 1983:7–8).[1]

Strategic and military concerns also contributed to the development of the TVA. America's decision to enter World War I made Congress fear that the nation's access to nitrates—an essential ingredient in the production of explosives—would be terminated by German naval operations. The United States still relied on Chilean guano—essentially bat dung—as the source of this critical military resource. In response to this potentially disastrous problem, the National Defense Act of 1916 authorized immediate construction of two nitrate plants to be powered by an adjacent hydroelectric facility. Government engineers selected Muscle Shoals, Alabama, located on the Tennessee River, as the construction site. Surveys noted that it had the most potential for the development of water power east of the Rockies. Construction on the dam began in 1918. The war ended, however, before the facilities could begin production (Hubbard 1961).

For the next 15 years, Congress struggled over what to do with the Muscle Shoals properties. Hydroelectric power could easily be used to promote economic development and nitrates, manufactured in the plants, could be used to produce fertilizer. Thus the proposed purpose of the facility shifted from national defense to domestic production. It was at this time that Henry Ford made a much publicized offer to purchase the $130 million complex for $5 million. Ford promised to make Muscle Shoals the "Detroit of the South," and many locals, as well as the labor unions, backed Ford's vision. However, Ford faced a strong opponent in Senator George W. Norris of Nebraska. Norris opposed Ford's offer because he felt the public sector should control the development of natural resources. He proposed that the Alabama facility be utilized as part of a plan for unified resource development of the Tennessee River. Congress debated the auto tycoon's offer, but he ultimately withdrew his bid, citing seemingly endless delays (Hubbard 1961). The debate over Muscle Shoals continued until the advent of the Depression, when national priorities, and the political climate, underwent a dramatic change.

After the economic boom of the 1920s came to a crash in 1929, the country entered the Great Depression, an unprecedented economic disaster. Nationally statistics were grim: one in four workers was unemployed; many of those employed had only part-time work. Because they had no income or their income had decreased, many people could not pay their mortgages and lost their homes. Others lost their life savings as banks across America failed. Farm prices dropped by 55 percent between 1929 and 1932 (Himmelberg 2001). While the nation endured hard times, it was especially difficult living in the Tennessee Valley. Dr. Arthur E.

Morgan, TVA's first chairman, testified that in the fall of 1933 there were counties in the Southern Highlands with more than 50 percent of the families on relief. Morgan pointed out that there were many "prosperous communities" in the valley region, but that "a considerable part of the population is on the verge of starvation." Morgan characterized the problem as "a very desperate economic situation" (Duffus 1946:53).

Starvation was not the only problem for the people of the Tennessee Valley. Many suffered from "debilitating diseases such as malaria and hookworm" (Huxley 1959:10). Primitive farming practices resulted in soil depletion and erosion. It was not unexpected that half of the valley population was on relief; the per capita income of those in the Tennessee Valley region was half that of the country as a whole. The birthrate was one-third above the national average. Levels of literacy were low, and the labor force was largely unskilled. Only three farms in 100 had electricity. Unchecked fires burned 10 percent of the region's woodlands every year, and poor logging practices had nearly denuded forests that once offered endless miles of virgin timber (TVAb 1983:9). A Florence, Alabama, newspaper editor's assessment of the valley in 1933 was that "we were flat on our backs in the street and there were no cars to run over us" (Krutch 1969:2).

Therefore, in 1933 the political and economic climate, both nationally and regionally, was ripe for the creation of TVA. FDR quickly threw his support behind the Norris plan as part of his New Deal program to revitalize the economy. Following the principles of unified resource development, or integrated resource management, as it is known today, Congress gave TVA broad charges. The agency was to regulate the flow of the Tennessee River system to create a deep-water navigation channel in the Tennessee River and to regulate flood waters in the Tennessee and lower Mississippi valleys. As a by-product of flood control, TVA would also produce inexpensive electrical power. The agency would provide for reforestation and for the agricultural and industrial development of the valley. National defense measures and the operation of experimental chemical plants for the development of new fertilizer materials and for manufacture of munitions in times of national emergency also remained an important concern. In addition, TVA was charged with caring for conservation and development of natural resources in the Tennessee River basin (TVA Act 1933). Roosevelt stated in a 1933 visit to Muscle Shoals that "With the help of Congress, we are going to put the Tennessee Valley back on the map. We will make Muscle Shoals a part of an even greater development that will take in all the Tennessee

River from the mountains of Virginia to the Ohio River. . . . We will tie industry, agriculture, forestry and flood control into one great develop- ment" (Roosevelt 1938:886–888).

Taking the president's words to heart and hoping for a more pros- perous future, residents of East Tennessee embraced the TVA. As soon as the *Knoxville News-Sentinel* distributed an extra edition announcing the newly created agency, the town of Coal Creek in Anderson County, Tennessee, went wild. "Whistles blew and church bells rang. A parade of 100 cars and trucks carrying jubilant Coal Creek citizens went to Clinton, then back to Coal Creek to dance in downtown" (*Knoxville News-Sentinel* May 19, 1933:1). Almost immediately the city of Knox- ville, Tennessee, turned its energies toward a giant celebration. "I don't care how much suds flows [*sic*]," shouted Dr. W. S. Nash, a former coun- cilman, as he pleaded for an immediate celebration. "This is the time of all times to rejoice," he declared. "Is there any reason why we shouldn't jump and crack our heels together?" (*Knoxville News-Sentinel* May 19, 1933:1) And the people of Knoxville did rejoice. City and county offices closed as the "Let's Go East Tennessee" Depression Funeral Parade made its way up Gay Street. Bands played, girls marched, and men wearing red, white, and blue hats carried noisemakers. The postmaster of Coal Creek drove his car in the parade with banners proclaiming Coal Creek as "the best town by a dam site." After the parade the festivities contin- ued as Knoxville played Chattanooga in a ballgame, and there was an open-air dance at Market Square to end the evening (*Knoxville News Sentinel* May 22, 1933:1).

While East Tennessee celebrated the new agency, George Norris expressed what the TVA might mean to the nation: "It establishes a new governmental policy which, when carried to its logical end, will bring blessings of peace and comfort to all of our people." He went on to say that "generations now unborn, assembled around millions of happy firesides will thank God for the vision of President Roosevelt and render praise to his memory for signing this bill" (*New York Times* 1933).

FDR appointed and the Senate confirmed three men to lead the agency: Dr. Arthur E. Morgan, president of Antioch College and well- known hydroelectric engineer of the Miami Conservancy; Dr. H. A. Morgan, president of the University of Tennessee, well known in the field of agricultural studies and a highly regarded friend of the farmer; and David E. Lilienthal, a graduate of Harvard Law School and attor- ney for the Wisconsin Public Power Board. With this first TVA Board meeting held in Washington, D.C., in June 1933, TVA began its legacy of change in the valley, transforming the Tennessee Valley from a rural, backward region to a more urban, industrialized area. The agency, acting alone or in conjunction with other federal, state, or local agencies, tackled the problems that led to its creation. By June 1940, a short seven years after its creation, TVA had completed six multipurpose dams and had four more under construction. From Muscle Shoals, Alabama, to Chattanooga, Tennessee, the navigation channel was 2 feet deep when TVA was created. By 1940 the same stretch of river now had a navigable waterway with a depth of at least 6 feet. As a result river traffic increased from 22,482,000 ton-miles in 1933 to 70,700,000 in 1939. The six completed reservoirs also provided approximately 4,000,000 acre-feet of controlled storage for flood waters. By 1939 TVA's power system was the largest in the South and one of the 10 largest in the United States (TVA 1969).

In a short time TVA had completed some amazing tasks, but it must be noted that its achievements were not without personal cost and sacrifice for many in the valley region. Families who had farmed the same land for generations were suddenly confronted with the realization that their farms would soon be underwater. Besides the removal of thousands of families from their homes, thousands of graves were also relocated, according to the wishes of the next of kin when possible. While TVA paid fair market value for property and tried its best to appease families in the relocation process, many resented the sacrifices they had made (TVA 1939:485–538).[2]

TVA was making great strides in fulfilling its mission, but by the 1940s the agency's attention quickly turned from improving the Tennessee Valley to assisting in the war effort. David Lilienthal, then the chairman of the agency's Board of Directors, placed TVA into the wartime perspective: "We have transformed the ploughshares of peace into a sword of war in defense of democracy, and our blows are felt around the world—in airplanes over Berlin, in bombs rocking the docks in Palermo, in merchant ships carrying military supplies to far-off ports. Because of our labors of peacetime, the Tennessee Valley has become a sturdy weapon of war" (*Nashville Tennessean* 1943:2).

Because TVA was already in place and functioning, the agency was able to provide enormous contributions to the war effort. TVA, in order to supply additional electric power for war industries, engaged in one of the largest construction programs ever undertaken in the United States. At its wartime peak in 1942, TVA had under construction 12 hydroelectric projects and a large steam plant (TVA 1954). Tied directly to the construction of the power facilities was the need to provide enough cheap electricity to power various war industries. At war's end the TVA system was producing power at a rate approaching 12 billion kilowatt hours annually, approximately 75 percent of which was devoted to war production. TVA power went into aluminum, chemical, electrometallurgical, and munitions plants, the products of which were essential in war. While the agency was not directly involved in the development of the atomic bomb, TVA's Project Planning Branch was unknowingly involved in determining the eventual site of the Manhattan Project facilities in nearby Oak Ridge, Tennessee. In fact, if TVA had not already been in place in the region, it is doubtful that the site would have been selected. In explaining the birth of Oak Ridge, an Atomic Energy official stated: "We needed an isolated location. And the valley beneath Black Oak Ridge in Tennessee gave us that. We needed labor. And the people of Tennessee gave us that. But most of all we needed electric power, an enormous amount of electric power to supply the electric-magnetic process involved in producing the atom bomb. And the Tennessee Valley Authority gave us that" (McBride 1975).

Besides supplying power to wartime industries, TVA contributed to the national defense in other ways. For example, the agency supplied more than 60 percent of the elemental phosphorus required by our armed forces for use in smoke and incendiary bombs, shells, tracer bullets, and other munitions. The agency's Maps and Surveys Branch mapped nearly one-half million square miles of foreign territory for the Army Map Service, and TVA developed mass-produced housing for war workers (TVA 1987). A *New York Times* editorial eloquently summed up TVA's significance to the war effort: the Tennessee Valley Authority was "worth to the country many divisions of troops, many ships, and many airplanes. What it does and can do might make the difference between victory and defeat or even between peace and war" (*New York Times* 1954:12).

TVA's war effort was successful, and so too was its reconversion to peacetime. The valley, like other parts of the nation, enjoyed the prosperity of the postwar economy. Industries moved into the region to take advantage of the cheap electricity offered by TVA, which averaged less than 1 cent per kilowatt-hour. Other incentives for industrial relocation included a dependable year-round navigation channel, flood-free building sites, and a cheap and abundant labor force. However, by the early 1950s TVA discovered that the demand for electricity was outpacing the capacity of the dams and the river system to produce it. As a result the agency began building coal-fired steam plants, and by 1955 coal surpassed hydropower as the system's primary source of energy (TVA 1969).

At the same time, a revolution was taking place on Tennessee farms. TVA-developed fertilizers and improved management techniques for both row-crop and livestock agriculture helped valley farmers heal the ravaging erosion of the 1930s, restore soil fertility, and increase agricultural production. For example, in the 25 years between 1934 and 1960, the area planted to corn dropped from 3.5 million acres to 1.8 million acres, or 49 percent, while the average yield per acre increased more than 78 percent. During the same period the value of livestock and livestock products sold increased 559 percent, from $49.3 million to $324 million. TVA's agricultural programs became a model for agricultural extension services, and the agency's new fertilizers and its test-demonstration method of introducing new farming practices were adopted throughout the nation (TVA 1969).

As 40-hour workweeks and time-saving electric appliances became commonplace in most homes, a growth in the recreational and tourism industries followed. With its many TVA reservoirs, the valley was able to take advantage of this national trend. By 1963 the water surface on the TVA reservoirs had increased to 600,000 acres with 10,000 miles of shoreline. Many types of water sports, as well as picnicking and camping, became popular activities for families in the region. To demonstrate the recreation potential, TVA built five parks with overnight accommodations on its reservoirs' shoreline—some of the first such parks in the nation. It turned these parks over to the states, which used them in later years as a springboard for developing their own park systems. TVA also began construction of its own national recreation area, Land Between the Lakes (LBL). Within a day's drive for 70 million people located in the large industrial centers of the East and Midwest, LBL was the prototype for outdoor recreation in the United States (TVA 1969).

Also during the postwar period, national and international interest in TVA's regional approach to development increased. TVA, long studied as a regional development agency, began training others in unified resource management planning. Agency power-generating plants also became a regular stop for many foreign dignitaries. In 1963 TVA entertained 2,597 visitors from 88 foreign countries, and the agency began to influence international planning and development. For example, the plan for Damodar Valley in India, aimed at irrigation, power production, navigation, and the reduction of floods, was modeled closely after TVA (TVA 1963).[3] On the national level, Congress approved an amendment to the TVA Act that gave the agency authority to issue bonds to finance the construction of its own power plants. Until then TVA had relied on congressional appropriations to supply the funds needed for new plants. The new legislation, signed in 1959, made the TVA power system self-financing. This amendment also defined the geographic limits of the TVA power service area and prohibited territorial expansion into areas served by private companies.

Thus, by 1963, 30 years after the creation of the agency, TVA, as President John F. Kennedy remarked at TVA's thirtieth anniversary celebration, stood for progress, and this progress was evident throughout the Tennessee Valley. A stairway of nine dams and reservoirs provided a continuous 9-foot river navigation channel permitting the movement of more than 13 million tons of commercial freight traffic annually. TVA's multiple-use reservoir system also provided 12 million acre-feet of water storage, making serious floods a thing of the past. Average annual home use of electricity in the TVA region exceeded 10,000 kilowatt-hours per customer during fiscal year 1963, a dramatic contrast with 600 kilowatt-hours per customer in 1933. TVA generated 46 times as much power in 1963 as it did in 1933—power used in homes, on farms, and in business and industry. The agency, which began work on one kind of fertilizer, concentrated superphosphate, in the 1930s, now produced large quantities of 10 different fertilizer materials. Educational programs using TVA fertilizers operated in four-fifths of the states in cooperation with land-grant agricultural colleges and industry. The agency had also provided more than 570 million seedlings for reforestation, restoring large tracts of the southern landscape.[4]

TVA, partnering with state and local governments and other federal agencies, transformed the Tennessee Valley region.[5] In many ways the first 30 years proved to be a golden age for the agency. It accomplished what it set out to do: improve navigation, control flooding, and provide affordable electricity to the people of the Tennessee Valley. Certainly the agency was not without its problems during these years: the issue of its constitutionality, the personality clashes of the first board members, the family removals and grave relocations, for example, were but a few of the controversies faced in the first decades. However, these early controversies paled in comparison to what TVA would face later.

In 1964 the agency's focus remained on many of the same issues that it had been working on since its creation: improving (and increasing navigation) on the Tennessee River, providing flood control, and cheap electricity. Agricultural and fertilizer research continued to be a major responsibility, but forestry, recreation, fish and wildlife, and tributary area development became more important to the TVA organization (TVA 1969). By 1967 a subtle shift in the agency's priorities can be seen: a chapter in that year's annual report is titled "Conservation in the 'New Generation.'" Issues addressed include steam-plant improvement, strip-mine reclamation, fertilizer-plant modernization, and halting out-migration. By the next year, the cover-photo caption on the first page of the report states that the "giant cooling towers at Paradise Steam Plant reflect one aspect of TVA's concern for maintaining the quality of the environment" (TVA 1969).

While the 1960s and 1970s were decades of social and economic turmoil throughout the United States, environmental issues soon became the focus in the Tennessee Valley. In 1967 TVA began construction of two facilities: Browns Ferry, the agency's first nuclear-powered plant, and Tellico Dam. The first of many TVA rate increases, caused by rising coal, labor, and interest costs occurred in 1967. The environmental problems associated with coal were becoming more apparent while nuclear energy was perceived to be an economical, environmentally sound method for generating electricity. Thus TVA began a program to supplement its hydroelectric and fossil-fueled plants with nuclear plants. Commercial operation of Browns Ferry in 1974 allowed TVA to enter the nuclear age (TVA 1983a).

However, TVA soon realized that nuclear power had its own share of environmental problems. In an agency report outlining the state of the valley's environment in 1983, certain issues with nuclear energy were listed: "the thermal discharges from a nuclear plant are much greater than those from a comparably sized coal-fired plant. Mining and milling of uranium produces impacts on land, water, and air. Nuclear plants also produce low level radioactive wastes and spent reactor fuel, both of which require extreme care in handling, transportation, and disposal. And finally, disposal technologies and locations are extremely emotional, controversial issues" (TVA 1983a). TVA would begin construction on seven nuclear plants but would ultimately operate only three. TVA completed and operates Browns Ferry, Sequoyah, and Watts Bar Nuclear Plants. The agency deferred construction and later cancelled Hartsville, Yellow Creek, and Phipps Bend Nuclear Plants. TVA is currently reevaluating plans for completion of a nuclear generator at the partially constructed Bellefonte Plant, including the addition of two new reactors in order to address the growing need for power generation in the Tennessee Valley. TVA applied for a combined construction and operating license (COL) for BLN in 2008. It is one of several power companies to submit a new COL application to the NRC for alternative sources of energy in what appears to be a new twenty-first-century push for nuclear power.

Though TVA's nuclear plants were controversial, so too was the construction of Tellico Dam. The location of Fort Loudoun Dam, above the junction of the Tennessee and Little Tennessee rivers, ultimately led to the construction of Tellico; the two had been linked as early as 1936 (Wheeler and McDonald 1986). While on the drawing board for years, it was not until 1965 that TVA announced the project to the public, and, to the agency's surprise, the public balked (Callahan 1980). The agency explained how Tellico would add to the water-control system and would increase economic development in the Tennessee Valley, but many people did not agree that the benefit outweighed the loss of many farms. Furthermore many archaeological sites were situated in the area where the reservoir was to be built, and the preservation of these sites had to be addressed (Callahan 1980; Wheeler and McDonald 1986). In 1976, acknowledging the importance of the sites, TVA reported that "excavations at the Icehouse Bottoms site produced the earliest known human skeletal material from Tennessee and the earliest known use of textiles in the eastern United States."[6]

But while the Tellico Project resulted in many controversies, one of the most contentious involved a small fish. In 1973 the snail darter was discovered in the Little Tennessee River. That same year the Endangered Species Act of 1973 was passed. One of the provisions of this legislation included section 7, which stated that "all Federal agencies were required to undertake programs for the conservation of endangered and threatened species, and were prohibited from authorizing, funding, or carrying out any action that would jeopardize a listed species or destroy or modify its 'critical habitat'" (ESA 1973). In 1975 the first listing of endangered species, which included the snail darter, was released. The Tellico Dam project was about 75 percent complete at this time. When the dam was finished, almost all of the known habitat of the fish would be impounded, leading to possible extinction. A suit seeking preliminary and permanent injunctions against further construction of Tellico Dam was filed against TVA. The case was ultimately heard by the Supreme Court, which upheld a lower court ruling that the dam would destroy the only known habitat of the snail darter. In 1979 Congress exempted the dam from the Endangered Species Act and President Carter signed a bill that allowed closing of the gates (TVA 1983a). It should be noted that during 1974 and 1975 TVA transplanted a population of 710 snail darters to the Hiwassee River. By 1983 this initial population had expanded to 3,000. Since that time other natural populations of the snail darter have been discovered in other parts of the Eastern Valley (TVA 1983a).

By the early 1980s TVA was seen as an off-track, bloated bureaucracy. Like most of America, TVA was struggling with a recession. In 1982 power sales to TVA's large, industrial direct-served customers slumped to their lowest levels in 20 years (TVA 1983b). The Board of Directors adopted a three-pronged plan to get the agency back on course. The first was to reduce the need for more borrowing, which meant the agency would defer three nuclear units and cancel four units already deferred. The agency had amassed tremendous debt as a result of expenditures for the nuclear program. The second was to decrease employment by 20 percent. TVA employment dropped from a peak of 53,000-plus in April 1981 to less than 40,000 by September 1982. The final prong was to slow the growth of power costs and rates. The 1983 rate increase was 4 percent, the smallest increase in 12 years (TVA 1983b).

Even with these changes, TVA continued to struggle. In their annual "state of the agency" letter to the president, the Senate, and the House of Representatives, Directors C. H. Dean, Jr., and John Waters wrote that "by making progress toward solving some of the most complex problems this agency has faced in recent years . . . TVA helped lay a stronger foundation for the region's growth." They go on to mention that they were "pleased to welcome Marvin Runyon to TVA as Chairman. We look forward to serving with him as TVA builds on its accomplishments as a national laboratory and pursues its goal of becoming a model of government quality, productivity, and innovation" (TVA 1987b).

With the charge to make TVA more competitive, Marvin Runyon, a former Ford and Nissan Motors executive, wasted no time in bringing about change. Runyon, who earned the name "Carvin' Marvin" for his massive layoffs in 1988, worked to streamline the agency and to incorporate business trends into day-to-day management. With Runyon as chairman, TVA began its transition from bureaucracy to a customer-focused, total quality management corporation. For example, Runyon's 1991 letter to Congress regarding the state of the agency stands in stark contrast to earlier letters: "In fiscal year 1991, TVA's employees worked hard to keep power rates constant, cut overhead expenses, and adopt more efficient and competitive business practices. We also strengthened the human and natural resources of the region through innovative and cost-efficient programs. Now with our total quality initiative underway, we are gaining a clearer focus on what it takes to meet our customers' needs. . . . We are dedicating ourselves to customer satisfaction and to constantly improving the efficiency and quality of everything we do for the people of the Tennessee Valley, the nation, and the world."[7]

TVA has continued to downsize since 1988. The agency remains competitive with less than 13,000 full-time employees. Since fiscal year 1999, TVA has not received appropriated dollars; power revenues fund all activities. Much emphasis is placed on reducing the agency's debt and retaining its 159 power distributors. One of the most significant changes to the agency in recent years has been in its governance structure—from a three-member, full-time Board of Directors to a nine-member, part-time board.[8] For the first time in its history, there is a president and a chief executive officer of the authority.

There is no question that TVA has played an important role in the development of the Tennessee Valley. Although much has changed in this region since 1933, TVA remains a viable, innovative, and controversial force in the region. Former chairman Gordon Clapp (1955) once remarked that "TVA is controversial because it is consequential; let it become insignificant to the public interest, an agency of no particular account, and people will stop arguing about it." After 75 years, TVA remains significant to the region and its people.

Notes

1. For more information regarding conservation, Franklin Roosevelt, and Gifford Pinchot see Franklin D. Roosevelt, *Franklin D. Roosevelt and Conservation 1911–1945*, comp. and ed. Edgar B. Nixon (Hyde Park, NY: General Services Administration, National Archives and Records Service, Franklin D. Roosevelt Library, 1957).

2. For most of the hydro projects that TVA completed, there exists a project book that details every aspect of the project including land acquisition, family relocation, and cemetery removal. Specific numbers regarding family relocation and cemetery removal are found in these books. *The Norris Project* (TVA 1939) is the first report completed by the agency and details the procedures used for subsequent projects. For a more personal rendition of family removal see Marshall A. Wilson, *Tales from the Grass Roots of TVA, 1933–1952* (N.p.: privately published, 1982); Michael J. McDonald and John Muldowny, *TVA and the Dispossessed* (Knoxville: University of Tennessee Press, 1982).

3. *1963 Annual Report of the Tennessee Valley*, 13–14. TVA library.

4. Ibid., 1–15.

5. Not all believe that TVA enhanced the Tennessee Valley. For an in-depth argument see William U. Chandler, *The Myth of TVA: Conservation and Development in the Tennessee Valley, 1933–1983* (Cambridge, MA: Ballinger Publishing Company, 1984). Chandler challenges the idea that TVA's work in navigation, flood control, and hydroelectric power created unprecedented economic prosperity in the Tennessee Valley. He asserts that instead of aiding the valley, government by authority may have impeded economic growth in the region.

6. *Annual Report of the Tennessee Valley Authority*, vol. 1, text (Knoxville, TN: TVA, 1976), p. 24. TVA library.

7. *1991 TVA Annual Report*, p. 1. TVA library.

8. *Knoxville News-Sentinel*, April 1, 2006.

References Cited

CALLAHAN, NORTH
1980   *TVA: Bridge over Troubled Waters*. A. S. Barnes and Co., South Brunswick, NJ.

CHANDLER, WILLIAM U.
1984   *The Myth of TVA: Conservation and Development in the Tennessee Valley, 1933–1983*. Ballinger Publishing Company, Cambridge, MA.

CLAPP, GORDON R.
1955   *The TVA: An Approach to the Development of a Region*. University of Chicago Press, Chicago.

DUFFUS, R. L.
1946   *The Valley and Its People*. Alfred A. Knopf, New York.

ENDANGERED SPECIES ACT OF 1973, AS AMENDED
1973   (16 U.S.C. 1531–1544, 87 Stat. 884)–Public Law 93–205.

HARGROVE, ERWIN C., AND PAUL K. CONKIN (EDITORS)
1983   *TVA: Fifty Years of Grass Roots Bureaucracy*. University of Illinois Press, Urbana.

HIMMELBERG, ROBERT F.
2001   *The Great Depression and the New Deal*. Greenwood Press, Westport, CT.

HUBBARD, PRESTON J.
1961   *Origins of the TVA: The Muscle Shoals Controversy, 1920–1932*. Vanderbilt University Press, Nashville.

HUXLEY, JULIAN
1959   *TVA, Adventure in Planning*. Architectural Press, London.

Kneburg, Thomas M. N., and Madeline Lewis Kneburg
1972   Interview by Charles W. Crawford. Tape recording transcript. 19 November 1972. Mississippi Valley Collection, John Willard Brister Library, University of Memphis, Memphis, Tennessee.

Knoxville *(TN) News-Sentinel*
1933a   19 May:1. Knoxville, Tennessee.
1933b   22 May:1. Knoxville, Tennessee.

Krutch, Charles
1969   Interview by Charles W. Crawford. Tape recording transcript. 10 November 1969. Mississippi Valley Collection, John Willard Brister Library, University of Memphis, Memphis, Tennessee.

McBride, Don
1975   TVA and the National Defense. TVA Corporate Library, Knoxville, TN, 1975. Photocopy. Unpublished manuscript.

McDonald, Michael J. and John Muldowny
1982   *TVA and the Dispossessed: The Resettlement of Population in the Norris Dam Area.* University of Tennessee Press, Knoxville.

Nashville Tennessean
1943   TVA Declared National Asset. 19 May, Nashville, Tennessee.

New York Times
1933   Misuse Charged at Muscle Shoals. 19 May, New York.
1954   [description] Editorial 31 December. New York.

Roosevelt, Franklin D.
1938   *The Public Papers and Addresses of Franklin D. Roosevelt,* vol. 1, *The Genesis of the New Deal.* Compiled by Samuel I. Rosenman. Random House, New York.
1957   *Franklin D. Roosevelt and Conservation 1911–1945.* Compiled and edited by Edgar B. Nixon. General Services Administration, National Archives and Records Service, Franklin D. Roosevelt Library. Hyde Park, NY.

Tennessee Valley Authority Act of 1933, as amended
1933   16 USC Section 831, 831c, 831d-831h-1, 831I-831ed.

Tennessee Valley Authority (TVA)
1939   *The Norris Project.* U.S. Government Printing Office, Washington, DC.
1954   *Tennessee Valley Authority Handbook.* TVA Information Office, Knoxville.
1969   *Annual Reports of the Tennessee Valley Authority, 1933–1968.* Reprinted, Arno Press, New York.
1983a   *The First Fifty Years: Changed Land, Changed Lives.* Knoxville.

1983b   *A History of the Tennessee Valley Authority.* TVA Information Office, Knoxville.

1985   *Tellico Project Final Design Report.* Division of Engineering, Knoxville.

1987   *Tennessee Valley Authority Handbook.* TVA Corporate Library, Knoxville.

1987b   *Tennessee Valley Authority Annual Report,* Knoxville.

1998   *Answers to the Most Frequently Asked Questions about TVA.* TVA Information Office, Knoxville.

2006a   TVA, What is TVA? Electronic document, http://www.tva.gov/about tva/index.htm, accessed May 30, 2006.

2006b   Energy, Environment, Economic Development. Electronic document, http://www.tva.gov/abouttva/index.htm, accessed May 30, 2006.

WHEELER, WILLIAM B., AND MICHAEL J. MCDONALD

1986   *TVA and the Tellico Dam, 1936–1979: A Bureaucratic Crisis in Post-Industrial America.* University of Tennessee Press, Knoxville.

WILSON, MARSHALL A.

1982   *Tales from the Grass Roots of TVA, 1933–1952.* Privately Published.

2
In the Beginning . . .

Danny E. Olinger and A. Eric Howard

THE TENNESSEE RIVER IS FORMED by the confluence of the Holston and French Broad rivers at Knoxville, Tennessee, and flows 650 miles through Tennessee, Alabama, Mississippi, and Kentucky to its mouth on the Ohio River at Paducah, Kentucky. The drainage basin covers 40,910 square miles (105,956 sq. km) including portions of seven states; Virginia, North Carolina, Georgia, Tennessee, Alabama, Mississippi, and Kentucky. Once this wild river was almost impossible to navigate and flooded its banks regularly, causing damage and havoc to adjacent communities. This all changed with the passing of the Tennessee Valley Authority Act in 1933.

The Tennessee Valley Authority, commonly known by its initials "TVA," was created by an act of Congress in May 1933 as part of newly inaugurated Franklin D. Roosevelt's New Deal program for economic recovery from the Great Depression. Almost immediately the new agency began plans, in part adopted from previous United States Corps of Engineers (USACE) studies, to construct a series of dams on the Tennessee River and its tributaries for the multiple purposes of flood control, navigation, and hydroelectric power production. The first two projects constructed under this grand scheme were a dam across the Clinch River, a tributary in east Tennessee, and a dam across the Tennessee River in Lauderdale and Lawrence counties, Alabama above the existing USACE-built Wilson Dam.

Not long after TVA was formed, David L. DeJarnette from the University of Alabama, received a letter from Dr. William S. Webb at the University of Kentucky. Webb related to DeJarnette that there was a new government agency in the Tennessee Valley called the TVA and that he wanted to meet with its leader to discuss archaeology. Webb invited DeJarnette to accompany him to a meeting in Knoxville with the chairman of the TVA, A. E. Morgan, in August 1933. At the meeting Webb informed Morgan that the new dams being planned for the Tennessee River would immerse many important archaeological sites and destroy all records of prehistoric occupation and that samples of these sites should be recovered. Morgan replied that it sounded like a good idea, noting that the other board members would agree and that money and labor to support the effort could be obtained. The chairman instructed the archaeologists to put together a proposal and get back to him. At that point Webb removed a sheaf of papers from his coat pocket and said, "I just happen to have a proposal right here." Morgan was so impressed, he assured DeJarnette and Webb then and there they would have the support of the other two members of the TVA Board (anecdote provided by J. Bennett Graham regarding personal communication with DeJarnette in 1974).

In December 1933 a conference was held in Knoxville to organize the archaeological studies and the preservation of prehistoric materials. Representatives from TVA, the University of Tennessee, the University of Alabama, and Neil Judd, curator of Archaeology of the National Museum (later known as the Smithsonian), were in attendance. Webb was hired by TVA to provide overall supervision of the program, and individual projects were portioned out to the state universities corresponding to the locations of the dam projects (Webb 1938; Lyon 1996).

Construction on the Clinch River dam (later named Norris Dam in honor of the author of the TVA Act, Senator George W. Norris of Nebraska) began in October 1933. The archaeological survey of the Norris basin began in January 1934 and continued through July under the overall supervision of Webb and direct field supervision by Thomas M. N. Lewis of the University of Tennessee (Webb 1938). Webb (1938) remarked of Lewis, "In the face of many physical handicaps, he initiated both the survey and the work of excavation and carried them to a successful conclusion. The region under investigation was rugged; the roads [were] very poor. In addition, work was begun in the middle of the winter and was continued in spite of snow and zero degree weather, in the winter months and excessive rains and river floods in the spring."

The results of the work were published as the Bureau of American Ethnology (BAE) Bulletin 118. The TVA Norris Project technical report (TVA 1940a) describes the archaeological project thus: "The survey revealed 23 sites showing definite evidence of prehistoric occupation."

It also states, with an obvious disregard to political correctness, that "It has been possible to identify three classes of civilization in the area, one low in cultural development and two well up in barbarism." The two "advanced" civilizations are described as the *small-log town house people* and the *large-log town house people*.

Such statements may seem naive and overly simplified to archaeologists working in the region today, but we must keep in mind that up to this point little formal archaeological research had been conducted in the Tennessee Valley. Most of the previous investigations in the Southeast focused on mortuary patterns and mound construction and not on prehistoric occupational use of the river basins. A comparison of other traits identified for Norris basin sites indicates the small-log townhouse people may be equated to the Early Mississippian Period Hiwassee Island phase and the large-log townhouse people to the Late Mississippian Dallas phase. The walls of small-log townhouses and dwellings were always constructed in trenches, but the wall posts of large-log structures were always set in individual postholes. Ceramic vessels from the "small-log" sites are characterized by the presence of loop handles while the vessels from "large-log" sites possess strap handles.

In addition, three specialized studies were undertaken on the Norris basin materials: skeletal analysis, dendrochronology, and ceramic analysis. William D. Funkhouser's 1938 University of Kentucky study of the osteological material provided important initial data regarding the physical anthropology and pathology of prehistoric populations in East Tennessee. Logging activities cleared the reservoir bed in the region, giving Florence Hawley (1938) of the University of New Mexico an opportunity to study tree rings and humidity patterns of hardwoods at southeastern burial mound locations and compare the dendrochronology record to that of the Southwest. Lastly, although there was a limited amount of comparative material, James B. Griffin (1938, 1939), University of Michigan, utilized the Norris ceramic data and combined it with the material recovered during the Wheeler basin survey to develop a nomenclature that is still used today. Griffin recognized that the temper, or paste, pattern of the Tennessee Valley ceramics consisted of fiber ware, sand ware, clay ware, clay-grit ware, limestone tempered ware, and shell tempered ware. He further deduced that clay, clay-grit, and limestone tempered ware were temporally parallel. This was a very significant discovery in southeastern archaeology.

During early years of these large-scale archaeological investigations, multiple New Deal agencies participated in providing labor and funding.

The Norris basin sites were excavated with Civil Works Authority (CWA) and Federal Emergency Relief Administration (FERA) labor and the costs were absorbed by those agencies. TVA's funding of $4,161.34 was primarily used for administration of the program (TVA 1940a).

TVA continued to select dam locations and build the reservoir system. The next construction project, Wheeler Dam, named after Confederate and Spanish-American War general Joe Wheeler, was started in November of 1933. The Corps of Engineers was already building a navigation lock at the dam site, and when TVA took over the project, the lock and dam design were increased 14 feet in height to provide a longer, deeper navigation channel, thus creating a reservoir pool of more than 68,000 acres (TVA 1940b).

Archaeological studies began in December 1933 and continued through July 1934 under the field supervision of DeJarnette with overall program supervision by Webb. The Alabama Museum of the University of Alabama, under a grant from the National Research Council, had already conducted an archaeological survey in northern Alabama including the Wheeler area in the summer of 1932 (Webb 1939; TVA 1940b). Together with the previous survey work, 237 sites were located in the basin, and 19 were selected as a representative sample for excavation, again using CWA and FERA labor. Project results were published in Bulletin 122 of the BAE (Webb 1939). Again other agencies provided the labor, and TVA's expenditure on administration of the archaeology program was $2,955.67 (TVA 1940b).

Although excavations in the Tennessee Valley during the late nineteenth and early twentieth centuries by Cyrus Thomas, C. B. Moore, Gerard Fowke, and others had focused on mound sites, some effort was made to investigate other types of sites such as villages, lithic workshops, and one cave site. However, 12 of the 19 excavated sites were described as mounds, of which two general types were recognized: shell mounds and earth mounds. It was also recognized that the shell mounds were essentially massive refuse middens, and the earth mounds were primarily burial mounds although one pyramidal substructure mound was investigated on Hobbs Island (Webb 1939).

According to the 1940 TVA Wheeler Project technical report, the investigations "led to significant additions to the prehistory of southeastern United States. One of the most important was the discovery of a people not previously known in the lower region of the shell mounds, who not only antedated the use of pottery but were even of a preflint culture . . . [and] used implements fashioned of bone" (TVA 1940b). This was a misinterpretation in the technical report regarding the material identified at the base of a shell mound at 1LU86. In reality, Webb (1939) states, "From a careful investigation of the occurrence of these flint spear points and their association, the author is convinced that a spear-throwing, hunting and fishing people who made no pottery and used no bows and arrows, laid down the great shell midden at the base of Lu°86."

The second (and accurately) described discovery (TVA 1940b) was that the earth mounds yielded another new complex, which has been termed the *Copena*. "Copena" was coined from the words *copper* and *galena*, as these two substances were commonly found as burial accompaniments and in other contexts. Webb saw a strong relationship between the Copena complex of north Alabama and the Hopewell culture of the Ohio Valley. Today we recognize Copena as a phase of the Middle Woodland period associated with the Hopewellian ceremonial complex (Bense 1994; Walthall 1973).

In rapid succession construction was started on other dams across the Tennessee River to utilize further the energy production potential and flood control: Pickwick Landing Dam and Guntersville Dam in 1935, Hiwassee Dam on the Hiwassee River and Chickamauga Dam in 1936, Watts Bar Dam and Gilbertsville (later renamed Kentucky) Dam in 1939, and Ft. Loudoun Dam in 1940. Because of the rapid pace, it was not easy for the archaeologists to keep up with the speed of dam construction and river valley inundation. Edwin Lyon's thoroughly researched treatise on New Deal archaeology in the Southeast describes the many difficulties in trying to manage such a massive salvage archaeology program (Lyon 1996). The University of Tennessee conducted the field excavations and artifact and data curation for projects in Tennessee, and the University of Alabama was responsible for those in Alabama. Work on the 160,000-acre Kentucky Lake was divided along the state line between the University of Tennessee and the University of Kentucky.

Although the surveys of the Pickwick and Guntersville basins in Alabama were published in 1942 and 1951, respectively (Webb and DeJarnette 1942; Webb and Wilder 1951), the University of Tennessee was ill equipped to handle the volume of artifacts and data being generated by the excavations conducted in Tennessee. While there was an abundant supply of field labor through New Deal public works programs such as CWA and WPA, there was a critical shortage of trained staff to work on the analysis and report preparations. With the exception of a few site specific but extremely significant reports, such as those on Hiwassee Island (Lewis and Kneberg 1946) and Eva (Lewis and Lewis 1961), the Norris basin report was the only one published on the reservoirs in

Tennessee until Lynne P. Sullivan of the University of Tennessee edited and published Thomas M. N. Lewis and Madeline Kneberg's manuscript on the survey of Chickamauga basin in 1995 (Sullivan 1995).

The pace of dam construction did not abate, as nine more projects began on Tennessee River tributaries between 1940 and 1942. The University of Tennessee excavated two large Mississippian villages along the proposed Douglas Reservoir on French Broad River, but little or no attention was given to the archaeological resources at most of the other sites. After investigating the monumental sites along the main channel of the Tennessee River, it seems that the archaeologists had become somewhat jaded. The TVA technical report (TVA 1958) on the upper Holston reservoirs makes the following statement: "A reconnaissance survey of the South Holston and Watauga Reservoirs by the Division of Anthropology of the University of Tennessee indicated that there were no archaeological manifestations of any importance in the area and, therefore, that no extensive excavations were justified."

The lack of archaeological investigations on these latter projects is attributable in part to the agency's, and indeed the entire nation's, attention being diverted to the war effort. Many of the New Deal economic recovery programs were being terminated as federal budget appropriations were increased for the military. Some of the dam construction projects were mothballed while others were accelerated to completion to provide power for wartime industries such as the Alcoa aluminum plant in Blount County, Tennessee, and the government's secret Manhattan Project near Knoxville. In particular TVA concentrated its construction efforts on the completion of three dams in a very short time: Douglas, Cherokee, and Fontana. Douglas was completed within 13 months, at that time a record for a project of its scale (TVA 1949). There was some interest paid to archaeological data recovery on Douglas and Cherokee at the time but none to that on Fontana. Once dam construction began on Fontana, efforts continued 24 hours a day until it was completed (TVA 1950). TVA also constructed its first coal-fired power plant near Watts Bar Dam in 1942, mainly to ensure a continuous power supply to the Manhattan Project and the Alcoa plant.

After the war, dam construction continued but at a much slower rate. TVA built two tributary dams in the early 1950s (Boone and Fort Patrick Henry), and another began in 1960 (Melton Hill). A new dam, Nickajack, was also started on the Tennessee River in 1964 to improve navigation through a stretch of the river that had marginal channel depth. Apparently TVA abandoned its previous commitment to the documentation of archaeology during this period. Some salvage excavations, largely through volunteer efforts, were conducted at Melton Hill Reservoir and a new coal-fired plant (Bull Run), built in conjunction with the reservoir. One of the salvage operations conducted in 1960 was at the Cox site (40AN19), which was first recorded as the Cox Mound (Mississippian Period) and excavated in the initial Norris basin survey (Webb 1938); The adjacent village site was not investigated in the 1930s because it was being actively farmed. The 1960 study provided information that demonstrated that the more intense occupational use of the site was in the Woodland Period and not the Mississippian (McNutt and Fischer 1960). However, no complete report of this work has ever been published. Archaeological salvage conducted by the University of Tennessee on Nickajack Reservoir was limited to four sites and funded by the National Park Service (NPS) and the Tennessee Department of Transportation (Faulkner and Graham 1965, 1966a, 1966b).

TVA began to focus on construction projects that involved less acreage but provided more electrical power. TVA built several coal-fired power plants in the 1950s and 1960s to meet the rapidly growing demand for electricity in the Tennessee Valley and surrounding areas. Seven plants were built in eight and a half years, beginning with Johnsonville in 1949 and culminating with the Gallatin Plant on the Cumberland River (TVA 1958, 1967). Three more plants were built between 1959 and 1968: the Paradise Plant on the Green River in Muhlenberg County, Kentucky, Bull Run Plant on Melton Hill Reservoir, and the Cumberland Plant on Cumberland River in Stewart County, Tennessee. The Paradise Plant is immediately across the river from Indian Knoll (150H2). The reservations for these power plants range from 800 acres to nearly 2,000 acres. No archaeological surveys or excavations were conducted prior to the initial construction phase of any of these plants except Bull Run.

TVA continued its concentrated effort on power production and began construction of its first nuclear power plant, Browns Ferry, near Decatur, Alabama, in 1966 and its second, Sequoyah, above Chattanooga, in 1969. Early in the construction of Browns Ferry, DeJarnette at the University of Alabama got a call requesting that he come inspect some bones that had been unearthed. DeJarnette went to the site with graduate student J. Bennett Graham. After they briefly surveyed the devastation being wrought by heavy earthmoving machinery, Graham turned to him and said, "They've fucked everything up anyway, let's just get out of here" (J. Bennett Graham, personal communication).

There were few exceptions of archaeological investigations until the passage of the Reservoir Salvage Act in 1960 and the National Historic Preservation Act in 1966, both of which had a significant impact on the revival of archaeological data recovery at TVA projects. When TVA began construction of Tims Ford Reservoir on Elk River in 1966, an archaeological team from the University of Tennessee conducted salvage excavations at three sites under contract to the NPS (Faulkner 1968). When TVA started construction of Tellico Dam in 1967, the agency had little expectation that the project would not get final completion authorization until 1979 (TVA 1987). This long delay allowed archaeologists from the University of Tennessee a unique opportunity to study the lower Little Tennessee River basin in great detail. The many volumes and thousands of pages of excavation reports and master's theses and Ph.D. dissertations that emanated from this project are too lengthy to enumerate here, but some of the more significant sites investigated are:

- the eighteenth century Overhill Cherokee towns of Citico, Chota, Tanasee, Toqua, Tomotley, Tuskegee, and Mialoquo by numerous investigators (Salo 1969, Gleeson 1970, 1971, Guthe and Bistline 1978, Baden 1983, Russ and Chapman 1984, Schroedl 1986, Polhemus 1987)
- the deeply stratified Early Archaic Rose Island Site by Jeff Chapman (Chapman 1975)
- the transitional Woodland/Mississippian Martin Farm Site by Charles Faulkner (Salo 1969) and later by Gerald Schroedl (Schroedl et al. 1985)
- British colonial Ft. Loudoun by Carl Kuttruff (1989)
- the early Federal Period Tellico Blockhouse trading post by Richard Polhemus (Polhemus 1979)
- the Late Mississippian Dallas mound and village component at Toqua by Polhemus (Polhemus 1987).

Numerous other contributions include plant domestication and geomorphological studies (Chapman and Crites 1987; Delcourt 1980). Through 1974 the Tellico project was funded by NPS through its Interagency Archaeological Services program and later by TVA.

In 1972 TVA started construction on Normandy Dam on Duck River in Middle Tennessee and the following year started Columbia Dam 112 miles downstream (TVA 1987). In late 1970 and 1971, Charles H. Faulkner undertook a survey of the Normandy basin with a small grant from the University of Tennessee. Using data from this survey, proposals to test numerous sites and conduct data recovery at the Banks site (Faulkner and McCollough 1973, 1974) were submitted to and approved by NPS and TVA. Fieldwork continued on the Normandy project through 1975, and the dam's gates were closed in January 1976. Ultimately eight large volumes reporting the archaeological project were published by the University of Tennessee and TVA (Faulkner and McCollough 1977, 1978a, 1978b, 1982a, 1982b; McCollough and Faulkner 1976).

The year 1972 marks the beginning of an ambitious nuclear construction program at TVA. Construction started on five nuclear power plants and continued until 1978: Watts Bar (1972), Bellefonte (1973), Hartsville (1976), Phipps Bend (1978), and Yellow Creek (1978). All these plants involved land reservations of a thousand acres or more. At Watts Bar test and data recovery excavations were conducted by the University of Tennessee–Knoxville in 1971, and the following year the University of Tennessee–Chattanooga conducted excavations at 40RH6, a multi-component habitation site (Calabrese 1976). The University of Alabama conducted data recovery at the Bellefonte site, 1Ja300, in 1973 and 1974 (Futato 1977). Middle Tennessee State University and the University of Memphis surveyed, tested, and excavated sites at the Hartsville plant site on the Cumberland River (Blanchard and Spires 1984; McNutt and Weaver 1983; McNutt and Lumb 1987). The University of Alabama conducted the archaeological data recovery program at Phipps Bend (Lafferty 1981), and the University of Mississippi conducted the work at Yellow Creek (Thorne, Broyles, and Johnson, 1981; Johnson 1981).

Passage of the Archeological and Historic Preservation Act of 1974, commonly known as the Moss-Bennett Act, brought about significant changes in the way TVA approached its preservation responsibilities. Actually an amendment to the Reservoir Salvage Act of 1960, the Moss-Bennett Act expanded data recovery authority to all types of federal construction projects, authorized federal agencies to spend up to 1 percent of project costs for historic preservation and authorized agencies to implement their own preservation program as an alternative to transferring funds to NPS to conduct these activities. Because of the passing of this and previous federal legislation, in 1974 TVA hired its first staff archaeologist, J. Bennett Graham—perhaps not unexpectedly, given his association with Webb, who had worked for TVA during the New Deal era.

The last reservoir construction project to be undertaken by TVA was Columbia Dam. The University of Tennessee, originally under the direction of Bruce Dickson and later Walter Klippel, began archaeological research in the project area in 1972 and continued fieldwork until 1985, when the Columbia project was suspended because of environmental issues (Dickson 1976; Turner and Klippel n.d.; Entorf n.d.). Although the planned archaeological program was never carried to completion because of the work stoppage, several significant contributions of paleontological, botanical, and zooarchaeology studies of early hunter-gatherer cultures in the Nashville basin area were published that increased the knowledge of Middle Tennessee prehistory (Klippel and Parmalee 1982; Turner and Klippel n.d.; Crites 1983).

Since the mid-1980s, TVA has focused attention on the stewardship of the remaining archaeological resources on the lands it holds in public trust. These efforts have included archaeological surveys of reservoir shorelines and winter drawdown zones, of TVA land above reservoir pool, and occasionally of normally inundated lands at reservoirs dewatered for dam inspections and repairs (Solis and Futato 1987; Smith 1988 and 1990; Meyer 1995; Herrmann and Frankenberg 2000; Riggs and Shumate 2002; and Wampler, Deter-Wolf, and L. McKee 2002) Furthermore TVA has undertaken a stabilization program to protect sites along shorelines from further damage caused by reservoir erosion. From 1992 to 2007 TVA stabilized 75 miles of critically eroding reservoir shoreline for environmental protection, with a high priority given to preservation of significant archaeological resources. However, where preservation in situ has not been feasible, data recovery excavations have led to significant contributions to valley prehistory at other sites. Prominent examples are the Snodgrass Small Mound on Wheeler Reservoir, investigated by Richard Krause (Krause 1988); Dust Cave on Pickwick Reservoir, excavated under the direction of Boyce Driskell (Goldman-Finn and Driskell 1994); and the problem-oriented studies of Removal Period Cherokee sites on the reservoirs in the mountains of western North Carolina, by Brett Riggs (Riggs 1999).

In the twenty-first century TVA has continued the studies along shoreline drawdown zones to address reservoir operations and residential development (Alhman 2002; Gage 2005; Gage and Herrmann 2006 and 2007). These studies may not compare to the grand scale of labor used during the beginning of TVA, but the information being collected still has the original premise by Webb—to record all archaeological sites within a survey area. With more systematic testing procedures than those used in the 1930s, more than 500 archaeological sites have been recorded on Norris Reservoir, compared to Webb's 23 sites. In fact TVA's commitment to this regard has risen from its original investment of $4,161.34 for administrational purposes in 1933 to a budget of $280,000 for archaeological inventory in 2007. Continued recording and researching archaeological resources along the Tennessee River Valley will provide future archaeological study opportunities to scholars who in turn will help upcoming generations to understand and appreciate their heritage.

References Cited

AHLMAN, TODD M.
2002   Archaeological Identification Survey of the Ocoee No. 1 (Parksville) Reservoir, Polk County, Tennessee. Submitted to the Tennessee Valley Authority.

BADEN, WILLIAM W.
1983   Tomotley: An Eighteenth Century Cherokee Village. Department of Anthropology, University of Tennessee, Report of Investigations 36.

BENSE, JUDITH A.
1994   Archaeology of the Southeastern United States PaleoIndian to World War I. Academic Press, San Diego, CA.

BLANCHARD, KENDALL, AND DONALD SPIRES
1984   The Hartsville Sites: Prehistoric Adaptations in Smith and Trousdale Counties, Middle Tennessee. Report on file, Tennessee Valley Authority, Norris.

CALABRESE, FRANCIS A.
1976   Excavations at 40RH6, Watts Bar Area, Rhea County, TN. Tennessee Valley Authority, Knoxville.

CHAPMAN, JEFFERSON
1975   The Rose Island Site and the Bifurcate Point Tradition. Report of Investigations No. 14, Department of Anthropology, University of Tennessee, Knoxville, and Publications in Anthropology No. 8, Tennessee Valley Authority.

CHAPMAN, JEFFERSON, AND GARY C. CRITES
1987   Evidence of early maize (Zea mays) from the Icehouse Bottom Site, Tennessee. American Antiquity, 52:352–54.

CRITES, GARY D.
1983   Woody Vegetation in the Inner Nashville Basin: An Example from the Cheek Bend Area of the Central Duck River Valley. Ethnobotany Laboratory Report No. 2 for the Columbia Reservoir Research Project.

DELCOURT, PAUL A.
1980   Quaternary alluvial terraces of the Little Tennessee River Valley, East Tennessee. In The 1979 Archaeological and Geological Investigations in the Tellico Reservoir, edited by Jefferson Chapman, pp. 110–121. Reports of Investigations No. 29, Department of

Anthropology, University of Tennessee, Knoxville and Publications in Anthropology No. 24, Tennessee Valley Authority.

DICKSON, D. BRUCE

1975   *Final Report on the 1972–1973 Archaeological Site Reconnaissance in the Proposed TVA Columbia Reservoir, Maury and Marshall Counties, Tennessee.* Submitted to the Tennessee Valley Authority.

ENTORF, ROBERT F.

n.d.   *Final Report on Archaeological Test Excavations at Six Stratified Rockshelters on Fountain Creek, Maury County, Tennessee.* Submitted to the Tennessee Valley Authority.

FAULKNER, CHARLES H.

1968   *Archaeological Investigations in the Tims Ford Reservoir, Tennessee, 1966.* Report of Investigation No. 6, Department of Anthropology, University of Tennessee, Knoxville.

FAULKNER, CHARLES H., AND J. B. GRAHAM

1965   *Excavations in the Nickajack Reservoir: Season I.* Miscellaneous Paper No. 7, Tennessee Archaeological Society. Knoxville.

1966a   *Westmoreland-Barber Site (40Mi-11) Nickajack Reservoir: Season II.* Department of Anthropology, University of Tennessee. Knoxville.

1966b   *Highway Salvage in the Nickajack Reservoir.* Department of Anthropology, University of Tennessee, Knoxville.

FAULKNER, CHARLES H., AND MAJOR C. R. McCOLLOUGH

1973   *Introductory Report of the Normandy Reservoir Salvage Project: Environmental Setting, Typology, and Survey.* Normandy Archaeological Project 1. Report of Investigations No. 11, Department of Anthropology, University of Tennessee, Knoxville.

1974   *Excavations and Testing, Normandy Reservoir Salvage Project: 1972 Season.* Normandy Archaeological Project Volume 2. Report of Investigations No. 12, Department of Anthropology, University of Tennessee, Knoxville.

FAULKNER, CHARLES H., AND MAJOR C. R. McCOLLOUGH (EDITORS)

1976   *Fourth Report of the Normandy Archaeological Project: 1973 Excavations of the Hicks I, Eoff I, and Eoff III Sites.* Normandy Archaeological Project, vol. 4. Report of Investigations No. 19, Department of Anthropology, University of Tennessee, Knoxville.

1978a   *Fifth Report of the Normandy Archaeological Project: 1973 Excavations at the Banks V Site (40CF111).* Normandy Archaeological Project Volume 5. Report of Investigations No. 20, Department of Anthropology, University of Tennessee, Knoxville.

1978b   *Sixth Report of the Normandy Archaeological Project: 1974 Excavations at the Nowlin II Site (40CF35), 1975 Excavations at the Wiser-Stephens I Site (40CF81).* Normandy Archaeological Project Volume 6. Report of Investigations No. 21, Department of Anthropology, University of Tennessee, Knoxville, Notes in Anthropology No.4, Laboratory of Anthropology, Write State University and Publications in Anthropology No. 19, The Tennessee Valley Authority.

1982a   *Seventh Report of the Normandy Archaeological Project: 1974 Excavations at the Ewell III Site (40CF118), Jernigan II Site (40CF37), and the Parks Site (40CF5).* Normandy Archaeological Project Volume 7. Report of Investigations No. 32, Department of Anthropology, University of Tennessee, Knoxville, and Publications in Anthropology No. 29, Tennessee Valley Authority.

1982b   *Eighth Report of the Normandy Archaeological Project.* Normandy Archaeological Project Volume 8. Report of Investigations No. 33, Department of Anthropology, University of Tennessee, Knoxville, and Publications in Anthropology No. 30, Tennessee Valley Authority.

FUNKHOUSER, WILLIAM D.

1938   A Study of the Physical Anthropology and Pathology of the Osteological Material From the Norris Basin. From *An Archeological Survey of the Norris Basin in Eastern Tennessee.* Smithsonian Institution Bureau of American Ethnology, Bulletin 118.

FUTATO, EUGENE M.

1977   *Bellefonte Site 1JA300.* Research Series No.2 Office of Archaeological Research, University of Alabama.

GAGE, MATTHEW D.

2005   Archaeological Site Identification and Erosion Monitoring for the TVA Reservoir Operations Study: The 2005 Field Season on Portions of Cherokee, Norris, Pickwick, and Wheeler Reservoirs. Submitted to the Tennessee Valley Authority.

GAGE, MATTHEW D., AND NICHOLAS P. HERRMANN

2006   Archaeological Site Identification and Erosion Monitoring for the TVA Reservoir Operation Compliance Project: The 2006 Field Season on Portions of Blue Ridge, Chatuge, Cherokee, Fontana, Hiwassee, Norris, Nottely, Pickwick, South Holston, Watauga, and Wheeler Reservoirs. Submitted to the Tennessee Valley Authority.

2007   Archaeological Site Identification and Erosion Monitoring for the TVA Reservoir Operation Compliance Project: The 2007 Field Season on Portions of Fontana, Hiwassee, Norris, and Wheeler Reservoirs. Submitted to the Tennessee Valley Authority.

GLEESON, PAUL. F. (EDITOR)

1970   *Archaeological Investigations in the Tellico Reservoir: interim Report 1969.* Department of Anthropology, University of Tennessee. Report of Investigations, 8.

1971   *Archaeological Investigations in the Tellico Reservoir: Interim Report 1970*. Department of Anthropology, University of Tennessee. Report of Investigations, 9.

GOLDMAN-FINN, NURIT S., AND BOYCE N. DRISKELL (EDITORS)
1994   *Journal of Alabama Archaeology: Preliminary Archaeological Papers on Dust Cave, Northwest Alabama*. Volume 40 (1–2). The Alabama Archaeological Society, Moundville.

GUTHE, ALFRED K., AND E. MARIAN BISTLINE
1978   *Excavations at Tomotley, 1973–74, and the Tuskegee Area: Two Reports*. Department of Anthropology, University of Tennessee, Report of Investigations, 24.

GRIFFIN, JAMES B
1938   The Ceramic Remains from Norris Basin. From *An Archeological Survey of the Norris Basin in Eastern Tennessee*. Smithsonian Institution Bureau of American Ethnology, Bulletin 118.

1939   Report on the Ceramics of Wheeler Basin. From *An Archeological Survey of the Wheeler Basin on the Tennessee River in Northern Alabama*. Smithsonian Institution Bureau of American Ethnology, Bulletin 122.

HAWLEY, FLORENCE M.
1938   Tree Ring Dating for Southeastern Mounds. From *An Archeological Survey of the Norris Basin in Eastern Tennessee*. Smithsonian Institution Bureau of American Ethnology, Bulletin 118.

HERRMANN, NICHOLAS P., AND SUSAN R. FRANKENBERG
2000   *Archaeological Reconnaissance Survey of Tennessee Valley Authority Lands on the Melton Hill Reservoir*. Submitted to the Tennessee Valley Authority.

JOHNSON, JAY K.
1980   *The Yellow Creek Archaeological Project*, vol. 2, *Lithic Procurement and Utilization Trajectories: Analysis, Yellow Creek Nuclear Power Plant Site, Tishomingo County, Mississippi*. Archaeological Papers of the Center for Archaeological Research, No.1 University of Mississippi, and Publications in Anthropology No.28, Tennessee Valley Authority.

KLIPPEL, WALTER E., AND PAUL W. PARMALEE
1982   *The Paleontology of Cheek Bend Cave: Phase II*. Report to the Tennessee Valley Authority.

KRAUSE, RICHARD A.
1988   *The Snodgrass Small Mound and Middle Tennessee Valley Prehistory*. Publications in Anthropology No. 52, Tennessee Valley Authority.

Kuttruff, Carl

1994   Fort Loudoun, Tennessee, a mid-18th Century British Fortification: A case study in research archaeology, reconstruction, and interpretative exhibits. In *Conflict in the Archaeology of Living Traditions*, edited by Robert Layton, pp. 265–83. Unwin Hyman, London.

Lafferty, Robert H., III

1981   *Phipps Bend Archaeological Project*. Research Series No. 4, Office of Archaeological Research, University of Alabama, and Publications in Anthropology No.26, Tennessee Valley Authority.

Lewis, Thomas M. N., and Madeline Kneberg

1946   *Hiwassee Island: An Archaeological Account of Four Tennessee Indian Peoples*. University of Tennessee Press, Knoxville.

Lewis, Thomas M. N., and Madeline K. Lewis

1961   *Eva: An Archaic Site*. University of Tennessee Press, Knoxville.

Lyon, Edwin A.

1996   *A New Deal for Southeastern Archaeology*. University of Alabama Press, Tuscaloosa.

McCollough, Major C. R., and Charles H. Faulkner (editors)

1976   *Third Report of the Normandy Reservoir Salvage Project: 1973 Testing Program, Lithic Resource Survey, Lithic Annealing Project, and Report on Plant and Faunal Remains from the Banks III Site*. Normandy Archaeological Project Volume 3 and Report of Investigations No. 16, Department of Anthropology, University of Tennessee.

McNutt, Charles H., and F. William Fischer

1960   *Archaeological Investigations in the Upper Melton Hill Reservoir, Anderson County, Tennessee, 1960*. Submitted to the Tennessee Valley Authority.

McNutt, Charles H., and Lisa C. Lumb

1987   *Three Archeological Sites Near Hartsville: Smith and Trousdale Counties, Tennessee, Dixon Creek (40SM113), Oldham (40SM108), Celsor (40TR20)*. Anthropological Research Center Occasional Papers No. 14, Memphis State University, and Publications in Anthropology No. 48, Tennessee Valley Authority.

McNutt, Charles H., and Guy G. Weaver

1983   *The Duncan Tract Site (40TR27), Trousdale County, Tennessee*. Publications in Anthropology No. 33, Tennessee Valley Authority.

Meyer, Catherine C.

1995   *Cultural Resources in the Pickwick Reservoir*. Submitted to the Tennessee Valley Authority.

POLHEMUS, RICHARD R.
1979   *Archaeological Investigations of the Tellico Blockhouse Site: A Federal Military and Trade Complex.* Report of Investigations No. 26, Department of Anthropology, University of Tennessee, Knoxville, and Publications in Anthropology No. 8, Tennessee Valley Authority.

POLHEMUS, RICHARD R. (EDITOR)
1987   *Toqua Site—40MR6: A Late Mississippian Dallas Phase Town.* Report of Investigations No. 41, Department of Anthropology, University of Tennessee, Knoxville, and Publications in Anthropology No. 44, Tennessee Valley Authority.

RUSS, KURT C., AND JEFFERSON CHAPMAN
1984   *Archaeological Investigations at the Eighteenth Century Overhill Cherokee Town of Mialoquo (40MR3).* Department of Anthropology, University of Tennessee, Repot of Investigations 37.

RIGGS, BRETT H.
1999   *Removal Period Cherokee Households in Southwestern North Carolina: Material Perspectives on Tradition and Westernization.* Ph.D. dissertation, Department of Anthropology, University of Tennessee, Knoxville.

RIGGS, BRETT H., AND SCOTT SHUMATE
2002   *Archaeological Data Recovery at 31SW365 Lemmons Branch Boat Ramp, Fontana Reservoir, Swain County, North Carolina.* Submitted to the Tennessee Valley Authority.

SALO, LAWRENCE W. (EDITOR)
1968   *Archaeological Investigations in the Tellico Reservoir, Tennessee 1967–1968: An Interim Report.* Report of Investigations No. 7, University of Tennessee, Knoxville.

SCHROEDL, GERALD F. (EDITOR)
1986   *Overhill Cherokee Archaeology at Chota-Tanasee.* Department of Anthropology, University of Tennessee, Report of Investigations 38.

SCHROEDL, GERALD F., R. P. STEPHEN DAVIS JR., AND C. CLIFFORD BOYD JR.
1985   *Archaeological Contexts and Assemblages at Martin Farm.* Report of Investigations No. 39, Department of Anthropology, University of Tennessee, Knoxville, and Publications in Anthropology No. 37, The Tennessee Valley Authority.

SMITH, MARVIN T.
1988   *Archaeological Survey of Portions of the Chickamauga Reservoir, Tennessee 1987–1988.* Submitted to the Tennessee Valley Authority.

1990   *Survey Report of Archaeological Resources in Portions of the Chickamauga Reservoir 1987, 1988, and 1989 Field Seasons.* Submitted to the Tennessee Valley Authority.

SOLIS, CARLOS, AND EUGENE M. FUTATO
1987   *Cultural Resource Investigations in the Guntersville Reservoir Area,
        Marshall and Jackson Counties, Alabama and Marion County,
        Tennessee.* Submitted to the Tennessee Valley Authority.

SULLIVAN, LYNNE P. (EDITOR)
1995   *The Prehistory of the Chickamauga Basin in Tennessee,* 2 vols.
        University of Tennessee Press, Knoxville.

TENNESSEE VALLEY AUTHORITY
1940a   *The Norris Project: A Comprehensive Report on the Planning,
        Design, Construction, and Initial Operations of the Tennessee Valley
        Authority's First Water Control Project.* Technical Report No. 1.
        U.S. Government Printing Office, Washington, DC.

1940b   *The Wheeler Project: A Comprehensive Report on the Planning,
        Design, Construction, and Initial Operations of the Wheeler
        Project.* Technical Report No. 2. U.S. Government Printing Office,
        Washington, DC.

1949   *The Douglas Project: A Comprehensive Report on the Planning,
        Design, Construction, and Initial Operations of the Douglas
        Project.* Technical Report No. 10. U.S. Government Printing Office,
        Washington, DC.

1950   *The Fontana Project: A Comprehensive Report on the Planning,
        Design, Construction, and Initial Operations of the Fontana
        Project.* Technical Report No. 12. U.S. Government Printing Office,
        Washington, DC.

1958   *The Upper Holston Projects: Watauga, South Holston, Boone, and
        Fort Patrick Henry: A Comprehensive Report on the Planning,
        Design, Construction, Initial Operations and Costs of Four Hydro
        Projects in the Holston Basin at the Eastern Tip of Tennessee.*
        Technical Report No. 14. U.S. Government Printing Office,
        Washington, DC.

1967   *Gallatin Steam Plant: A Report on the Planning, Design,
        Construction, Costs, and First Power Operations of the Initial
        Four-Unit Plant.* Technical Report 36. Tennessee Valley Authority,
        Knoxville, TN.

1987   *TVA Handbook.* Edited by D. D. Mills. TVA Technical Library,
        Knoxville, TN.

THORNE, ROBERT M., BETTY J. BROYLES, AND JAY K. JOHNSON
1980   *The Yellow Creek Archaeological Project,* vol. 1, *Lithic Procurement
        and Utilization Trajectories: Archaeological Survey and Excavations,
        Yellow Creek Nuclear Power Plant Site, Tishomingo County,
        Mississippi.* Archaeological Papers of the Center for Archaeological
        Research No. 1, University of Mississippi, and Publications in
        Anthropology No. 27, Tennessee Valley Authority.

TURNER, WILLIAM B., AND WALTER E. KLIPPEL

n.d.   Archaeological Investigations of Prehistoric Hunter-Gatherers in Cheek and Cannon Bends of the Proposed Columbia Reservoir. Submitted to the Tennessee Valley Authority.

WAMPLER, MARK A., AARON DETER-WOLFE, AND LARRY McKEE

2002   *Phase I Archaeological Survey of Tennessee Valley Authority Property (C.A. 1500 Acres) Along Tims Ford Reservoir, Franklin County, Tennessee.* Submitted to the Tennessee Valley Authority.

WATHALL, JOHN A.

1973   *Copena: A Tennessee Valley Middle Woodland Culture.* Ph.D. dissertation. Department of Anthropology, University of North Carolina, Chapel Hill.

WEBB, WILLIAM S.

1938   *An Archeological Survey of the Norris Basin in Eastern Tennessee.* Smithsonian Institution Bureau of American Ethnology, Bulletin 118.

1939   *An Archeological Survey of Wheeler Basin on the Tennessee River in Northern Alabama.* Smithsonian Institution Bureau of American Ethnology, Bulletin 122.

WEBB, WILLIAM S., AND DAVID L. DEJARNETTE

1942   *An Archeological Survey of Pickwick Basin in the Adjacent Portions of the States of Alabama, Mississippi, and Tennessee.* Smithsonian Institution Bureau of American Ethnology, Bulletin 129.

WEBB, WILLIAM S., AND CHARLES G. WILDER

1951   *An Archaeological Survey of Guntersville Basin on the Tennessee River in Northern Alabama.* University of Kentucky Press, Lexington.

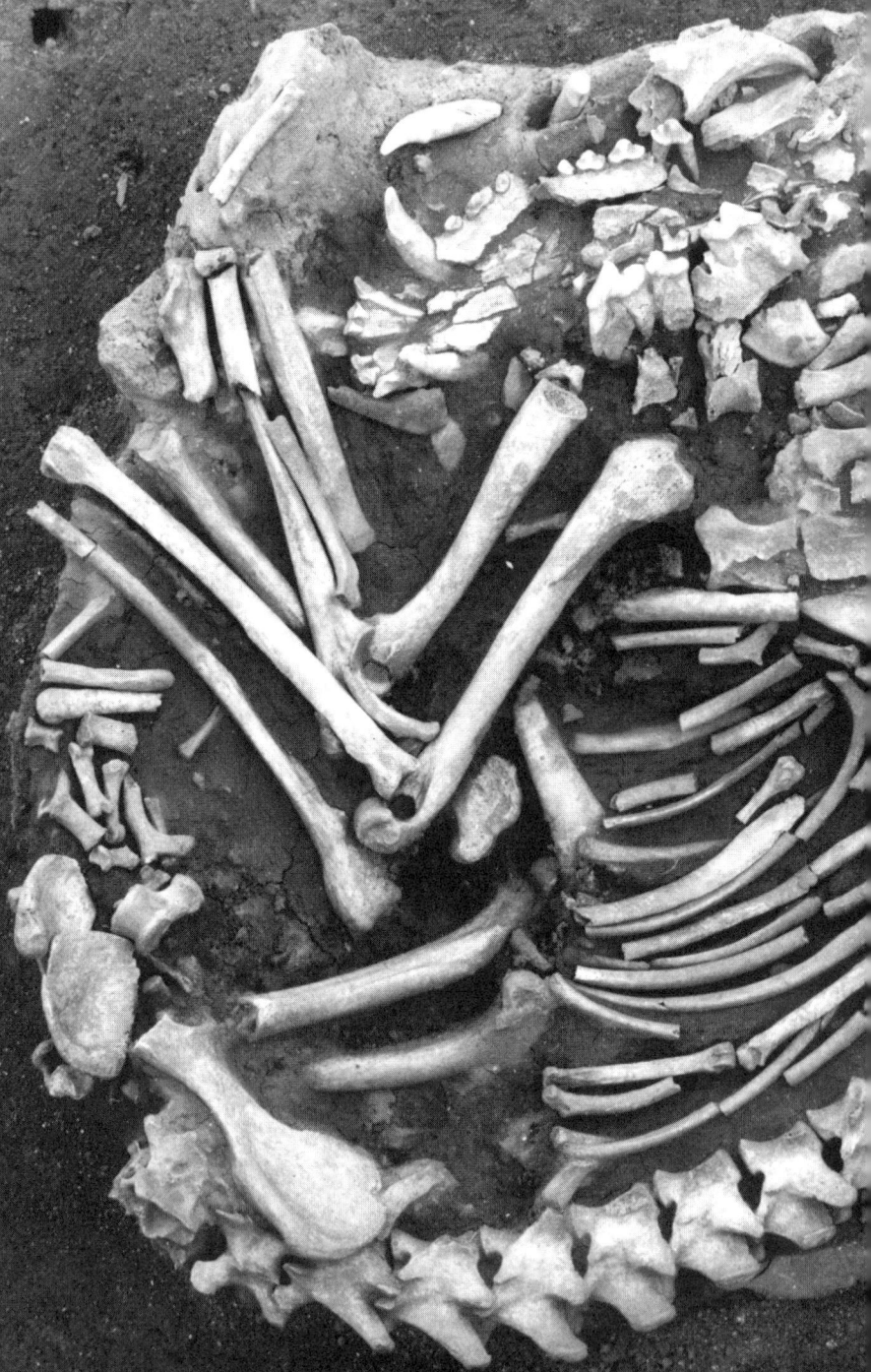

PART II
SCIENTIFIC BREAKTHROUGHS IN SOUTHEASTERN ARCHAEOLOGY

3
The Normandy Archaeological Project
Charles H. Faulkner

FEDERALLY FUNDED ARCHAEOLOGY in the TVA reservoirs from 1933 to 1942 produced the largest data base of regional prehistoric cultural chronologies and taxonomy in the Southeast up to that time (Stoltman 1973). This research also provided the earliest training ground for dozens of young men and women to become professionally trained field archaeologists and teachers in our colleges and universities. The scope of their work was unprecedented, with an inventory of thousands of archaeological sites that would never be accessible again. A result of this formidable task of preserving these archaeological data was to begin immediately the large-scale excavation of the largest habitation sites and mounds within the flood zone, since there was little time to conduct adequate survey or testing to determine the true nature and significance of the majority of these sites. This approach was truly "salvage" archaeology since little was known about Tennessee Valley prehistory, and the research on large, productive sites would provide a baseline for the culture history of this region. However, as the paradigm of North American archaeology changed in the 1960s and 1970s from a focus on culture history to the agenda of culture process, what is now called conservation archaeology began to shift to the role of the environment and technology in the study of past cultures. When it was learned in 1970 that TVA would soon construct a dam on the upper Duck River at mile 248.6 in Coffee County, Tennessee, flooding a surface area of about 3,200 acres, plans were made at the University of Tennessee to initiate an archaeological study of the envisioned Normandy Reservoir (Figure 3.1).

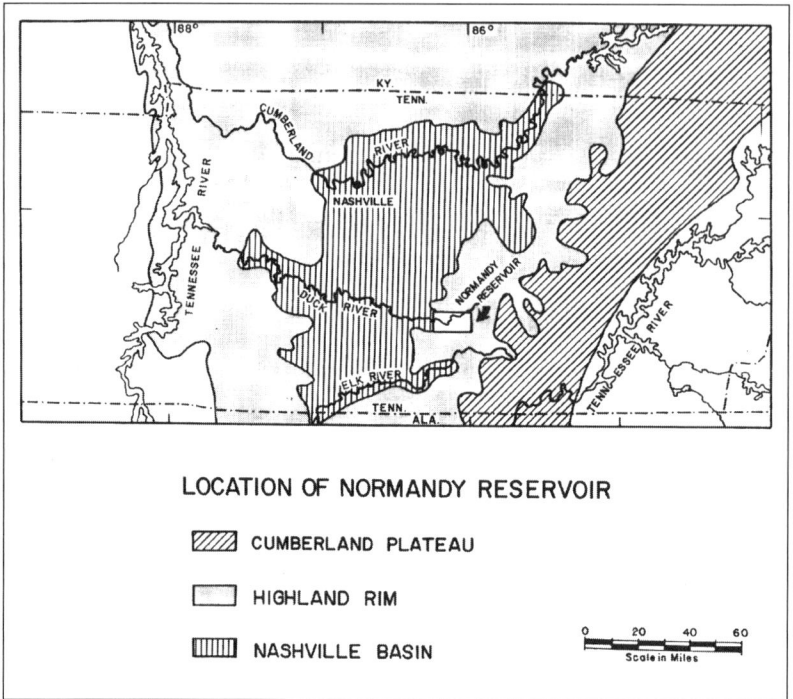

LOCATION OF NORMANDY RESERVOIR

▨ CUMBERLAND PLATEAU

▢ HIGHLAND RIM

▥ NASHVILLE BASIN

0   20   40   60
Scale in Miles

Fig. 3.1. Location of the Normandy Reservoir.

From the beginning these plans were systematically problem-oriented with the goal of methodically recording archaeological data by taking the following steps: 1) visiting the planned reservoir area as soon as possible to assess its archaeological potential and obtain help from the Coffee County chapter of the Tennessee Archaeological Society (TAS) to locate sites; 2) surveying and testing the area that would be immediately affected by the construction of the Normandy Dam as soon as possible; 3) using these data to apply to the Tennessee Valley Authority and the National Park Service for funds to conduct large scale survey and excavation in the planned reservoir; 4) publishing the first volume of the Normandy Archaeological Project encompassing the environmental setting of the reservoir area, the initial site survey of this area, and the typology used to analyze the artifacts found in the survey (Faulkner and McCollough 1973); 5) developing a research design for testing and intensive excavation focusing on the close articulation between the environment and the subsistence and settlement patterns of the prehistoric Native people who inhabited the upper Duck Valley; and 6) publishing detailed volumes for each season of archaeological research in the reservoir.

The axis of the Normandy Dam would eventually cross the Joe Barton farm, with the earth fill being removed from the adjacent Randall Banks farm. Information from local collectors/avocational archaeologists indicated large, multicomponent prehistoric sites on these farms. On November 21, 1970, permission was granted by Randall Banks for testing on his property, and during the next year surface collections began on previously recorded sites in the reservoir by the author, his students, and members of the Coffee County chapter of the TAS. In February, 1971, the author received a faculty grant from the graduate school of the University of Tennessee–Knoxville to fund the survey, and the Department of Anthropology helped prepare a preliminary survey report (Faulkner 1971). This report accompanied a proposal to TVA for funding the immediate testing of the dam axis area (Barton Farm) and the Banks site in the spring of 1972, and that June contracts were received from TVA and NPS for the further testing and extensive excavation program in the Normandy Reservoir, based on the archaeological data thus far recovered. These contracts continued through 1975, the reservoir being filled in January 1976.

The environmental study of the upper Duck Valley revealed that the Normandy Reservoir was located in two major topographical areas, a lower reservoir zone (Central Basin) where the floodplain becomes wider and the adjacent upland (Highland Rim) is deeply dissected with long narrow sloping ridgetops separated by narrow steep-sided valleys, and an upper reservoir zone where a narrow floodplain is bordered by the broad rolling Highland Rim. In addition, both areas were divided into four major biogeographic zones: the floodplain, older alluvial terraces, valley slopes and bluffs, and uplands. Location of sites and subsistence activities in these zones would be studied from both the broader aspect of cultural adaptation in the regional ecotone of the Highland Rim/Central Basin and the more localized aspect of prehistoric utilization of the four biogeographic zones (Faulkner and McCollough 1973).

Field Methodology

The Phase I archaeological survey of the Normandy Reservoir recorded 168 sites with 245 identifiable components. Cultural components were largely identified by diagnostic projectile point/biface and ceramic types. When concentrations of artifacts from distinct components or natural divisions could be discerned on site topography, separate areas designated by alphabet letters (*a, b, c*) accompanied the site number. Components (phases in parentheses) included six Paleo-Indian (Clovis); 10 Transitional Paleo-Archaic (Dalton, Big Sandy); 23 Archaic; 36 Early Archaic (Kirk, Bifurcate); 17 Middle Archaic (Stanley, Eva/Morrow Mountain, White Springs/Three Mile); 51 Late Archaic (Benton, Ledbetter); 24 Terminal Archaic (Wade); six Early Woodland (Watts Bar, Long Branch); 40 Middle Woodland (McFarland, Neel, Owl Hollow); 16 Late Woodland (Mason) 10 Woodland; four Mississippian (Banks/Langston); and four late-eighteenth-to-nineteenth-century Euro-American sites.

Six areas on the Barton site (40CF102) were tested in spring, 1972 (Faulkner and McCollough 1974:47–79). Later testing in 1972 was confined to the lower reservoir zone and included the investigation of seven sites in the summer and seven sites in the fall. Testing was based on a Cartesian grid of 5 x 5 foot units rather than on the use of shovel tests to collect more comprehensive data on stratigraphy and the concentration and types of features on these sites. Sites were divided into four quadrants, a table of random numbers was consulted, and a series of random numbers was chosen corresponding to the units within each quadrant. The plow zone was removed as a single unit; if an undisturbed midden was encountered, it was removed in arbitrary 0.5 foot levels until subsoil was reached (Faulkner and McCollough 1974:47–175).

Of the six sites tested in the summer of 1972, five were recommended for further excavation. A block excavation proceeded on the Banks I site (40CF34), where a Late Archaic structure was located (Faulkner and McCollough 1974:176–258). Block excavation was considered a Phase III intensive continuation of Phase II testing in which contiguous blocks or squares were opened to further test middens and expose feature clusters and structures. Soil from middens and features was waterscreened through 1/4-inch and 1/16-inch mesh screen, and flotation samples were taken from charcoal-enriched features.

Testing revealed an extensive midden under the plow zone on the Banks III site (40CF108), which was further exposed by block stripping and removal of the plow zone by mechanical means (in this case a road patrol grader) in large blocks and then extensively hand-excavated. Soil was processed as in block excavation. Significant features included Middle Woodland Owl Hollow–phase summer and winter houses and early Mississippian Banks–phase domestic installations (Faulkner and McCollough 1974:259–570). Woodland middens were also discovered on the Eoff I site (40CF32), and three areas of this large site were recommended for block excavation in 1973.

Three Archaic sites were also recommended for further study. The Eoff III site (40CF107) was the only intensively occupied site found in the floodplain zone, producing a number of Middle Archaic projectile points. Although deep soundings in two units did not indicate buried strata, additional testing was proposed at this site. The Hicks site (40CF62) produced evidence of a Late Archaic Ledbetter component and was recommended for further study in 1973. Several features and a burial attributed to a Terminal Archaic Wade occupation at the Nowlin II site (40CF35) required further block excavation (Faulkner and McCollough 1974:81–175).

Testing continued on seven sites in the lower reservoir in fall 1972, the most important being the Banks V site (40CF111) and Rhoton Cave (40CF46). Test units on Banks V revealed an extensive midden preserved under the plow zone dating to the Middle Woodland period, which was studied by shallow plowing with controlled surface collection and the removal of the plow zone from a cruciform pattern of intersecting trenches using a TVA provided smooth-bladed Tournapull pan. Block stripping of Banks V was planned for 1973 (Faulkner and McCollough 1974). Rhoton Cave was first tested in 1968–69 by local members of the Tennessee Archaeological Society. After removing several tons of surface rock fall, excavation of two units in 1972 revealed a stratified sequence of Woodland components with excellent faunal preservation. Further testing was recommended, but time did not permit returning to the cave (Faulkner and McCollough 1974).

In addition to the above two sites, a large area called the Banks floodplain, or "West Bottom," was also tested in fall 1972. Five 3 x 3 foot test pits were placed on prominences in this floodplan zone. All were excavated to the water table with negative results; no deeply buried arti-facts or archaeological deposits were found (Faulkner and McCollough 1974:132).

After the 1972 excavation season, the Normandy Archaeological Project laboratory was established in the Department of Anthropol-ogy of the University of Tennessee–Knoxville, funded by National Park Service contracts. Prior to analysis, comprehensive lithic and ceramic typologies were established to insure consistency in artifact identification (Faulkner and McCollough 1973:63–327; Faulkner and McCollough 1974:19–45). In 1973 coprincipal investigator McCollough began the Normandy Lithic Resource Survey to collect samples of raw materi-als from primary context in the Highland Rim area to serve as a basis for research into prehistoric lithic utilization in the upper Duck Valley (Penny and McCollough 1976:140–194). Paul Parmalee, curator of the department's extensive faunal type collection, directed the faunal analysis and Andrea Shea and Gary Crites assembled a floral collection for archaeo-botanical research (Shea 1977). Artifact analysis was largely conducted by graduate students in the Normandy Research Assistantship program with the proviso that they use the data for M.A. theses and Ph.D. dissertations. Twelve theses and three dissertations resulted from this research.

Phase I site survey continued in the reservoir during the 1973 field seasons. Phase II testing continued on four sites in the lower reservoir zone, two of these identified as large and intensively occupied loci based on the surface collections. The Jernigan II site (40CF37) covered approximately two acres and was divided into seven contiguous horizontal testing areas that were controlled surface collected before unit excavation. Scattered midden deposits and an unusual shaft and chamber burial dated to the Mason-phase occupation, and Ledbetter-phase features were numerous on the site (McCollough and Duvall 1976:27–58). On the Parks site (40CF5), one of the largest sites in the upper Duck Valley, cultural material was thickly spread over an area of 20 to 25 acres. Four areas were chosen, based on plowed-out midden deposits and artifact distribution, and then delimited on the site and tested through the summer and fall of 1973. Late Archaic through Mississippian components were well represented on the Parks site, and intensive excavation was planned for the following year (McCollough and Duvall 1976:116–133).

Phase II in the upper reservoir zone began in 1973 with the testing of four large sites; Riddle (40CF59), Boyd II (40CF68), Wiser-Stephens (40CF81), and Anthony II (40CF104). In addition, one of the largest sites in the upper reservoir, Ewell III (40CF118) was discovered in an area that had not been cultivated for several years. Testing of the Wiser-Stephens site revealed components dating from the Late Archaic period to the Late Woodland period, with an especially intensive occupation during the latter period. Further excavation was recommended on this site. Additional excavation was also planned for the Boyd II site, the largest and one of the most significant habitation sites in the upper reservoir zone.

Phase III block excavation proceeded on three sites during the spring, summer, and fall of 1973. The Hicks I site was excavated in the spring with units and a 5 x 70 foot trench through the Archaic midden. Four levels were removed from this deeply buried horizon containing widely scattered Ledbetter-phase basin hearths (Faulkner 1977a).

Phase III excavation at the Eoff I site was accomplished in two areas of midden deposits. Area A on the north end of the site was excavated

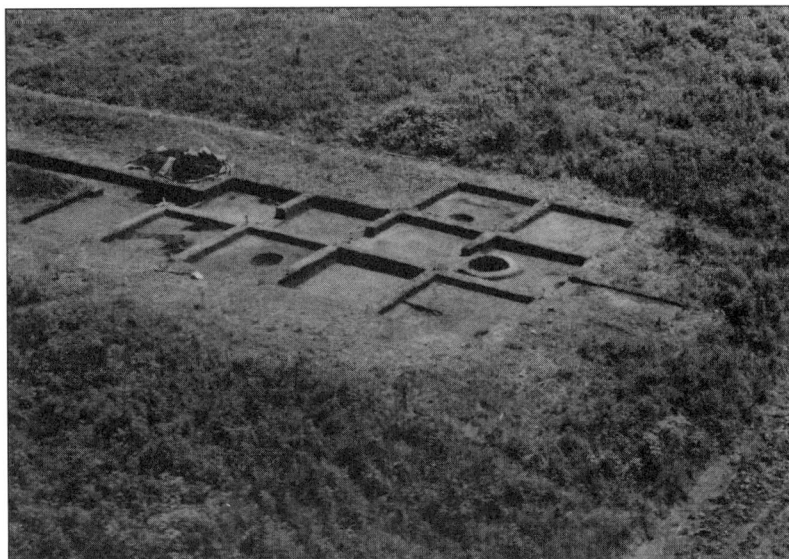

Fig. 3.2. Block excavation on the Eoff I site.

with a large block exposing a Neal-phase dwelling. Trench 1 was placed through a stratified earth midden that reached a thickness of as much as two feet below the plow zone, the strata containing largely Mason-phase features and artifacts. The major excavation in this Area B originally consisted of a 5 x 90 foot trench that was later expanded into a block of 20 10 x 10 foot units (Figure 3.2). Seventeen features were exposed in Area B representing the Ledbetter, Wade, and McFarland phases, the most informative being an irregular large and deeply stratified conical pit that was so large, its total diameter and depth could not be determined. However, the configuration and artifact association indicated this was an ancient spring/solution cavity that had been filled during the early Ledbetter phase, radiocarbon dated between 3500 and 3000 B.C. (Faulkner 1977b).

On the floodplain adjacent to Eoff I is the Eoff III site (40CF107), tested in 1972 and found to contain a Middle Archaic component. Since this was the earliest site surveyed in the reservoir that produced enough diagnostic artifacts to suggest a more intensive occupation, two 30 x 30 foot blocks were opened in areas where another controlled surface collection was made. Three features were exposed, a shallow basin providing a radiocarbon date of 4575 B.C. In addition, one 5 x 10 foot unit was taken down to a depth of eight feet below surface; however, no evidence of human occupation was found below the base of the plow zone (Faulkner 1977c).

An entire volume was devoted to the investigation of the Banks V site (40CF111) during the summer and fall of 1973 and continuing into the 1974 field season (Faulkner and McCollough, eds. 1978). Research involved a combination of continued controlled surface collecting, power strip trenches, and finally total removal of the plow zone from a 2.36-acre area with intensive excavation of features in a .66-acre area (Figure 3.3). Numerous features were revealed, many of them associated with a large (50 x 35 foot) Owl Hollow winter house (Figure 3.4) and an early Mississippian hamlet (Faulkner and McCollough, eds. 1978). Beginning with the 1974 field season, a change in field strategy was initiated since only two years remained before the reservoir would be filled. It was obvious from the testing and block excavation phase that the majority of the sites did not have deep middens, but features remained well preserved beneath the plow zone. Also features dating earlier than the Late Archaic period were rare to absent so virtually no data on settlement/ community patterning and subsistence would be forthcoming from the earlier periods. It was decided that the last two years would be spent stripping large areas of those sites containing substantive features to enable the continuation of testing hypotheses about culture process during the 4,500 years from the Late Archaic through the Mississippian periods. Four sites were extensively machine stripped in 1974. These included the Nowlin II site in the lower reservoir and the Ewell III site in the upper reservoir. Nowlin II was excavated by a field school from Wright State University directed by Bennie C. Keel. The site continued to be tested in June and July, and 14,500 square feet of plow zone were removed in August. Features and burials from the Wade, Watts Bar, and McFarland phases were well represented (Keel 1978). The Ewell III site was further tested in the spring and .643 acres of this site on a narrow alluvial terrace were stripped in June, revealing community patterns of the Wade, McFarland, and Mason phases (DuVall 1982). Jernigan II, the largest site on the right bank of the lower reservoir zone, was excavated in the summer with a main block of 1.3 acres stripped and three deep backhoe transects dug revealing that no in situ deposits remained dating earlier than the Late Archaic. Feature clusters dating from the Ledbetter, Long Branch, and Mason phases were excavated (Figure 3.5). A midden containing the cultural remains of an historic sawmill was also tested (Faulkner and McCollough 1982a).

Areas A through C on the Parks site continued to be tested in the spring including a sinkhole, with fill dating to 3930 B.C. Deep units were

Fig. 3.3. Visit of the TVA Consulting Board to the Banks V site, August 1973. Left to right: not identified, Major McCollough, Robert Stephenson, Bruce Dickson, John Corbett, Lloyd Chapman (foreground), John Brew, Corydon Bell, and Charles Faulkner.

also sunk on the Parks floodplain but with negative results. During the summer and fall 5.8 acres of plow zone were removed, exposing numerous features, burials, and structures from the Ledbetter, Neel, McFarland, Mason, and Banks phases (Faulkner and McCollough 1982b). The Coffee County chapter of the TAS continued to excavate features on the Parks site until the reservoir was flooded (Bacon 1982). There were also plans for extensive excavation of the Boyd II site in the upper reservoir, but permission could not be obtained from the owner, who still farmed the property.

Excavation in 1975 concentrated on two large sites, Eoff I in the lower reservoir and Wiser-Stephens in the upper reservoir. About 10 acres of the Eoff I site were stripped, the most significant discoveries being community patterning of McFarland, Owl Hollow, and Banks structures (Chapman 1978, 1982; Cobb 1982, 1985). The Wiser-Stephens site was excavated by the Wright State University field school under the direction of Keel, initially with 5 x 5 foot units, a hand-excavated control block, and finally plow zone removal of more than 5,000 square feet of the site where clusters of Ledbetter, Wade, and McFarland features were excavated (Davis 1976, 1978).

Fig. 3.4. Large Owl Hollow double-oven winter house, Banks V site.

Two smaller upland sites in the lower reservoir were also studied in 1975. The Aaron Shelton site (40CF69), located on a 50-foot-high bluff, was tested in the spring, and four areas were stripped later in the year. A trench was also dug to locate possible buried early horizons since late Paleo to Middle Archaic artifacts had been found in the 1971 survey. No early features were found, most of the occupation occurring during the Ledbetter and Long Branch phases (Wagner 1980, 1982). The other excavated upland site was Duke I, a historic farmstead that was tested with 16 5 x 5 foot units producing a late nineteenth–early twentieth century artifact assemblage (Faulkner 1982).

Culture History in the Normandy Reservoir

Eighty-two radiocarbon dates and seven archaeomagnetic dates were obtained from features on the Normandy Reservoir sites. The earliest radiocarbon date is 4575 B.C. +\ -165 from a Middle Archaic Eva/Morrow Mountain feature on the Eoff III site. Three dates span the fourth millennium B.C. from 3930 B.C. +/- to 3105 B.C. +/- 105 dating an early Late Archaic phase tentatively named the Hicks phase (Bowen 1975). Although this 1,000-year span should include the White Springs/Three Mile and Benton phases, no diagnostic projectile points/knives

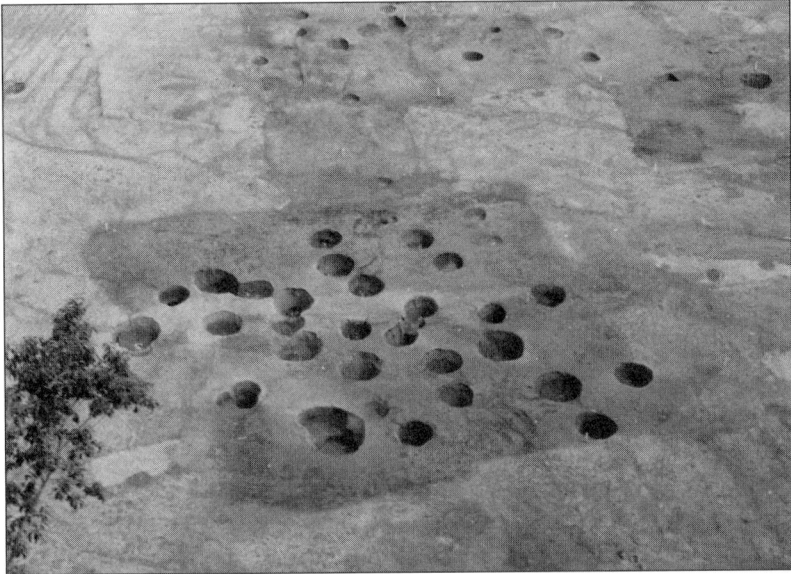

Fig. 3.5. Late/Terminal Archaic pit cluster on the Jernigan II site.

from these phases were associated with dated features. Late/Terminal Archaic dates include three from the Ledbetter phase from 2080 B.C. +/- 260 and 900 B.C. +/- 870 and four from the Wade phase from 1075 B.C. +/- 75 to 840 B.C. +/80. Early Woodland period dates range from 675 B.C. +/- 140 to 390 B.C. +/- 90 for the Watts Bar phase (3 dates) and from 215 B.C. +/- 110 (three acceptable dates) for the Long Branch phase. Three dates for the Neel phase fall between 255 B.C. +/- 125 and 115 B.C. +/- 60). Six early Middle Woodland McFarland dates range from 90 B.C. +/- 95 to A.D. 155 +/- 110, and 19 acceptable late Middle Woodland Owl Hollow dates range from A.D. 150 +/- to A.D. 710 +/- 140. Four of six archaeomagnetic dates from Owl Hollow features at the Eoff I site are from A.D. 565 +/- 29 years to A.D. 625 +/- 25. Seven Mason-phase dates range from A.D. 660 +/- 160 to A.D. 1190 +/- 170. Sixteen Mississippian dates range from A.D. 745 +/- 195 to A.D. 1344 +/- 134. Two clusters of dates indicate an Emergent Mississippian phase about A.D. 700–A.D. 1000 and an Early Mississippian phase at around A.D. 1000–A.D. 1300.

The relationship of the Normandy prehistoric phases to cultural manifestations outside the Eastern Highland Rim area after the Middle Archaic period can be generally attributed to shifting culture contact and probably even movement of populations. Interaction with the Ledbetter culture of the western Tennessee Valley (Lewis and Kneberg 1959) and the closely related Lauderdale culture of the middle Tennessee River Valley of northern Alabama (Walthall 1980:69) is evident during the Late Archaic period, with close ties to the south continuing through the Long Branch phase with the Colbert culture of the middle Tennessee Valley (Walthall 1980:112–16). Contact with the Watts Bar culture in the eastern Tennessee Valley (Lewis and Kneberg 1957) is also indicated very early in the Woodland period and interaction with the eastern valley continues into the Long Branch phase.

There is strong evidence of cultural continuity between the Early Woodland Long Branch and Middle Woodland McFarland phases. The McFarland phase proper appears closely related to the domestic aspects of the Copena culture of northern Alabama. However, an assemblage called the Neel phase overlaps both Long Branch and McFarland based on radiocarbon dates from Normandy and from the Yearwood site in the adjacent Elk River Valley (Butler 1979). Ties to Scioto and Havana Hopewell in Ohio and Illinois and Hopewellian related sites to the south such as Tunacunnhee in northern Georgia (Jeffries 1976, 1979) are indicated by exotic grave goods, elaborate burial practices, and construction of earthworks, suggesting the Neel phase is a mortuary component within a late Long Branch–early McFarland settlement system (Faulkner 2002:190–191). The C-14 dates for Neel components also imply Hopewellian influences appeared earlier in the Eastern Highland Rim than they did in the Connestee culture of the eastern Tennessee Valley (Chapman and Keel 1979).

A cultural discontinuity occurs in the Middle Woodland period after ca. A.D. 200 with the appearance of the Owl Hollow culture. This culture, which shows little or no connection to Hopewell, may be most closely related to the La Motte culture of the lower Wabash Valley (Pace 1973; Winters 1963). There also appears to be little direct relationship between the Owl Hollow and Mason phases, the latter sharing a number of traits with the Late Woodland Hamilton culture of the eastern Tennessee Valley (Lewis and Kneberg 1946) and McKelvey culture of northern Alabama (Walthall 1980). Mason cultural traits such as net-impressed pottery and shaft-and-chamber graves are also found in Late Woodland cultures in the Carolina Piedmont (McCollough et al. 1979).

The Emergent Mississippian Banks phase also appears to be a site-intrusive culture, the C-14 dates in the eighth and ninth centuries being some of the earliest dates for Mississippian in the mid-South. Its contemporanity with the Mason phase is indicated by features containing ceramics from both cultures. Architecture and other material traits, especially ceramics, suggest Banks is closely associated with the Langston culture of northern Alabama (Walthall 1980). Some ceramics in the Early Mississippian (A.D. 1000–A.D. 1300) indicate closer ties with the Middle Cumberland culture in the Cumberland Valley to the north. There is yet no evidence of a late or protohistoric Mississippian occupation of the Normandy Reservoir area.

Culture Process in the Normandy Reservoir

Following the decision to test hypotheses about the relationship of environment and culture in the upper Duck Valley during the past 4,000 years, special emphasis was placed on fine water screening and flotation. A major hypothesis that was tested was whether the utilization of fauna changed from a diffuse pattern practiced by Late Archaic hunters and gatherers to a focal pattern employed by the agricultural Mississippian people. Faunal analysis indicates that white-tailed deer was the primary meat source with small vertebrates providing a minor but consistent percentage of the diet through time, with little difference in faunal exploitation occurring from the Late Archaic through the Mississippian periods. Though shellfish were not important in the diet, all of the biogeographic zones were exploited during this time (Robison 1977, 1978, 1986).

Examination of recovered plant foods during this same period revealed significant subsistence developments. One was the increasing importance of gardening from the Late Archaic through the Mississippian period with utilization of herbaceous annuals and their eventual domestication from the Late Archaic through the Middle Woodland. Squash and gourd rind was found as early as the Late/Terminal Archaic, and maize was discovered in Owl Hollow context. Another development was the intensive utilization of herbaceous annuals such as chenopodium, marsh elder, and the domestication of some of these plants in the Middle Woodland period (Crites 1978, 1985; Shea 1977, 1978). More intensive gardening appears to have been a major factor in a shift from settlement throughout both the upper and lower reservoir zones from Ledbetter through McFarland times to the exclusive establishment of communities in the broad and fertile floodplain of the lower reservoir zone in the Owl Hollow and Banks phases.

Settlement and community patterns during the past 4,000 years were also a major focus in this study. In looking at coarse-grained settlement patterns, the concern was with testing two settlement models: the mobile dispersed model (shifting hunting and gathering camps) and the nuclear model (permanent villages). Both pertained to the long-term settlement of the lower and upper reservoir zones and the fine-grained shift from a mobile dispersed pattern to the nuclear pattern in the shorter term waxing and waning of cultural phases (Prescott 1978). In the early Middle Woodland period, settlements were found throughout both reservoir zones, although by late McFarland times, larger permanent domestic sites were located in the upper reservoir zone. This may have been an effect of the construction of the Old Stone Fort ceremonial enclosure further upstream. In the Owl Hollow and Mississippian cultures, permanent settlements are found only in the lower reservoir zone. As discussed above, this settlement shift can be largely explained by the more intensive growing of herbaceous annuals and some maize by the Owl Hollow people and the intensive maize farming of the Mississippians.

The intensity of site occupation based on numbers of food preparation and storage facilities and permanency of dwellings was primarily used to indicate short-term settlement shifts and changing community patterns. The earliest evidence of Archaic features is in the Eva-Morrow Mountain phase at Eoff III. It might be significant that this is the only site found on the floodplan with intact features, suggesting that later groups abandoned this flood-prone zone as seasonal camps involved less mobility. This certainly seems to be the case with the appearance of the Ledbetter phase (after ca. 2000 B.C.), when clusters of cylindrical storage pits (or "silos"), shallow processing pits, burials (both flesh inhumations and cremations), and postholes are found on sites on the older, higher terraces. Other Ledbetter sites do not have storage facilities, suggesting seasonal occupation by nuclear or extended families, as does the typical open windbreak or "cabana" structure. Such small, seasonally occupied sites continue in the Wade phase although a greater degree of sedentism is signaled by fully enclosed wall-roof framework houses (Figure 3.6). A greater complexity in this phase is also seen in an increased frequency of exotic materials such as steatite and Dover chert, often accompanying flesh inhumations.

Little change can be discerned in the community patterning of the Early Woodland period. Sites remain small, with pit clusters now including rock-filled earth ovens. No structures have been identified. Since only one site, Jernigan II, shows evidence of repeated occupation, it appears that the population of the upper Duck Valley actually declined during this time.

The densest population of the upper Duck Valley appears in the Middle Woodland period, but even at that time most settlements probably did not exceed three extended family households, or approximately 25–30 persons. The early McFarland settlement pattern was nuclear

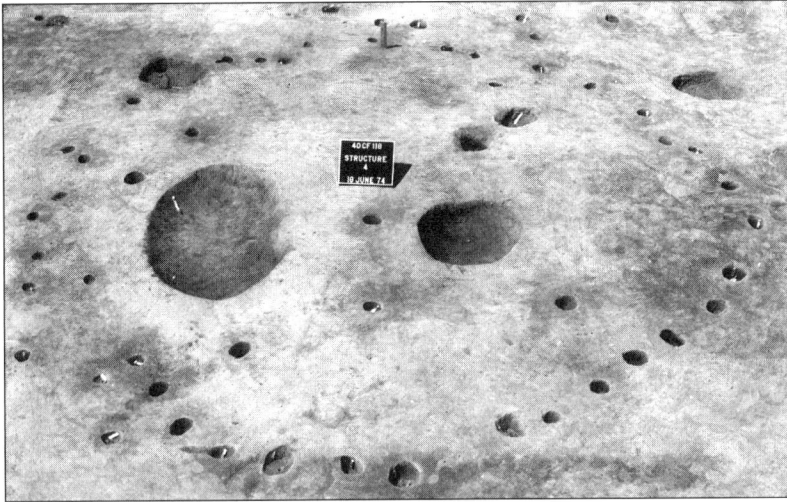

Fig. 3.6. Wade phase structure on the Ewell III site.

in that individual families occupied small permanent "villages" during most of the year but seasonally congregated at special mortuary sites such as Parks or the Old Stone Fort ceremonial enclosure. An early Middle Woodland component such as that on the former site is believed to represent an early influence of the Hopewellian mortuary practices and trade called the Neel phase, with construction of the latter site commencing at a slightly later date (Faulkner 1996). The "village" aspect of the McFarland phase consisted of warm season windbreaks and fully enclosed cold-season structures with discrete dwelling and food processing zones. Absence of substantial middens and infrequent rebuilding of dwellings indicate these villages were frequently moved.

True nucleated settlements or villages are found in the succeeding Owl Hollow phase, a long-term and intense occupation being indicated by deep refuse middens, substantially constructed double earth-oven winter lodges, and companion enclosed summer structures, with these buildings often arranged around an open, plazalike area (Cobb 1985; Faulkner 2002). No seasonal camps of the Owl Hollow people have been identified although large numbers of their lanceolate notched and "spike" points were found on most sites in the reservoir, suggesting local hunting stands. Burials include cremations and flesh inhumations (Brown 1982), and although the Old Stone Fort appears to have been used until the end of the fifth century A.D., there is little evidence of Hopewellian influence on this culture.

The organized, permanent villages of the McFarland and Owl Hollow phases were eventually replaced by what appear to be seasonal encampments of the intrusive Late Woodland Mason phase. While the scattered pits and more open, poorly constructed dwellings of this phase might suggest a population decline during this time, a more likely interpretation is that the community patterning reverted back to what has been described as the mobile dispersed model. Since maize has been found in some Mason features, it is likely that gardening was conducted at central base camps such as Parks, where simple burial of the dead also took place (Duggan 1982; McMahan 1983).

The Mississippian occupation, also believed to be phase intrusive, apparently shared the upper Duck Valley with the Mason culture during the ninth and tenth centuries A.D. with the more formal and permanent wall-trench houses scattered on sites in the lower reservoir zone. Although several houses may have been located on the Eoff I site, these settlements were more likely family farmsteads where maize was by then a principal crop. The presence of large storage pits on this site also suggests that some type of seasonal movement was practiced. By the fifteenth century A.D., the upper Duck River Valley appears to have been abandoned with the Mississippian populations then congregating in large villages in the lower Duck and Elk river valleys and the Cumberland drainage.

Normandy Reservoir Archaeology: The Legacy

Briefly, what is the legacy of the Normandy Archaeological Project? Two aspects of this research come to mind. One is procedural. Large scale projects such as Normandy must be conducted within a measured time frame that allows the research to evolve through thorough survey, testing, and intensive excavation phases with the concomitant development of a research design that builds on the results of each phase. It is fortunate that the reservoir was small enough so that the focus could be on testable hypotheses allowed by the accumulating data. This is not to say that more could not have been done had more time been available. For example, more effort would have been made to delineate earlier prehistoric components and the historic occupation of the reservoir, had time permitted.

Another legacy is that although earlier TVA reservoir mitigation provided a window into the prehistory of a river valley, sites in the surrounding uplands were usually not included in the surveys, thus causing a skewed interpretation of regional cultural patterns. It was only with the relatively recent large-scale mitigation on federal highway projects that the presence of important sites in the uplands became known in many areas of Tennessee. Reservoir archaeology should not be an end in itself but a means to the end from which to test further hypotheses about regional subsistence and settlement patterns in the surrounding uplands. Testing deductive models about Middle Woodland subsistence and settlement patterns in the upland areas around the Duck and Elk River valleys continued from 1976 to 1982 with National Foundation grants (Cobb 1985; Cobb and Faulkner 1978; Faulkner 1988, 2002; Kline et al. 1982).

Acknowledgments

First and foremost, I want to thank my coprincipal investigator, Major C. R. McCollough for his steadfast commitment to the Normandy project. Without his perseverance and guidance, this project would not have been possible. I also want to thank Bennie C. Keel for his professional guidance and for bringing two fine Wright State University field schools to the reservoir in 1974 and 1975. Unfortunately, space will not allow the names of many persons at the University of Tennessee–Knoxville, TVA, and the Park Service who assisted us to appear here, but I must mention the invaluable support of Bill Bass, former head of the Anthropology Department, Corydon Bell and J. Bennett Graham at TVA, and Richard Faust at the National Park Service. It is also impossible to thank all the local residents and landowners who helped us in so many ways, but I can not forget the contributions of Will and Bonnie Bacon, Travis and Helga Binion, Raymond and Carolyn Duke, Greg and Penny Kline, and Leo and Blossom Merryman who also treated us like family.

It is also impossible to list the more than 200 students and volunteers who worked in the field and lab during the five years of the Normandy project. At the risk of missing someone, however, I must acknowledge the following field and lab supervisors and assistants whose dedication and expertise were the glue holding the project together, many of them going on to become professional anthropologists/archaeologists: Hugh Berryman, Michael Binion, Lloyd Chapman, Jim Cobb, B. I. Coblentz, Cliff Coney, Steve Davis, Glyn DuVall, Jason Fenwick, Nick Fielder, Pat Fisher, Stan Guffy, Karen Gunn, Victor Hood, Carroll Kleinhans, Larry Kimball, Susan Kluge, Joy Medford, Robert Murphy, Jim Penny, Joanne Mueller Penny, Richard Roberts, Neil Robison, Doug Prescott, Andrea Brewer Shea, Michael Smolek, Jim Walden, Lee Wallace, Rick Ward, Dennis Wentworth, and P. Willey.

References Cited

BACON, WILLARD S.

1982 Structural Data Recovered from the Banks III Site (40CF108) and the Parks Site (40CF5B), Normandy Reservoir, Coffee County, Tennessee. *Tennessee Anthropologist* 7(2):176–197.

BOWEN, WILLIAM R.

1975 Late Archaic Subsistence and Settlement in the Western Tennessee Valley. M.A. thesis, Department of Anthropology, University of Tennessee, Knoxville.

BROWN, TRACY C.

1982 Prehistoric Mortuary Patterning and Change in the Normandy Reservoir, Coffee County, Tennessee. M.A. thesis, Department of Anthropology, University of Tennessee, Knoxville.

BUTLER, BRIAN M.

1979 Hopewell Contacts in Southern Middle Tennessee. In *Hopewell Archaeology: The Chillecothe Conference,* edited by David Brose and Naomi Greber, pp. 150–156. Kent State University Press, Kent, Ohio.

CHAPMAN, LLOYD N.

1978 The Mississippian Component at the Eoff I Site. M.A. thesis, Department of Anthropology, University of Tennessee, Knoxville.

1982 The Mississippian Component at the Eoff I Site. In *Eighth Report of the Normandy Archaeological Project,* edited by Charles H. Faulkner and Major C. R. McCollough, pp. 1–148. University of Tennessee, Department of Anthropology, Report of Investigations No. 33 and TVA Publications in Anthropology No. 30. Knoxville.

CHAPMAN, JEFFERSON, AND BENNIE C. KEEL

1979 Candy Creek—Connestee Components in Eastern Tennessee and Western North Carolina and Their Relationship with Adena-Hopewell. In *Hopewell Archaeology: The Chillecothe Conference,* edited by David Brose and Naomi Greber, pp. 157–161. Kent University Press, Kent, Ohio.

COBB, JAMES E.

1978 The Middle Woodland Occupations of the Banks V Site, 40CF111. In *Fifth Report of the Normandy Archaeological Project,* edited by Charles H. Faulkner and Major C. R. McCollough, pp. 72–327. University of Tennessee, Department of Anthropology, Report of Investigations No. 20. Knoxville.

1982 The Late Middle Woodland Occupation of the Eoff I Site, 40CF32. In *Eighth Report of the Normandy Archaeological Project,* edited by Charles H. Faulkner and Major C. R. McCollough, pp. 149–301.

University of Tennessee, Department of Anthropology, Report of
Investigations No. 33 and TVA Publications in Anthropology No.
30. Knoxville.

1985   Late Middle Woodland Settlement and Subsistence Patterns on the
Eastern Highland Rim of Middle Tennessee. Ph.D. dissertation,
Department of Anthropology, University of Tennessee, Knoxville.

COBB, JAMES E., AND CHARLES H. FAULKNER
1978   *The Owl Hollow Project: Middle Woodland and Subsistence
Patterns in the Eastern Highland Rim of Tennessee.* Final report
submitted to the National Science Foundation in accordance with
the requirements of Grant BNS 76–11266.

CRITES, GARY D.
1978   Paleoethnobotany of the Normandy Reservoir in the Upper Duck
River Valley, Tennessee. M.A. thesis, Department of Anthropology,
University of Tennessee, Knoxville.

1985   Middle Woodland Paleoethnobotany of the Eastern Highland Rim
of Tennessee: An Evolutionary Perspective on Change in Human-
Plant Interaction. Ph.D. dissertation, Department of Anthropology,
University of Tennessee, Knoxville.

DAVIS, R. P. STEPHEN, JR.
1976   The Wiser-Stephens Site—40CF81. M.A. thesis, Department of
Archaeology, University of Calgary, Alberta, Canada.

1978   Excavations at the Wiser-Stephens I Site. In *Sixth Report of
the Normandy Archaeological Project,* edited by Major C. R.
McCollough and Charles H. Faulkner, pp. 291–547. University of
Tennessee, Department of Anthropology, Report of Investigations
No. 21, Wright State University/Laboratory of Anthropology/Notes
in Anthropology No. 4, TVA Publications in Anthropology No. 19.
Chattanooga.

DUGGAN, BETTY J.
1982   A Synthesis of the Late Woodland Mason Phase in the Normandy
and Tims Ford Reservoirs in Middle Tennessee. M.A. thesis,
Department of Anthropology, University of Tennessee, Knoxville.

DUVALL, GLYN D.
1977   The Ewell III Site (40CF118): An Early Middle Woodland
McFarland Phase Site in the Normandy Reservoir, Coffee County,
Tennessee. M.A. thesis, Department of Anthropology, University of
Tennessee, Knoxville.

1982   The Ewell III Site (40CF118). In *Seventh Report of the Normandy
Archaeological Project,* edited by Charles H. Faulkner and Major
C. R. McCollough, pp. 8–151. University of Tennessee, Department

of Anthropology, Report of Investigations No. 32, TVA Publications in Anthropology No. 29.

FAULKNER, CHARLES H.

1971 *An Archaeological Survey of the Proposed Normandy Reservoir: Interim Report.* On file in the Department of Anthropology, University of Tennessee, Knoxville.

1977a The Hicks Site (40CF62). In *Fourth Report of the Normandy Archaeological Project,* edited by Charles H. Faulkner and Major C. R. McCollough, pp. 9–63. University of Tennessee, Department of Anthropology, Report of Investigations No. 19. Knoxville.

1977b Eoff I Site (40CF32). In *Fourth Report of the Normandy Archaeological Project,* edited by Charles H. Faulkner and Major C. R. McCollough, pp. 64–278. University of Tennessee, Department of Anthropology, Report of Investigations N0.19. Knoxville.

1977c Eoff III Site (40CF107). In *Fourth Report of the Normandy Archaeological Project,* edited by Charles H. Faulkner and Major C. R. McCollough, pp. 279–299. University of Tennessee, Department of Anthropology, Report of Investigations No. 19. Knoxville.

1982 The Duke I Site (40CF97). In *Eighth Report of the Normandy Archaeological Project,* edited by Charles H. Faulkner and Major C. R. McCollough, pp. 527–541. University of Tennessee, Department of Anthropology, Report of Investigations No. 33, TVA Publications in Anthropology No. 30. Knoxville.

1988 Middle Woodland Community and Settlement Patterns on the Eastern Highland Rim of Tennessee. In *Middle Woodland Settlement and Ceremonialism in the Mid-South and Lower Mississippi Valley,* edited by Robert C. Mainfort, Jr., pp. 76–98. Archaeological Report 22, Mississippi Department of Archives and History, Jackson.

1996 The Old Stone Fort Revisited: New Clues to an Old Mystery. In *Mounds, Embankments, and Ceremonialism in the Midsouth,* edited by Robert C. Mainfort and Richard Walling, pp. 7–11. Arkansas Archaeological Survey, Research Series No. 46, Fayetteville.

2002 Woodland Cultures of the Elk and Duck River Valleys, Tennessee: Continuity and Change. In *The Woodland Southeast,* edited by David G. Anderson and Robert C. Mainfort, Jr., pp. 185–203. University of Alabama Press, Tuscaloosa.

FAULKNER, CHARLES H., AND MAJOR C. R. McCOLLOUGH

1973 *Introductory Report of the Normandy Reservoir Salvage Project: Environmental Setting, Typology, and Survey.* Normandy Archaeological Project, vol. 1. University of Tennessee, Department of Anthropology, Report of Investigations No. 11. Knoxville.

1974 *Excavations and Testing, Normandy Reservoir Salvage Project: 1972 Seasons.* Normandy Archaeological Project, vol. 2, University of Tennessee, Department of Anthropology, Report of Investigations No. 12. Knoxville.

1982a   Excavation of the Jernigan II Site (40CF37). In *Seventh Report of the Normandy Archaeological Project,* edited by Charles H. Faulkner and Major C. R. McCollough, pp. 153–311. University of Tennessee, Department of Anthropology, Report of Investigations No. 32 and TVA Publications in Anthropology No. 29. Knoxville.

1982b   The Investigation of the Parks Site (40CF5). In *Seventh Report of the Normandy Archaeological Project,* edited by Charles H. Faulkner and Major C. R. McCollough, pp. 313–352. University of Tennessee, Department of Anthropology, Report of Investigations No. 32, and TVA Publications in Anthropology No. 29. Knoxville.

FAULKNER, CHARLES H., AND MAJOR C. R. MCCOLLOUGH, EDS.
1978   *Fifth Report of the Normandy Archaeological Project,* edited by Charles H. Faulkner and Major C. R. McCollough. University of Tennessee, Department of Anthropology, Report of Investigations No. 20. Knoxville.

JEFFRIES, RICHARD W.
1976   *The Tunacunnhee Site: Evidence of Hopewellian Interaction in Northwest Georgia.* Anthropological Papers of the University of Georgia No. 1. Athens.

1978   The Tunacunnhee Site: Hopewell in Northwest Georgia. In *Hopewell Archaeology: The Chillicothe Conference,* edited by David S. Brose and N'omi Greber, pp. 162–170. Kent State University Press, Kent, Ohio.

KEEL, BENNIE C.
1978   Excavations at the Nowlin II Site. In *Sixth Report of the Normandy Archaeological Project,* edited by Major C. R. McCollough and Charles H. Faulkner, pp. xi–290. University of Tennessee, Department of Anthropology, Report of Investigations No. 21, Wright State University, Laboratory of Anthropology, Notes in Anthropology No. 4, TVA Publications in Anthropology No. 19. Chattanooga.

KLINE, GERALD W., GARY D. CRITES, AND CHARLES H. FAULKNER
1982   *The McFarland Project: Early Middle Woodland Settlement and Subsistence in the Upper Duck Valley in Tennessee.* Tennessee Anthropological Association, Miscellaneous Paper No. 8. Knoxville.

LEWIS, THOMAS N. M., AND MADELINE KNEBERG
1946   *Hiwassee Island.* University of Tennessee Press, Knoxville.

1957   The Camp Creek Site. *Tennessee Archaeologist* 13(1):1–48.

1959   The Archaic Culture in the Middle South. *American Antiquity* 25(1):161–183.

MCCOLLOUGH, MAJOR C. R., AND GLYN D. DUVALL
1976   Results of 1973 Testing. In *Third Report of the Normandy Reservoir Salvage Project*, edited by Major C. R. McCollough and Charles H. Faulkner, pp. 27–139. University of Tennessee, Department of Anthropology, Report of Investigations No. 16. Knoxville.

MCCOLLOUGH, MAJOR C. R., GLYN D. DUVALL, CHARLES H. FAULKNER, AND TRACY C. BROWN
1979   A Late Woodland Shaft and Chamber Grave in the Normandy Reservoir, Tennessee. *Tennessee Anthropologist* 4(2):175–188.

MCMAHAN, JOE DAVID
1983   Paleoethnobotany of the Late Woodland Mason Phase in the Elk and Duck River Valleys, Tennessee. M.A. thesis, Department of Anthropology, University of Tennessee, Knoxville.

PACE, ROBERT E.
1973   *Archaeological Salvage, Daughtery-Monroe Site: Island Levee Local Protection Project, Sullivan County, Indiana.* Submitted to the Northeast Regional Office, National Park Service.

PENNY, JAMES S., JR., AND MAJOR C. R. MCCOLLOUGH
1976   The Normandy Lithic Resource Survey. In *Third Report of the Normandy Reservoir Salvage Project*, edited by Major C. R. McCollough and Charles Faulkner, pp. 140–194. University of Tennessee, Department of Anthropology, Report of Investigations No. 16. Knoxville.

PRESCOTT, WILLIAM D.
1978   Analysis of Surface Survey Data from the Normandy Reservoir. M.A. thesis, Department of Anthropology, University of Tennessee, Knoxville.

ROBISON, NEIL D.
1977   Zooarchaeological Analysis of the Mississippian Faunal Remains from the Normandy Reservoir. M.A. thesis, Department of Anthropology, University of Tennessee, Knoxville.

1978   A Zooarchaeological Analysis of the Mississippian Faunal Remains from the Normandy Reservoir. In *Fifth Report of the Normandy Archaeological Project*, edited by Charles H. Faulkner and Major C. R. McCollough, pp. 498–595. University of Tennessee, Department of Anthropology, Report of Investigations No. 10. Knoxville.

1986   An Analysis and Interpretation of the Faunal Remains from Eight Late Middle Woodland Owl Hollow Phase Sites in Coffee, Franklin and Bedford Counties. Ph.D. dissertation, Department of Anthropology, University of Tennessee, Knoxville.

SHEA, ANDREA B.
1977   Comparison of Middle Woodland and Early Mississippian Subsistence Patterns: Analysis of Plant Remains from an

Archaeological Site in the Duck River Valley, Tennessee, Supplemented by the Potentially Exploitable Native Flora. M.S. thesis, Department of Botany, University of Tennessee, Knoxville.

1978   An Analysis of Plant Remains from the Middle Woodland and Mississippian Components on the Banks V Site and a Paleoethnobotanical Study of the Native Flora of the Upper Duck Valley. In *Fifth Report of the Normandy Archaeological Project,* edited by Charles H. Faulkner and Major C. R. McCollough, pp. 596–699. University of Tennessee, Department of Anthropology, Report of Investigations No. 20. Knoxville.

STOLTMAN, JAMES B.
1973   The Southeastern United States. In *The Development of North American Archaeology,* edited by James E. Fitting, pp. 117–150. Anchor Books, Garden City, New York.

WAGNER, MARK J.
1980   The Aaron Shelton Site (40CF69): A Multicomponent Site in the Lower Normandy Reservoir. M.A. thesis, Department of Anthropology, University of Tennessee, Knoxville.

1982   The Aaron Shelton Site (40CF69): A Multicomponent Site in the Lower Normandy Reservoir. In *Eighth Report of the Normandy Archaeological Project,* edited by Charles H. Faulkner and C. R. McCollough, pp. 389–526. University of Tennessee, Department of Anthropology, Report of Investigations No. 33, TVA Publications in Anthropology No. 30. Knoxville.

WALTHALL, JOHN A.
1980   *Prehistoric Indians of the Southeast: Archaeology of Alabama and the Middle South.* University of Alabama Press, Tuscaloosa.

WINTERS, HOWARD D.
1963   *An Archaeological Survey of the Wabash Valley in Illinois.* Illinois State Museum, Report of Investigations 10. Springfield.

4
The Tellico Archaeological Project
Gerald F. Schroedl

THE TENNESSEE VALLEY AUTHORITY first proposed construction of the Tellico Reservoir in the 1930s as an extension of the Fort Loudoun Dam. Its construction was completed in the early 1940s, but the planned extension was postponed until the 1960s, when it was rechristened the Tellico Reservoir Project. Construction of the dam at the river's mouth eventually flooded the lower 33 miles of the Little Tennessee River and the lower 22 miles of the Tellico River. Construction began in 1967, was originally scheduled for completion in 1971 (TVA 1967), was subsequently delayed until 1975 (TVA 1972:Vol. I, Pt. 1:1), was further interrupted until 1977 (TVA 1978:6–7), and was postponed again until 1979, when the project was finished. As documented by Wheeler and McDonald (1986), intense debate over social, economic, political, and environmental issues plagued the project from its inception. In the 1970s there were various lawsuits focusing on TVA's compliance first with the National Environmental Policy Act (NEPA), then the Endangered Species Act, and finally the American Indian Religious Freedom Act.

Wheeler and McDonald (1986) include the archaeological work in their broader discussion of the public debate over the project and the ensuing litigation. Chapman's (1994:14–18) popular book includes an overview of the development of archaeology in the Tennessee Valley, how TVA and the University of Tennessee became involved in archaeological research, and how a variety of federal laws shaped the conduct and outcome of the Tellico Archaeological Project. Chapman (1988) discusses the Tellico and contemporary Normandy and Columbia projects in the broader context of Tennessee archaeology from 1966 to 1986, and Lyon (1996) provides an account of the historical foundation of southeastern archaeology as developed during the Depression. Although archaeology has changed in many ways since the 1930s, there is no question that current research questions, goals, and interpretations are linked to past efforts. The Tellico project was no exception.

Kimball (1985:11–38) gives a detailed review and evaluation of the kinds of work conducted in the Tellico Reservoir through 1977. He identifies early research goals and explains how, when the Tellico Archaeological Project began in 1967, additional research goals were established, how those goals changed, and how archaeologists attempted to implement a variety of research strategies to achieve their goals. Kimball (1985) and Chapman (especially 1980a:1–6) fully appreciate how the Tellico archaeological studies were involved in ongoing litigation and public debate, and in turn how these activities influenced the outcome of the archaeological studies.

The Tellico Archaeological Project unfolded at the interface of two major changes in American archaeology. The Tellico Archaeological Project began in the tradition of the 1930s, focused on culture history. By the time the project concluded, the transition to processual archaeology that had begun in the 1960s was evident. The second major change was the development of modern cultural resource management. When the Tellico Archaeological Project began, few federal laws, save the Reservoir Salvage Act, were routinely implemented on federally financed projects. From 1966 through 1979, far-ranging legislation established modern cultural resource management and the Tellico Archeological Project changed accordingly. Finally and most important, selectively reviewing some of the project's research results bears out that the Tellico Archeological Project made lasting and significant contributions to the archaeology of North America and the Southeast and that this work still influences contemporary research nearly 30 years after its conclusion.

Prelude to the Tellico Project

Cyrus Thomas's Indian mound survey in eastern North America in the late nineteenth century helped initiate what became more than a half century later the Tellico Archaeological Project. Thomas's work first identified 25 distinctive mounds, mound groups, or village sites that he clearly located on an accompanying map of the Little Tennessee and Tellico rivers (Thomas 1894:Plate XXV). Second, excavations at some of the sites revealed the characteristics of the archaeological record and showed what future archaeologists could anticipate finding. The third and most significant contribution Thomas made to archaeological studies in the lower Little Tennessee River was his attempt to correlate archaeological sites with Overhill Cherokee villages recorded by Lieutenant Henry Timberlake in 1762 (Williams 1927). Thomas (1894:Plate XXVI) reproduced Timberlake's map of the village locations. He specifically identified the Hardin Mound with the Cherokee town of Tallasee and proposed that other villages corresponded to some of the sites he investigated (Thomas 1894:367). By doing so, Thomas made the study of the archaeological record of the historic Cherokee a primary research goal. Working in 1914–1915, Harrington furthered this goal but confined his investigations to the area near the confluence of the Little Tennessee and Tennessee rivers (Harrington 1922).

Archaeologists embraced this goal again in the 1930s, when considerable work was done by Works Progress Administration (WPA) researchers at large mound and village sites in the Chickamauga Reservoir and elsewhere in the Tennessee River Valley (see Chapman 1994:16–17). The best known of these sites was Hiwassee Island, but extensive work was also carried out at the Hixon, Dallas, Mouse Creeks, and others sites (Lewis and Kneberg 1946; Lewis and Lewis 1995). The goal of this work, in keeping with the culture historical paradigm and direct historical method of the day, was to link distinctive archaeological manifestations with known Native American ethnic groups. Consequently Lewis and Kneberg (1946: 5,8) using the McKern or Midwestern Taxonomic Method (McKern 1939) for defining and naming archaeological cultures, correlated their early Watts Bar, Candy Creek, and Hamilton cultures with unknown but possibly Algonquian peoples. They identified the later Hiwassee Island and Dallas cultures with Muskogean or Creek people, and they interpreted the Mouse Creeks site as evidence of the historic Yuchi (Lewis and Kneberg 1946:10–14). They recognized, however, that there was little historical or archaeological evidence for placing the Cherokee in the Chickamauga Basin until the late eighteenth century. Consequently Lewis and Kneberg turned their attention to the Little Tennessee River, Timberlake's map, and other historical records to account for the Cherokee in East Tennessee. In 1939 they assigned archaeological site numbers to all the Overhill Cherokee villages even though their locations were unconfirmed by archaeological survey and excavations, and excavations were made at Chota and Fort Loudoun the same year (Lewis and Kneberg 1946:17; Schroedl and Russ 1986:19–20).

In the late 1950s and early 1960s, members of the Tennessee Archaeological Society, under the supervision of Lewis and Kneberg, conducted additional, much smaller investigations in the Tellico area (Kimball 1985:17–18). They had worked immediately upstream in the Chilhowee Reservoir at the Cherokee towns of Chilhowee and Tallasee. Not only did they appreciate the rich archaeological record of the lower Little Tennessee River, but by the early 1960s they undoubtedly were aware of TVA's plans to complete the Tellico project. A 10 by 70 ft excavation was made at Citico, test pits were dug to locate the Chota townhouse, and test excavations were made at four other Mississippian sites, including Martin Farm (Kimball 1985:17–18).

Archaeological Resource Management

When Cyrus Thomas worked in the lower Little Tennessee River Valley, there were no federal or state laws regulating or mandating the conduct of archaeological research. By the time WPA excavations were initiated, the federal government had passed the Antiquities Act (1906) and the Historic Sites Act (1935), but these had little impact on the conduct of archaeology in eastern Tennessee. Instead the creation of the WPA and the TVA, by providing a mechanism to employee large numbers of workers, was ideally suited for the large-scale excavations (see Lyon 1996). The investigations were organized, administered, and carried out mostly by academic institutions such as the University of Tennessee. How this approach helped define salvage archaeology in the United States is well established (see Lyon 1996:201–202; King et al. 1977:11–44; Peebles 1988:53–60). Provisions for analyzing the materials and publishing the results of the work were given less consideration, and the eventual outbreak of World War II brought virtually all archaeological fieldwork to a halt. The relationship established between TVA and WPA archaeology set an important precedent. Not only did the two cooperate to undertake archeological studies, but TVA established a record of direct support for its conduct. This precedent was a key element in the future funding, organization, and eventual outcome of the Tellico Archaeological Project.

In the early 1960s public concern with environmental protection grew rapidly in the United States. By the late 1960s and early 1970s, Congress began to enact important legislation to address a wide range of environmental issues, from endangered plants and animals to cultural resources. Just before construction of the Tellico Dam commenced, archaeological sites came under the purview of the National Historic Preservation Act

(1966); as the project continued, the National Environmental Policy Act (1969), the Archaeological and Historic Preservation Act (1974), and eventually the Archaeological Resources Protection Act (1979) all came into play. Before this, only the Antiquities Act (1906) and the Reservoir Salvage Act (1960) were directly relevant to archaeological studies in Tellico. Implementation of both environmental and cultural legislation in Tellico, as in many areas, did not happen immediately. There were serious questions about the applicability of various laws and about the procedures for carrying them out, since the project had started prior to the passage of most laws. This of course became the subject of a variety of lawsuits in which archaeology was implicated as documented by Wheeler and McDonald (1986).

Fowler (1986:148–149) and others (e.g., King, Hickman, and Berg 1977:11–44; Knudson 1986) show that archaeologists in the early 1970s began to embrace a conservation ethic as espoused in the National Historic Preservation Act (NHPA) and endorsed at the 1974 cultural resources meeting in Denver, but these aspirations at first had small effect on archaeology's long history of commitment to salvage archaeology. Archaeologists, as a result, found the mandates of the National Environmental Policy Act and the Archeological and Historic Preservation Act more appealing (King, Hickman, and Berg 1977:35). The former forced federal agencies to consider their impacts on the environment, including archaeological resources, and archaeologists could obtain research funding from agencies needing to comply with the law. The latter made it possible for all federal agencies—not just the National Park Service—to fund archaeological investigations directly. For Tellico archaeologists this raised the real possibility of conducting well-funded, large-scale excavations. Eventually archaeological conservation and cultural resource management perspectives, as directed by the National Historic Preservation Act and Executive Order 11593 (1971), caught up with the project by the time of its completion (see Chapman 1980a). The ironic result, when combined with the history of dam construction and associated litigation, was that many activities such as comprehensive site survey and inventory that should have occurred early in the project were not seriously undertaken until near the end of the project. The further irony, however, is that had this been done at the beginning of the project, culture historical perspectives and techniques would have prevailed. As it was, these activities all took place in a decidedly processual manner and thus produced research results that might otherwise have never been realized.

Archaeological Method and Theory

The culture historical method, archaeology's interest in describing archaeological cultures and determining their spatial and temporal occurrences, was developed in the 1930s and 1940s, became well established by the 1950s, and was regarded widely as the acceptable way to conduct archaeology by the 1960s (see Willey and Sabloff 1993; O'Brien, Lyman, and Schiffer 2005:8–35; Binford 1968). Practicing archaeologists and their students were committed to the culture historical method. When the Tellico project was federally funded in 1967, archaeological work was guided by this approach. In the early 1960s, as is well known in the history of archaeology, processual archaeology (or at the time "new archaeology") was offered as a radically different if not alternative approach to the conduct of archaeology (O'Brien, Lyman, and Schiffer 2005). Among the tenets of this approach that found their way into Tellico archaeology were the emphasis on research design, regional and intrasite sampling, focus on the reconstruction of subsistence and settlement patterns, attempts to decipher activity areas and site function, and the interpretation of human adaptation (Schroedl, Chapman, and Polhemus 1975). A processual perspective had considerable impact on the conduct and results of the Tellico project although the vision of a culture historical perspective that had guided the project at its inception was never lost.

A Project Overview

The combination of environmental awareness, federal legislation relating to environmental issues and cultural resources, and the development and implementation of new approaches to archaeological research came together in the Tellico Archaeological Project. In 1967, when the project began, it was understood that the Tellico Dam would be built quickly and that there would be no more than three or four years to complete the archaeological work. The occurrence of historic Overhill Cherokee sites, particularly the important town of Chota, was well known, and research questions relating to Cherokee origins and culture were well established going all the way back to Thomas (1894). Contributing to the further interest in the Overhill Cherokee was the University of North Carolina's Cherokee Project, investigating the archaeological record of the Cherokee and their ancestors in western North Carolina (Coe 1961; Dickens 1976; Keel 1976). It was no surprise that the Tellico project at first focused almost exclusively on the Cherokee. TVA land acquisition had just begun, and none of the known locations of Cherokee towns, especially Chota, had been purchased. Many landowners were reluctant to have archaeologists disturb their fields and crops, but, using National Park Service funding made available through the Reservoir Salvage Act, some archaeological survey was conducted and excavations were undertaken at several Woodland and Mississippian period sites (Salo, ed. 1969).

Still operating under the assumption that Tellico Dam would be completed quickly, the greatest effort was directed at Chota, where permission to excavate had been obtained, and work was conducted in 1969 and 1970 (Gleeson 1970, 1971). Interest in other aspects of the archaeological record, however, were taking shape, and the work at Icehouse Bottom produced important Middle Woodland materials relating to both Ohio Hopewell cultures and Connestee culture found in western North Carolina, neither of which had been recognized previously in East Tennessee (Gleeson 1970; Chapman 1973; Chapman and Keel 1979). This and the fact that the excavations included the use of water flotation to recover botanical remains clearly connected the work to research interests and questions beyond East Tennessee and beyond purely culture historical concerns. In 1971 University of Tennessee field investigations took place at Harrison Branch because of the stratified Woodland and Archaic deposits and at Bat Creek because there were burial mounds and a platform mound and village with abundant Mississippian cultural materials (Schroedl 1975). This is where Cyrus Thomas had recovered the now famous Bat Creek Stone (1894:391–393 and Figure 273; Mainfort and Kwas 1991, 1993, 2004). A small crew of Cherokee Indians worked at Chota, initiating their direct participation in the project (Schroedl and Russ 1986:25, 29). Archaeological survey work continued during the winter and early spring months, but because this was poorly implemented, numerous sites were overlooked or poorly documented (Kimball 1985:18–25). This situation was not corrected until large-scale systematic and probabilistic surveys were undertaken in 1977 and 1979 (Davis 1990; Kimball 1985).

Significant changes in the Tellico project occurred in 1972 and 1973. Two University of Tennessee excavation crews engaged in fieldwork, as had occurred in 1967–1968. This was increased in subsequent years, so that as many as four excavation teams carried out work for much of May through September or even later into the fall. This required considerable increase in funding and logistical support. TVA at first participated by directly providing all the field equipment necessary for the work. This

was followed soon after by TVA's helping to fund the project in cooperation with National Park Service, Interagency Archeological Services. At
this time too, there was deliberate recognition and concerted effort to
investigate the full range of archaeological cultures represented in the
project area. This included multisite studies to reveal the full breadth
and detail of Archaic period occupation (Chapman 1975; 1977; 1978;
1979; 1981) as well as focused investigations on selected Woodland
period sites to describe individual cultures, investigate plant domestication, and determine the relationships with Ohio Hopewell and North
Carolina Middle Woodland cultures (Chapman 1973; Cridlebaugh
1981; Schroedl 1975, 1978b). Two Mississippian sites, Toqua and Martin Farm were chosen for study. Martin Farm was selected for its relevance to issues of Mississippian origins (Schroedl, Davis, and Boyd
1985), and Toqua was investigated for the information it contained
respecting late Mississippian culture (Polhemus 1987). Investigations
of Cherokee sites also were greatly expanded after 1976 to include
large-scale work at Tomotley (Baden 1983) and smaller but significant
excavations at Mialoquo (Russ and Chapman 1983), Toqua (Polhemus
1987), and Citico (Chapman and Newman 1979). Tellico Blockhouse
excavations began in 1973 (Polhemus 1978) and large-scale excavation
was started at Fort Loudoun in 1975 (Kutruff and Bastian 1977). As
reservoir construction and litigation came to an end in the later 1970s,
TVA had acquired virtually all the project land it required. This facilitated archaeological site reconnaissance and testing unencumbered by
patterns of private land ownership. Systematic testing for deeply buried
sites began in 1977 as did a comprehensive evaluation of recorded sites
and systematic below pool archaeological survey (Chapman ed. 1980;
Kimball 1985). This was followed by further systematic testing for buried
sites and a stratified probabilistic survey of the above pool area (Davis
1980; Kimball 1980, 1985).

Despite the unusual, and in retrospect, somewhat convoluted way
in which the Tellico project unfolded, it made numerous significant and
lasting contributions to virtually all aspects of East Tennessee and southeastern prehistoric and historic archaeological studies. These include, for
example, clear revisions to the regional culture history respecting both
the dating and definition of archaeological cultures. Accomplishments
relating to the interpretation of cultural adaptation and the nature of
economic, social, and ideological institutions for a variety of cultures
were considerable. The Tellico research furthermore produced important
interpretations regarding culture development and change. Briefly dis-

cussed and summarized below are some of the project's most significant and lasting research results.

Tellico Survey

The Tellico Reservoir Area includes 14,400 acres of land and streams now inundated and another 20,044 acres purchased by TVA for economic development (Davis 1990:23). This incorporates the lower 33 miles of the Little Tennessee River below Chilhowee Dam and the lower 22 miles of the Tellico River. Over this area 624 aboriginal archaeological sites were recorded through 1982 and more sites are identified each time a particular parcel is scheduled for development (e.g., Frankenberg and Herrmann 2000). Until the late 1970s, particularly as the emphasis remained on intensive excavations of a few large sites, site survey and record keeping were irregular, cursory, or at times inadequate (Kimball 1985:11–38). Archaeological sites, in keeping with culture historical approaches, were assessed almost exclusively on the basis of containing sufficiently dense occupations, abundant cultural remains, and distinct culture diagnostic types to warrant full scale excavation. When these conditions were not met, further site evaluation was not made or not fully reported. The survey implemented in 1977 reviewed all then currently available site data and systematically examined all the below pool area of the reservoir. This work identified 129 new sites and included the first systematic effort to document lithic source areas. Analysis of the survey data established the chronological framework and criteria for recognizing specified archaeological components for all subsequent survey and test excavations.

In 1979 a probabilistic survey was conducted using a stratified random sampling procedure to fully assess the archaeological record of the entire reservoir area (Davis 1980, 1985, 1990; Kimball 1985). The design of this work was influenced by a nonsite approach pioneered by Thomas (1973, 1975) and elaborated by others (e.g., Dunnell and Dancey 1983). The entire reservoir was divided into nine sampling strata and 12,663 sampling units each measuring 300 by 300 ft. A total of 425 sample units were examined. Each sample unit was plowed in a pattern of six 20 ft by 300 ft strips 100 ft apart, with three strips intersecting the other three perpendicularly. This exposed 0.74 acres that were collected in 10 ft squares following sufficient rainfall to adequately reveal artifacts on the surface. This work produced 358 new sites and, when combined with all previous work, made it possible to produce an overall settlement pattern study for the area (Davis 1990). These analyses utilized contemporary theoretical concepts relating to site activities and site function. From a culture resource management perspective, this provided TVA a baseline predictive model that was subsequently used to determine the likely occurrence of cultural resources and the need for further survey, testing and excavation in areas subject to recreational, industrial, and suburban development.

Chronology and Culture History

The prevailing culture chronology when the Tellico project commenced had changed little since first established by Lewis and Kneberg (1946). The Tellico work was the first large project in East Tennessee where the opportunity was presented to obtain large numbers of radiocarbon dates, and this was accomplished by dating numerous site components representing nearly the complete record of human occupation. Especially notable were dates that established the Early, Middle, and Late Archaic period sequence (Chapman 1976, 1985). This chronology was poorly dated anywhere in the Southeast prior to the Tellico work. Dates were also secured for virtually all other culture manifestations identified in the project area. As each site investigation proceeded, individual researchers placed their data and associated dates in a comparative regional context, but the goal of constructing a comprehensive chronology and overall cul-ture history did not become a priority until late in the project. The need to do so was prompted first by the simple fact that so many dates had been obtained for poorly dated or previously undated cultural manifestations. Second, the dates suggested that previous chronologies required revision, and, third, the Tellico project needed to date the Middle Woodland Con-nestee and emergent Mississippian or Martin Farm cultures that had never been formally included in the East Tennessee culture history.

A primary goal of the 1977 systematic survey was to describe a comprehensive set of diagnostic lithic and ceramic artifacts from which to date uniformly all identified site occupations. These data were cross-referenced to all available radiocarbon dates from the region (Kimball 1985). Until Chapman's work at Rose Island, Icehouse Bottom, and elsewhere in the reservoir, the Archaic chronology for East Tennessee was derived from artifact comparisons from dated contexts at sites such as Hardaway in North Carolina (Coe 1964), St. Albans in West Virginia (Broyles 1966, 1970, 1971), and Russell Cave in Alabama (Griffin 1974). A Woodland and Mississippian chronology was better established in East

Tennessee, but, prior to the Tellico project, few radiocarbon dates were available for these periods (Faulkner 1967; Kneberg 1961; McCollough and Faulkner 1973).

At the time of the survey, East Tennessee culture history consisted of a temporally ordered series of named archaeological phases. Most of these had first been defined using the Midwestern Taxonomic System and then were redefined or relabeled using the Willey and Philips (1958) approach in the 1960s. The chronology proposed by Kimball uses many of the same culture labels but designates them only as temporal units or periods.

Table 4.1 shows diagnostic projectile points for each cultural period and temporal unit; diagnostic ceramics that in addition define each Woodland and Mississippian period temporal unit are presented in Table 4.2. The time ranges shown in these tables are established from an evaluation of 147 radiocarbon dates, 63 of which were secured from excavations in the Tellico area, and the remainder of which come from sites mostly in East Tennessee (Table 4.3). The individual corrected dates are given in Kimball (1985:Tables 69 and 70).

This chronology is different from previously proposed chronologies. First, it is based on statistical measures of assemblage variability to establish the characteristics of sherd assemblages, and, second, it provides uniform statistical evaluations of all the radiocarbon dates (Kimball and Baden 1985). The chronology is developed strictly as a dating tool and posits no culture phases. Where data are insufficient, no temporal unit is proposed although diagnostic artifact types may occur. Conversely there are distinctive but unnamed diagnostic projectile points for some temporal units, and some types may occur in more than one temporal unit. This is especially true for the Mississippian period. The data are fine grained enough to distinguish three Woodland periods that include five temporal units. These do not necessarily correspond to previous Early, Middle, and Late Woodland divisions (Kimball 1985:292). This fully integrates sand tempered types associated with Connestee culture and makes finer distinctions in the earlier portions of the Woodland period. There are no data reflecting a traditional Late Woodland, Hamilton, or Hamilton Burial Mound complex. Burial mounds, most of which presumably are Hamilton, occur in the Tellico area and were recorded or excavated by Thomas (1894). No burial mounds were investigated during the Tellico project except for obtaining a radiocarbon date from the Pate Mound (Davis, Kimball, and Baden 1982:546–556) and excavation and dating of the Middle Woodland Kittrell mound (Chapman

Table 4.1: Diagnostic Projectile Points for Recognized Temporal Units		
Temporal Unit	**Diagnostic Projectile Point**	**Time Range**
PaleoIndian Period		
Undesignated Unit	Clovis	c. 11,000–8000 B.C.
Early Archaic Period		
Undesignated Unit	Dalton	7,900–7,500 B.C.
Lower Kirk	Lower Kirk Corner Notched	c. 7,500 B.C.
Upper Kirk	Upper Kirk Corner Notched	7,400–7,000 B.C.
	Decatur	7,400–7,000 B.C.
St. Albans	St. Albans Side Notched	7,000–6,600 B.C.
LeCroy	LeCroy Bifurcated Stem	6,500–6,100 B.C.
Kanawha	Kanawha Stem	6,500–6,100 B.C.
Middle Archaic Period		
Stanly/Kirk Stemmed	Kirk Stemmed/Stanly Stemmed	6,000–5,500 B.C.
Morrow Mountain	Morrow Mountain I Stemmed	5,400–5,000 (?) B.C.
	Morrow Mountain II Stemmed	5,400–5,000 (?) B.C.
Undesignated Units	Guilford Lanceolate	undetermined
	Halifax Side Notched	c. 4,300 B.C.
	Sykes	undetermined
Late Archaic Period		
Undesignated	Savannah River Stemmed	3,000–2,500 B.C.
Undesignated	Iddins Undifferentiated Stemmed	2,200–900 B.C.
Woodland I Period		
Bacon Bend	Undetermined	900–200 B.C.
Woodland II Period		
Patrick	Greeneville	200 B.C.–A.D. 350
	Camp Creek	
	Nolichucky	
Woodland III Period		
Icehouse Bottom	Connestee Triangular	A.D. 350–900
	Bradley Spike	
Mississippian I Period		
Martin Farm	Hamilton	A.D. 900–1000
Mississippian II Period		
Hiwassee Island I	Hamilton	A.D. 1000–1300
Hiwassee Island II	Undesignated Triangular	
	Undesignated Triangular	

	Mississippian II Period	
	Madison	
	Pentagonal	
	Mississippian III	
Dallas and Mouse Creek	Dallas Excurvate	A.D. 1300–1600
	Undesignated Triangular	
	Undesignated Triangular	
	Madison	
	Mississippian IV	
Overhill	Undesignated Triangular	A.D. 1600–1819
	Undesignated Triangular	
	Madison	

Source: After Kimball 1985: Table 66

Table 4.2: Diagnostic Ceramic Sherd Categories for Recognized Temporal Units

Temporal Unit	Diagnostic Ceramic Category	Time Range
Woodland I		900–200 B.C.
Bacon Bend	Coarse crushed quartz temper— fabric marked	
	Coarse crushed quartz temper— cord marked	
Woodland II		200 B.C.–A.D. 350
Patrick I	Limestone temper—fabric marked	
	Medium crushed quartz temper— check stamped	
Patrick II	Limestone temper—check stamped	
	Medium crushed quartz temper— plain	
Woodland III		A.D. 350–900
Icehouse Bottom	Sand temper—all surfaces	
	Limestone temper—simple stamped	
Woodland III		A.D. 350–900
	Limestone temper— complicated stamped	
	Limestone temper—incised decoration	
	Limestone temper— punctate decoration	

Table 4.2 (continued)		
Temporal Unit	**Diagnostic Ceramic Category**	**Time Range**
	Limestone temper—red filmed	
	Medium crushed quartz temper— simple stamped	
Westmoreland Barber	Limestone temper—plain	
	Limestone temper—brushed	
Mississippian I		A.D. 900–1000
Martin Farm	Limestone temper—cord marked	
	Shell temper—plain	
Mississippian II		A.D. 1000–1300
Hiwassee Island	Shell temper—fabric marked	
	Shell temper—red filmed	
	Shell temper—rectilinear complicated stamped	
Mississippian III		A.D. 1300–1600
Dallas and Mouse Creek	Shell temper—cord marked	
	Shell temper—modeled	
	Shell temper—incised decoration	
	Shell temper—fillet applique	
	Grit temper—incised decoration	
Mississippian IV		A.D. 1600–1819
Overhill Cherokee	Shell temper—simple stamped	
	Shell temper—check stamped	
	Shell temper—curvilinear complicated stamped	
	Shell temper—fillet applique	
	Grit temper—plain	
	Grit temper—cord marked	
	Grit temper—simple stamped	
	Grit temper—check stamped	
	Grit temper—complicated stamped	

Source: After Kimball 1985: Table 68

Table 4.3: Temporal Units, Numbers of Radiocarbon Dates, and Age Estimates for Cultural Periods Represented in the Tellico Project Area

Temporal Period	Tellico Dates	Dates from Region	Estimated Age Range
Early Archaic	18	15	7,900–6,100 B.C.
Middle Archaic	6	7	6,000–4,300 B.C.
Late Archaic	9	11	3,000–900 B.C.
Early Woodland	3	27	900 B.C.–A.D. 350
Middle Woodland	10	2	A.D. 350–900
Late Woodland	0	18	C. A.D. 900
Emergent and Early Mississippian	11	4	A.D. 900–1,300
Late Mississippian	6	0	A.D. 1,300 -1,600
Historic Cherokee	0	0	A.D. 1600 -1819
Total	63	84	

Source: After Kimball 1985: Tables 69 and 70

1987). No diagnostic projectile points or ceramics are distinctive enough to define a Woodland IV or Hamilton temporal unit. The possible need for doing so is discussed by Schroedl and Boyd (1991).

Respecting the Mississippian period, the Martin Farm temporal unit (A.D. 900–1000) is included in the chronology. Its constituent assemblages are described elsewhere (Schroedl, Davis, and Boyd 1985; Schroedl, Boyd, and Davis 1990). The Late Mississippian is dated to A.D. 1600, and reference to Dallas/Mouse Creek is intended to allow for a distinctive protohistoric occupation and transition to a Cherokee archaeological record dating prior to A.D. 1670. Cherokee culture is included as Mississippian IV to recognize it as a terminal Mississippian culture having ancestral continuity with prehistoric and protohistoric cultures in the region.

Tellico Settlement Patterns

The 1977 and 1979 (Kimball 1985; Davis 1990) archaeological surveys and reexamination of all previously excavated-site data became the basis for a comprehensive settlement pattern study. The radiocarbon chronology and diagnostic artifact categories established by Kimball provide the temporal criteria for the patterning (Davis 1985). The temporal units, however, are redefined as 16 archaeological phases, composed of 894 site components with each phase having 7 to 102 site components (Table 4.4). (Other slightly different culture histories, based on the same data, have also been published [e.g., Chapman and Shea 1981:Table 1].) The spatial occurrence of sites as represented in the nonprobabilistic and probabilistic data sets as well as contemporary theory respecting settlement use, intensity, location, and landscape features guided the analysis. Binford's (1980, 1982) foragers-collector model is the organizational framework for addressing Archaic and Woodland period pat-

Table 4.4: Summary of Cultural Components Identified in the Tellico Reservoir Area			
Temporal Period	Cultural Phase	No. of Site Components	%
PaleoIndian	(Clovis)*	7	0.78
Early Archaic	(Dalton)*	15	1.68
	Lower Kirk	55	6.15
	Upper Kirk	101	11.30
	St. Albans	31	3.47
	LeCroy	23	2.57
	Kanawha	17	1.90
Middle Archaic	Kirk Stemmed/Stanly	64	7.16
	Morrow Mountain	72	8.05
	(Guilford)*	12	1.34
	(Sykes)*	51	5.70
Late Archaic	Savannah River	22	2.46
	Iddins	102	11.41
Early Woodland	Watts Bar	54	6.04
Middle Woodland	Patrick	62	6.94
	Icehouse Bottom	87	9.73
Early Mississippian	Martin Farm	17	1.90
	Hiwassee Island	42	4.70
Late Mississippian	Dallas	27	3.02
Historic Cherokee	Overhill	33	3.69
Total		894	99.99

Source: After Davis 1990: Table 71
Note *Diagnostic artifacts present, but phase not formally recognized or defined for the project area

terning while the Mississippian settlement criteria are derived from a variety of sources (e.g., Peebles 1978; Price 1978; Steponaitis 1978) to reflect greater residential sedentism, the use of agriculture, and settlement hierarchies (Davis 1990: 17–19).

Table 4.5 shows the distribution of site components according to the sampling strata where they occur. Most sites occur on the first river terrace (T-1 Terrace) or the uplands. Between 18 and 51 sites occur in each of the remaining seven strata. Evaluation of these data suggests that site occurrences on older alluvial terraces (higher terraces) are underrepresented in the sample possibly affecting "perceived patterns of residential site location" (Davis 1990:194). Overrepresentation of upland sites is less of a concern since these sites represent extractive activities that cannot be attributed to a specific archaeological phase.

Archaic site distributions are summarized in Table 4.6. All site types are represented for each phase. Diagnostic Clovis, Dalton, Guilford, and Sykes projectile points occur, but no distinctive site types are evident, and no phases are formally identified in these data. During the Upper and Lower Kirk phases, residential base camps, some of which were repeatedly and intensely used, are found in the T-1 Terrace. Logistical camps occur in a variety of locations, and overall use of upland areas for hunting characterizes these phases (Davis 1990:210). Subsequent Early Archaic cultures exhibit similar site types, but there are fewer such sites,

Table 4.5: Actual and Expected Distribution of Site Components by Landform				
Landform	Total Site Inventory		Expected Site Distribution	
	n	%	n	%
T-1 Terrace	130	20.8	137.3	22.0
T-2 Terrace	28	4.5	18.7	3.0
Higher Terraces	51	8.2	162.2	26.0
LTRV	47	7.5	43.7	7.0
Tellico River Valley	50	8.0	37.4	6.0
Tellico River Slope	18	2.9	18.7	3.0
Tributary Valley	37	5.9	25.0	4.0
Tributary Slope	43	6.9	25.0	4.0
Upland	220	35.3	156.0	25.0
Total	624	100.0	624.0	100.0

SOURCE: After Davis 1990: Table 72
LTRV = Little Tennessee River Valley

Table 4.6: Function of Archaic Period Sites						
Temporal Period	Cultural Phase	Base Camp	Logistical Camp	Activity Locus	Indeter-minate	Total
PaleoIndian	(Clovis)*	0	0	0	0	7
Early Archaic	(Dalton)*	0	0	0	0	15
	Lower Kirk	12	7	21	15	55
	Upper Kirk	20	21	51	9	101
	St. Albans	10	3	9	9	31
	LeCroy	8	2	9	4	23
	Kanawha	4	3	10	0	17
Middle Archaic	Kirk Stemmed/ Stanly	11	18	27	8	64
	Morrow Mountain	7	17	43	5	72
	(Guilford)*	3	9	0	0	12
	(Sykes)*	2	13	36	0	51
Late Archaic	Savannah River	5	7	8	2	22
	Iddins	44	20	35	3	102
Total		126	120	249	55	572

SOURCE: Compiled from Davis 1990: Tables 73–84
Note *Diagnostic artifacts present, but phase not formally recognized or defined for the project area

and their distribution suggests much greater focus of activities along the Little Tennessee River.

Davis (1990:219) identifies two distinctive trends in the Middle Archaic settlement data. The declining numbers of base camps suggest less intense use of the region and greater focus on resource procurement by groups residing outside the area. The second trend in the Middle Archaic data is increased utilization of the Tellico River Valley compared to the Early Archaic. The Late Archaic, Savannah River phase, with low site densities and evidence of group mobility, is comparable to the Middle Archaic period. In contrast the Iddins phase shows a local adaptation and intense exploitation of the area with a strong riverine emphasis and frequent use of upland areas (Davis 1990:226).

Early Woodland occupation in the Tellico reservoir area (see Table 4.7), although marked by the occurrence of ceramics suggesting residential camps, also shows a strong riverine orientation and pattern of land-

Table 4.7: Function of Woodland Period Sites							
Temporal Period	Cultural Phase	Large Base Camp	Small Base Camp	Logistical Camp/ Residence	Logistical Camp/ Activity Locus	Indeter-minate	Total
Early Woodland	Watts Bar	22	5	25	0	2	54
Middle Woodland	Patrick	17	8	26	11	0	62
	Icehouse Bottom	21	7	43	16	0	87
Total		60	20	94	27	2	203

Source: Compiled from Davis 1990: Tables 85–87

scape use not greatly different from the preceding Iddins phase (Davis 1990:230). Both the Patrick and Icehouse Bottom phases, representing Middle Woodland period occupation, exhibit similar kinds and numbers of sites, reflecting comparable patterns of landscape use and environmental exploitation. As Davis (1990:238) argues, both phases "reflect greater residential activity and imply greater residential population" than earlier Woodland occupations. An important difference between the phases is in mortuary patterning and cultural connections beyond East Tennessee. Connestee ceramics and mica, found with Icehouse Bottom sites, demonstrate connections with North Carolina and Hopewell pottery, and Flint Ridge flint shows interaction with cultures in Ohio (see Chapman 1973). Patrick-phase base camps produced many burials, but none occurs with Icehouse Bottom occupations. The preferred mortuary pattern probably was the use of upland mounds, but few of these are identified and only one site, Kittrell Mound was excavated (Chapman 1987).

Mississippian settlement in the Tellico project area, shown in Table 4.8, like that in much of the Southeast, exhibits a hierarchy of sites consistent with agricultural development and increased sociopolitical complexity. As this pattern took hold, there was a distinct settlement shift from first terrace locations in the Martin Farm phase to second and higher terraces in the Hiwassee Island phase (Davis 1990: 247). This is attributed to settlement movement away from flood-prone first terrace locations and the utilization of these rich soils for corn agriculture. The further elaboration of this patterning is represented in the Dallas phase. Permanent communities were larger but fewer in number, with much

Table 4.8. Function of Mississippian Period sites

Temporal Period	Culture Phase	Center	Hamlet	Home-stead	Logistical Camp	Activity Locus	Total
General Missis-sippian	—	0	0	28	14	45	87
Early Missis-sippian	Martin Farm	3	9	5	0	0	17
	Hiwassee Island	5	11	12	0	0	42*
Late Missis-sippian	Dallas	3	3	21	0	0	27
Historic Cherokee	Overhill	6	5	22	0	0	33
Total		17	28	88	14	45	206

Source: Compiled from Davis 1990: Tables 88–92
*Total includes 14 mortuary sites. These are Hamilton Burial Mound complex sites.

greater internal complexity than earlier Mississippian centers. Hamlets, homesteads, and logistical camps appear to have been less formally organized than local centers and, although less visible and underrepresented in the survey data, probably were numerous throughout the study area.

Archaic Settlement-Subsistence

Work at Rose Island, Icehouse Bottom, and Bacon Farm, as well as deep testing using heavy equipment and corroborating geoarchaeological studies of alluvial sediments, firmly established a remarkable stratigraphic record of Early Archaic period settlement that is well known and well described (e.g., Chapman 1975, 1977, 1978, 1979). Lithic tools were found in sufficient quantities to enable description with great precision of the associated diagnostic projectile points and the range of assemblage variability (Chapman 1985). This represents some of the most detailed data anywhere in eastern North America for Early Archaic period Kirk, St. Albans, LeCroy, and Kanawha materials. The excavations were large enough at Rose Island and Icehouse Bottom to produce associated cultural features such as hearths, small pits, and artifact clusters from which to interpret activity areas. Among the associated features are remarkably well preserved textile-impressed hearths representing some of the earliest indirect evidence for perishable fabrics anywhere in eastern North America (Chapman 1977:98–102; Chapman and Adovasio 1977; Sherwood and Chapman 2005). Enough sites were sampled to suggest a settlement pattern of seasonally occupied large base camps (e.g., Rose Island) and a variety of smaller special purpose occupations (Chapman 1976, 1985).

Binford's (1978, 1979) site structure model was used to further evaluate these ideas by using a variety of statistical measures to examine spatial relationships of artifacts and the activities they represented for the Le Croy occupation (Stratum VIIA) at Rose Island (Kimball 1993). The analysis included 5,914 lithic artifacts and 10 features. Propositions respecting site activities were assessed quantitatively with cluster analysis and analysis of variance. Six distinctive spatial clusters were interpreted as places where primary and secondary flint knapping, probable bone and hide working, and additional hide working and plant processing were conducted and as the location of a warm weather shelter (Kimball 1993:109–112).

In a subsequent study the broader patterns of settlement-subsistence were further examined for Early Archaic components using Binford's (1980, 1982) forager-collector model. This study utilized 42 assemblages from excavations at Rose Island, Icehouse Bottom, Patrick, Calloway Island, and Bacon Farm as well as 156 locations producing Early Archaic projectile points in the 1977 below pool survey and from 62 sample units in the 1979 probabilistic survey (Kimball 1996:169–170). These data show that Kirk occupations are found over a diversity of landforms (all river terraces and uplands), while LeCroy and St. Albans occupations are concentrated at the front edge of the first river terrace (T-1). These distributions suggest greater logistical organization (following Binford) characterized by base camps such as at Rose Island and a wide range of logistical camps and activity loci distributed across much of the area in many different topographic settings (Kimball 1996:173). LeCroy and St. Albans settlement appear more residentially organized. Fewer and less diverse assemblages found on higher terraces and uplands likely are the result of foraging trips from residential bases. Changing settlement dynamics may reflect in addition differences in overall population density as well as adjustment to initial Middle Holocene climatic conditions. Kimball makes the important point that, no matter which variables are examined, Early Archaic settlement cannot be regarded as a single homogeneous settlement system (Kimball 1996:184).

Environmental Reconstruction and Plant Utilization

Paleoenvironmental studies were in their infancy in the Southeast when the Tellico project began and the systematic recovery of plant remains to elucidate past environments, processes of plant domestication, and patterns of agricultural development were comparatively new. Contemporary work on prehistoric plant use at the Koster site, Illinois (Asch and Asch 1985), Salts Cave, Kentucky (Yarnell 1974), and along the Green River, Kentucky (Watson 1985) influenced the Tellico investigations as they did in much of the Southeast. Water flotation to recover plant materials (the so-called flotation revolution), essential to pursuing these goals, was applied mostly but not exclusively to Archaic and Woodland contexts in Tellico. Fine water screening (using window-screen-size mesh) rather than flotation was used with more regularity at Mississippian and Overhill Cherokee sites. The reasons for this were, first, the logistics of processing such large quantities of sediments at these sites and, second, the belief that most subsistence questions for the late archaeological cultures could be addressed with historical and ethnological references rather than archaeological materials.

More than 1,000 samples totaling nearly 23,000 grams of carbonized plant remains were analyzed from 17 sites (Chapman and Shea 1981:65). Early cultigens or potential cultigens come from 16 Late Archaic, Early Woodland, Middle Woodland, Mississippian, or Historic Cherokee contexts (Table 4.9). Although some of these were among the earliest dated cultigens in eastern North America when first reported in the 1980s, earlier occurrences have now been documented elsewhere (Smith 1992). Besides the seeds and fruits shown in Table 4.9, Chapman and Shea (1981:70) report Cucurbitaceae remains (squash, gourds, and pumpkins) dating between 2540 and 1255 B.C. in Late Archaic contexts at the Bacon Bend and Iddins sites and their presence in Early Mississippian, Late Mississippian, and Historic Cherokee contexts. Cucurbitaceae rinds and seeds also occur with Early and Middle Woodland occupations (Schroedl 1978b: 212–231). Middle Woodland period maize dated to the fifth century at Icehouse Bottom remains among the earliest recorded in eastern North America (Chapman and Crites 1987; Smith 1992:110). Corn becomes common from the Early Mississippian through Historic Cherokee occupations; whereas beans are not seen until the Late Mississippian.

The paleobotanical data show widespread use of hickory nuts, walnuts, and acorns throughout the prehistoric period, with no decline until

Table 4.9: Identified Whole and Fragmented Seeds and Fruits from Cultigens and Potential Cultigens Late Archaic through Historic Cherokee Contexts

Taxa	Late Archaic	Early Woodland	Middle Woodland	Early Mississippian	Late Mississippian	Historic Cherokee	Total
Chenopodium sp. (Goosefoot)	48	1431	60	250	32	175	1996
Polygonum sp. (Knotweed)	4	0	10	385	13	347	759
Phalaris caroliniana (Maygrass)	131	0	131	40	0	27	329
Amaranthus sp. (Pigweed)	1	1	9	0	0	0	11
Ambrosia sp. (Ragweed)	1	0	0	7	3	34	45
Helianthus annus (Sunflower)	0	14	13	6	2	77	112
Iva annua (Sumpweed)	0	26	1	21	447	2	497
Phaseolus vulgaris (Beans)	0	0	0	0	157	822	979
Total	185	1472	224	709	654	1484	4728

Source: After Chapman and Shea 1981: Table 4
Late Archaic = Bacon Bend (40MR25) and Iddins (40LD38)
Early Woodland = Patrick (40MR40), Calloway Island (40MR41), Rose Island(40MR44)
Middle Woodland = Icehouse Bottom (40MR23)
Early Mississippian = Martin Farm (40MR20), Jones Ferry (40MR76)
Late Mississippian = Toqua (40MR6)
Historic Cherokee = Chota (40MR2), Tomotley (40MR5), Toqua (40MR6), Citico (40MR7) Tuskegee (40MR24) Tansee (40MR62), Wear Bend (40LD107)

extensive maize cultivation began in the Mississippian period. Beginning in the Late Archaic, cultigens and potential cultigens such as Cucurbitaceae, *Chenopodium* sp. (chenopod), *Phalaris caroliniana* (maygrass), *Amaranth* sp. (pigweed), *Iva annua* (sumpweed) and *Helianthus annus* (sunflower) are regularly associated with most archaeological phases and with the exception of Iva continue to occur with some regularity after maize and beans became well established after A.D. 1000 (Chapman and Shea 1981:77–79). This general pattern is now widely recognized in the Midwest and throughout the Midsouth and is the basis for identifying premaize plant domestication and the independent development of agriculture in eastern North America (Gremillion 2002). In contrast, early plant domestication played much less of a role in the subsistence economies of Native Americans living in the Lower Mississippi River Valley, the Gulf and Atlantic coasts, and the Piedmont east of the Appalachians. Agriculture did not take on great importance in these areas until maize and beans became common after A.D. 1000.

In the mid-1960s, geoarchaeology was in its infancy and was barely known in the Southeast. The need for geoarchaeology studies became obvious in the Tellico project when deep excavations revealed a stratified archaeological record for most of the Holocene. As a result detailed studies of site sediments were conducted at the Howard site, Calloway Island, Icehouse Bottom, Harrison Branch, and the Patrick site (Chapman 1977; Foley and Chapman 1977). This was followed by geomorphological studies made during systematic testing with a backhoe to locate buried archaeological sites (Delcourt 1980:110–121). Nine river terraces were mapped between river miles 19.0 and 23.5. Terraces 2 through 9 all accumulated before 15,000 years ago, and although containing no evidence of buried human occupation, their surfaces and topography are related to all subsequent human exploitation (Delcourt 1980:117). Terrace 1 (T-1) accumulated in response to increased early Holocene warming and greater precipitation after 15,000 years ago. Sedimentation rates diminished, the river incised its channel, and the T-0, or active floodplain, was established between 4,000 and 3,500 years ago (Chapman et al. 1982:117–119). Complementary pollen studies were made at Tuskegee Pond, and these data were integrated with analysis of wood charcoal fragments and carbonized fruits and seeds from flotation and waterscreen samples (Cridlebaugh 1984). These data suggest that from about 10,000 to 4,000 years ago prehistoric residents utilized bottom land and higher terrace trees for fuel. Disturbed habitat species such as pine (*Pinus* sp.) and red cedar (*Juniperus* sp.) comprise only about

10 percent of the samples. Evidence for bottom land forest species is greatly reduced in the analyzed samples dating after 4,000 years ago, while disturbance-related taxa increase. This suggests reduction in the extent of bottom land forests related to river incising and increasing use of first terrace soils for domestic plant cultivation that appear in the archaeological record at this time. By 2,000 years ago plant cultivation probably occurred on second and higher terraces. Pollen data indicate even more prevalent disturbed habitats by the Late Mississippian period and a low (1 to 2 percent) incidence of maize pollen throughout the last 1,600 years. The geomorphological, pollen, and wood charcoal data indicate a closed canopy deciduous forest in the early to mid Holocene. "The late Holocene landscape, however, was a mosaic of (1) croplands near permanent Indian settlements, (2) early-successional forests with disturbance-favored taxa invading both abandoned Indian old-fields and areas of timber exploitation, and (3) deciduous forest remnants on high terraces and bedrock interfluves" (Chapman et al. 1982:118). Chapman et al. (1982:118) make two additional important points: first, that after the mid Holocene, Native American settlement and agriculture had a profound effect on the Little Tennessee River Valley and, second, that by creating disturbed habitats, Native Americans may have helped increase the diversity of plants and animals so important to their lifeway.

Mississippian Origins

Population migration was established in the 1930s as the culture historical explanation for the origins of Mississippian cultures in East Tennessee and was widely applied throughout the Southeast, remaining popular even today (see Schroedl, Boyd, and Davis 1990; Smith 1984). Culture replacement was marked by the change from grit- and limestone-tempered ceramics to shell-tempered ceramics and the attendant development of large village and platform mound complexes. When both kinds of ceramics as well as limestone-tempered sherds exhibiting Mississippian vessel forms were recovered together at Martin Farm, interpretations at first embraced culture historical views (Faulkner 1975:27–28; Salo 1969:138). The ceramics represented a transition from Woodland culture (limestone-tempered ceramics) to Mississippian culture (shell-tempered) as the resident population learned or were forced to alter their ceramics and their lifeway as new people entered the region. It was proposed that the archaeological data monitored the "Mississippianization" of the Woodland cultures.

An alternative perspective came from processual archaeology as assemblages and contexts comparable to those from Martin Farm and labeled emergent Mississippian were identified in many areas of the Southeast (see Smith 1990). This designation reflected the idea that Mississippian cultures had developed in many different areas of the Southeast as different populations turned to agriculture. Martin Farm, in addition to recording ceramic development, is the earliest recorded village with domestic structures and a platform mound comparable in form and permanence to later Mississippian settlements (Schroedl 1998:66–67). The Martin Farm site in this regard is but one example of culture evolution and the widespread economic and social adaptation of indigenous populations. Neither the culture historical nor processual approaches are the final word respecting Mississippian origins. The Martin Farm research provides the best-documented occurrence of these transitional cultures in East Tennessee. Exhaustive analysis of the associated artifacts, especially the ceramics, made it possible to identify similar occupations elsewhere in Tellico (Davis 1990:238–243). Rather than rare or isolated, these data suggest that emergent Mississippian communities existed throughout much of East Tennessee. Thus the foundation for initiating newer research agendas focusing on Mississippian origins, based, for example, in evolutionary theory or evolutionary ecology, is firmly in place for future archaeologists.

Late Mississippian

During the heyday of WPA era archaeological studies large-scale excavations were directed at Late Mississippian mounds and villages. This work produced an incredible wealth of materials from sites such as Hiwassee Island, Dallas, Hixon, Davis, and Mouse Creeks (Lewis and Lewis 1995). Citico and Toqua were two such mound center sites located in the Tellico Reservoir where considerable work was accomplished. Much less was done at a third Late Mississippian mound center on Bussell Island. A Late Mississippian village occupation with no associated mound also was investigated near Tomotley (Guthe and Bistline 1981). Considerable numbers of burials were removed from the Citico site, even before the Tellico project commenced. Work there in 1967 produced additional burials and some information regarding the mound, domestic structures, and the village palisade (King, Olinger, and Salo 1969:26–84). Tellico archaeologists returned to Citico in 1978 for the purpose of investigating the Cherokee occupation that had been largely ignored by earlier work at the site (Chapman and Newman 1979). Attention turned to Toqua as the primary candidate for obtaining evidence of late Mississippian culture comparable to what had been found in the 1930s at Hiwassee Island and elsewhere.

TVA acquired the Toqua property late in the Tellico project, and up to that time permission to work there had not been forthcoming (Chapman and Polhemus 1987:12). Neither had relic collectors gained access to the site, and the expectation that Toqua would produce as much or more information than had come from any Dallas culture site was more than met. The trade off was that, when the Toqua excavations started in 1975—again anticipating imminent completion of the dam and flooding of the reservoir—compromises were required respecting what could be reasonably excavated and properly recorded. This necessitated using a variety of earth-moving machines, working into the late fall and early winter, and maintaining a much larger number of field-workers.

Nevertheless the Toqua work produced a nearly complete stratigraphic record of Mound A, revealing a complex building sequence of 12 multiple mound summits with associated structures and human interments (Polhemus 1987). Two other mounds are related to mortuary activities. More than 100 domestic structures representing primary as well as summer dwellings, hundreds of human burials, a sequence of three palisades, a large borrow pit, and village plaza, along with an extraordinarily large sample of features and artifacts were recovered at Toqua. There is no question that the Toqua data form one of the most comprehensive records available for Dallas-phase town planning, village organization (Polhemus 1987; Schroedl 1998), mortuary patterning (Parham 1987; Scott and Polhemus 1987), subsistence patterns (Shea, Polhemus, and Chapman 1987; Bogan 1987), and technological organization (Reed 1987; Roberts 1987). Many of these kinds of data are unavailable from earlier excavations or are compromised for a variety of reasons. Toqua constitutes a critical benchmark for any late Mississippian research focus in East Tennessee.

Historic Cherokee

Through 1974 virtually all investigations relating to the historic Overhill Cherokee were at Chota (Schroedl, ed. 1986). The objectives of the Chota work, as had been established as far back as Cyrus Thomas (1894) and taken up by Lewis and Kneberg (1946), were to elucidate, if possible, the origin and antiquity of the Cherokee in East Tennessee and to describe the character of their material culture. By the mid 1970s, as a more processual approach took hold, the additional goal of understanding Cherokee culture development and change in relationship to European contact (Schroedl 2000, 2001) was established. At first it was assumed that other Cherokee villages exhibited patterning comparable to Chota. Subsequent investigations at Tomotley (Baden 1983), Mialoquo (Russ and Chapman 1983), Toqua (Schroedl 1978a; Polhemus 1987), and Citico (Chapman and Newman 1979) showed that this was not the case and that variability in culture patterning was far greater than represented at Chota alone (Schroedl 1986). Collectively the Cherokee village investigations covered nearly 7 ha and recorded six townhouses, 74 domestic structures, more than 1,300 features, and 212 burials (Schroedl 1986:538–539). To address the goal of describing Cherokee culture change, the historical record was employed to define seven distinctive episodes of culture contact beginning with Spanish contact through the postremoval period. Archaeological assemblages representing each period were identified, described, and compared to show how the Overhill Cherokee had changed from the late seventeenth through the early nineteenth centuries as a response to Euro-American contact (Schroedl 2000:212).

These data indicate that the Overhill Cherokee were successful in maintaining much of their cultural integrity and heritage through the 1760s. The Cherokee were caught up in the deer-hide trade, and this initiated dramatic change in their technology as they adopted European iron technology. Stone tool use diminished greatly but was never replaced. Ceramic technology remained unchanged, but some new vessel forms were developed. Village patterning and both public and domestic architecture were uncompromised, although some variation in household design in the mid eighteenth century may be related to movements of Cherokee people from South and North Carolina. Change in subsistence also was minimal, although consumption of chickens and pigs became common and European-introduced plants such as peaches, Irish potatoes, sweet potatoes, and cowpeas also were incorporated in the diet. The essential elements of social, political, and religious life remained stable, although pressure to change was intensified as the Cherokee became more entangled with the British and French (Schroedl 2000).

There is ample archaeological and historical evidence that the American Revolutionary War and its aftermath were devastating to the Cherokee. By the beginning of the nineteenth century, the Overhill Cherokee villages were greatly depleted in size and population, some were abandoned, and all were ceded to the United States by 1819. Traditional

Cherokee architecture was replaced with rail cabins and eventually by log cabins. Hunting and farming came to depend almost entirely on Euro-American technology as traditional Cherokee settlement and subsistence came to resemble early-nineteenth-century American culture.

A small number of Cherokee hamlets or isolated houses were investigated in the course of other reconnaissance, testing, or excavation activities (Milligan 1969; Chapman 1980b). When additional survey of the above pool portions of the reservoir were initiated in 1979, however, it became quickly apparent from both archaeological and historical sources that there were individual domestic households associated with late-eighteenth- and early-nineteenth-century Federal period and Removal period Cherokee occupation, kinds of manifestations not known or poorly represented in village site excavations (Davis 1990:256; Riggs 1987, 1989; Ford 1982). Recognition and investigation of these sites was instrumental in establishing a research agenda for contemporary sites in western North Carolina (Riggs 1996, 1999).

Euro-American Sites

Excavations were conducted at four Euro-American sites important in the early history of Tennessee. Fort Loudoun was constructed at the confluence of the Tellico and Little Tennessee rivers in 1756 and was abandoned by the British and then looted by the Cherokee in 1760. Excavations were conducted first in 1936–1937, again in 1957–1958 (Kunkel 1960), and then in 1966–1967, before the Tennessee State Division of Archaeology completely excavated the site in 1975–1976 (Kuttruff and Bastian 1977:11–23). Large areas surrounding the fort (subsequently utilized for borrow to raise the land surface so that the fort could be rebuilt at its original location and contour only at a higher elevation) also were investigated. This work produced structures and features representing probable early Mississippian occupation and additional domestic buildings and associated features representing remnants of the Cherokee town of Tuskegee. Reports on the animal remains (Parmalee 1960; Breitburg 1983) are available and so is a summary of the investigations (Kutruff and Bastian 1977). As important as Fort Loudoun is in the archaeology and early history of Tennessee, it is regrettable, however, that full descriptions of the excavations, recorded buildings and features, the artifacts, and their interpretation remain unpublished.

The Virginia Fort also was constructed in 1756 and abandoned shortly thereafter. It was fortunate that the location of this important historical site was identified, but because of its short occupation, few artifacts and only incomplete remnants of its associated structures were found (Polhemus 1977).

Tellico Blockhouse, constructed in 1793 and abandoned in 1807, served to monitor nearby Cherokee towns and provide their residents access to Euro-American technology during implementation of federal programs to assimilate the Cherokee. The site was fully excavated in 1972–1973, revealing three phases of construction activities, represented by 13 distinctive structures, 5 privies, a well, a blacksmith shop, a series of palisades and gates, and a variety of other features (Polhemus 1978). More than 40,000 historic artifacts, 39,000 animal bones, and 13,000 aboriginal lithic and ceramic artifacts were identified. This research, along with analysis of historic artifacts from Cherokee towns, employed South's (1972, 1977) functional classification, mean ceramic dating, and pattern recognition procedures. At Tellico Blockhouse artifact frequencies and spatial distributions were interpretable as organizational developments from a Frontier pattern to a Carolina pattern. Pattern recognition studies, when applied to historical Cherokee contexts, permitted definition of a Frontier Aboriginal Artifact pattern for describing the process of acquiring Euro-American technology, showing shifting patterns of technological changes, and elaborating the full pattern of technological acculturation including how aboriginal technological systems represented by lithic and ceramic artifacts were altered accordingly (see Newman 1977, 1986).

Perhaps the single greatest oversight of the Tellico Archaeological Project was that so little effort was made to identify and document nineteenth- and twentieth-century Euro-American sites. Households identified, for example, at Harrison Branch and Citico were significant to analysis of late-eighteenth and early-nineteenth-century white settlement and its comparison to contemporary Cherokee occupation at sites such as Bell Rattle's (Ford 1982; Riggs 1987, 1989). These sites, however, were largely accidentally encountered in the course of pursuing other research goals. As a result virtually all of the houses and farm buildings in the reservoir, some of which surely dated to early Euro-American settlement and all of which reflected growth, development, and change to the rural landscape of East Tennessee were bulldozed during reservoir clearing or in other cases torn down by landowners or burned by vandals. There was no systematic effort to record the buildings prior to their demolition, and no accompanying archaeological work was included. Partly to blame for this was the reluctance of archaeologists and historians to embrace nineteenth- and twentieth-century rural farms and settlement as cultural resources and archaeological sites. TVA also shares some blame because of its reluctance to accept responsibility for such resources under the National Historic Preservation Act and Executive Order 11593 in a more timely fashion.

Archaeological interests in the nineteenth- and twentieth-century rural landscape and TVA's commitment to such resources was initiated in the late 1970s but did not become common in East Tennessee until the 1980s. This is illustrated first by archaeological excavations in 1979 at Morganton, a prominent town on the banks of the Little Tennessee River in the first half of the nineteenth century (Polhemus 1980). A controlled surface collection was made in 10 ft squares over 7.15 acres or about 23 percent of the town area. Backhoe assisted excavations made in 13 areas totaled 1.18 acres and revealed 10 structures and 790 additional features and postholes. These data trace the formal establishment of the town in 1813 and show the pattern of its growth as well as gradual demise as economic conditions declined and the town experienced repeated flooding in the mid and late nineteenth century. The Morganton work is important because it chronicles early urban development in East Tennessee that occurred as Cherokee occupation dwindled and rapid growth in white settlement ensued.

The second example focusing on Euro-American settlement in the nineteenth and twentieth centuries is the systematic archaeological survey of a 2,600-acre area set aside for industrial development (Carnes 1980). Survey of this parcel for historic sites was guided by a variety of archival sources and personal interviews with former residents and included examination of 28 sampling units from the probabilistic site survey. This identified 52 farm or residence sites, most of which had been razed by TVA prior to the survey, and three family cemeteries. These sites mostly represent occupation after the 1870s, but some produced artifacts dating earlier in the nineteenth century. It is obvious that this work would have been far more productive had it been done before the buildings were demolished and had archaeological test excavations been included. Some sense of what might have been recorded elsewhere is that this historic survey covered only about 8 percent of the total Tellico Project area.

Summary and Conclusions

Archaeological studies in the lower Little Tennessee River Valley, beginning with the work of Thomas (1894) and Harrington (1922) and taken up by Lewis and Kneberg (1946), set the initial culture historical research agenda for the Tellico Archaeological Project. When the project began in 1967, the focus was mostly on late prehistoric and early historic cultures, particularly the rich and well-known Overhill Cherokee towns so well documented, for example, by Timberlake and many others (Williams 1927). At the time it was thought that the Tellico Dam would be completed within a few years and that it was likely that only a small or moderate portion of the archaeological record could be studied. Funding for the conduct of the studies was modest and made possible through the National Park Service, Interagency Archaeological Services. A perennial problem was obtaining landowner permission to investigate site areas not yet acquired by TVA.

From the beginning the Tellico Dam Project was controversial. Federal environmental laws, passed in the late 1960s and early 1970s, included statutes relating to cultural resources and began to affect the project and the conduct of archaeology. TVA at first provided equipment and supplies to support the archaeological field and laboratory work and then eventually funded much of the research investigations. While the fundamental culture historical perspective was never lost, the project began to take on distinctive characteristics of processual archaeology. This ranged from efforts to articulate research designs, to devise and implement intra-site and regional-site sampling, and to address contemporary research problems such as activity areas, spatial organization, subsistence-settlement patterns, sociopolitical patterns, and questions relating to culture development and change from a culture evolutionary perspective. Litigation that delayed dam construction seven years beyond its scheduled completion allowed for far more archaeological work than was ever anticipated in 1967. Multiple delays and the unpredictable nature of their duration and eventual resolution, however, often made it difficult to plan and conduct fieldwork very far in advance.

For its time the Tellico Archaeological Project was among the largest and costliest archaeological programs ever conducted in the Southeast (Chapman 1988). The project generated hundreds of public lectures, professional presentations, technical reports, monographs, book chapters, and journal articles (for a listing of publications see Riggs and Chapman 1983 and Chapman 1994). Archaeological materials from the project are prominently included in public exhibits at the Sequoyah Birthplace Museum, Vonore, Tennessee, and the Frank H. McClung Museum, University of Tennessee–Knoxville. Today the Tellico data remain a significant source for scholarly research and publication (e.g., Schroedl 2008; Chapman 2008; Sherwood and Chapman 2005)

The Tellico investigations made lasting and significant contributions to archaeological chronology and culture history. Notable in this regard is the Archaic period research. Virtually every discussion of the Archaic period in eastern North America now acknowledges the Tellico work (e.g., Bense 1994:65–72; Fagan 2005:377–382). Woodland period materials added much to defining regional Hopewell- and Connestee-related cultural manifestations, and the Martin Farm data have helped define the Woodland-Mississippian transition. A defining goal of the Tellico Archaeological Project was to describe the culture manifestations of the Overhill Cherokee, and because of the Tellico work, there is now comprehensive documentation for this era in Native American history.

The Tellico Archeological Project from a processual perspective is equally noteworthy. The Tellico survey and resulting settlement pattern studies firmly established a quantitative and replicable approach to prehistoric landscape use. These data, when connected to geomorphology, wood charcoal, and pollen studies, place the settlement data in its environmental context. Models of site structure and hunter-gatherer mobility, particularly applied to Early Archaic data, represent detailed quantitative studies of site activities, site use, and changes in landscape utilization. Botanical remains recovered from Tellico project excavations have played a major role in defining patterns of plant domestication and agricultural development in eastern North America. Establishment of a zooarchaeological studies program at the University of Tennessee in the early 1970s ensured detailed identification and comparative analysis of faunal remains (e.g., Bogan 1982, 1987; Bogan, LaValley, and Schroedl 1986; Cridlebaugh 1981:162–164; Schroedl 1975:270–273; 1978:192–211; Robison 1981:179–200). The Martin Farm work contributed fundamental information respecting the origin and development of Mississippian culture. In turn the Toqua studies provide the best understanding of Late Mississippian town planning and organization available in East Tennessee. Skeletal materials from the site have contributed greatly to regional studies of human biology and mortuary patterning (Boyd and Boyd 1991). The Overhill Cherokee and associated Euro-American sites' research documents one of the most extraordinary record of historic settlement and Native American culture change found anywhere.

The Tellico Project pioneered many approaches now used in cultural resource management. The project was not the first to use heavy equipment in the conduct of archaeology, but its application at so many sites and under so many different circumstances was unique. Water screening to process vast volumes of sediments also made the Tellico Project distinctive, particularly when it is recognized that screening was not in common use when the project began. The probabilistic survey was a major innovation for the Southeast. The project routinely hired women in field and supervisory positions when it was uncommon to do so. Cherokee Indian participation, although limited to the Chota site, was certainly unique.

The Tellico Archaeological Project started out informed by culture historical theory and salvage archeology and concluded by incorporating numerous elements of processual archaeology and modern cultural resource management. Given current cultural resource and environmental law, the Tellico Dam Project, if conducted at all today, would be very different than it was 40 years ago. The expense of doing archaeology would be perhaps 10 or 20 times the cost then. Most archaeological techniques employed then would be employed now, but many technological innovations, alternative theoretical perspectives, or cultural resource management procedures, not available or in practice, would have to be incorporated. Regardless, the Tellico Archaeological Project for its time and circumstance produced a remarkable record of human habitation in East Tennessee, and its many research results surely will remain current and relevant for generations to come.

Acknowledgments

I thank Todd M. Ahlman and Erin Pritchard for asking me to contribute this chapter. I am grateful to the hundreds of individuals who in one way or another contributed to archaeological research in the Tellico Reservoir Area (see Chapman 1994: v-vi for additional names). Alfred K. Guthe (deceased) was principal investigator for much of the project's history. I especially appreciate the contributions of my Tellico project associates Jefferson Chapman, Richard Polhemus, Larry R. Kimball, R. P. Stephen Davis, Jr., and C. Clifford Boyd, Jr. Contained in this essay is research developed by many individuals. I have done my best to represent their scholarship accurately, but I alone am responsible for any deletions or misrepresentations of their work. The Tellico project was funded by numerous contracts with the Tennessee Valley Authority and the National Park Service. The success of the Tellico work owes much to the dedication of J. Bennett Graham at TVA and Bennie C. Keel at NPS.

References Cited

ASCH, DAVID, AND NANCY ASCH
1985   Prehistoric Plant Cultivation in West Central Illinois. In *Prehistoric Food Production in North America*, edited by Richard I. Ford, pp. 149–203. Anthropological Papers No. 75. Museum of Anthropology, University of Michigan, Ann Arbor.

BADEN, WILLIAM W.
1983   *Tomotley: An Eighteenth Century Cherokee Village.* Report of Investigations No. 36. Department of Anthropology, University of Tennessee, Knoxville.

BENSE, JUDITH A.
1994   *Archaeology of the Southeastern United States.* Academic Press, New York.

BINFORD, LEWIS R.
1968   Archaeological Perspectives. In *New Perspectives in Archaeology,* edited by Sally R. Binford and Lewis R. Binford, pp. 5–32. Aldine, Chicago.

1978   Dimensional Analysis of Behavior and Site Structure: Learning from an Eskimo Hunting Stand. *American Antiquity* 43:330–361.

1979   Organization and Formation Processes: Looking at Curated Technologies. *Journal of Anthropological Research* 35:255–273.

1980   Willow Smoke and Dogs' Tails: Hunter-Gatherer Settlement Systems and Archaeological Site Formation. *American Antiquity* 45:4–20.

1982   The Archaeology of Place. *Journal of Anthropological Archaeology* 1:5–31.

BOGAN, ARTHUR E.
1982   Archeological Evidence of Subsistence Patterns in the Little Tennessee River Valley. *Tennessee Anthropologist* 7:38–50.

1987   Faunal Analysis: A Comparison of Dallas and Overhill Cherokee Subsistence Strategies. In *The Toqua Site: A Late Mississippian Dallas Phase Town,* vol. 2, edited by Richard Polhemus, pp. 971–1111. Report of Investigations No. 41, Department of Anthropology, University of Tennessee, Knoxville.

BOGAN, ARTHUR E., LORI LAVALLEY, AND GERALD F. SCHROEDL
1986   Faunal Remains. In *Overhill Cherokee Archaeology at Chota-Tanasee,* edited by Gerald F. Schroedl, pp. 469–514. Report of Investigations No. 38, University of Tennessee, Department of Anthropology, University of Tennessee, Knoxville.

BOYD, C. CLIFFORD, JR., AND DONNA C. BOYD
1991   A Multidimensional Investigation of Biocultural Relationships among Three Late Prehistoric Societies in Tennessee. *American Antiquity* 56:75–88.

BREITBURG, EMMANUEL
1983 Bone Discardment Patterns and Meat Procurement Strategies at British Fort Loudoun (Tennessee). M.A. thesis, Department of Anthropology, Vanderbilt University, Nashville.

BROYLES, BETTYE J.
1966 Preliminary Report: The St. Albans Site (46KA27), Kanawha County, West Virginia. *West Virginia Archaeologist* 19:1–43.
1970 New Dates Received for St. Albans Site. *West Virginia Archaeological Society Newsletter* 12(4):6.
1971 *Second Preliminary Report: The St. Albans Site, Kanawha County, West Virginia*. Report of Archaeological Investigations No. 3, West Virginia Geological and Economic Survey, Morgantown.

CARNES, LINDA F.
1980 A Summary of Historic Archaeological Resources Located Within Tellico Industrial Area II. Department of Anthropology, University of Tennessee, Knoxville.

CHAPMAN, JEFFERSON
1973 *The Icehouse Bottom Site, 40MR23*. Report of Investigations No. 13, Department of Anthropology, University of Tennessee, Knoxville.
1975 *The Rose Island Site and the Bifurcate Point Tradition*. Report of Investigations No. 14, Department of Anthropology, University of Tennessee, Knoxville.
1976 The Archaic Period in the Lower Little Tennessee River Valley: The Radiocarbon Dates. *Tennessee Anthropologist* 1:1–12.
1977 *Archaic Period Research in the Lower Little Tennessee River Valley-1975: Icehouse Bottom, Harrison Branch, Thirty Acre Island, Calloway Island*. Report of Investigations No. 18, Department of Anthropology, University of Tennessee, Knoxville.
1978 *The Bacon Farm Site and a Buried Site Reconnaissance*. Report of Investigations No. 23, Department of Anthropology, University of Tennessee, Knoxville.
1979 *The Howard and Calloway Island Sites*. Report of Investigations No. 27, Department of Anthropology, University of Tennessee, Knoxville.
1980a Introduction. In *The 1979 Archaeological and Geological Investigations in the Tellico Reservoir*, edited by Jefferson Chapman, pp. 1–6. Report of Investigations No. 29, Department of Anthropology, University of Tennessee, Knoxville.
1980b Wear Bend Site, 40LD107. In *The 1979 Archaeological and Geological Investigations in the Tellico Reservoir*, edited by Jefferson Chapman, pp. 32–42. Report of Investigations No. 29, Department of Anthropology, University of Tennessee, Knoxville.

1981   *The Bacon Bend and Iddins Sites: The Late Archaic Period in the Lower Little Tennessee River Valley.* Report of Investigations No. 31, Department of Anthropology, University of Tennessee, Knoxville.

1985   Archaeology and the Archaic Period in the Southern Ridge-and-Valley Province. In *Structure and Process in Southeastern Archaeology,* edited by Roy S. Dickens, Jr., and H. Trawick Ward, pp. 137–153. University of Alabama Press, Tuscaloosa.

1987   The Kittrell Mound and an Assessment of Burial Mound Construction in the Southern Ridge and Valley Province. *Tennessee Anthropologist* 12:51–73

1988   The Federal Archaeological Program in Tennessee, 1966–1986: An Archaeological Second Coming. In *Advances in Southeastern Archaeology 1966–1986: Contributions of the Federal Archaeological Program,* edited by Bennie C. Keel, pp. 46–49. Southeastern Archaeological Conference Special Publication No. 6.

1994   *Tellico Archaeology: 12,000 Years of Native American History,* revised edition. University of Tennessee Press, Knoxville.

2008   Tellico Archaeology: Tracing Timberlake's Footsteps. In *Culture, Crisis, and Conflict: Cherokee British Relations 1756–1765,* edited by Anne F. Rogers and Barbara R. Duncan, Museum of the Cherokee Indian Press, Cherokee, NC.

CHAPMAN, JEFFERSON (EDITOR)
1980   *The 1979 Archaeological and Geological Investigations in the Tellico Reservoir.* Report of Investigations No. 29, Department of Anthropology, University of Tennessee, Knoxville.

CHAPMAN, JEFFERSON, AND JAMES M. ADOVASIO
1977   Textile and Basketry Impressions from Icehouse Bottom Tennessee. *American Antiquity* 42:620–25.

CHAPMAN, JEFFERSON, AND GARY CRITES
1987   Evidence for Early Maize (*Zea mays*) from the Icehouse bottom Site. *American Antiquity* 52:352–354.

CHAPMAN, JEFFERSON, AND BENNIE C. KEEL
1979   Candy Creek-Connestee Components in Eastern Tennessee and Western North Carolina and Their Relationship with Adena-Hopewell. In *Hopewell Archaeology: The Chillicothe Conference,* edited by David S. Brose and N'omi Greber, pp. 157–161. Kent State University Press, Kent, Ohio.

CHAPMAN, JEFFERSON, AND ROBERT D. NEWMAN
1979   Archaeological Investigations at the Citico Site. In *The 1978 Archaeological Investigations at the Citico Site (40Mr7),* edited by Jefferson Chapman, pp. 1–4. Report submitted to the Tennessee Valley Authority, Knoxville.

CHAPMAN, JEFFERSON, AND RICHARD R. POLHEMUS

1987   Introduction. In *The Toqua Site: A Late Mississippian Dallas Phase Town*, 2 vols., edited by Richard Polhemus, pp. 1–30. Report of Investigations No. 41, Department of Anthropology, University of Tennessee, Knoxville.

CHAPMAN, JEFFERSON, AND ANDREA B. SHEA

1981   The Archaeobotanical Record: Early Archaic Period to Contact in the Lower Little Tennessee River Valley. *Tennessee Anthropologist* 6:61–84.

CHAPMAN, JEFFERSON, PAUL A. DELCOURT, PATRICIA A. CRIDLEBAUGH, ANDREA B. SHEA, AND HAZEL R. DELCOURT

1982   Man-Land Interaction: 10,000 Years of American Indian Impact on Native Ecosystems in the Lower Little Tennessee River Valley, Eastern Tennessee. *Southeastern Archaeology* 1:115–121.

COE, JOFFRE

1961   Cherokee Archaeology. In *Symposium on Cherokee and Iroquois Culture*, edited by William Fenton and John Gulick, pp. 53–60. Bureau of American Ethnology Bulletin 180. Washington, DC.

1964   *The Formative Cultures of the Carolina Piedmont*. Transactions of the American Philosophical Society 54(5).

CRIDLEBAUGH, PATRICIA A.

1981   *The Icehouse Bottom Site (40MR23): 1977 Excavations*. Report of Investigations No. 34, Department of Anthropology, University of Tennessee, Knoxville.

1984   American Indian and Euro-American Impact upon Holocene Vegetation in the Lower Little Tennessee River Valley. Ph.D. dissertation, Department of Anthropology, University of Tennessee, Knoxville.

DAVIS, R. P. STEPHEN, JR.

1980   A Summary Report of Probabilistic "Non Site" Sampling in Tellico Reservoir, 1979. In *The 1979 Archaeological and Geological Investigations in the Tellico Reservoir*, edited by Jefferson Chapman, pp. 59–90. Report of Investigations No. 29, Department of Anthropology, University of Tennessee, Knoxville.

1985   Intersite Assemblage Variability in the Lower Little Tennessee River Valley: Exploring Extinct Settlement Systems through Probabilistic Sampling. In *Structure and Process in Southeastern Archaeology*, edited by Roy S. Dickens, Jr., and H. Trawick Ward, pp. 154–179. University of Alabama Press, Tuscaloosa.

1990   *Aboriginal Settlement Patterns in the Little Tennessee River Valley*. Report of Investigations No. 50, Department of Anthropology, University of Tennessee, Knoxville.

DAVIS, R. P. STEPHEN, JR., LARRY R. KIMBALL, AND WILLIAM W. BADEN
1982   An Archaeological Survey and Assessment of Aboriginal Settlement within the Lower Little Tennessee River Valley. Report submitted to the Tennessee Valley Authority by the Department of Anthropology, University of Tennessee, Knoxville.

DELCOURT, PAUL A.
1980   Quaternary Alluvial Terraces of the Little Tennessee River Valley, East Tennessee. In *The 1979 Archaeological and Geological Investigations in the Tellico Reservoir*, edited by Jefferson Chapman, pp. 110–121. Report of Investigations No. 29, Department of Anthropology, University of Tennessee, Knoxville.

DICKENS, ROY S.
1976   *Cherokee Prehistory: The Pisgah Phase in the Appalachian Summit Region.* University of Tennessee Press, Knoxville.

DUNNELL, ROBERT C., AND WILLIAM S. DANCEY
1983   The Siteless Survey: A Regional Scale Data Collection Strategy. In *Advances in Archaeological Method and Theory*, vol. 6, edited by Michael B. Schiffer, pp. 267–287. Academic Press, New York.

FAGAN, BRIAN M.
2005   *Ancient North America*, fourth edition. Thames & Hudson, London.

FAULKNER, CHARLES H.
1967   Tennessee Radiocarbon Dates. *Tennessee Archaeologist* 23:12–30.
1975   The Woodland-Mississippian Transition in the Eastern Tennessee Valley. *Southeastern Archaeological Conference Bulletin* 18:19–30.

FOLEY, LUCY, AND JEFFERSON CHAPMAN
1977   Appendix: Stratigraphy and Geomorphology of the Icehouse Bottom, Harrison Branch and Patrick Sites. In *Archaic Period Research in the Lower Little Tennessee River Valley—1975: Icehouse Bottom, Harrison Branch, Thirty Acre Island, Calloway Island*, edited by Jefferson Chapman, pp. 179–206 Report of Investigations No. 18, Department of Anthropology, University of Tennessee, Knoxville.

FORD, THOMAS B.
1982   An Analysis of Anglo-American–Cherokee Culture Contact during the Federal Period, the Hiwassee Tract, Eastern Tennessee. M.A. thesis, Department of Anthropology University of Tennessee, Knoxville.

FOWLER, DON D.
1986   Conserving American Archaeological Resources. In *American Archaeology Past and Future*, edited by David J. Meltzer, Don D.

Fowler, and Jeremy A. Sabloff, pp. 135–162. Smithsonian Institution Press, Washington DC.

FRANKENBERG, SUSAN R., AND NICHOLAS P. HERRMANN

2000   *Archaeological Reconnaissance Survey of Tennessee Valley Authority Lands on the Tellico Reservoir.* Report submitted to the Tennessee Valley Authority by the Department of Anthropology, University of Tennessee, Knoxville.

GLEESON, PAUL F. (EDITOR)

1970   *Archaeological Investigations in the Tellico Reservoir, Interim Report, 1969.* Report of Investigations No. 8, Department of Anthropology, University of Tennessee, Knoxville.

1971   *Archaeological Investigations in the Tellico Reservoir, Interim Report, 1970.* Report of Investigations No. 9, Department of Anthropology, University of Tennessee, Knoxville.

GREMILLION, KRISTEN J.

2002   The Development and Dispersal of Agricultural Systems in the Woodland Period Southeast. In *The Woodland Southeast,* edited by David G. Anderson and Robert C. Mainfort, pp. 483–501. University of Alabama Press, Tuscaloosa.

GRIFFIN, JOHN W.

1974   *Investigations in Russell Cave: Russell Cave National Monument, Alabama.* Publications in Archaeology No. 13, National Park Service.

GUTHE, ALFRED K., AND E. MARIAN BISTLINE

1981   *Excavations at Tomotley, 1973–74, and the Tuskegee Area: Two Reports.* Report of Investigations No. 24, Department of Anthropology, University of Tennessee, Knoxville.

HARRINGTON, M. R.

1922   *Cherokee and Earlier Remains on the Upper Tennessee River.* Indians Notes and Monographs No. 24, Museum of the American Indian, Heye Foundation, New York.

KEEL, BENNIE C.

1976   *Cherokee Archaeology: A Study of the Appalachian Summit.* University of Tennessee Press, Knoxville.

KIMBALL, LARRY R.

1980   A Summary Report of Probabilistic Sampling of Selected Excavated Sites in Tellico Reservoir, 1979. In *The 1979 Archaeological and Geological Investigations in the Tellico Reservoir,* edited by Jefferson Chapman, pp. 91–109. Report of Investigations No. 29, Department of Anthropology, University of Tennessee, Knoxville.

1985   *The 1977 Archaeological Survey: An Overall Assessment of the Archeological Resources of Tellico Reservoir.* Report of Investigations No. 40, Department of Anthropology, University of Tennessee, Knoxville.

1993   Rose Island Revisited: The Detection of Early Archaic Site Structure Using Grid Count Data. *Southeastern Archaeology* 12:93–116.

1996   Early Archaic Settlement and Technology: Lessons from Tellico. In *The Paleoindian and Early Archaic Southeast,* edited by David G. Anderson and Kenneth E. Sassaman, pp. 147–186. University of Alabama Press, Tuscaloosa.

KIMBALL, LARRY R., AND WILLIAM BADEN
1985   Quantitative Model of Woodland and Mississippian Ceramic Assemblages for the Identification of Surface Collections. In *The 1977 Archaeological Survey: An Overall Assessment of the Archaeological Resources of Tellico Reservoir,* edited by Larry R. Kimball, pp. 121–274. Report of Investigations No. 40, Department of Anthropology, University of Tennessee, Knoxville.

KING, DUANE H., DANNY OLINGER, AND LAWR V. SALO
1969   Citico Site (40MR7). In *Archaeological Investigations in the Tellico Reservoir, Tennessee, 1967–1968: An Interim Report,* edited by Lawr V. Salo, pp. 26–84. Report of Investigations No. 7, Department of Anthropology, University of Tennessee, Knoxville.

KING, THOMAS F., PATRICIA PARKER HICKMAN, AND GARY BERG
1977   *Anthropology in Historic Preservation.* Academic Press, New York.

KNEBERG, MADELINE D.
1961   Four Southeastern Limestone-Tempered Pottery Complexes. *Southeastern Archaeological Conference Newsletter* 7(2):3–14.

KNUDSON, RUTH ANN
1986   Contemporary Cultural Resource Management. In *American Archaeology Past and Future,* edited by David J. Meltzer, Don D. Fowler, and Jeremy A. Sabloff, pp. 395–414. Smithsonian Institution Press, Washington, DC.

KUNKEL, PETER H.
1960   *Fort Loudoun Archaeology: A Summary of the Structural Problem.* Miscellaneous Paper No. 6, Tennessee Archaeological Society.

KUTRUFF, KARL, AND BEVERLY BASTIAN
1977   Fort Loudoun Excavations: 1975 Season. *Conference on Historic Sites Archaeology Papers* 10:11–23.

LEWIS, THOMAS M. N., AND MADELINE KNEBERG
1946   *Hiwassee Island: An Archaeological Account of Four Tennessee Peoples.* University of Tennessee Press, Knoxville.

LEWIS, THOMAS M. N., AND MADELINE D. KNEBERG LEWIS
1995   *The Prehistory of the Chickamauga Basin in Tennessee,* vols. 1 and
        2. Compiled and edited by Lynne P. Sullivan, University of Tennessee
        Press, Knoxville.

LYON, EDWIN A.
1996   *A New Deal for Southeastern Archeology.* University of Alabama
        Press, Tuscaloosa.

MAINFORT, ROBERT C., AND MARY L. KWAS
1991   The Bat Creek Stone: Judeans in Tennessee. *Tennessee
        Anthropologist* 16:1–19.

1993   The Bat Creek Stone: A Final Statement. *Tennessee Anthropologist*
        18:87–93.

2004   The Bat Creek Stone Revisited: A Fraud Exposed. *American
        Antiquity* 69:761–769

McCOLLOUGH, C. R., AND CHARLES H. FAULKNER
1973   *Excavation of the Higgs and Doughty Sites I-75 Salvage
        Archaeology.* Miscellaneous Paper No. 12, Tennessee Archaeological
        Society.

McKERN, W. C.
1939   The Midwestern Taxonomic Method as an Aid to Archaeological
        Culture Study. *American Antiquity* 4:301–313.

MILLIGAN, JOSEPH W.
1969   The Starnes Site (40MR32). In *Archaeological Investigations in the
        Tellico Reservoir, Tennessee, 1967–1968: An Interim Report,* ed-
        ited by Lawr V. Salo, pp. 166–178. Report of Investigations No. 7,
        Department of Anthropology, University of Tennessee, Knoxville.

NEWMAN, ROBERT D.
1977   An Analysis of the European Artifacts from Chota-Tanasee:
        An Eighteenth-Century Overhill Cherokee Town. M.A. thesis,
        Department of Anthropology, University of Tennessee, Knoxville.

1986   "Euro-American Artifacts." In *Overhill Cherokee Archaeology at
        Chota-Tanasee,* edited by Gerald F. Schroedl, pp. 415–468. Report
        of Investigations No. 38. Department of Anthropology, University of
        Tennessee, Knoxville.

O'BRIEN, MICHAEL J. R., LEE LYMAN, AND MICHAEL BRIAN SCHIFFER
2005   *Archaeology as Process: Processualism and Its Progeny.* University
        of Utah Press, Salt Lake City.

PARHAM, KENNETH
1987   Toqua Skeletal Biology: A Biocultural Approach. In *The Toqua
        Site: A Late Mississippian Dallas Phase Town,* vol. I, edited by
        Richard Polhemus, pp. 431–551. Report of Investigations No. 41,
        Department of Anthropology, University of Tennessee, Knoxville.

PARMALEE, PAUL
1960   Vertebrate Remains from Fort Loudoun, Tennessee. In *Fort
        Loudoun Archaeology: A Summary of the Structural Problem*,
        edited by Peter H. Kunkel, pp. 26–29. Miscellaneous Paper No. 6,
        Tennessee Archaeological Society.

PEEBLES, CHRISTOPHER S.
1978   Determinants of Settlement Size and Location in the Moundville
        Phase. In *Mississippian Settlement Patterns*, edited by Bruce D.
        Smith, pp. 369–416. Academic Press, New York.
1988   Federal Archaeology in the Southeast: Practice, Product and
        Promise. In *Advances in Southeastern Archaeology 1966–1986:
        Contributions of the Federal Archaeological Program*, edited by
        Bennie C. Keel, pp. 53–60. Southeastern Archaeological Conference
        Special Publication No. 6.

POLHEMUS, RICHARD R.
1977   The Virginia Fort. Ms. on file, Frank H. McClung Museum,
        University of Tennessee, Knoxville.
1978   *Archaeological Investigations of the Tellico Blockhouse Site: A
        Federal Military and Trade Complex*. Report of Investigations
        No. 26, Department of Anthropology, University of Tennessee,
        Knoxville.
1980   Preliminary Report on the Archaeological Investigation of the
        19th Century Town of Morganton. In *The 1979 Archaeological
        and Geological Investigations in the Tellico Reservoir*, edited by
        Jefferson Chapman, pp. 122–163. Report of Investigations No. 29,
        Department of Anthropology, University of Tennessee, Knoxville.
1987   *The Toqua Site: A Late Mississippian Dallas Phase Town, 2 Vols.*
        Report of Investigations No. 41, Department of Anthropology,
        University of Tennessee, Knoxville.

PRICE, JAMES E.
1978   The Settlement Pattern of the Powers Phase. In *Mississippian
        Settlement Patterns*, edited by Bruce D. Smith, pp. 201–231.
        Academic Press, New York.

REED, ANN
1987   Ceramic Artifacts. In *The Toqua Site: A Late Mississippian Dallas
        Phase Town*, vol. 1, edited by Richard Polhemus, pp. 553–687.
        Report of Investigations No. 41, Department of Anthropology,
        University of Tennessee, Knoxville.

RIGGS, BRETT H.
1987   Socioeconomic Variability in Federal Period Overhill Cherokee
        Archaeological Assemblages. M.A. thesis, Department of
        Anthropology, University of Tennessee, Knoxville, Tennessee.

1989   Interhousehold Variability among Early Nineteenth-century
        Cherokee Artifact Assemblages. In *Households and Communities:
        Proceedings of the 21st Annual Chacmool Conference,* edited by
        Scott MacEachern, David Archer, and Richard Garvin, pp. 328–338.
        Calgary, Alberta, Canada.

1996   *Removal Period Cherokee Households and Communities in
        Southwestern North Carolina (1835–1838).* Report submitted to the
        North Carolina Division of Archives and History, Raleigh, North
        Carolina.

1999   Removal Period Cherokee Households in Southwestern North
        Carolina: Material Perspectives on Ethnicity and Cultural
        Differentiation. Ph.D. dissertation, Department of Anthropology,
        University of Tennessee, Knoxville.

RIGGS, BRETT H., AND JEFFERSON CHAPMAN

1983   *A Bibliography for the Tellico Archaeological Project.* Department
        of Anthropology, University of Tennessee, Knoxville.

ROBERTS, WAYNE

1987   Lithic Artifacts. In *The Toqua Site: A Late Mississippian Dallas
        Phase Town,* vol. 2, edited by Richard Polhemus, pp. 689–909.
        Report of Investigations No. 41, Department of Anthropology,
        University of Tennessee, Knoxville.

ROBISON, NEIL

1981   An Analysis of the Faunal Remains. In *Excavations at Tomotley,
        1973–74, and the Tuskegee Area: Two Reports,* edited by Alfred K.
        Guthe and E. Marion Bistline, pp. 179–200. Report of Investigations
        No. 24, Department of Anthropology, University of Tennessee,
        Knoxville.

RUSS, KURT C., AND JEFFERSON CHAPMAN

1983   *Archaeological Investigations at the 18th Century Overhill
        Cherokee Town of Mialoquo.* Report of Investigations No. 37,
        Department of Anthropology, University of Tennessee, Knoxville.

SALO, LAWR V.

1969   Martin Farm. In *Archaeological Investigations in the Tellico
        Reservoir, Tennessee, 1967–1968: An Interim Report,* edited
        by Lawr V. Salo, pp. 87–150. Report of Investigations No. 7,
        Department of Anthropology, University of Tennessee, Knoxville.

SALO, LAWR V. (EDITOR)

1969   *Archaeological Investigations in the Tellico Reservoir, Tennessee,
        1967–1968: An Interim Report,* Report of Investigations No. 7,
        Department of Anthropology, University of Tennessee, Knoxville.

SCHROEDL, GERALD F.
1975   *Archaeological Investigations at the Harrison Branch and Bat Creek Sites.* Report of Investigations No. 10, Department of Anthropology, University of Tennessee, Knoxville.

1978a   Louis-Phillipe's Journal and Archaeological Investigations at the Overhill Cherokee Town of Toqua. *Journal of Cherokee Studies,* 3(4):206–220.

1978b   *The Patrick Site (40MR40), Tellico Reservoir, Tennessee.* Report of Investigations No. 25. Department of Anthropology, University of Tennessee, Knoxville.

1986   Overhill Cherokee Archaeology from the Perspective of Chota-Tanasee. In *Overhill Cherokee Archaeology at Chota-Tanasee,* edited by Gerald F. Schroedl, pp. 531–551. Report of Investigations No. 38. Department of Anthropology, University of Tennessee, Knoxville.

1998   Mississippian Towns in the Eastern Tennessee Valley. In *Mississippian Towns and Sacred Spaces,* edited by Barry Lewis and Charles Stout, pp. 64–92. University of Alabama Press, Tuscaloosa.

2000   Cherokee Ethnohistory and Archaeology from 1540 to 1838. In *Indians of the Greater Southeast during the Historic Period,* edited by Bonnie McEwan, pp. 204–241. University Press of Florida, Gainesville.

2001   Cherokee Archaeology since the 1970s. In *Archaeology of the Appalachian Highlands,* edited by Lynne P. Sullivan and Susan C. Prezzano, pp. 278–297. University of Tennessee Press, Knoxville.

2008   Overhill Cherokee Architecture and Village Organization. In *Culture, Crisis, and Conflict: Cherokee British Relations 1756–1765,* edited by Anne F. Rogers and Barbara R. Duncan, Museum of the Cherokee Indian Press, Cherokee, NC.

SCHROEDL, GERALD F. (EDITOR)
1986   *Overhill Cherokee Archaeology at Chota-Tanasee,* Report of Investigations No. 38. University of Tennessee, Department of Anthropology, Knoxville.

SCHROEDL, GERALD F., AND C. CLIFFORD BOYD, JR.
1991   Late Woodland Period Culture in East Tennessee. In *Stability, Transformation, and Variation: The Late Woodland Southeast,* edited by Michael S. Nassaney and Charles R. Cobb, pp. 69–90. Plenum Press, New York.

SCHROEDL, GERALD F., AND KURT RUSS
1986   An Introduction to the Ethnohistory and Archaeology of Chota and Tanasee. In *Overhill Cherokee Archaeology at Chota-Tanasee,* edited by Gerald F. Schroedl, pp. 1–42. Report of Investigations

No. 38. Department of Anthropology, University of Tennessee, Knoxville.

SCHROEDL, GERALD F., C. CLIFFORD BOYD, JR., AND R. P. STEPHEN DAVIS, JR.

1990   Explaining Mississippian Origins in East Tennessee. In *The Mississippian Emergence*, edited by Bruce D. Smith, pp. 175–196. Smithsonian Institution Press, Washington, DC.

SCHROEDL, GERALD F., JEFFERSON CHAPMAN, AND RICHARD POLHEMUS

1975   *A Comprehensive Research Design for Archaeological Investigations in the Tellico Reservoir, 1975–1980.* Report submitted to the Tennessee Valley Authority and the National Park Service.

SCHROEDL, GERALD F., R. P. STEPHEN. DAVIS, JR., AND C. CLIFFORD BOYD, JR.

1985   *Archaeological Contexts and Assemblages at Martin Farm.* Report of Investigations No. 39. Department of Anthropology, University of Tennessee, Knoxville.

SCOTT, GARY, AND RICHARD POLHEMUS

1987   Mortuary Patterning. In *The Toqua Site: A Late Mississippian Dallas Phase Town*, vol. 1, edited by Richard Polhemus, pp. 378–431. Report of Investigations No. 41, Department of Anthropology, University of Tennessee, Knoxville.

SHEA, ANDREA B., RICHARD POLHEMUS, AND JEFFERSON CHAPMAN

1987   The Paleoethnobotany of the Toqua Site. In *The Toqua Site: A Late Mississippian Dallas Phase Town*, vol. 2, edited by Richard Polhemus, pp. 1113–1207. Report of Investigations No. 41, Department of Anthropology, University of Tennessee, Knoxville.

SHERWOOD, SARAH C., AND JEFFERSON CHAPMAN

2005   The Identification and Potential Significance of Early Holocene Prepared Clay Surfaces: Examples from Dust Cave and Icehouse Bottom. *Southeastern Archaeology* 24:70–82

SMITH, BRUCE D.

1984   Mississippian Expansion: Tracing the Historical Development of an Explanatory Model. *Southeastern Archaeology* 3:13–32.

1992   Prehistoric Plant Husbandry in Eastern North America. In *The Origins of Agriculture*, edited by C. Wesley Cowan and Patty Jo Watson, pp.101–119. Smithsonian Institution Press, Washington DC.

SMITH, BRUCE D. (EDITOR)

1990   *The Mississippian Emergence.* Smithsonian Institution Press, Washington, DC.

SOUTH, STANLEY A.
1972   Evolution and Horizon as Revealed in Ceramic Analysis in Historical Archaeology. *The Conference on Historic Site Archaeology Papers* 6:71–116.
1977   *Method and Theory in Historical Archaeology.* Academic Press, New York.

STEPONAITIS, VINCAS
1978   Location Theory and Complex Chiefdoms: A Mississippian Example. In *Mississippian Settlement Patterns,* edited by Bruce D. Smith, pp. 417–453. Academic Press, New York.

TENNESSEE VALLEY AUTHORITY (TVA)
1967   *Budget Program: Justification of Programs and Estimates for the Fiscal Year Ending June, 30, 1968.* Report submitted to the United States Congress.
1972   *Final Environmental Statement,* Tellico Project Vol. I, Part 1. Tennessee Valley Authority, Chattanooga.
1978   *Alternatives for Completing the Tellico Project.* Tennessee Valley Authority, Knoxville.

THOMAS, CYRUS
1894   Report on Mound Explorations of the Bureau of Ethnology. In *Twelfth Annual Report of the Bureau of American Ethnology,* pp. 3–730. Smithsonian Institution, Washington, DC.

THOMAS, DAVID H.
1973   An Empirical Test for Steward's Model of Great Basin Settlement Patterns. *American Antiquity* 38:155–176.
1975   Nonsite Sampling in Archaeology: Up the Creek without a Site. In *Sampling in Archaeology,* edited by Jon W. Mueller, pp. 61–81. University of Arizona Press, Tucson

WATSON, PATTY JO
1985   The Impact of Early Horticulture in the Upland Drainages of the Midwest and Midsouth. In *Prehistoric Food Production in North America,* edited by Richard I. Ford, pp. 99–148. Anthropological Papers No. 75. Museum of Anthropology, University of Michigan, Ann Arbor.

WHEELER, WILLIAM BRUCE, AND MICHAEL J. MCDONALD
1986   *TVA and the Tellico Dam, 1936–1979.* University of Tennessee Press, Knoxville.

WILLEY, GORDON R., AND PHILIP PHILLIPS
1958   *Method and Theory in American Archaeology.* University of Chicago Press, Chicago.

WILLEY, GORDON R., AND JEREMY A. SABLOFF
1993   *A History of American Archaeology,* third edition. W. H. Freeman, New York.

WILLIAMS, SAMUEL COLE (EDITOR)
1927   *Lieutenant Henry Timberlake's Memoirs, 1756–1765.* Watauga Press, Johnson City, TN.

YARNELL, RICHARD
1974   Plant Food and Cultivation of the Salts Cavers. In *Archaeology of the Mammoth Cave Area,* edited by Patty Jo Watson, pp. 113–122. Academic Press, Orlando, FL.

5
The Geoarchaeology of the Tennessee Valley: Methodological and Archaeological Milestones

Sarah C. Sherwood

As a GENERAL RULE the geomorphic history of a region can have a profound effect on both the spatial and temporal distribution of archaeological sites and the geologic processes of site formation that influence their preservation and discovery (Butzer 1982; Goldberg et al. 1993; Leach and Jackson 1987; Schiffer 1987). The Tennessee Valley is no exception. Geoarchaeology is an interdisciplinary approach that delves into the link between geology and archaeology, addressing archaeological questions using methods and theories from the earth sciences. Though few, the geoarchaeological studies in the Tennessee Valley in the last four decades have been milestones in the discipline. In particular these studies have taken on the issue of geomorphic history as it relates to archaeological site location. These studies have attempted to explain the timing of late Quaternary landscape stability by constructing models generally focused on landscape response to cycles of climatic change. Several of these studies advance the way we conceive of the archaeological record in this temperate region (expanding survey methods in alluvial valleys) while enhancing our understanding of southeastern prehistory. The earliest studies were conducted in conjunction with reservoir mitigation, with large archaeological research programs that were sponsored by TVA prior to inundation. The later studies are examples of geoarchaeological research conducted postinundation that generally seek to refine these earlier models and provide site-specific depositional histories.

Despite the historic interest in resource development throughout the Tennessee River Valley (and therefore at least some attention to the regional geology), surprisingly few studies have targeted the Quaternary history of the landforms. One of the only review articles that covers the Quaternary geomorphology of the Appalachian Highlands and Interior Low Plateau, of which much of the Tennessee River Valley is a part, was published by Mills and Delcourt in 1991. The paper emphasizes the absence of available data to describe and interpret stratigraphy, sedimentology, and the age of surficial deposits in this region. This deficiency results in part from difficulties in identifying past geomorphic processes and establishing exact ages for surficial deposits, since the depositional history of an alluvial valley is typically reconstructed based on the chronometric, morphologic, and lithologic correlation of stream terraces (Mills and Delcourt 1991). Throughout the Tennessee River Valley, terrace correlation is complicated to impossible, given the present-day erosion and flooding of the valley floor. The raised water levels from inundation have covered the lowest portions of the original floodplain and other early erosional and depositional features. Even before inundation, terrace surfaces seldom continued longitudinally, making it difficult to correlate such features across the valley. In addition, exposures that could aid in such correlations are rare in this richly vegetated temperate region. For these reasons the details of the geomorphic models that do exist in the valley are often fairly localized and cannot be universally applied. This general deficiency of Quaternary geomorphology studies in the valley highlights the importance and cross-disciplinary significance of the geoarchaeological studies cited in this review.

Little Tennessee River

The current models for the early depositional history of the valley, in particular the upper valley, focus on landscape response to cycles of Quaternary climatic change. Delcourt (1980) developed one such model while conducting alluvial geomorphic research along the lower Little Tennessee River Valley, a large Tennessee River tributary located at the boundary between the Ridge and Valley and the Blue Ridge provinces in East Tennessee (Figure 5.1). Delcourt's work was conducted in conjunction with the TVA-funded Tellico Reservoir archaeological investigation (under the direction of Jefferson Chapman), in order to offer a strategy for the identification of deeply stratified sites within the terrace system (Chapman 1973; 1980; 2001). Though developed for the Little Ten-

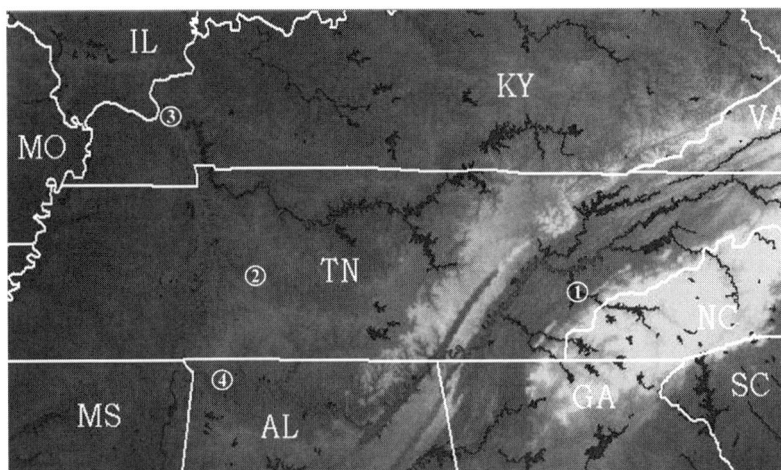

Fig. 5.1. DEM of the Tennessee River Valley: (1) Tellico Archaeological Project, Little Tennessee River, (2) Columbia Archaeological Project, Central Duck River Valley, (3) Lower Cumberland Archeological Project, Lower Tennessee and Cumberland Rivers, (4) Dust Cave Archaeological Project, western Middle Tennessee River Valley.

nessee River, this model is generally applicable to the Upper Tennessee River Valley.

Delcourt's (1980) model begins in the Cenozoic Era, when the Tennessee River progressively cut down along the edge of the Appalachian Interior Low Plateau, creating the initial valley. The landscape reflected the impact of full glacial conditions far to the north, influencing both the local geomorphology and the vegetation. The freeze-thaw conditions of the Late Pleistocene interglacial periods extensively weathered the exposed bedrock, resulting in massive colluvial fans extending down the slopes and foothills of the Appalachian boreal forests (Braun 1989; Daniels et al. 1987; Eaton 1999; Shafer 1988). Sediment weathered from the bedrock and these colluvial fans was transported down slope by gravity and slopewash, rapidly aggrading the valleys below (Delcourt 1980).

The lithology of the Tennessee River alluvium is a direct result of this periglacial weathering of the igneous and metamorphic rocks that make up the Southern Appalachians. Sand-size micas and to a lesser degree pyroxene/amphibole are a signature in the alluvial lithology (Collins, Gose, and Shaw, 1994; Sherwood et al. 2004). The identification of this signature has been instrumental in the reconstruction of the fluvial history of the river in relation to archaeological deposits as observed today in sediments of the upper valley (Delcourt 1980; Sherwood and Kocis

2006; Simek et al. 1997), the Middle Valley (Collins, Gose, and Shaw, 1994; Sherwood et al. 2004), and in the lower valley (Sherwood 2005; Sherwood and Kocis 2004).

Radiocarbon dates from terraces in the Little Tennessee River Valley placed the peak sediment accumulation during the Late Pleistocene at just over 30,000 BP, and Delcourt (1980:121) associates these accumulations with the transition from the Late Altonian Stadial to the Early Farmdalian Interglacial. There are no known early Late Pleistocene radiocarbon dates for terraces in the Middle or Lower Tennessee River Valley primarily because, as noted above, few studies have targeted Quaternary geomorphology. The remnants of alluvial lithostratigraphic units derived from this phase in the river's history are typically deeply buried in the current floodplain. The only descriptions of this material are usually restricted to engineering drill logs (e.g., Gallet and Associates 1997; Kellberg and Benziger 1956). Such logs from the Middle Tennessee River indicate massive to moderately bedded deposits of micaceous, quartzose silts and fine sands, manifesting an accretional topography composed of fining upward sequences that are suggestive of overbank deposition. Beneath the bedded overbank deposits, there are typically channel lag deposits (ranging in size from boulders and gravel to sand) that overlie bedrock. The top of this sequence (above pool level) consists of brown clayey silts and silt loams in which soils are actively forming. In most cases there are multiple buried soils, and therefore deposits containing archaeological materials can be found well below the current surface.

Within these buried alluvial deposits lie narrow channels identified at different depths across the valley floor. These extinct channels can be filled with organic rich clay and organic debris, suggesting abandoned sloughs or braided channels (e.g., Kellberg and Benziger 1956, Kocis and Sherwood 2006). These deposits, as well as paleosols, are currently being targeted by innovative research using compound specific stable isotope analysis to decipher high resolution climatic and even seasonal signals that can inform detailed paleoenvironmental reconstructions (Driese et al. 2007; Kocis 2007; Kocis et al. 2007).

During the Pleistocene the wider sections of the river valley most likely consisted of a braided drainage pattern with relatively steep gradient and increased sediment load (e.g., Leigh et al. 2004; Leopold and Wolman 1957). Valley aggradation continued in the upper valley into the early Holocene. Precipitation was greater and temperatures cooler than today (Delcourt and Delcourt 1985), and as a result the Tennessee River in general probably flooded frequently. Delcourt (1980:121)

Fig. 5.2. Profile photograph of deep alluvial deposits in the Little Tennessee Valley, Icehouse Bottom. (Courtesy of the Frank H. McClung Museum, University of Tennessee, Knoxville.)

deduced that further aggradation of the floodplain in the Little Tennessee River Valley occurred relatively rapidly from 15,000 to 7,000 years BP, burying a nearly continuous archaeological record in the first terrace. Archaeological excavations at the Icehouse Bottom and Rose Island sites expanded this time line with Early Archaic through Late Archaic deposits buried in the first terrace (Figure 5.2; Chapman 1973, 1975, 1977). Geoarchaeological research was instrumental in the identification of these early sites, whose excavation results remain landmark studies in the Archaic of the southeastern United States (e.g., Chapman 2001; Chapman and Crites 1987; Davis et al. 1982).

Central Duck River

Turning to another large tributary of the Tennessee River, Brakenridge (1982, 1984) proposed a model for the Central Duck River Basin that suggests local geomorphic response to direct and indirect effects of climate change. The central section is located in the Nashville Basin region of Middle Tennessee where the Duck River creates a meandering ingrown bedrock valley (Figure 5.1). This study was part of the Columbia Archaeological Project directed by Walter E. Klippel and sponsored by the TVA in an effort to mitigate the effects of the proposed Columbia Dam (Hall 1992; Turner and Klippel 1989).

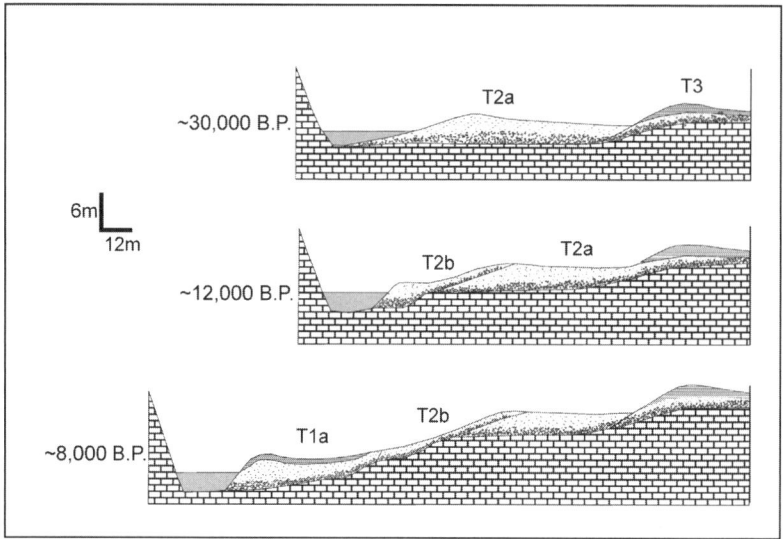

Fig. 5.3. Diagrammatic sedimentary history of the Central Duck River Valley (modified from Brakenridge 1984; Schumm and Brakenridge 1987).

Brakenridge created broadly defined lithostratigraphic "formations" in order to facilitate facies mapping of backhoe trenches profiles. The lithostratigraphic units consisted of four fine-grained informally defined "formations" with subordinate "members," or chronostratigraphic units, defined by radiocarbon dates and diagnostic artifacts (Table 5.1; Figure 5.3). These units were delineated in the field by color, texture, pedogenic structure, sedimentary structures, redoximorphic features, and artifact composition and generally correspond to terrace designations as defined by Hack (1965; Brackenridge 1984:13). By and large these formations consist of paleosols derived from fining upward channel–overbank deposits. Brackenridge does point out, however, that there is no direct one-to-one relationship in the Duck River Valley "between terraces as geomorphic surfaces and the age and lithology of the underlying alluvium" (1984:24). The T1 surface, in particular, can vary slightly in age throughout the valley.

In the Duck River Valley around 30,000 years ago, peak sediment accumulation resulted in the formation of a T2, with the bedrock floor of the valley about 5 m higher than it is today. At the end of the Pleistocene, extensive fluvial erosion resulted in further entrenchment of the valley and the removal of much of this Late Wisconsin sedimentary record (Brakenridge 1982, 1984; Schumm and Brakenridge 1987). Brakenridge

Table 5.1: Informal Lithostratigraphic "Formations" Defined by Brakenridge (1982, 1984) in Order to Map the Valley Fills of the Central Duck River Basin

Formation (F.) and Member (M.)	Terrace Surface	Chronology (BP)	Archaeology
Cheek Bend F. Lower M.	T2a	?32,000–14,000	Late Pleistocene–precultural
Cheek Bend F. Upper M.	T2b	?14,000–10,000	Paleoindian?
Cannon Bend F. Lower M.	T1a1	10,000–8000	E. Archaic
Cannon Bend F. Upper M.	T1a2	8000–6400	E. Archaic
Leftwich Formation Lower M.	T1b1	6400–3900	M. to L. Archaic
Leftwich F. Upper M.	T1b2, T1b3	3900–150	Woodland through L. Archaic
Sowell Mill F.	T0	150 BP–modern	Historic

(1982, 1984) reports remnants of the now partially buried Late Pleistocene floodplain (T2b) along the T2, containing artifacts associated with 12,000 to 10,000 years ago (Figure 5.3). Following the terminal Pleistocene erosion, a lower (T1) terrace formed, with artifacts and radiocarbon dates suggesting stability as early as 10,000 years ago. Climate change during the Holocene, while not causing valleywide floodplain transformation, did result in localized variable and episodic floodplain stability and pedogenesis followed by overbank deposition, coupled with channel migration and erosion (Brakenridge 1984:24–25). By the historic era, climatic change is trumped by Euro-American intensive land-use practices that resulted in significant overbank sedimentation, further burying prehistoric deposits on the T0 and T1 surfaces. This phenomenon is observed on these landforms in many areas throughout the Tennessee River Valley (Figure 5.4).

Lower Tennessee River

Geoarchaeological investigations conducted through the Lower Cumberland Archaeological Project (LCAP), under the direction of Jack D. Nance, focused on the reconstruction of the landscape in the lower Tennessee and Cumberland rivers. They emphasized the potential for

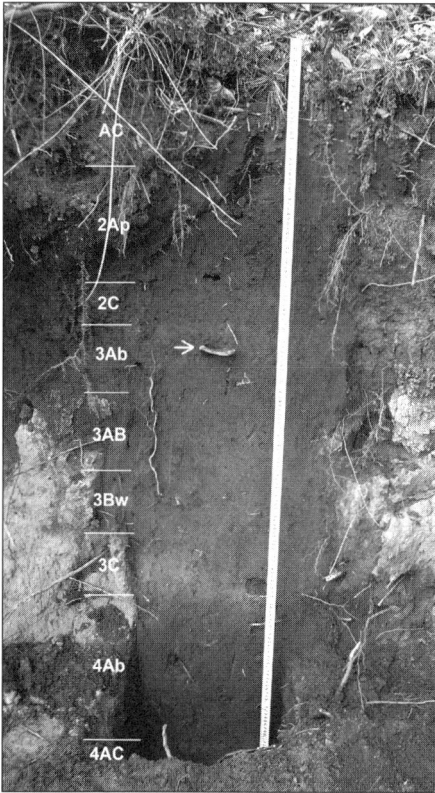

Fig. 5.4. Soil horizons labeled in a south bank profile on the eastern end of Seven Mile Island, Lauderdale County, Pickwick Reservoir (profile 3 described in Sherwood 2004, Table A3). The arrow points to a historic salt-glazed earthenware sherd (2C) clearly demonstrating the recent alluvial deposition burying older soils. A buried surface (4Ab) is recorded containing artifacts (probably Late Archaic) at approximately 130–160 cmbs. These examples illustrate the unfortunate futility of shovel testing to efficiently and reliably explore the full potential for archaeological deposits across many areas of the valley floor.

surface versus buried sites and the proposition and designation of the Pinckneyville Terrace (Leach and Jackson 1987; Nance 1987a, 1987b; Figure 5.1). This research was supported by a range of sources including TVA, Simon Fraser University, National Geographic Society, Kentucky Heritage Council, and the National Science Foundation. Much of the work done in the LCAP focused on the Archaic period and the identification of "small sites." For example, Leach (1981) conducted geoarchaeological research at the Morrisroe site, providing the geomorphic context for this Archaic midden site just over 10 river miles upstream from the confluence with the Ohio.

In a more broadly scaled study, Leach and Jackson (1987) used a combination of sediment descriptions from cores, topographic mapping and magnetic properties to map the age and extent of the T2, T1, and T0 terraces in the region. Their reconstruction began with the deposition of lacustrine sediments into the Tennessee and Cumberland River valleys above their confluence with the Ohio. Prior to 18,000 BP the Lower Cumberland and Tennessee valleys contained backwater lakes resulting from impoundment by the Ohio River Valley. This resulted in deep fine-grained lacustrine deposits in this portion of the valley, preserved in upper terraces (ca. 340 ft / 104 m contour) in Kentucky. Elevated base levels existed in the Ohio River system after 15,000 BP, corresponding to melt water draining down the Ohio River system caused by a readvancement of ice. This elevated base level "downstream" resulted in the Lower Tennessee and Cumberland rivers aggrading until approximately 11,000 BP, when they adjusted to lower local base levels and began downcutting (Leach and Jackson 1987:104–105). This study suggests that only the earliest sites are buried in terraces in these portions of the valley, while in the Holocene floodplain, there is a high potential for sites younger than 9000 BP (Leach and Jackson 1987:107).

Middle Tennessee River

The Middle Tennessee River Valley appears to have undergone similar transformations in response to climate change during the Pleistocene/Holocene transition. Collins and Goldberg (2000) conducted a brief geoarchaeological assessment of the regional geomorphology in the Wheeler basin as part of an archaeological survey conducted in the reservoir during winter drawdown. The project was conducted by the Office of Archaeological Services at the University of Alabama under the direction of Carey Oakley, Scott Shaw, and others (Shaw 2000). In the relatively wide (~19 km) portion of the eastern Middle Valley, increased precipitation and rising sea levels during the Pleistocene/Holocene transition resulted in adjustments in the load and flow characteristics initiating incision, followed by a reduced flow that resulted in lateral progradation (Collins and Goldberg 2000; Collins, Goldberg, and Gose 1995). This response is clearly visible in the Wheeler basin as progradational sequences discernible near Decatur, Alabama. This is further documented in the broadest sense in archaeological surveys on the Wheeler and Pickwick reservoirs, where site distributions on first terraces are restricted to later component sites (Middle and Late Archaic, Woodland, and Mississippian periods), while early period sites are located on the second and third levees (Meyer 1995; Shaw 2000; Sherwood 2001). In some instances Paleoindian and Early Archaic period deposits dating to the Pleistocene/Holocene transition ca. 12,000–10,000 BP are buried in the second terraces (where these geologic features are discernable). The

well-known Late Paleoindian sites referred to as the Quad Locale suggest that the second levee, located approximately 200 m from the first
levee, represents the river bank at the end of the Pleistocene (Hubbert
1989). These temporal versus spatial distributions further support a
progradational sequence for this relatively broad portion of the Middle
Tennessee River Valley. In the western Middle Valley, the geomorphic
alluvial history manifests itself in a slightly different way, a result of the
increased gradient and the narrow morphology of the overall valley.

Geoarchaeological research conducted in the context of the Dust
Cave Project in the western Middle Tennessee River Valley exemplifies
the postinundation study of the geomorphology of the valley as it relates
to archaeological site distribution. Postinundation research often relies
on nontraditional approaches that can include cave stratigraphy (e.g.,
Dust Cave), or underwater coring such as was recently conducted in
Jackson County, Alabama, by the Alabama Department of Transportation, the University of Alabama Office of Archaeological Research, and
the University of Tennessee Archaeological Research Laboratory (Kocis
2005). Continuous coring was carried out using a barge-mounted coring rig to test the now-inundated site 1JA77 that would be affected by
proposed bridge construction. A geoarchaeological study of the cores
provided a general reconstruction of the fluvial geomorphology on the
north bank of the river through the description and dating of intact
paleosols. This study also indicated that archaeological deposits buried
in inundated sites can be intact, with the potential to provide significant
archaeological and paleoenvironmental data.

The Dust Cave Project, under the direction of Boyce Driskell, was
supported by the TVA, as well as research grants from the National
Science Foundation, National Geographic Society, Alabama Historical
Commission, and others (see Driskell, this volume, for details on the
project). An abiding archaeological theme in the vicinity of Dust Cave
is the concentration of Paleoindian fluted point finds in Lauderdale
and Colbert counties, located on either side of the river (Anderson and
Sassaman 1996; Futato 1982). This area is well known for the availability of high quality blue/gray Fort Payne chert that drew early prehistoric
peoples to this portion of the valley (Johnson and Meeks 1994; Meeks
1994). But what is not well understood is the distribution of fluted points
in the valley, specifically if those finds from the valley floor, relative
to the adjacent uplands, are in their original context. A model for the
overall depositional history of the valley floor in this area was first proposed by Collins, Gose, and Shaw (1994) and later refined by Sherwood

The Profile of the Tennessee River System

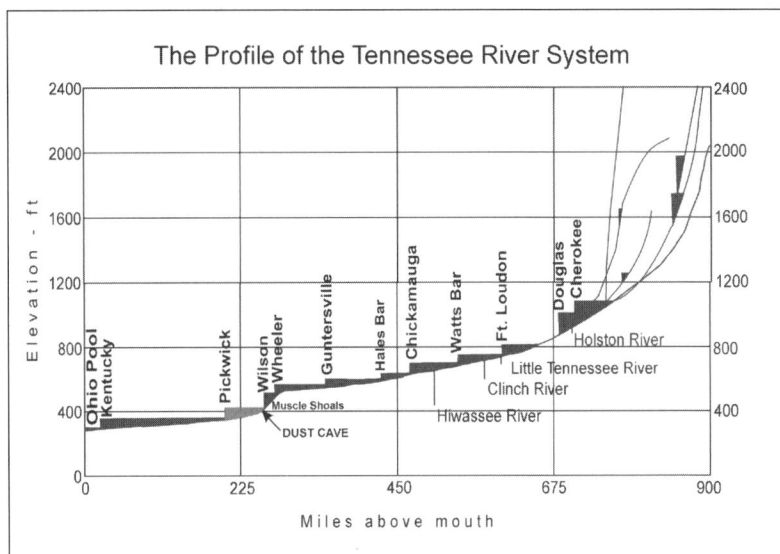

Fig. 5.5. Tennessee River System and the descent related to the reservoirs.

(2001) and Sherwood et al. (2004). Data are derived from detailed sedi-mentological and micromorphological study of cave stratigraphy and radiocarbon dates from excavations in Dust and Basket Caves. This model suggests that the fluted point finds on the currently eroding T1 are not in their original context.

Located in the north valley wall where the river cuts down through horizontal Mississippian age rock, the entrances of Dust Cave (130.5 m amsl) and Basket Cave (136.5 m amsl) are located approximately 6 m vertical and horizontal distance from one another. This relatively narrow section of the river (1–3 km wide) is located immediately downriver from Muscle Shoals, which marks the steepest descent in the main Tennessee River system, with a drop of about 40 m over 55 km (Figure 5.5). Coffee Slough is located in front of the cave, at the base of the talus slope (ca. 10 m from the entrance, and 2 m lower in elevation). The slough is a drowned spring-fed creek bed (once part of Cypress Creek) that trends west, paralleling the Tennessee River until it intersects the main channel 7 km below the cave (Figure 5.6).

During the Late Pleistocene, the Tennessee River base level and the valley floor through this narrow section of the valley were at least 6 m higher than they are today. Dust Cave would have been completely full of alluvial sediment, while Basket Cave contained Tennessee River

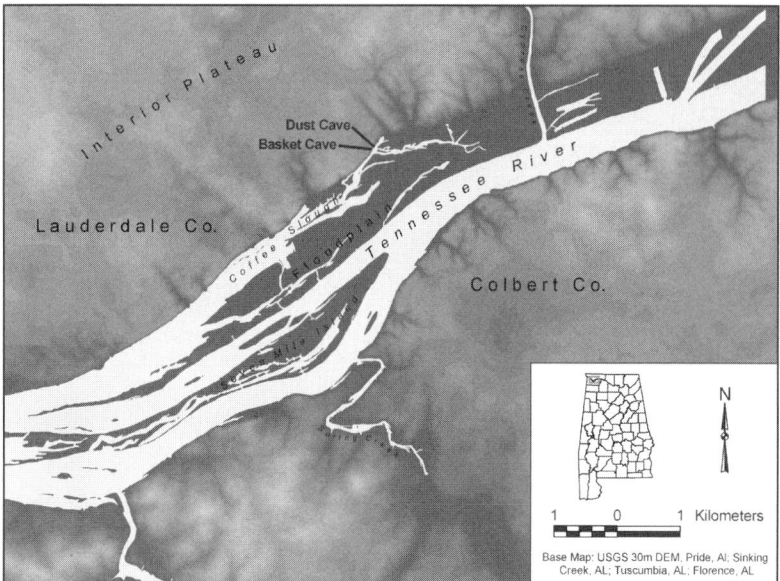

Fig. 5.6. Location of Dust and Basket caves (modified from Sherwood et al. 2004).

overbank deposition (topped off with slack water deposits). This sequence is now buried below 2 m of red clay and rock (derived from the cave interior). A radiocarbon date of 15,630 B.P. was collected from these alluvial deposits, indicating that at the end of the Pleistocene the valley floor was significantly higher than it is today (Sherwood et al. 2004).

The Pleistocene/Holocene transition is marked by a lowering base level, as well as increased precipitation at the end of the Pleistocene (Delcourt and Delcourt 1985), which would have directly affected the karstic drainage system and the spring surges at the base of the escarpment. As local groundwater base level began to lower, it was likely accelerated by the narrow valley and steep descent associated with Muscle Shoals. This major Terminal Pleistocene erosional phase is suggested by the shift in source material in the Basket Cave sequence noted above (Sherwood et al. 2004: 541). Below this elevation, the caves in the valley wall acted as major spring conduits flushing sediments as the valley floor lowered (Collins, Gose, and Shaw 1994). Dust Cave, once filled, was left with only a remnant of ancient alluvial deposits in the back passage. The earliest date in Dust Cave, 11,000–10,350 cal. B.C., comes from sediments that accumulated on the bedrock floor in the entrance chamber (Sherwood et al. 2004:542).

This study indicates that a slightly different scenario associated with the Pleistocene/Holocene transition occurred in the western portion of the Middle Tennessee River Valley west of Muscle Shoals, relative to the progradational model for the Eastern Middle Tennessee River Valley. The cave stratigraphy signifies a relatively rapid degradation of this section of the valley, resulting in the probable removal of most of the Late Pleistocene surfaces. Elsewhere in the area near Dust Cave, data suggest that landscapes were stable along a prograding floodplain beginning in the early Holocene by the Early and Middle Archaic (see Hubbert et al. 1978; Waselkov and Morgan 1983). The poorly defined levee and overbank deposition began on the north side, against the escarpment in the vicinity of Coffee Slough, and the associated channel prograded toward the south wall until it settled in its current location against the steep southern escarpment.

There are no other well-documented terrace remnants visible along the valley walls, suggesting that at the end of the Pleistocene, as in the Duck River basin, extensive fluvial erosion resulted in further entrenchment of the valley and removal of this early sedimentary record. There may be remnants preserved under steep colluvial deposits along the escarpment or in caves high in the valley walls, such as Basket Cave. This model of high energy and the lowering of the valley floor during the Pleistocene/Holocene transition suggests that the numerous diagnostic Paleoindian artifacts recovered along the floodplain margins cannot be in their original context. Important to this model and to Paleoindian studies in general are the significant numbers of Paleoindian artifacts recovered in the uplands adjacent to the escarpment, often near large sinks. These upland sites have been reduced to gravel lag deposits primarily caused by deleterious farming practices (Goldman-Finn 1995; Waselkov and Hite 1987). Many of these artifacts have probably joined the gravels transported during storm events, down the small steep upland drainages where they are deposited in gravel bars and small alluvial fans. This model of landscape response to Quaternary climatic change at the Pleistocene/Holocene transition in this narrow section of the valley has significant consequences both to the interpretation of the Paleoindian artifact distributions and in site survey strategies.

Discussion

The geoarchaeological studies reviewed here represent both archaeological and methodological milestones within the discipline. The financial support and commitment of TVA have facilitated these studies and as a result significantly contributed to how archaeology in the temperate river valleys of North America is conducted in addition to expanding our knowledge of prehistory. Prior to the work of Delcourt and Chapman, there was a paucity of early archaeological sites known on the valley floor. Through their willingness to dig deeper (literally and figuratively) and explore the Quaternary fluvial history of the valley, we have a far greater understanding of Archaic land use, both in and beyond the Tennessee Valley.

We now know that sites and significant portions of the landscapes occupied by the earliest Late Pleistocene and early Holocene peoples are either buried or have been removed. The valley changes as the river travels through different geological landscapes with variable bedrock structure and composition, sedimentology, and gradients. As a result of these differences, there are variable responses to all scales of climatic change. Thus no one model can explain the geomorphological variation of the valley as it relates to the distribution of archaeological sites. What is consistent, however, is that the current surface configuration does not directly correlate to the stable surfaces at different times in prehistory.

The future for geoarchaeology in the Tennessee River Valley is both exciting and promising. Techniques such as hydraulic coring are enhancing our ability to efficiently expand our survey methodology, allowing for the exploration of deeply buried sites with minimal impact to surface sites and also providing important data toward the reconstruction of the fluvial geomorphology and regional paleoclimate (Kocis and Sherwood 2006; Sherwood and Kocis 2006). Geoarchaeological research in the river valleys of the midwestern United States and in the Great Plains have already made great strides with the application of such techniques (e.g., Artz 1995; Bettis 2003; Bettis and Hajic 1995; Holliday 1997; Kidder et al. 2008; Mandel 1995, 2000; Stafford et al. 1992). With more regular attention to the potential for buried sites, soil morphology, and radiocarbon dating in the valley, we should be able to refine current models and develop new ones as we correlate colluvial, fan, and alluvial depositional histories (Ferring 2001). With better and increased digital access to geodata sources for soil, geology, and hydrology, paleoenvironmental models will be more comprehensive, and predictive models will be better informed and therefore will facilitate the design of more effective survey protocols to aid in better protection of the Tennessee Valley's cultural resources.

Cultural resource management, tethered as it is to development and resource use, is, for better or worse, opportunistic. For the most part this is for the better, as the primary goal of CRM is to mitigate the impacts of development. But a consequence of this opportunistic nature is the fact that there are portions of the Tennessee Valley where little is known about the Quaternary geomorphology in relation to prehistory. In spite of significant and intriguing resources such as the upper two-thirds of Kentucky Lake where there is a rich Paleoindian record (Broster and Norton 1993, 2001; Broster et al. 1994), Guntersville with its abundant Copena sites (Walthall and DeJarnette 1974; Webb and Wilder 1951), and Cherokee and Norris Reservoirs where extensive lithic resource sites are distributed across the upland landscape (Gage 2005; Gage and Herrmann 2007), little data exist to place these sites in a comprehensive geomorphic context or to model other site locations. The future of the cultural resources and their successful protection and research potential in the Tennessee Valley lies in the integration of the earth sciences into management plans and research designs, ultimately revealing and contextualizing the valley's rich and diverse prehistory.

Acknowledgments

Thanks are owed to Bennett Graham and the TVA archaeologists who for many years have remained stalwart stewards of the cultural resources in the valley. I am grateful to all the archaeologists and earth scientists with whom I have had the good fortune to work along the Tennessee River—(to name but a few) David Anderson, Mike Collins, Boyce Driskell, Matt Gage, Paul Goldberg, Lara Homsey, James Kocis, Nicholas Herrmann, Kandace Hollenbach, Scott Meeks, Richard Polhemus, Asa Randall, Scott Shaw, Jan Simek, and Renee Walker. Finally, I gratefully acknowledge the constructive comments on this manuscript by Todd Ahlman, Boyce Driskell, Erin Pritchard, Hector Qirko, and two anonymous reviewers.

References Cited

ANDERSON, DAVID G., AND KENNETH. E. SASSAMAN
1996   Modeling Paleoindian and Early Archaic Settlement in the
        Southeast: A Historical Perceptive. In *The Paleoindian and Early
        Archaic Southeast,* edited by D. G. Anderson, and K. E. Sassaman,
        pp. 16–28. University of Alabama, Tuscaloosa.
ARTZ, J. A.
1995   Geological Contexts of the Early and Middle Holocene Archae-
        ological Record in North Dakota and Adjoining Areas of the

Northern Plains. In *Archaeological Geology of the Archaic Period in the United States,* edited by E. A. Bettis III, pp. 67–86. Geological Society of America, Boulder, CO. Special Paper 297.

BETTIS, E. ARTHUR, III
2003   Patterns in Holocene Colluvium and Alluvial Fans across the Prairie-forest Transition in the Midcontinent USA. *Geoarchaeology* 18: 779–797.

BETTIS, E. ARTHUR, III, AND EDWARD R. HAJIC
1995   Landscape Development and the Location of Evidence of Archaic Cultures in the Upper Midwest. In *Archaeological Geology of the Archaic Period in the United States,* edited by E. Arthur Bettis III, pp. 87–113. Geological Society of America, Boulder, CO. Special Paper 297.

BRAKENRIDGE, G. ROBERT
1982   Alluvial Stratigraphy and Geochronology along the Duck River, Central Tennessee: A History of Changing Floodplain Sedimentary Regimes. Ph.D. dissertation. University of Arizona.

1984   Alluvial Stratigraphy and Radiocarbon Dating along the Duck River, Central Tennessee: Implications Regarding Flood-Plain Origin. *Geological Society of America Bulletin* 95:9–25.

BRAUN, D. D.
1989   Glacial and Periglacial Erosion of the Appalachians. *Geomorphology* 2(1–3):233–256.

BROSTER, JOHN. B., AND MARK R. NORTON
1993   The Carson-Conn-Short Site (40BN190): An Extensive Clovis Habitation in Benton County, Tennessee. *Current Research in the Pleistocene* 10:3–5.

2001   Update on Archaeological Investigation at Site 40BN190, A Study of Clovis Lithic Technology. Paper presented at the Thirteenth Annual Current Research in Tennessee Archaeology Meeting.

BROSTER, J. B., M. R. NORTON, D. J. STANFORD, C. V. HAYNES JR., AND M. A. JOBRY
1994   Eastern Clovis Adaptations in the Tennessee River Valley. *Current Research in the Pleistocene* 11:12–14.

BUTZER, KARL W.
1982   *Archaeology as Human Ecology.* Cambridge University Press, New York.

CHAPMAN, JEFFERSON
1973   *The Icehouse Bottom Site, 40MR23.* Report of Investigations No. 13, Department of Anthropology, University of Tennessee, Knoxville.

1975   *The Rose Island Site and the Bifurcate Point Tradition.* Report of
        Investigations No. 14. Department of Anthropology, University of
        Tennessee, Knoxville.

1977   *Archaic Period Research in the Lower Little Tennessee River
        Valley—1975: Icehouse Bottom, Harrison Branch, Thirty Acre
        Island, Calloway Island.* University of Tennessee, Department of
        Anthropology, Report of Investigations No. 18, Knoxville.

1980   *The 1979 Archaeological and Geological Investigations in the
        Tellico Reservoir.* Tennessee Valley Authority, Publications in
        Anthropology No. 24, University of Tennessee, Department
        of Anthropology Report of Investigations No. 29, Knoxville,
        Tennessee.

2001   *Tellico Archaeology: 12,000 Years of Native American History,*
        Revised Edition. Publications in Anthropology No. 41, Tennessee
        Valley Authority, Knoxville, Tennessee.

CHAPMAN, JEFFERSON, AND GARY CRITES
1987   Evidence of Early Maize (*Zea mays*) from the Icehouse Bottom Site,
        Tennessee. *American Antiquity* 52:352–54

COLLINS, MICHAEL. B., AND PAUL GOLDBERG
2000   Geoarchaeological Observations at Wheeler Reservoir. In *Cultural
        Resources in the Wheeler Reservoir,* edited by Scott Shaw, pp.
        193–204. University of Alabama, Alabama Museum of Natural
        History, Division of Archaeology, Moundville, Alabama.

COLLINS, MICHAEL B., PAUL GOLDBERG, AND WOLF GOSE
1995   Geoarchaeology on the Middle Tennessee Valley of Northern
        Alabama. Published Abstracts with Program. Geological Society of
        America Annual Meeting, North-Central and South-Central Section.
        Geological Society of America, Boulder, Colorado.

COLLINS, MICHAEL B., WULF A. GOSE, AND SCOTT SHAW
1994   Preliminary Geomorphological Findings at Dust and Nearby Caves.
        Journal of Alabama Archaeology 40(1&2):35–56.

DANIELS, W. L., C. J. EVERETT, AND L. W. ZELAZNY
1987   Virgin Hardwood Forest Soils of the Southern Appalachian
        Mountains: I. Soil Morphology and Geomorphology. *Soil Science
        Society of America Journal* 51(3):722–729.

DAVIS, STEPHEN, JR., LARRY R. KIMBALL, AND WILLIAM W. BADEN
1982   *An Archaeological Survey and Assessment of Aboriginal
        Settlement within the Lower Little Tennessee River Valley.* Tellico
        Archaeological Survey Report No. 3, Department of Anthropology,
        University of Tennessee, Knoxville.

DELCOURT, H. R., AND P. A. DELCOURT
1985   Quaternary Palynology and Vegetational History of the South-
        eastern United States. In *Pollen Records of Late-Quaternary North*

American Sediments, edited by V. M. Bryant, and R. G. Holloway, pp. 1–37. American Association of Stratigraphic Palynologists Foundation, Dallas.

DELCOURT, PAUL A.

1980   Quaternary Alluvial Terraces of the Little Tennessee River Valley, East Tennessee. In *The 1979 Archaeological and Geological Investigations in the Tellico Reservoir,* edited by J. Chapman, pp. 110–121. Tennessee Valley Authority, Publications in Anthropology No. 24, University of Tennessee, Department of Anthropology Report of Investigations No. 29.

DRIESE, STEVEN G., ZHENG-HUA LI, AND LARRY D. MCKAY

2007   Evidence for Multiple, Episodic, Mid-Holocene Hypsithermal Recorded in Two-Soil Profiles along an Alluvial Floodplain Catena, Southeastern Tennessee, USA. *Quaternary Research* 69(2):276–291.

EATON, LOUIS SCOTT

1999   Debris Flows and Landscape Evolution in the Upper Rapidan Basin, Blue Ridge Mountains, Central Virginia. Ph.D. dissertation, Department of Environmental Sciences. University of Virginia, Charlottesville, Virginia.

FERRING, C. REID

2001   Geoarchaeology in Alluvial Landscapes. In *Earth Sciences and Archaeology,* edited by Paul Goldberg, Vance T. Holliday, and C. Reid Ferring, pp.77–106. Kluwer Academic/Plenum Publishers, New York.

FUTATO, EUGENE. M.

1982   Some Notes on the Distribution of Fluted Points in Alabama. *Archaeology of Eastern North America* 10:30–33.

GAGE, MATTHEW

2005   *Archaeological Site Identification and Erosion Monitoring for the TVA Reservoir Operation Study: The 2005 Field Season on Portions of Cherokee, Norris, Pickwick, and Wheeler Reservoirs—Draft.* Technical report submitted to the Tennessee Valley Authority, Cultural Resources, Knoxville, Tennessee.

GAGE, MATTHEW, AND NICHOLAS P. HERRMANN

2007   *Archaeological Site Identification and Erosion Monitoring for the TVA Reservoir Operation Study: The 2006–7 Field Seasons on Portions of Norris, Fontana, Pickwick, and Wheeler Reservoirs— Draft.* Technical report submitted to the Tennessee Valley Authority, Cultural Resources, Knoxville, Tennessee.

GALLET AND ASSOCIATES

1997   *Geotechnical Exploration Proposed Planned Upgrades Cypress Creek Waste Water Treatment Plant.* Report prepared by Gallet and Associates, Inc., Birmingham, Alabama. City of Florence, Alabama.

GOLDBERG, PAUL, DAVID T. NASH, AND MICHAEL D. PETRAGLIA (EDS.)
1993   *Formation Processes in Archaeological Context.* Prehistory Press, Madison, Wisconsin.

GOLDMAN-FINN, NURIT S.
1995   *Archaeological Survey in the Middle Tennessee River Uplands, Colbert and Lauderdale Counties, Alabama.* University of Alabama Museums Report of Investigations Vol. 74. Moundville, Alabama.

HACK, JOHN T.
1965   *Geomorphology of the Shenandoah Valley, Virginia and West Virginia and the Origin of the Residue Ore Deposits,* US Geological Survey Professional Paper 484.

HALL, CHARLES LINDEN
1992   Exploring Archaic Settlement in the Midsouth: The Surface Archaeology of Cannon and Cheek Bends of the Duck River, Tennessee. Doctoral dissertation, Department of Anthropology, University of Tennessee, Knoxville.

HOLLIDAY, VANCE T.
1997   Paleoindian Geoarchaeology of the Southern High Plains. University of Texas Press, Austin.

HUBBERT, CHARLES M.
1989   Paleo-Indian Settlement in the Middle Tennessee River Valley: Ruminations from the Quad Paleo-Indian Locale. *Tennessee Anthropologist* 14(2):148–164.

HUBBERT, C. M., R. H. LAFFERTY III, AND TVA ARCHAEOLOGY STAFF AND THE OFFICE OF ARCHAEOLOGICAL RESEARCH STAFF AT THE UNIVERSITY OF ALABAMA
1978   *Seven Mile Island Archaeological District.* National Register of Historic Places Inventory—Nomination Form.

JOHNSON, HUNTER, AND SCOTT MEEKS
1994   Source Areas and Prehistoric Use of Fort Payne Chert. *Journal of Alabama Archaeology* 40(1 & 2):66–78.

KELLBERG, J. M., AND C. P. BENZINGER
1956   *Geology of the Proposed New Wilson Lock and Canal Relocation.* Tennessee Valley Authority, Division of Water Control Planning, Geologic Branch. Knoxville, Tennessee.

KIDDER, TRISTRAM R., KATHERINE A. ADELSBERGER, LEE J. ARCO, AND TIMOTHY M. SCHILLING
2008   Basin-Scale Reconstruction of the Geological Context of Human Settlement: An Example from the Lower Mississippian Valley, USA. *Quaternary Science Reviews* 27:1255–1270.

Kocis, James J.
2005   Geoarchaeological Examination of Site 1Ja77: An Inundated Site in Guntersville Reservoir, Jackson County, Alabama. Report submitted to Office of Archaeological Research, University of Alabama.
2007   Holocene Climate Dynamics Recorded by Tennessee River Floodplain Paleosols. Poster presented at the 2006 Southeastern Archaeological Conference Annual Meeting, Knoxville, Tennessee.

Kocis, James J., and Sarah C. Sherwood
2006   Geoarchaeological Examination of Sites 1Ma141 and 1Ma285 along the Tennessee River in Redstone Arsenal, Madison County, Alabama. Technical Report submitted to Alexander Archaeological Consultants, Wildwood, Georgia.

Kocis, James J., Sarah C. Sherwood, and Lawrence S. Alexander
2006   Development and Occupation of a Mid-Holocene Floodplain along the Tennessee River Interpreted from Geoarchaeology Deep-Testing at Site 40Ha524. Poster presented at the 2005 Southeastern Archaeological Conference Annual Meeting, Little Rock, Arkansas.

Leach, Elizabeth K.
1981   The Archaeological Geology of the Archaic Morrisroe Site, Tennessee River, Western Kentucky. M.S. thesis, Department of Anthropology, University of Minnesota

Leach, Elizabeth K., and Michael J. Jackson
1987   Geomorphic History of the Lower Cumberland and Tennessee Valleys and Implications for Regional Archaeology. Southeastern Archaeology 6(2):100–107.

Leigh, David S, Pradeep Srivastava, and George A. Brook
2004   Late Pleistocene Braided Rivers of the Atlantic Coastal Plain, USA. Quaternary Science Reviews 23(1–2):65–84.

Leopold, L. B., and M. G. Wolman
1957   River Channel Patterns; Braided, Meandering Straight. U.S. Geological Survey Professional Paper 282–B.

Mandel, Rolfe
1995   Geomorphic Controls of the Archaic Record in the Central Plains of the United States. In Archaeological Geology of the Archaic Period in the United States, edited by E. A. Bettis III, pp. 37–66. Geological Society of America, Boulder, CO. Special Paper 297.
2000   Geoarchaeology in the Great Plains. University of Oklahoma Press, Norman.

Meeks, Scott C.
1994   Lithic Artifacts from Dust Cave. Journal of Alabama Archaeology 40(1&2):79–106.

MEYER, CATHERINE C.
1995   *Cultural Resources in the Pickwick Reservoir.* Report of
        Investigations 75. University of Alabama, Alabama Museum of
        Natural History, Division of Archaeology, Moundville, Alabama.

MILLS, H. H., AND P. DELCOURT
1991   Quaternary Geology of the Appalachian Highlands and Interior
        Low Plateaus. In *Quaternary Nonglacial Geology: Coterminous
        U.S., The Geology of North America,* vol. K-2, edited by R. B.
        Morrison. Geological Society of America, Boulder, Colorado.

NANCE, JACK D.
1987a   Research into the Prehistory of the Lower Tennessee-Cumberland-
        Ohio Region. *Southeastern Archaeology* 6(2):93–100.

1987b   The Archaic Period in the Lower Tennessee-Cumberland-Ohio
        Region. In *Paleoindian and Archaic Period Research in Kentucky,* ed-
        ited by C. D. Hockensmith, D. Pollack, and T. W. Sanders. Kentucky
        Heritage Council, Frankfort, Kentucky.

SCHIFFER, MICHAEL B.
1987   *Formation Processes of the Archaeological Record.* University of
        New Mexico Press, Albuquerque.

SCHUMM, S. A., AND G. R. BRAKENRIDGE
1987   River Responses. In *North America and Adjacent Oceans During
        the Last Deglaciation,* edited by W. F. Ruddiman, and H. E. Wright
        Jr., pp. 221–240. Geological Society of America, Boulder, Colorado.

SHAFER, D. S.
1988   Late Quaternary Landscape Evolution at Flat Laurel Gap,
        Blue Ridge Mountains, North Carolina. *Quaternary Research*
        30(1):7–11.

SHAW, SCOTT
2000   *Cultural Resources in the Wheeler Reservoir.* Report of Investi-
        gations 79. Technical report prepared by the University of Alabama,
        Office of Archaeological Services for the Tennessee Valley Authority,
        Norris, Tennessee.

SHERWOOD, SARAH C.
2001   The Geoarchaeology of Dust Cave: A Late Paleoindian through
        Middle Archaic Site in the Middle Tennessee River Valley. Ph.D.
        dissertation, Department of Anthropology, University of Tennessee,
        Knoxville.

2004   *Geoarchaeological Assessment of the Potential for Buried Sites for
        3,150 Acres in the Vicinity of the Seven Mile Island Archaeological
        District, Pickwick Lake, Lauderdale and Colbert Counties,
        Alabama.* Technical report submitted to TRC Inc., Atlanta, Georgia.

2005   *A Geoarchaeological Study of the Mound A Stratigraphy, Shiloh National Military Park, Hardin County, Tennessee.* Report submitted to the Southeast Archeology Center, National Park Service, Tallahassee, Florida.

SHERWOOD, SARAH C., BOYCE N. DRISKELL, ASA R. RANDALL, AND SCOTT C. MEEKS

2004   Chronology and Stratigraphy at Dust Cave, Alabama. *American Antiquity* 69(3):533–554.

SHERWOOD, SARAH C., AND JAMES J. KOCIS

2004   *Deep Testing Assessment of Sites 40DR102 and 40DR226 within the Forrest Crossing Real Estate Development, along the Tennessee River in Decatur County, Tennessee.* Report submitted to TRC Inc., Nashville.

2006   Deep Testing Methods in Alluvial Environments: Coring vs. Trenching on the Nolichucky River. Tennessee Archaeology 2(2). 107–119.

SIMEK, J. F., C. H. FAULKNER, S. R. FRANKENBERG, W. E. KLIPPEL, T. M. AHLMAN, N. P. HERRMANN, S. C. SHERWOOD, R. B. WALKER, W. M. WRIGHT, AND R. YARNELL

1997   A Preliminary Report on the Archaeology of a New Mississippian Cave Art Site in East Tennessee. *Southeastern Archaeology* 16(1):51–73.

STAFFORD, C. RUSSELL, DAVID S. LEIGH, DAVID L. ASCH

1992   Prehistoric Settlement and Landscape Change on Alluvial Fans in the Upper Mississippi River Valley. *Geoarchaeology* 7(4):287–314.

TURNER, WILLIAM B., AND WALTER E. KLIPPEL

1989   Hunter-Gatherers in the Nashville Basin: Archaeological and Geological Evidence for Variability in Prehistoric Land Use. *Geoarchaeology* 4(1):43–67.

WALTHALL, JOHN A., AND DAVID L. DEJARNETTE

1974   Copena Burial Caves. *Journal of Alabama Archaeology* 20:1–59.

WASELKOV, G. A., AND S. HITE

1987   Paleo-Indians in the Tennessee Valley: A Preliminary Report to the National Geographic Society (#3246–85). Manuscript in possession of the author.

WASELKOV, G. A., AND R. T. MORGAN

1983   *The Archaeology of Seven Mile Island: A Cultural Resources Survey of the National Register District.* Auburn University Archaeological Monograph 8. Auburn, Alabama.

WEBB, W. S., AND C. G. WILDER

1951   *An Archaeological Survey of Guntersville Basin on the Tennessee River in Northern Alabama.* University of Kentucky Press, Lexington.

Cairo

Ohio

KE

Paducah

KENTUCKY

River

Mississippi

Tennessee River

Nashvi

TENNESS

Memphis

PICKWICK

WHEELER

MISS.

WILSON

ALABAMA

GUN

The TVA
REGION

Birmin

Map of the TVA Region. (Courtesy of the Tennessee Valley Authority.)

An unidentified sharecropper family, East Tennessee, 1936. (Photograph courtesy of the Tennessee Valley Authority.)

Top: First TVA Board. Left to right, H. A. Morgan, A. E. Morgan, and David Lilienthal, 1933. (Photograph courtesy of the Tennessee Valley Authority.) Bottom: Franklin Delano Roosevelt, Eleanor Roosevelt, and A. E. Morgan, chairman of the TVA at Norris Dam, 1934. (Photograph courtesy of the Tennessee Valley Authority.)

Top: Douglas Basin Survey. Fains Island (1JE1[B]). WPA workers posing in archaeological features, 1935. (Photograph courtesy of the Frank H. McClung Museum, University of Tennessee, Knoxville.) Bottom: Wilson Dam, Muscle Shoals, Alabama, 1934.

Guntersville Basin Survey. Ross Site (28MS134), August 1939. (Courtesy of the University of Alabama Museums, Tuscaloosa, AL.)

Top: Pickwick Basin Survey. Excavations at cave site (1CT65) after completion of block excavation, February 19, 1939. (Courtesy of the University of Alabama Museums, Tuscaloosa, AL.) Bottom: Watts Bar Basin Survey. Montgomery Site (77RE8 and 239RE8) mound excavation, 1941, showing unique technique used for trenching during this period. (Photograph courtesy of the Frank H. McClung Museum, University of Tennessee, Knoxville.)

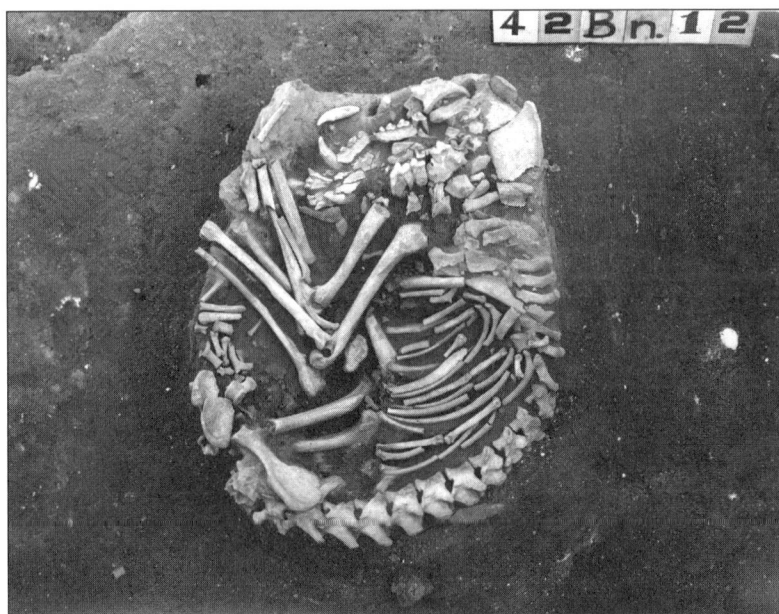

Top: Chickamauga Basin Survey. Hiwassee Island Site (37MG31). Earthen Mound, Level E, Southeast Corner of Feature 39, which consists of a pyramidal substructure and associated ramp and platform. March 20, 1938. (Photograph courtesy of the Frank H. McClung Museum, University of Tennessee, Knoxville.) Bottom: Kentucky basin. Eva Site (42BN12) photograph depicting a dog burial, October 9, 1940. (Courtesy of the Frank H. McClung Museum, University of Tennessee, Knoxville.)

PART III
HISTORY REVISITED

6
Viewing Jonathan Creek through Ceramics and Radiocarbon Dates: Regional Prominence in the Thirteenth Century

Sissel Schroeder

THE LARGE JONATHAN CREEK SITE, located in western Kentucky (Figure 6.1), was partially excavated in the early 1940s with Civilian Conservation Corps (CCC) labor in collaboration with the Tennessee Valley Authority (TVA), which sponsored survey and large-scale excavations throughout the valley in advance of dam construction projects (Milner and Smith 1986:11–12; Lyon 1996; Schroeder 2005:55–56; Tennessee Valley Authority 1983; Webb 1952; see chapter 1, this volume). The Jonathan Creek project was conducted under the direction of William S. Webb, who, from his office at the University of Kentucky in Lexington more than 250 miles away, kept up with activities at the site through his correspondence with the site supervisors, Harold F. Dahms, James R. Foster, Glenn E. Martin, and Joseph Spears. The site attracted Webb's attention because of seven earthen mounds, which were first documented in the late nineteenth century (Figure 6.2; Loughridge 1888). Six of these mounds were located on the terrace and arranged around an open plaza, conforming to a layout typical of Mississippian town-and-mound centers across the Southeast (Lewis and Stout 1988). The seventh mound was located nearby in the floodplain of Jonathan Creek. The plan had been to excavate the site in its entirety, but excavations terminated prematurely on March 20, 1942, when the CCC crew and site supervisors were

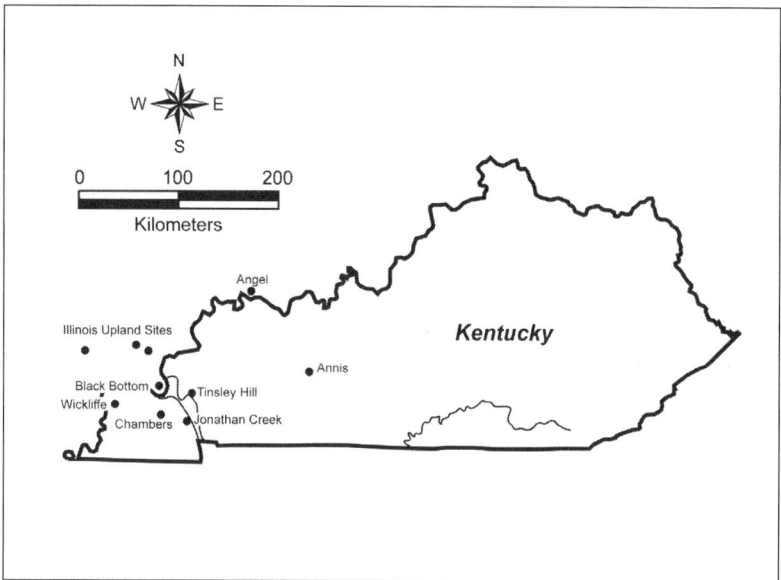

Fig. 6.1. Location of the Jonathan Creek and other sites.

mobilized for World War II. Less than half the site had been excavated, revealing 89 house structures and at least eight stockade lines with bastions (Webb 1952; Figure 6.3), the largest quantity of walls documented at a single site in the Southeast.

Jonathan Creek is considered to be one of the most significant archaeological sites in the lower Tennessee, Cumberland, and Ohio valleys and the central Mississippi Valley. The site has lent its name to an archaeological phase (Butler 1991; Clay 1979, 1997) and is referred to in nearly every publication that deals with the Mississippian period in the Ohio Confluence region and western Kentucky (e.g., Butler 1991; Clay 1979, 1997; Cobb and Butler 2002; Lewis 1986, 1990, 1991, 1996; Moore 1915; Wesler 2001). And yet the site excavations have never been fully reported, nor has a comprehensive inventory of artifacts ever been accomplished. These circumstances prompted a reinvestigation of Jonathan Creek with the broad goals of resolving issues about the occupation history of the site, clarifying how the site grew or contracted in size, exploring whether or not the site went through periods of occupation and abandonment, and investigating how events at Jonathan Creek relate to social, political, and historical developments elsewhere in western Kentucky, western Tennessee, and southern Illinois. Focus-

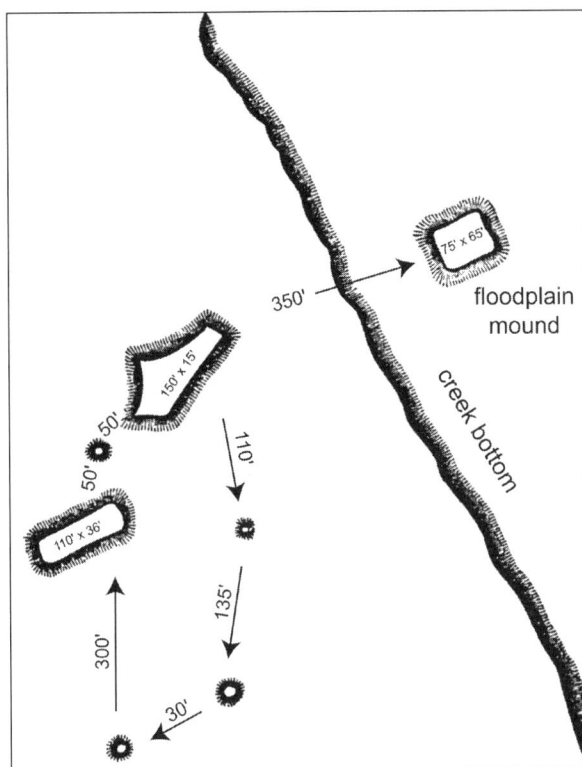

Fig. 6.2. Early map of the Jonathan Creek site (adapted from Loughridge 1888).

ing on the regional ceramic chronology and the radiocarbon dates from Jonathan Creek and other Mississippian sites in western Kentucky and southern Illinois helps clarify the chronology and occupation history of the site and its place within the regional sociopolitical landscape of the midcontinent.

Architecture and the Occupation History of Jonathan Creek

In 1952 Webb published a general account of the CCC project at Jonathan Creek. The artifact analyses presented in the report are based on a small fraction of the cultural materials recovered during excavation, with only 150 stone artifacts and 2,685 ceramic sherds and objects tabulated in the report (Webb 1952:87, 109). Although a complete analysis of the materials from Jonathan Creek has not yet been accomplished, it

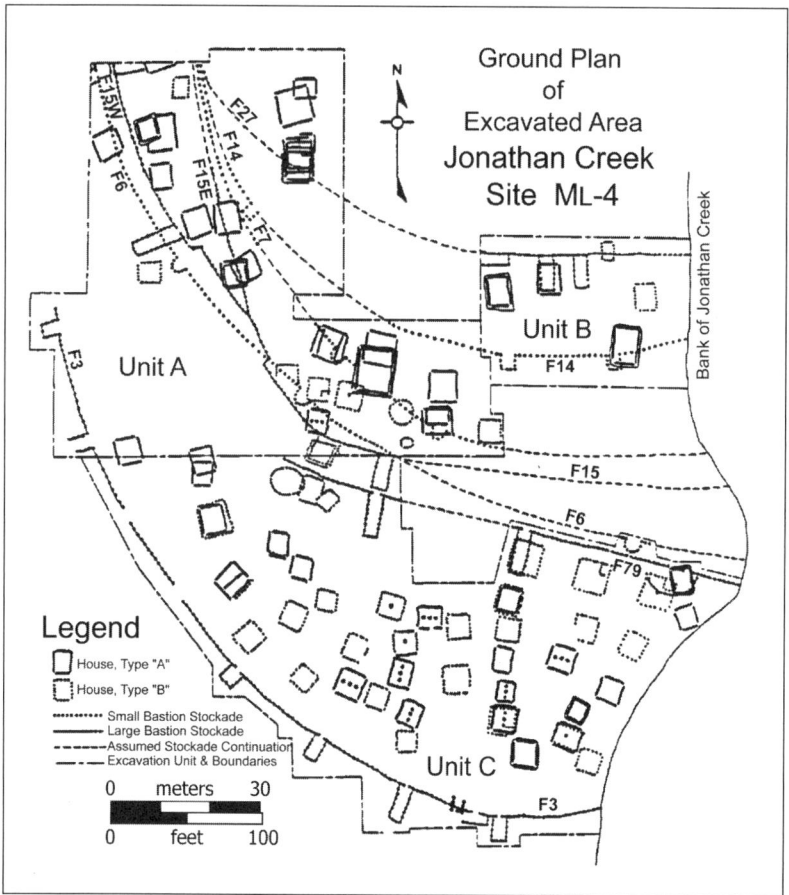

Fig. 6.3. Excavation plan map of the Jonathan Creek site (adapted from Webb 1952).

is likely that Webb analyzed about 3.5% of the collection. This report includes an inventory of about 12% of the collection. Webb's investigation of these items is largely descriptive, with some limited functional interpretation of certain artifact types, and there are no references to the contexts from which the inventoried objects came. Webb did not use the artifacts to address any questions related to chronology; instead he focused on posited temporal relationships between palisades with short and long bastions and between structures of different architectural styles as revealed by the superpositioning of features (Figure 6.3; Webb 1952:67–74). Webb concluded that the site had been occupied by two distinct groups of people. The first occupants were responsible for

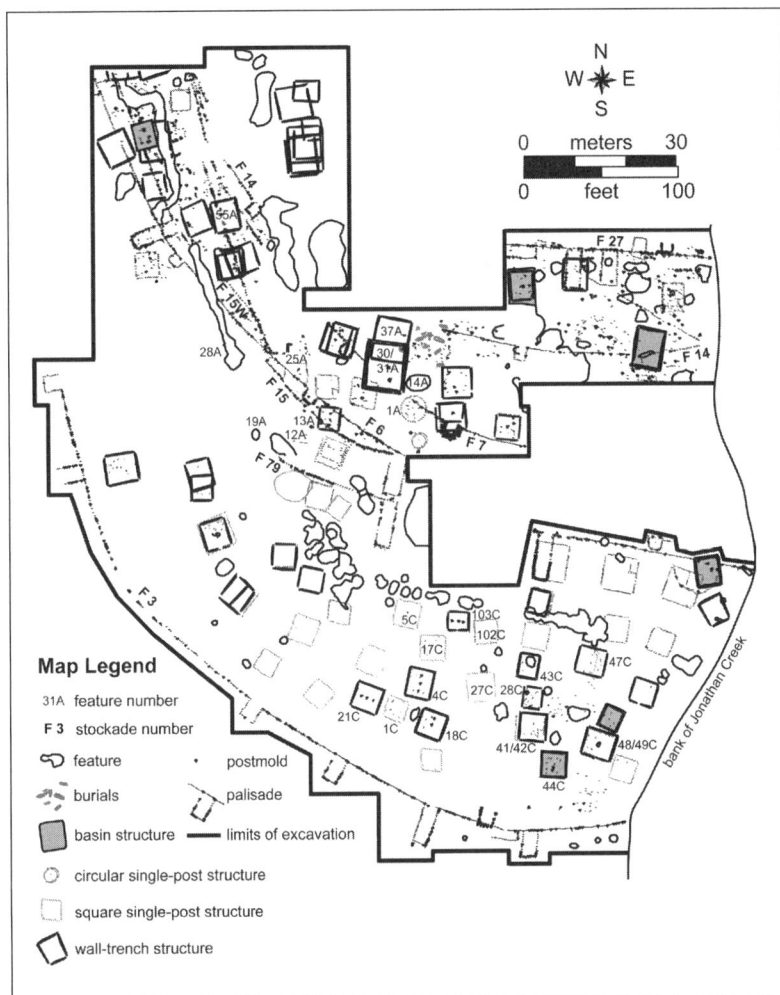

Fig. 6.4. Comprehensive plan map of the Jonathan Creek site showing features with analyzed ceramic assemblages or radiocarbon dates.

building wall-trench structures and pit houses and constructed palisade lines with large rectangular bastions (Webb 1952:70–71). After a period of abandonment, the site was reoccupied by people who built square and rectangular, single-post structures and palisades with small bastions (Webb 1952:72–74).

The reanalysis of Jonathan Creek began with digitizing the field maps to make it possible to manage the data in a Geographic Information System (Figure 6.4), and, like Webb, using architecture to construct a series of hypotheses about the occupation history of the site (Schroeder 2005, 2006). Most significantly, it was not possible to confirm the construction sequence of occupation, abandonment, and reoccupation proposed by Webb (Schroeder 2005:62–63). Although time may account for some differences, some of the origins of Jonathan Creek's architectural variability perhaps may be attributable to functional distinctions among relatively contemporaneous winter houses, summer houses, and corn houses (Brouwer and Schroeder 2005; Schroeder 2005:52–63; for ethnohistoric examples, see Bartram 1791:189–190, 365; Hall 1801:3–4; Waselkov and Braund 1995:154–186; Woods 1979:14) or may represent kin-based or ethnic differences among the residents of the site—people who joined the community to seek protection or affiliation with the leaders at Jonathan Creek or who were relocated as war captives, slaves, or remnants of a conquered and now-subordinate group.

One implication of these suggestions is that the occupation history of the excavated portion of the Jonathan Creek site was fairly short, lasting perhaps less than a century. Because the northern part of the site was unexcavated, a full understanding of the settlement history of the site may never be reached, but this hypothesis does conform to a recognition that Mississippian chiefdoms were highly dynamic and unstable entities that, once established, went through processes of fusion, fission, and disintegration, or cycling, experiences that may be manifested in regionally variable settlement patterns through time and fluctuating occupation histories for individual sites (e.g., Anderson 1994a, 1994b; Blitz 1999; King 2003; Milner and Schroeder 1999). Furthermore, this question about the occupation history of the Jonathan Creek site can be explored through the analysis of two complementary lines of evidence: ceramics and radiocarbon dates. As with the reanalysis of architectural data, the new analysis of a small sample of ceramics from feature contexts, in conjunction with radiocarbon dates, does not support the occupation history presented by Webb.

Ceramic Chronology and the Occupation History of Jonathan Creek: The Prevailing View

Historically, archaeologists working in the lower Tennessee Valley have relied on ceramics to assess site occupation histories, and for those sites excavated prior to World War II, when samples of charred organics were not routinely collected, pottery generally is the only source of information that can be used to determine chronological placement. The ceramic chronology for this region that bears on the Jonathan Creek site initially was developed by R. Berle Clay (1963, 1979) in the 1960s on the basis of an analysis of excavated assemblages from two stratigraphically separated deposits at the Tinsley Hill site, located on the Cumberland River about 26 km from Jonathan Creek. The earlier assemblage was used to define the Jonathan Creek phase, and the later assemblage formed the basis of the Tinsley Hill phase. A gap between the two was subsequently filled by the Angelly phase, defined on the basis of excavated assemblages from three sites in the Black Bottom of the Ohio Valley (Riordan 1975). The sequence (Figure 6.5) begins with the Late Woodland Douglas phase (Butler 1991:266–267), which appears to have only a minor representation in the assemblage from the Jonathan Creek Site. The subsequent Jonathan Creek phase is the first fully Mississippian phase defined, and it dates roughly to A.D. 1000–1100, maybe extending to A.D. 1150. The Angelly phase is fairly securely dated to A.D. 1200–1300, although it may start somewhat earlier, at about A.D. 1150, thereby closing the gap between it and the Jonathan Creek phase (Clay 1979:19; 1997). The Tinsley Hill phase is dated to A.D. 1300–1450. The last phase, Caborn-Welborn, persists into the early historic era and is spatially restricted to the confluence of the Ohio and Wabash rivers (Pollack 2004). The Jonathan Creek collections lack the attributes characteristic of Caborn-Welborn assemblages, which include small triangular, or "thumbnail," endscrapers and jars with very wide strap handles and distinctive decorations composed of trailed or incised lines sometimes accompanied by punctations that are located between the neck and shoulder of the vessel (Pollack 2004:35, 38, 51–60, 134). Although there is considerable intersite variability, such decorations are fairly common within the Caborn-Welborn region, appearing on slightly more than 31 percent of the sherds, while plain surfaces are found on 52.7 percent of the sherds (Pollack 2004:37, 74).

The ceramic attributes for each of these phases have been used by other researchers to propose an occupation history for the Jonathan Creek site (Clay 1979; Wolforth 1987). For all the Mississippian phases of relevance here (Jonathan Creek, Angelly, and Tinsley Hill), the assemblages are dominated by shell-tempered pottery with plain surfaces (Mississippi Plain [coarse shell temper] and Bell Plain [fine shell temper] types together account for 90 percent or more of all assemblages; Clay 1963; Wolforth 1987). All phases have modest amounts of fabric impressed sherds and small numbers of sherds with a red film applied to the surface. Most notably, Jonathan Creek–phase assemblages lack decoration

Ceramic Chronology

Phase	Dates
Caborn-Welborn	AD 1450-1600
Tinsley Hill	AD 1300-1450
Angelly	c. AD 1200-1300
Jonathan Creek	c. AD 1000-1100
Douglas	AD 850-1000

Fig. 6.5. Ceramic chronology for the Lower Ohio, Tennessee, and Cumberland river valleys.

such as incising and painting, while these kinds of surface treatments are present in both Angelly- and Tinsley Hill–phase assemblages where they constitute less than 2 percent of the total ceramic assemblage (Clay 1979:116; Pollack and Railey 1987:94; Wolforth 1987:103). Obviously, with small assemblage sizes there is a good chance that decorated sherds will not be present (Butler 1991; Clay 1997), so decoration may not be the best attribute to rely on when trying to determine the phase, or phases, represented at a site, unless tens of thousands of sherds from contemporaneous contexts are available.

An attribute that archaeologists working in the region have found to be more useful is the form of the handle that occurs on some Mississippian jars (Butler 1991; Clay 1963, 1979; Hilgeman 2000:125–163; 212, 214–215, 218; Orr 1951:331; Phillips et al. 1951:152; Pollack and Railey 1987; Riordan 1975; Smith 1969; Wesler 1991). Early Mississippian Jonathan Creek–phase assemblages have loop handles on some jars,

Angelly-phase assemblages have loop and strap handles in roughly equal numbers, and Tinsley Hill–phase assemblages are dominated by wide strap handles (Butler 1991:266; Hilgeman 2000; Phillips et al. 1951). At the Angel site, Hilgeman associates loop handles (thickness:width ratios of 0.75–1.0) with A.D. 1100–1200, strap handles (thickness:width ratios of 0.1–0.38) with A.D. 1300–1450, and a type that is intermediate between loop and strap (thickness:width ratios of 0.39–0.74) with A.D. 1200–1325 (Hilgeman 2000:129, 215). The presence of certain vessel types also may be helpful. Although jars, bowls, and salt pans (typically fabric impressed) occur in all phases, hooded water bottles and plates are associated with Angelly- and Tinsley Hill–phase assemblages. Long- and short-neck bottles appear in Tinsley Hill–phase assemblages.

Everyone who has ever looked at the Jonathan Creek collections has commented on the abundance of plain, shell-tempered sherds, and all have drawn the conclusion that the major occupation of the site occurred during the Jonathan Creek phase. However, everyone with an interest in the site also has noted that there was a later occupation, represented by small numbers of incised sherds, sherds with a black or red slip on the surface, and painted sherds, as well as vessel forms such as hooded water bottles, bottles, and plates that are considered characteristic of both Angelly- and Tinsley Hill–phase assemblages, but they concluded that these materials were the product of a minor Tinsley Hill–phase occupation (Clay 1979:117; 1997:23; Wolforth 1987:117).

In brief, the prevailing view of the Jonathan Creek site, based on a limited investigation of the ceramic assemblage, is that it was a substantial early Mississippian, Jonathan Creek phase, community occupied sometime between A.D. 1000 and 1100 or 1150, probably deserted for a period of time, and then later reoccupied by a smaller group of people during the Tinsley Hill phase, after A.D. 1300, before being completely abandoned by A.D. 1450 (Butler 1991; Clay 1979, 1997; Wolforth 1987), an interpretation that is consistent with Webb's (1952:70–7) proposition of two separate occupations.

Ceramics from Jonathan Creek

By November 2006, 13,390 pieces of pottery associated with 24 different features at Jonathan Creek had been described in detail with regard to temper and surface treatment (see Tables 6.1–6.2 at the end of this chapter, after the references). This is still a small subset of the total ceramic assemblage recovered, but it is at least five times larger than the previously analyzed samples, which may be why some rare surface treatments and vessel types appeared in this analysis yet did not appear in the smaller assemblages that formed the basis of earlier studies. Of the 13,390 sherds, 725 were rims that also had been classified according to vessel type (see Table 6.3 at the end of chapter). Some caution is appropriate in exploring the patterns in these data. First, there is a high degree of variation in sample size among the features (Feature 1A, a single-post circular structure, produced a single sherd, while Feature 14A, a midden pit, yielded 4,097 sherds), making it difficult to directly compare assemblages, especially in terms of the more rarely represented types of surface treatments. Second, most structure floors (with the exception of pithouses and some of the wall trench structures) were destroyed by plowing; therefore a clear association of ceramics with most structures is not possible. Clear association between ceramics and features was possible for all midden (trash) pits (Features 12A, 14A, 19A, 28A) and for some wall trench and pithouse structures (Features 30/31/37A [structures on top of a small mound], 13A, 21C, 44C). In this study, all ceramics recovered from the excavation units that overlie individual structures are described and listed according to the associated structure. This is a far from ideal approach, and it certainly results in the inclusion of ceramics that were never behaviorally associated with a given structure, but it makes it possible to explore spatial variation in artifact distribution across the site (e.g., Brouwer and Schroeder 2005) that will become especially useful when the inventory of the full site assemblage is completed.

Based on the analyses conducted so far, the Jonathan Creek ceramics look typically Mississippian for the region and conform to impressionistic assessments of the collection, with shell temper and eroded and plain surfaces dominating the assemblage. Decorated and painted sherds are present in low numbers in most contexts, which is consistent with Angelly-phase and Tinsley Hill–phase assemblages, and atypical for a Jonathan Creek–phase assemblage. A very small sample of Mississippian jars is represented by rim segments with handles (N=33; Figure 6.6). Strap handles are present but are less common than loop and intermediate handles. Intermediate handles (N=16) slightly outnumber loop handles (N=12). Based on the temporal associations of handle types presented by Hilgeman (2000:129, 215), this handled-jar assemblage would most likely date between A.D. 1100 and 1325 and be associated with the Angelly phase and the very beginning of the Tinsley Hill phase, but some of the loop handles could be associated with the Jonathan Creek phase.

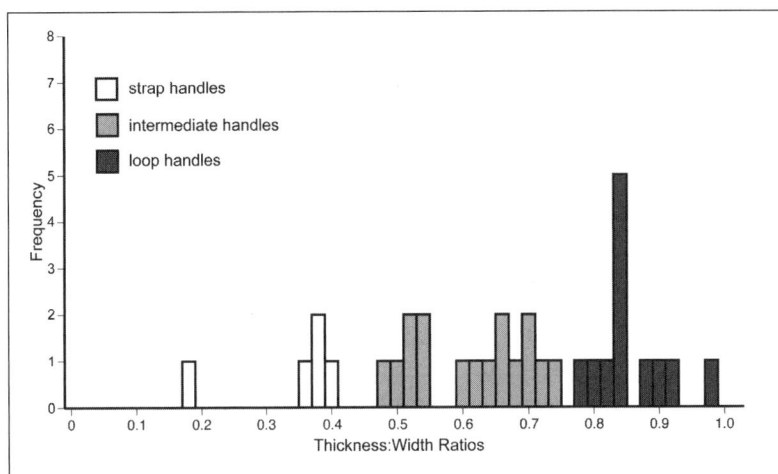

Fig. 6.6. Jar handle thickness:width ratios.

The diversity of vessel types present also conforms to expectations for the Angelly phase or Tinsley Hill phase, with small numbers of hooded water bottles, plates, and bottles present in the analyzed assemblage, which is otherwise dominated by jars, pans, and bowls.

Radiocarbon Dates and the Occupation History of Jonathan Creek

The initial process of sorting through and organizing the material from the CCC excavations of the Jonathan Creek site revealed charred corn cobs and wood from features scattered across the excavated portion of the site that had been retained by the excavators and had not been treated with preservatives or other chemicals (see Table 6.4 at end of chapter). AMS radiocarbon dates have been obtained for these materials, and the dates are tightly clustered, statistically indistinguishable from one another, and fall within the date range for the Angelly phase, supporting the conclusions about occupation history drawn from the limited ceramic analysis, but also matching up with a time when regional specialists have argued that the site was probably deserted (Schroeder 2006:Table 6.3).

The oldest of these dates (Beta-180076) comes from a large midden or trash pit (Feature 38C) located in the center of the excavated portion of the site (Figure 6.4). It appears that this pit was created sometime after Palisade Feature 79 because the postmolds from this wall do not extend across the feature. The fragments of charred wood collected from this feature had been so intensely burned that it was not possible to identify any wood structure. Consequently it was not feasible to isolate the outer rings of wood to submit for dating. The second date (Beta-180077) comes from wood charcoal lying on the floor of a pit house (Feature 44C) near the southern margins of the community, and the outermost rings of wood were submitted for dating. The third date (Beta-180074) is from a corn cob recovered from a small smudge pit or postmold in the floor of a wall trench structure with three large support posts running down the center (Feature 13A). And the fourth date (Beta-180075) is from the outer rings of a piece of wood charcoal that was associated with one of the wall-trench structures (Feature 31A) constructed on top of a small mound. All dates, at the one-sigma range, fall within the thirteenth century and clearly indicate a substantial and spatially extensive occupation at the site during the Angelly phase.

Jonathan Creek in Regional Context

Further ceramic analyses are still needed to refine our understanding of the occupation history of Jonathan Creek, but in light of the characteristics of the analyzed ceramic assemblage and the radiometric dates, all from widely distributed contexts, it becomes difficult to sustain the argument that the major occupation of the excavated portion of the site occurred in early Mississippian times, during the Jonathan Creek phase. Given the relative lack of overlapping structures, especially in the southern half of the excavated area, and the tight clustering of the available radiocarbon dates, it is possible that the occupation history of the excavated portion of the site falls within a relatively short span of time, primarily in the thirteenth century A.D. To investigate this proposition and its implications for regional sociopolitical conditions, 131 radiocarbon dates from 22 Mississippian mound and nonmound sites in western Kentucky and southern Illinois, including Jonathan Creek, were collected (Figure 6.7; Butler 1991; Cobb and Butler 2002; Edging 1990; Hammerstedt 2005:336; Hilgeman 2000; Kreisa 1998; Muller 1986; Pollack and Railey 1987; Wesler 2001; see also Schroeder 2006). These data were organized by river valley and physiographic region to emphasize regional patterns in occupation histories; however, individual sites have their own unique histories, which are only partially captured by this focus on radiocarbon dates. The 1–sigma ranges of the calibrated

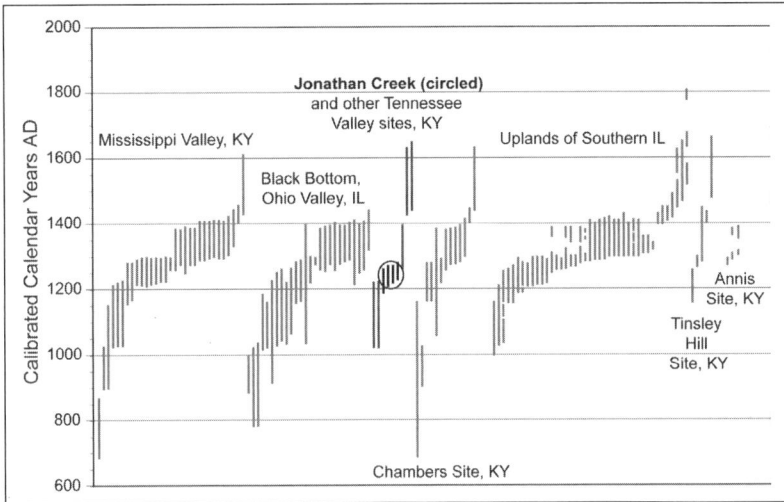

Fig. 6.7. Calibrated 1-sigma radiocarbon dates for Mississippian era sites in western Kentucky and southern Illinois.

dates were emphasized in this analysis with the goal of highlighting major similarities and differences in occupation histories as revealed by dated organic materials, which generally conform to the chronologic placement of the site on the basis of the analysis of ceramics.

Some of the earliest occupations are at Wickliffe, in the Mississippi Valley, and at Kincaid, in the Black Bottom of the Ohio Valley. Kincaid's genesis dates to around A.D. 1000, with its greatest florescence during the thirteenth century (Cobb and Butler 2002:627; 2006). The decline of Kincaid began around A.D. 1250, culminating in the complete collapse of the center around A.D. 1450—as inferred from the apparent abandonment of the site and immediate environs (Butler 1991; Cole et al. 1951; Muller 1986, 1993; Riordan 1975). The major florescence of the Wickliffe site falls between A.D. 1100 and 1250 with abandonment of the site occurring around A.D. 1350 (Wesler 2001; 2006). A couple of other small mound sites in the Mississippi Valley appear to have been founded after A.D. 1200 and occupations at these places may have continued until A.D. 1450 (Edging 1990; Kreisa 1998; Lewis 1986).

Elsewhere in the region, most of the radiometric evidence is for occupations dating between A.D. 1200 and A.D. 1400 or 1450. The excavated portion of Jonathan Creek indicates a substantial occupation between A.D. 1200 and 1300. At the Chambers site, situated in an upland drainage west of the Tennessee River, the main occupations fall between A.D.

1250 and 1350 (Pollack and Railey 1987). Dates from three non-mound sites in the uplands of southern Illinois indicate that these sites were essentially contemporaneous and were occupied between A.D. 1200 and 1450 (Cobb and Butler 2002, 2006). Tinsley Hill, a small mound site in the Cumberland Valley, was occupied primarily between A.D. 1200 and 1450 (Clay 1979, 1997; Hilgeman 2000). Dates for the Annis site, a small mound community along the Green River about 150 km east of Jonathan Creek, fall in the late 1200s and 1300s (Hammerstedt 2005:336).

The available radiocarbon dates for western Kentucky and southern Illinois indicate that only a few places, primarily in the Mississippi and Ohio valleys, had substantial Mississippian occupations before A.D. 1200. Sometime around A.D. 1200, Mississippian occupation in the region expanded, just as or shortly before Kincaid and Wickliffe began to decline (Clay 1997; Cobb and Butler 2002, 2006; Wesler 2001, 2006). Several new mound sites were established away from the Ohio and Mississippi valleys, and Jonathan Creek, which may have an earlier occupation, underwent a significant expansion. The Angel site, near the confluence of the Green and Ohio rivers, expanded at this time as well (Hilgeman 2000). In western Kentucky, few sites have produced radiometric evidence of occupations after about A.D. 1400 or 1450, supporting the notion of a "Vacant Quarter," or population abandonment of the Mississippi-Ohio confluence region (Cobb and Butler 2002; Williams 1990; *contra* Lewis 1990).

A Revised History of Jonathan Creek: The Legacy of the TVA

This new analysis of a small portion of the Jonathan Creek ceramic assemblage and the recently obtained radiocarbon dates from the site force a reconsideration of the occupation history of this prominent place in the late prehistoric landscape of western Kentucky. Although initial occupation of the site may have occurred earlier than A.D. 1200, possibly in the northern unexcavated area of the site, a significant part of the site's history falls between A.D. 1200 and 1300, during the Angelly phase. Jonathan Creek and the other sites in the region have their own unique occupation histories of varying durations, and all were part of a sociopolitical landscape that became particularly dynamic between A.D. 1200 and roughly 1400. The numerous walls that were built at Jonathan Creek are a testament to the social and political uncertainty of life in this era, as well as a manifestation of the regional status achieved by the leaders who lived at this site (Schroeder 2006). These data contribute to our growing understanding of chiefdom expansion, cycling, fission-fusion, collapse, migration, and abandonment in Mississippian societies (Anderson 1994a, 1994b; Blitz 1999; Milner and Schroeder 1999). Taking A.D. 1200 as a point of departure and moving beyond western Kentucky and southern Illinois, we see in many places similar patterns of a thirteenth-century florescence and dissolution of prominent communities, often fortified, including Towosahgy (also known as Beckwith's Fort) in Missouri (Price and Fox 1990) and Moundville in Alabama (Knight and Steponaitis 1998)—developments that occur just as many early Mississippian mound centers are slipping into decline and while regionwide phenomena, such as the Southeastern Ceremonial Complex, seem to be expanding (Brown and Kelly 2000; Muller 2007).

Finally, this research demonstrates the importance of curated collections, the wealth of untapped data that lurk within them, and the potential for new analyses of these data to modify significantly our understanding of the ancient occupation and dynamic sociopolitical landscape of the Southeast. The New Deal era saw numerous large-scale excavations in the river valleys affected by TVA dam development, projects that produced archaeological collections that cannot be duplicated today and helped define much of the culture history of the Southeast. The encouragement offered by the archaeologists of the agency to reanalyze existing collections is a continuation of this early commitment to stewardship and is helping to rewrite prehistory.

Acknowledgments

Bryan Haley assisted with the digitizing of the maps. Marieka Brouwer and Gwen O. Kelly played instrumental roles in the pottery analysis. The Webb Museum of Anthropology at the University of Kentucky has encouraged this research, and I am most grateful for all the assistance that has been provided by Nancy O'Malley and George Crothers. For their continued interest and encouragement of this research, I thank Todd Ahlman, Erin Pritchard, and the TVA archaeologists, especially J. Bennett Graham. Cliff Boyd, Robert H. Lafferty III, Marvin Smith, Alan Sullivan III, and one anonymous reviewer commented on an early draft of this paper, and I greatly appreciate their collegial suggestions. The research presented in this paper was funded in part by the graduate school and the Vilas Associates Program at the University of Wisconsin–Madison, and I am grateful for their support. In particular, the cost of the radiocarbon dates was covered by the Vilas Associates Program. This research also was funded in part by a grant from the National Park Service, U.S. Department of the Interior, and administered through the Kentucky Heritage Council. The use of federal funds does not imply endorsement of the content by the National Park Service or the Kentucky Heritage Council. All programs receiving federal funding are operated free from discrimination on the basis of race, color, national origin, age, or handicap. Any person who believes he or she has been discriminated against should write to Office of Equal Opportunity, U.S. Department of the Interior, P.O. Box 37127, Washington, DC, 20013–7127.

References Cited

ANDERSON, DAVID G.

1994a Factional Competition and Political Evolution of Mississippian Chiefdoms in the Southeastern United States. In *Factional Competition and Political Development in the New World,* edited by Elizabeth M. Brumfiel and John W. Fox, pp. 61–76. Cambridge University Press, Cambridge.

1994b *The Savannah River Chiefdoms: Political Change in the Late Prehistoric Southeast.* University of Alabama Press, Tuscaloosa.

BARTRAM, WILLIAM

1791 *Travels through North and South Carolina, Georgia, East and West Florida, the Cherokee Country, the Extensive Territories of the Muscogulges or Creek Confederacy, and the Country of the Chactaws.* James and Johnson, Philadelphia.

BLITZ, JOHN

1999 Mississippian Chiefdoms and the Fission-Fusion Process. *American Antiquity* 64:577–592.

BROWN, JAMES A., AND JOHN E. KELLY

2000 Cahokia and the Southeastern Ceremonial Complex. In *Mounds, Modoc, and Mesoamerica: Papers in Honor of Melvin L. Fowler,* edited by Steven R. Ahler. Illinois State Museum Scientific Papers, vol. 28, pp. 469–510. Springfield.

BROUWER, MARIEKA, AND SISSEL SCHROEDER

2005 Exploring Structural Variability at the Jonathan Creek Site, ca. AD 1200–1300, Kentucky, USA. *WISCI: Wisconsin Undergraduate Journal of Science* 1(1):40–45.

BUTLER, BRIAN M.

1991 Kincaid Revisited: The Mississippian Sequence in the Lower Ohio Valley. In *Cahokia and the Hinterlands: Middle Mississippian*

Cultures of the Midwest, edited by Thomas E. Emerson and R. Barry Lewis, pp. 264–273. University of Illinois Press, Urbana.

CLAY, R. BERLE

1963   Ceramic Complexes of the Tennessee-Cumberland Region in Western Kentucky. M.A. thesis, Department of Anthropology, University of Kentucky, Lexington.

1979   A Mississippian Ceramic Sequence from Western Kentucky. *Tennessee Archaeologist* 4:111–128.

1997   The Mississippian Succession on the Lower Ohio. *Southeastern Archaeology* 16:16–32.

COBB, CHARLES R., AND BRIAN M. BUTLER

2002   The Vacant Quarter Revisited: Late Mississippian Abandonment of the Lower Ohio Valley. *American Antiquity* 67:625–641.

2006   Mississippian Migration and Emplacement in the Lower Ohio Valley. In *Leadership and Polity in Mississippian Society*, edited by Paul Welch and Brian Butler, pp. 328–347. Center for Archaeological Investigations, Southern Illinois University, Carbondale.

COLE, FAY-COOPER, ROBERT BELL, JOHN BENNETT, JOSEPH CALDWELL, NORMAN EMERSON, RICHARD MACNEISH, KENNETH ORR, AND ROGER WILLIS (EDITORS)

1951   *Kincaid: A Prehistoric Illinois Metropolis.* University of Chicago Press, Chicago.

EDGING, RICHARD

1990   *The Turk Site: A Mississippi Period Town in Western Kentucky: Test Excavations and Mapping Project.* Kentucky Heritage Council, Frankfort.

HALL, JAMES

1801   *A Brief History of the Mississippi Territory: To Which is Prefixed a Summary View of Country between the Settlements on the Cumberland River and Territory.* Francis Coupée, Salisbury, North Carolina.

HAMMERSTEDT, SCOTT W.

2005   *Mississippian Construction, Labor, and Social Organization in Western Kentucky.* Ph.D. dissertation, Department of Anthropology, Pennsylvania State University, University Park.

HILGEMAN, SHERRI L.

2000   *Pottery and Chronology at Angel.* University of Alabama Press, Tuscaloosa.

KING, ADAM

2003   *Etowah: The Political History of a Chiefdom Capital.* University of Alabama Press, Tuscaloosa.

KNIGHT, VERNON J., JR., AND VINCAS P. STEPONAITIS
1998   A New History of Moundville. In *Archaeology of the Moundville Chiefdom*, edited by Vernon J. Knight, Jr., and Vincas P. Steponaitis, pp. 1–25. Smithsonian Institution Press, Washington, DC.

KREISA, PAUL
1998   Pottery, Radiocarbon Dates, and Mississippian-Period Chronology Building in Western Kentucky. In *Changing Perspectives on the Archaeology of the Central Mississippi River Valley*, edited by Michael J. O'Brien and Robert C. Dunnell, pp. 59–79. University of Alabama Press, Tuscaloosa.

LEWIS. R. BARRY
1990   The Late Prehistory of the Ohio-Mississippi Rivers Confluence Region, Kentucky and Missouri. In *Towns and Temples along the Mississippi*, edited by David H. Dye and Cheryl A. Cox, pp. 38–58. University of Alabama, Tuscaloosa.

1991   The Early Mississippi Period in the Confluence Region and its Northern Relationships. In *Cahokia and the Hinterlands: Middle Mississippian Cultures of the Midwest*, edited by Thomas E. Emerson and R. Barry Lewis, pp. 274–294. University of Illinois Press, Urbana.

1996   Mississippian Farmers. In *Kentucky Archaeology*, edited R. Barry Lewis, pp. 127–160. University Press of Kentucky, Lexington.

LEWIS, R. BARRY (EDITOR)
1986   *Mississippian Towns of the Western Kentucky Border: The Adams, Wickliffe, and Sassafras Ridge Sites.* Kentucky Heritage Council, Frankfort.

LEWIS, R. BARRY, AND CHARLES STOUT (EDITORS)
1988   *Mississippian Towns and Sacred Places.* University of Alabama Press, Tuscaloosa.

LOUGHRIDGE, ROBERT H.
1888   *Report on the Geological and Economic Features of the Jackson Purchase Region.* Kentucky Geological Survey, Lexington.

LYON, EDWIN A.
1996   *A New Deal for Southeastern Archaeology.* University of Alabama Press, Tuscaloosa.

MILNER, GEORGE R., AND SISSEL SCHROEDER
1999   Mississippian Sociopolitical Systems. In *Great Towns and Regional Polities in the Prehistoric American Southwest and Southeast*, edited Jill E. Neitzel, pp. 95–107. University of New Mexico Press, Albuquerque.

Milner, George R., and Virginia G. Smith
1986   *New Deal Archaeology in Kentucky: Excavations, Collections, and Research.* Occasional Papers in Anthropology No. 8, Program for Cultural Resource Assessment, University of Kentucky, Lexington.

Moore, Clarence B.
1915   Aboriginal Sites on Tennessee River. *Journal of the Academy of Natural Sciences of Philadelphia*, 2nd Series, 16:170–304.

Muller, Jon
1986   *Archaeology of the Lower Ohio River Valley.* Academic Press, New York.

1993   Lower Ohio Valley Mississippian Revisited: An Autocritique of "The Kincaid System." In *Archaeology of Eastern North America: Papers in Honor of Stephen Williams*, edited by James B. Stoltman, pp. 128–142. Archaeological Report No. 25. Mississippi Department of Archives and History, Jackson.

2007   Prolegomena for the Analysis of the Southeastern Ceremonial Complex. In *Southeastern Ceremonial Complex: Chronology, Content, Context*, edited by Adam King, pp. 15–37. University of Alabama Press, Tuscaloosa.

Orr, Kenneth
1951   Change at Kincaid: A Study of Cultural Dynamics. In *Kincaid: A Prehistoric Illinois Metropolis*, edited by Fay-Cooper Cole, Robert Bell, John Bennett, Joseph Caldwell, Norman Emerson, Richard MacNeish, Kenneth Orr, and Roger Willis, pp. 293–359. University of Chicago Press, Chicago.

Phillips, Philip, James A. Ford, and James B. Griffin
1951   *Archaeological Survey in the Lower Mississippi Alluvial Valley, 1940–1947.* Papers of the Peabody Museum of American Archaeology and Ethnology No. 25, Harvard University, Cambridge, MA.

Pollack, David
2004   *Caborn-Welborn: Constructing a New Society after the Angel Chiefdom Collapse.* University of Alabama Press, Tuscaloosa.

Pollack, David, and Jimmy A. Railey
1987   *Chambers (15ML109): An Upland Village in Western Kentucky.* Kentucky Heritage Council, Frankfort.

Price, James E., and Gregory L. Fox
1990   Recent Investigations at Towosahgy State Historic Site. *Missouri Archaeologist* 51:1–71.

RIORDAN, ROBERT
1975 *Ceramics and Chronology: Mississippian Settlement in the Black Bottom, Southern Illinois.* Ph.D. dissertation, Southern Illinois University, Carbondale.

SCHROEDER, SISSEL
2005 Reclaiming New Deal Era Civic Archaeology: Exploring the Legacy of William S. Webb and the Jonathan Creek Site. *CRM: The Journal of Heritage Stewardship* 2:53–71.

2006 Walls as Symbols of Political, Economic, and Military Might. In *Leadership and Polity in Mississippian Society,* edited by Paul Welch and Brian Butler, pp. 115–141. Center for Archaeological Investigations, Southern Illinois University, Carbondale.

SMITH, GERALD P.
1969 *Ceramic Handle Styles and Cultural Variation in the Northern Sector of the Mississippi Alluvial Valley.* Occasional Papers No. 3, Anthropological Research Center, Memphis State University, Memphis, TN.

STUIVER, MINZE , PAULA J. REIMER, EDOUARD BARD, J. WARREN BECK, G. S. BURR, KONRAD A. HUGHEN, BERND KROMER, GERRY MCCORMAC, JOHANNES VAN DER PLICHT, AND MARCO SPURK
1998 INTCAL98 Radiocarbon Age Calibration, 24,000–0 cal BP. *Radiocarbon* 40:1041–1083.

TENNESSEE VALLEY AUTHORITY (TVA)
1983 *A History of the Tennessee Valley Authority,* fiftieth anniversary edition. Tennessee Valley Authority, Knoxville.

WASELKOV, GREGORY A., AND KATHRYN E. HOLLAND BRAUND (EDITORS)
1995 *William Bartram on the Southeastern Indians.* University of Nebraska Press, Lincoln.

WEBB, WILLIAM S.
1952 *The Jonathan Creek Village.* Reports in Anthropology 7(1). University of Kentucky, Lexington.

WESLER, KIT W.
1991 Ceramics, Chronology, and Horizon Markers at Wickliffe Mounds. *American Antiquity* 56:278–290.

2001 *Excavations at Wickliffe Mounds.* University of Alabama Press, Tuscaloosa.

2006 Platforms as Chiefs: Comparing Mound Sequences in Western Kentucky. In *Leadership and Polity in Mississippian Society,* edited by Paul Welch and Brian Butler, pp. 142–155. Center for Archaeological Investigations, Southern Illinois University, Carbondale.

WILLIAMS, STEPHEN

1954   An Archaeological Study of the Mississippian Culture in Southeast Missouri. Ph.D. dissertation, Department of Anthropology, Yale University, New Haven.

1990   The Vacant Quarter and Other Late Events in the Lower Valley. In *Towns and Temples along the Mississippi,* edited by David. H. Dye and Cheryl A. Cox, pp. 170–180. University of Alabama Press, Tuscaloosa.

WOLFORTH, LYNNE M.

1987   Six House-Basin Structures: The Jonathan Creek Site and Its Depositional History. In *Current Archaeological Research in Kentucky,* vol. 1, edited David Pollack, pp. 101–119. Kentucky Heritage Council, Frankfort.

WOODS, PATRICIA D.

1979   *French-Indian Relations on the Southern Frontier, 1699–1762.* UMI Research Press, Ann Arbor, MI.

Table 6.1: Inventory of Ceramics (Dominant Temper)

Feature Number	Unit	Feature Type	Temper	Sherds (N)	Rims (N)	Total	%
1	A		Coarse shell	0	1		100.00
1	A		Fine shell	0	0		0.00
1	A		Grit-grog	0	0		0.00
1	A		Grog	0	0		0.00
1	A		Grit	0	0		0.00
1	A	Single post circular	TOTAL			1	
12	A		Coarse shell	535	46		92.52
12	A		Fine shell	40	4		7.01
12	A		Grit-grog	0	0		0.00
12	A		Grog	3	0		0.48
12	A		Grit	0	0		0.00
12	A	Midden pit	TOTAL			628	
13	A		Coarse shell	350	13		95.53
13	A		Fine shell	14	1		3.95
13	A		Grit-grog	0	0		0.00
13	A		Grog	2	0		0.53
13	A		Grit	0	0		0.00

Feature Number	Unit	Feature Type	Temper	Sherds (N)	Rims (N)	Total	%
Table 6.1 (continued): Inventory of Ceramics (Dominant Temper)							
13	A	Triple post wall trench	TOTAL			380	
14	A		Coarse shell	3460	188		89.04
14	A		Fine shell	411	26		10.67
14	A		Grit-grog	1	0		0.02
14	A		Grog	11	0		0.27
14	A		Grit	0	0		0.00
14	A	Midden pit (adjacent to small mound)	TOTAL			4097	
19	A		Coarse shell	425	27		96.17
19	A		Fine shell	13	1		2.98
19	A		Grit-grog	0	0		0.00
19	A		Grog	4	0		0.85
19	A		Grit	0	0		0.00
19	A	Midden pit	TOTAL			470	
25	A		Coarse shell	199	11		95.02
25	A		Fine shell	8	2		4.52
25	A		Grit-grog	0	0		0.00
25	A		Grog	1	0		0.45
25	A		Grit	0	0		0.00
25	A	Single post rectangle	TOTAL			221	
28	A		Coarse shell	3441	171		90.85
28	A		Fine shell	322	23		8.68
28	A		Grit-grog	0	0		0.00
28	A		Grog	11	2		0.33
28	A		Grit	2	3		0.13
28	A		No temper	0	1		0.03
28	A	Midden pit	TOTAL			3976	
30/31/37	A		Coarse shell	1448	68		72.57
30/31/37	A		Fine shell	508	27		25.61

30/31/37	A		Grit-grog	4	0		0.19
30/31/37	A		Grog	29	1		1.44
30/31/37	A		Grit	2	0		0.10
30/31/37	A		No temper	1	0		0.05
30/31/37	A		Grit (Late				
Wood-land)	1	0		0.05			
30/31/37	**A**	**Wall trench**	**Total**			**2089**	
55	A		Coarse shell	2	1		100.00
55	A		Fine shell	0	0		0.00
55	A		Grit-grog	0	0		0.00
55	A		Grog	0	0		0.00
55	A		Grit	0	0		0.00
55	**A**	**Wall trench**	**Total**			**3**	
1	C		Coarse shell	8	1		100.00
1	C		Fine shell	0	0		0.00
1	C		Grit-grog	0	0		0.00
1	C		Grog	0	0		0.00
1	C		Grit	0	0		0.00
1	**C**	**Single post square**	**Total**			**9**	
4	C		Coarse shell	12	0		75.00
4	C		Fine shell	3	0		18.75
4	C		Grit-grog	0	0		0.00
4	C		Grog	1	0		6.25
4	C		Grit	0	0		0.00
4	**C**	**Triple post wall trench**	**Total**			**16**	
5	C		Coarse shell	296	25		93.04
5	C		Fine shell	22	1		6.67
5	C		Grit-grog	0	0		0.00
5	C		Grog	1	0		0.29
5	C		Grit	0	0		0.00
5	**C**	**Single post square**	**Total**			**345**	
17	C		Coarse shell	118	4		84.72

Table 6.1 (continued): Inventory of Ceramics (Dominant Temper)							
Feature Number	Unit	Feature Type	Temper	Sherds (N)	Rims (N)	Total	%
17	C		Fine shell	18	0		12.50
17	C		Grit-grog	0	0		0.00
17	C		Grog	3	0		2.08
17	C		Grit	1	0		0.69
17	C	Single post square	TOTAL			144	
18	C		Coarse shell	81	4		84.16
18	C		Fine shell	11	1		11.88
18	C		Grit-grog	0	0		0.00
18	C		Grog	4	0		3.96
18	C		Grit	0	0		0.00
18	C	Triple post wall trench	TOTAL			101	
21	C		Coarse shell	24	4		77.78
21	C		Fine shell	7	0		19.44
21	C		Grit-grog	0	0		0.00
21	C		Grog	1	0		2.78
21	C		Grit	0	0		0.00
21	C	Triple post wall trench	TOTAL			36	
27	C		Coarse shell	84	0		81.55
27	C		Fine shell	14	4		17.48
27	C		Grit-grog	0	0		0.00
27	C		Grog	1	0		0.97
27	C		Grit	0	0		0.00
27	C	Single post square	TOTAL			103	
28	C		Coarse shell	65	6		94.67
28	C		Fine shell	4	0		5.33
28	C		Grit-grog	0	0		0.00
28	C		Grog	0	0		0.00
28	C		Grit	0	0		0.00
28	C	Wall trench	TOTAL			75	
41/42	C		Coarse shell	47	1		76.19

41/42	C		Fine shell	9	1		15.87
41/42	C		Grit-grog	1	0		1.59
41/42	C		Grog	1	1		3.17
41/42	C		Grog (Late Wood-land)	2	0		3.17
41/42	C		Grit	0	0		0.00
41/42	**C**	**Wall trench and single post square**	**Total**			**63**	
43	C		Coarse shell	117	8		93.98
43	C		Fine shell	2	0		1.50
43	C		Grit-grog	0	0		0.00
43	C		Grog	6	0		4.51
43	C		Grit	0	0		0.00
43	**C**	**Wall trench**	**Total**			**133**	
44	C		Coarse shell	25	1		100.00
44	C		Fine shell	0	0		0.00
44	C		Grit-grog	0	0		0.00
44	C		Grog	0	0		0.00
44	C		Grit	0	0		0.00
44	**C**	**Pit house**	**Total**			**26**	
47	C		Coarse shell	307	27		89.30
47	C		Fine shell	34	4		10.16
47	C		Grit-grog	0	0		0.00
47	C		Grog	2	0		0.53
47	C		Grit	0	0		0.00
47	**C**	**Wall trench**	**Total**			**374**	
48/49	C		Coarse shell	42	14		84.85
48/49	C		Fine shell	5	1		9.09
48/49	C		Grit-grog	1	0		1.52
48/49	C		Grog	3	0		4.55
48/49	C		Grit	0	0		0.00
48/49	**C**	**Wall trench and single post square**	**Total**			**66**	
102	C		Coarse shell	7	0		50.00

Table 6.1 (continued): Inventory of Ceramics (Dominant Temper)

Feature Number	Unit	Feature Type	Temper	Sherds (N)	Rims (N)	Total	%
102	C		Fine shell	7	0		50.00
102	C		Grit-grog	0	0		0.00
102	C		Grog	0	0		0.00
102	C		Grit	0	0		0.00
102	C	Single post square	TOTAL			14	
103	C		Coarse shell	14	0		70.00
103	C		Fine shell	5	0		25.00
103	C		Grit-grog	0	0		0.00
103	C		Grog	1	0		5.00
103	C		Grit	0	0		0.00
103	C	Triple post wall trench	TOTAL			20	
SUM TOTAL				12665	725	13390	

Table 6.2: Inventory of Ceramics (Surface Treatment)

Feature Number	Unit	Feature Type	Surface Treatment	Sherds (N)	Rims (N)	Total	%
1	A		Plain	0	0		0.00
1	A		Red	0	0		0.00
1	A		Black	0	1		100.00
1	A		Miss CM	0	0		0.00
1	A		Eroded	0	0		0.00
1	A		Decorated	0	0		0.00
1	A		Negative painted	0	0		0.00
1	A		Fabric	0	0		0.00
1	A		Unknown	0	0		0.00
1	A		Polished	0	0		0.00
1	A		Black and buff or buff	0	0		0.00
1	A	Single post circular	TOTAL			1	
12	A		Plain	371	33		64.33
12	A		Red	1	0		0.16

12	A		Black	15	5		3.18
12	A		Miss CM	0	0		0.00
12	A		Eroded	159	4		25.96
12	A		Decorated	3	0		0.48
12	A		Negative painted	0	0		0.00
12	A		Fabric	22	8		4.78
12	A		Unknown	0	0		0.00
12	A		Polished	5	0		0.80
12	A		Black and buff or buff	2	0		0.32
12	**A**		**Total**			**628**	
13	A		Plain	214	10		58.95
13	A		Red	5	0		1.32
13	A		Black	12	1		3.42
13	A		Miss CM	0	0		0.00
13	A		Eroded	109	1		28.95
13	A		Decorated	9	0		2.37
13	A		Negative painted	1	0		0.26
13	A		Fabric	16	2		4.74
13	A		Unknown	0	0		0.00
13	A		Polished	0	0		0.00
13	A		Black and buff or buff	0	0		0.00
13	**A**	**Triple post wall trench**	**Total**			**380**	
14	A		Plain	2024	129		52.55
14	A		Red	17	3		0.49
14	A		Black	233	16		6.08
14	A		Miss CM	0	0		0.00
14	A		Eroded	1388	20		34.37
14	A		Decorated	29	3		0.78
14	A		Negative painted	0	0		0.00
14	A		Fabric	166	34		4.88
14	A		Unknown	3	4		0.17
14	A		Polished	8	4		0.29
14	A		Black and buff or buff	5	1		0.15

Feature Number	Unit	Feature Type	Surface Treatment	Sherds (N)	Rims (N)	Total	%
Table 6.2 (continued): Inventory of Ceramics (Surface Treatment)							
14	A		Red over CM	10	0		0.24
14	A		TOTAL			4097	
19	A		Plain	240	15		54.26
19	A		Red	4	0		0.85
19	A		Black	34	4		8.09
19	A		Miss CM	0	0		0.00
19	A		Eroded	146	8		32.77
19	A		Decorated	0	0		0.00
19	A		Negative painted	5	0		1.06
19	A		Fabric	8	1		1.91
19	A		Unknown	0	0		0.00
19	A		Polished	2	0		0.43
19	A		White slip	3	0		0.64
19	A		TOTAL			470	
25	A		Plain	106	8		51.58
25	A		Red	0	0		0.00
25	A		Black	20	1		9.50
25	A		Miss CM	0	0		0.00
25	A		Eroded	69	4		33.03
25	A		Decorated	4	0		1.81
25	A		Negative painted	0	0		0.00
25	A		Fabric	9	0		4.07
25	A		Unknown	0	0		0.00
25	A		Polished	0	0		0.00
25	A		Black and buff or buff	0	0		0.00
25	A	Single post rectangle	TOTAL			221	
28	A		Plain	1929	86		50.68
28	A		Red	2	2		0.10
28	A		Black	110	18		3.22
28	A		Miss CM	1	1		0.05
28	A		Eroded	1618	65		42.33
28	A		Decorated	43	0		1.08

28	A		Negative painted	1	0		0.03
28	A		Fabric	57	23		2.01
28	A		Unknown	0	4		0.10
28	A		Polished	8	0		0.20
28	A		White slip	1	0		0.03
28	A		Modeled effigy	6	0		0.15
28	A		Red over CM	0	1		0.03
28	**A**		**Total**			**3976**	
30/31/37	A		Plain	917	65		47.01
30/31/37	A		Red	23	1		1.15
30/31/37	A		Black	91	1		4.40
30/31/37	A		Miss CM	1	0		0.05
30/31/37	A		Eroded	822	21		40.35
30/31/37	A		Decorated	28	0		1.34
30/31/37	A		Negative painted	2	0		0.10
30/31/37	A		Fabric	48	5		2.54
30/31/37	A		Unknown	1	2		0.14
30/31/37	A		Polished	31	0		1.48
30/31/37	A		Black and buff or buff	19	0		0.91
30/31/37	A		White slip	0	1		0.05
30/31/37	A		Modeled effigy	6	0		0.29
30/31/37	A		Black and brown	3	0		0.14
30/31/37	A		Eroded (Late				
Wood-land)	1	0		0.05			
30/31/37	**A**	**Wall trench**	**Total**			**2089**	
55	A		Plain	0	1		33.33
55	A		Red	0	0		0.00
55	A		Black	0	0		0.00
55	A		Miss CM	0	0		0.00
55	A		Eroded	2	0		66.67
55	A		Decorated	0	0		0.00
55	A		Negative painted	0	0		0.00

Feature Number	Unit	Feature Type	Surface Treatment	Sherds (N)	Rims (N)	Total	%
Table 6.2 (continued): Inventory of Ceramics (Surface Treatment)							
55	A		Fabric	0	0		0.00
55	A		Unknown	0	0		0.00
55	A		Polished	0	0		0.00
55	A		Black and buff or buff	0	0		0.00
55	**A**	**Wall trench**	**TOTAL**			**3**	
1	C		Plain	7	1		88.89
1	C		Red	0	0		0.00
1	C		Black	0	0		0.00
1	C		Miss CM	0	0		0.00
1	C		Eroded	1	0		11.11
1	C		Decorated	0	0		0.00
1	C		Negative painted	0	0		0.00
1	C		Fabric	0	0		0.00
1	C		Unknown	0	0		0.00
1	C		Polished	0	0		0.00
1	C		Black and buff or buff	0	0		0.00
1	**C**	**Single post square**	**TOTAL**			**9**	
4	C		Plain	12	0		75.00
4	C		Red	0	0		0.00
4	C		Black	0	0		0.00
4	C		Miss CM	0	0		0.00
4	C		Eroded	4	0		25.00
4	C		Decorated	0	0		0.00
4	C		Negative painted	0	0		0.00
4	C		Fabric	0	0		0.00
4	C		Unknown	0	0		0.00
4	C		Polished	0	0		0.00
4	C		Black and buff or buff	0	0		0.00
4	**C**	**Triple post wall trench**	**TOTAL**			**16**	
5	C		Plain	169	17		53.91

5	C		Red	1	0			0.29
5	C		Black	34	3			10.72
5	C		Miss CM	0	0			0.00
5	C		Eroded	100	4			30.14
5	C		Decorated	3	1			1.16
5	C		Negative painted	3	0			0.87
5	C		Fabric	9	1			2.90
5	C		Unknown	0	0			0.00
5	C		Polished	0	0			0.00
5	C		Black and buff or buff	0	0			0.00
5	**C**	**Single post square**	**TOTAL**				**345**	
17	C		Plain	52	3			38.19
17	C		Red	1	0			0.69
17	C		Black	1	0			0.69
17	C		Miss CM	0	0			0.00
17	C		Eroded	80	1			56.25
17	C		Decorated	0	0			0.00
17	C		Negative painted	1	0			0.69
17	C		Fabric	5	0			3.47
17	C		Unknown	0	0			0.00
17	C		Polished	0	0			0.00
17	C		Black and buff or buff	0	0			0.00
17	**C**	**Single post square**	**TOTAL**				**144**	
18	C		Plain	55	4			58.42
18	C		Red	0	0			0.00
18	C		Black	7	1			7.92
18	C		Miss CM	0	0			0.00
18	C		Eroded	30	0			29.70
18	C		Decorated	1	0			0.99
18	C		Negative painted	0	0			0.00
18	C		Fabric	2	0			1.98
18	C		Unknown	0	0			0.00
18	C		Polished	0	0			0.00

Table 6.2 (continued): Inventory of Ceramics (Surface Treatment)							
Feature Number	Unit	Feature Type	Surface Treatment	Sherds (N)	Rims (N)	Total	%
18	C		Modeled Effigy	1	0		0.99
18	C	Triple post wall trench	TOTAL			101	
21	C		Plain	26	0		72.22
21	C		Red	0	0		0.00
21	C		Black	0	0		0.00
21	C		Miss CM	0	0		0.00
21	C		Eroded	6	4		27.78
21	C		Decorated	0	0		0.00
21	C		Negative painted	0	0		0.00
21	C		Fabric	0	0		0.00
21	C		Unknown	0	0		0.00
21	C		Polished	0	0		0.00
21	C		Black and buff or buff	0	0		0.00
21	C	Triple post wall trench	TOTAL			36	
27	C		Plain	30	2		31.07
27	C		Red	0	0		0.00
27	C		Black	1	1		1.94
27	C		Miss CM	0	0		0.00
27	C		Eroded	65	1		64.08
27	C		Decorated	2	0		1.94
27	C		Negative painted	0	0		0.00
27	C		Fabric	1	0		0.97
27	C		Unknown	0	0		0.00
27	C		Polished	0	0		0.00
27	C		Black and buff or buff	0	0		0.00
27	C	Single post square	TOTAL			103	
28	C		Plain	25	1		34.67
28	C		Red	0	0		0.00
28	C		Black	10	0		13.33

28	C		Miss CM	o	o		0.00
28	C		Eroded	34	3		49.33
28	C		Decorated	o	o		0.00
28	C		Negative painted	o	o		0.00
28	C		Fabric	o	2		2.67
28	C		Unknown	o	o		0.00
28	C		Polished	o	o		0.00
28	C		Black and buff or buff	o	o		0.00
28	**C**	**Wall trench**	**TOTAL**			**75**	
41/42	C		Plain	16	1		26.98
41/42	C		Red	o	o		0.00
41/42	C		Black	6	2		12.70
41/42	C		Miss CM	o	o		0.00
41/42	C		Eroded	33	o		52.38
41/42	C		Decorated	o	o		0.00
41/42	C		Negative painted	o	o		0.00
41/42	C		Fabric	3	o		4.76
41/42	C		Unknown	o	o		0.00
41/42	C		Polished	o	o		0.00
41/42	C		Black and buff or buff	o	o		0.00
41/42	C		CM (Late Woodland)	2	o		3.17
41/42	**C**	**Wall trench and single post square**	**TOTAL**			**63**	
43	C		Plain	97	5		76.69
43	C		Red	o	o		0.00
43	C		Black	11	o		8.27
43	C		Miss CM	o	o		0.00
43	C		Eroded	11	1		9.02
43	C		Decorated	o	o		0.00
43	C		Negative painted	o	o	.	0.00
43	C		Fabric	6	2		6.02
43	C		Unknown	o	o		0.00
43	C		Polished	o	o		0.00

Feature Number	Unit	Feature Type	Surface Treatment	Sherds (N)	Rims (N)	Total	%
43	C		Black and buff or buff	0	0		0.00
43	**C**	**Wall trench**	**TOTAL**			**133**	
44	C		Plain	0	0		0.00
44	C		Red	0	0		0.00
44	C		Black	8	0		30.77
44	C		Miss CM	0	0		0.00
44	C		Eroded	14	1		57.69
44	C		Decorated	0	0		0.00
44	C		Negative painted	0	0		0.00
44	C		Fabric	3	0		11.54
44	C		Unknown	0	0		0.00
44	C		Polished	0	0		0.00
44	C		Black and buff or buff	0	0		0.00
44	**C**	**Pit house**	**TOTAL**			**26**	
47	C		Plain	183	12		52.14
47	C		Red	3	1		1.07
47	C		Black	42	4		12.30
47	C		Miss CM	1	0		0.27
47	C		Eroded	83	4		23.26
47	C		Decorated	1	0		0.27
47	C		Negative painted	0	0		0.00
47	C		Fabric	25	10		9.36
47	C		Unknown	0	0		0.00
47	C		Polished	5	0		1.34
47	C		Black and buff or buff	0	0		0.00
47	**C**	**Wall trench**	**TOTAL**			**374**	
48/49	C		Plain	22	8		45.45
48/49	C		Red	0	0		0.00
48/49	C		Black	1	0		1.52
48/49	C		Miss CM	1	0		1.52
48/49	C		Eroded	20	4		36.36
48/49	C		Decorated	1	0		1.52

Table 6.2 (continued): Inventory of Ceramics (Surface Treatment)

48/49	C		Negative painted	1	0		1.52
48/49	C		Fabric	5	3		12.12
48/49	C		Unknown	0	0		0.00
48/49	C		Polished	0	0		0.00
48/49	C		Black and buff or buff	0	0		0.00
48/49	C	Wall trench and single post square	Total			66	
102	C		Plain	5	0		35.71
102	C		Red	0	0		0.00
102	C		Black	4	0		28.57
102	C		Miss CM	0	0		0.00
102	C		Eroded	5	0		35.71
102	C		Decorated	0	0		0.00
102	C		Negative painted	0	0		0.00
102	C		Fabric	0	0		0.00
102	C		Unknown	0	0		0.00
102	C		Polished	0	0		0.00
102	C		Black and buff or buff	0	0		0.00
102	C	Single post square	Total			14	
103	C		Plain	15	0		75.00
103	C		Red	0	0		0.00
103	C		Black	0	0		0.00
103	C		Miss CM	0	0		0.00
103	C		Eroded	5	0		25.00
103	C		Decorated	0	0		0.00
103	C		Negative painted	0	0		0.00
103	C		Fabric	0	0		0.00
103	C		Unknown	0	0		0.00
103	C		Polished	0	0		0.00
103	C		Black and buff or buff	0	0		0.00
103	C	Triple post wall trench	Total			20	
Sum Total				12665	725	13390	

Table 6.3: Vessel Types

Vessel Type	N	%
Mississippian Jar	469	64.69
Pan	135	18.62
Bowl	75	10.34
Hooded Bottle	19	2.62
Plate	11	1.52
Bottle	8	1.10
Unknown (bowl, jar, or beaker)	5	0.69
Miniature Vessel	3	0.41
Total Rims	725	

Table 6.4: Jonathan Creek Charred Organics and C-14 Dates (cal. A.D.)

Sample #	2 sigma low	1-sigma low	Intercept	1-sigma high	2 sigma high	context
Beta-180076	1160	1190	1260	1230	1280	wood charcoal from Pit Fea. 38C (located in the center of the excavated portion of the site)
Beta-180077	1180	1210	1270	1250	1280	wood charcoal from structure Fea. 44C
Beta-180074	1180	1220	1270	1260	1290	corn from a postmold/smudge pit in the floor of structure feature 13A
Beta-180075	1190	1230	1280	1260	1290	wood charcoal from 1 ft. level of 70L7 which includes the floors of structure features 30 and 31 in Unit A
No date						Unit C, corn from 505R28 (FS#4); no features were mapped in this area, and sample is described as coming from disturbed soil so context of sample is uncertain
No date						Unit A, corn from postmold in Fea. 12; however, Fea. 12 is a midden pit without any postmolds recorded or mapped within it so context of sample is uncertain

Source: Calibrated using Stuiver et al., 1998.

7
Archaeological Time Constructs and the Construction of the Hiwassee Island Mound

Lynne P. Sullivan

GAPS IN CONSTRUCTION and use sequences of Mississippian platform mounds are common for numerous mounds in the Valley and Ridge province of northern Georgia (Hally 1996), including the large and impressive Etowah site (King 2001, 2003), and in eastern Georgia along the Savannah and Oconee Rivers (Anderson 1994a; Williams and Shapiro 1990). Anderson (1994a, 1994b) cites such mound sequences as evidence of chiefdom cycling, or the rise and fall of chiefly regimes. In the process of reconstructing mound sequences and proposed chiefdom cycling in northern Georgia, some researchers (Hudson et al. 1985; Smith 2000) have linked sites in the Upper Tennessee Valley to the Georgia sites and proposed that the Tennessee sites were subject to chiefdoms centered in northern Georgia. The sixteenth-century Coosa chiefdom described by de Soto specifically is proposed as extending from a capital at the Little Egypt site in northern Georgia well into the Upper Tennessee Valley (Hally, Smith, and Langford 1990; Smith 2000). Nonetheless, temporal placement for most of the Tennessee Valley sites is sketchy, and correlation with developments in Georgia remains speculative. Fine tuning the chronological placement of the Tennessee sites is a necessary step toward understanding the developmental dynamics of the Upper Tennessee Valley and, by extension, any relationship(s) these sites may have had with those of the proposed Coosa chiefdom.

Toward this goal, an examination of the sequences of Mississippian platform mounds in eastern Tennessee is essential to define more precisely their occupational histories and temporal placements. Some mounds were used sequentially (including gaps in use), such as the three platform mounds (one each) at the Davis, Hixon, and Dallas sites in the Chickamauga Basin of southeastern Tennessee (Lewis, Lewis, and Sullivan 1995; Sullivan 2001, 2007). These mounds are within one mile of each other and are situated on either side of the Tennessee River in the same river bottom. The serial use of these mounds at least partially correlates with political developments at Etowah (Sullivan 2007; Sullivan and Humpf 2001); the rise and demise of Hixon parallels the Early Wilbanks phase of Etowah's elaborate Mound C (King 2001, 2003). What follows are the results of a reexamination of the mound sequence at the Hiwassee Island site, an eminent mound site of the Eastern Woodlands. Lewis and Kneberg's (1946) initial study of this site provided the basis for definitions of the Mississippian period in eastern Tennessee and influenced archaeological thought in general about the Mississippian period throughout the Southeast.

Previous Research and Past Perceptions

Our perceptions of prehistory are based not only on the archaeological record and our own experiences and knowledge, but on the body of accumulated knowledge gained and crafted by the scholars who preceded us. Revising, refining, and sometimes replacing elements of this legacy all are part of the scholarly process of knowledge acquisition. This process of modification and correction is as integral to our continued improved understanding of prehistory as is augmenting our accumulated pool of data with newly collected information. Restudy of the data sets represented by older collections thus is extremely important for adjusting the foundations of our knowledge base and for advancing construction of better interpretations. Such restudy especially is crucial for those data sets that proved highly influential in shaping broadly based perceptions of regions or time periods. Revisiting eminent mound sites of the Eastern Woodlands not only presents an opportunity to make this important point about the value of older collections, but to apply these principles to the interpretation of "classic" sites that were instrumental in characterizing the Mississippian Period.

The site examined here, Hiwassee Island, provided one of the first regional chronologies in the Southeast, thus laying the foundation for future work in the Tennessee Valley and a comparative base for other areas. Brain and Phillips (1996:228) state, "the publication of the excavations [at Hiwassee Island] has been a cornerstone of the definition and chronology of Mississippian culture in the Mid-South and beyond." A significant part of the regional chronology established in Thomas M. N. Lewis and Madeline Kneberg's 1946 report is based on the stratigraphic sequence of the large substructure mound in the Mississippian town on the island. This sequence allowed Lewis and Kneberg to divide the Mississippian period into two phases (called "foci" during their time): the earlier named for the Hiwassee Island site itself, and the later for the Dallas site, another Mississippian town in the Chickamauga Basin.

The distinction between the phases still is recognized today as the major division between the early and late Mississippian occupations in the Upper Tennessee Valley, but several refinements have been made in the regional chronology for the Mississippian period. These are the segregation of the Martin Farm phase, a very early Mississippian phase that bridges the transition from Late Woodland (Faulkner 1972; Schroedl, Davis, and Boyd 1985; Schroedl, Boyd, and Davis 1990); the correlation of absolute dates to the two original phases (e.g., Faulkner 1967; Kimball 1985); and the correlation of Hamilton burial mounds with at least the early part of the Hiwassee Island phase (Schroedl 1973, 1978). Lewis and Kneberg (1946) thought these mounds dated solely to the Late Woodland period, and consequently were puzzled by the lack of burials in Hiwassee Island components. Absolute dates obtained by Schroedl (1973, 1978) showed that the Hamilton mounds were used until about A.D. 1200. The dates for the Mississippian phases in the Upper Tennessee Valley now are Martin Farm, A.D. 900–1000; Hiwassee Island, A.D. 1000–1300; and Dallas, A.D. 1300–1550, with the Mouse Creek phase on the Hiwassee River overlapping the latter part of Dallas (Schroedl, Boyd, and Davis 1990).

These refinements to the chronology are accompanied by new questions about the fit of the Hiwassee Island site itself into the regional chronology. James Hatch (1974:202) in his study of Dallas mortuary practices, states, "If there was some way to establish a 'norm' for Dallas burial patterning, Hiwassee Island would probably represent the most 'aberrant' case in comparison. It is therefore unfortunate that the Dallas component at Hiwassee Island was used by Lewis and Kneberg as the starting point for their discussion of Dallas burials in general." The lack of artifacts correlated with the Southeastern Ceremonial Complex (SECC) in the mound makes the site appear different and "out of step" with other sites assumed to date to the same period. Brain and Phillips (1996:228–233) also point out problems with attributions of pottery types with the phases and the lack of congruence of the architectural sequence in the mound with Lewis and Kneberg's (1946) own distinctions between the phases.

My efforts to refine our understanding of the periods of occupation of the major Mississippian sites in eastern Tennessee relies on the study of original collections and records from mound and other stratigraphic sequences. Where possible, I have correlated these sequences with absolute dates obtained for appropriate samples, when these can be found in the older collections. As mentioned above, one result of these efforts is a clarification of the temporal relationships of the Davis, Hixon, and Dallas sites, three other Mississippian mound centers in the Chickamauga Basin, all located about 15 miles down river from Hiwassee Island (Lewis, Lewis, and Sullivan, 1995; Sullivan 2001, 2007). These sites were occupied sequentially, and each has an occupation span that is shorter than that of Hiwassee Island. This work also demonstrates that the platform mounds at these sites were not used continuously but show periods of use and disuse.

Issues surrounding archaeological systematics are complex, and one certainly cannot assume change in material culture or cultural practices at consistent rates across time and space. Nevertheless, in a small region such as the Chickamauga Basin, where there is a high degree of similarity among assemblages and there undoubtedly was direct communication and interaction between the inhabitants of contemporary sites, the likelihood is high that trends would be fairly consistent among sites at any given time. A refined understanding of the temporal placement of the Hiwassee Island site thus can be gained by comparing the sequence represented by the Davis, Hixon, and Dallas sites with that of the Hiwassee Island mound. The first absolute date from the Hiwassee Island mound also provides a check on this placement. The comparison of these mound sequences sheds new light on Lewis and Kneberg's (1946) chronology and the original definitions of the Hiwassee Island and Dallas phases. Pottery, architecture, engraved shell gorget styles, and mortuary practices form the basis of this comparison.

The Hiwassee Island Site

Hiwassee Island (40MG31) is in Meigs County at the confluence of the Hiwassee and Tennessee rivers in southeastern Tennessee, about 20 miles north of present-day Chattanooga. Major excavations on the island were done from April 1937 to April 1939 by Works Progress Administration (WPA) crews under the direction of archaeologists from the University of

Tennessee (Lewis and Kneberg 1946). These efforts were in conjunction with construction of the Tennessee Valley Authority's (TVA) Chicka-mauga Dam and Reservoir on the Tennessee River. Hiwassee Island was one of 13 sites investigated throughout the reservoir area. Thomas M. N. Lewis, an apprentice of W. C. McKern at the Milwaukee Public Museum, was the principal investigator for the Chickamauga Basin project. Charles Nash, Wendell Walker, and Charles H. Fairbanks were the supervisory field archaeologists at Hiwassee Island. In 1938, Madeline Kneberg, a physical anthropologist and student of Faye-Cooper Cole at the University of Chicago, joined the team as supervisor of the main laboratory in Knoxville. She became highly influential in the analytical work and co-authored with Lewis (although she probably should have been listed as the senior author) the subsequent report on Hiwassee Island (Lewis and Kneberg 1946; Jennings 1994; Sullivan 1999).

A survey and records search of archaeological localities on the island by the WPA team identified at least 15 conical mounds, several small midden areas, and, on the north end of the island, a large village area with two substructure mounds. The team excavated five of the conical mounds, but the majority of their attention was devoted to investigations of sections of the large Mississippian village and, in particular, excavation of the entire main substructure mound. The nature of large southeastern mounds was incompletely understood in the 1930s. The idea that these mounds supported buildings was new, and techniques for excavating this type of mound were being developed (Fairbanks 1970; Lewis 1935, 1937). The Hiwassee Island mound was one of the first, if not the first, mound in North America to be dug using a horizontal stripping technique (Willey and Sabloff 1977:140). This technique exposed entire summits complete with building patterns so that it is possible to reconstruct how the mound appeared at various points in time. Plans of multiple buildings on the various summits were exposed, photographed, and mapped. Crews also kept detailed notes and records of artifact proveniences and other features such as burial and pit features. The collections from the WPA/TVA investigations of Hiwassee Island are curated by the Frank H. McClung Museum at the University of Tennessee.

Lewis and Kneberg's resulting report on Hiwassee Island, published in 1946, was innovative for its time. It was even praised by Walter Taylor (1948:9) as "quite possibly the best archaeological report I have had the occasion to read." Lewis and Kneberg attempted not only to describe the archaeological deposits and artifacts but to link these to patterns of human behavior. The report also provides one of the most comprehensive examples of the use of McKern's Midwest Taxonomic

Method (Willey and Sabloff 1977:112–113). Although certainly dated by today's standards, the Hiwassee Island report was a landmark for its time.

Major traits that Lewis and Kneberg used to distinguish the Hiwassee Island and Dallas phases, and that continue as defining characteristics of the phase today, are shown in Table 7.1. Lewis and Kneberg placed the break between the phases at Levels E-1 and D in the Hiwassee Island mound. This break mainly is based on the appearance of Dallas Decorated pottery in Level D (Lewis and Kneberg 1946:101, Table 19). Although they comment in the report's appendix that "Hiwassee Island is a typical example of multiple occupation where separation of two foci of the Mississippi pattern is difficult" (Lewis and Kneberg 1946:169), they make no explanation for the fact that the architecture does not change from the Hiwassee Island wall-trench style structures to Dallas single-post structures until Level A, the top layer of the mound. They also attribute several large, circular structures or rotundas in Levels E-2 and C to the seventeenth century, even though one rotunda is in a "Hiwassee Island" level and the others are in a "Dallas" level. This kind of discrepancy has plagued and confused subsequent interpretations of the site and hindered an understanding of larger-scale settlement patterns in the region.

The Davis, Hixon, and Dallas Sites

Before beginning the comparison, a review of the data from the Davis (40HA2), Hixon (40HA3), and Dallas (40HA1) sites is needed. The Davis site mound (Table 7.2, Figure 7.1a) dates between A.D. 1100

Table 7.1: Major Traits Used to Distinguish the Hiwassee Island and Dallas Phases		
	Hiwassee Island	Dallas
Architecture	Wall trench	Single post
Pottery	Hiwassee Island Red-Filmed	Dallas Decorated
	Hiwassee Island Red-on-Buff	Strap handles
	Loop handles	
Mortuary practices	Burial in burial mounds (early)	Burial in platform mds. & villages
	Burial in platform mounds and villages (late)	

and 1200, supported by a radiocarbon date of cal A.D. 1160 (intercept) for the second mound stage (Sullivan 2001:4, 2007:92–94). There was little evidence of a village (Figure 7.1b) surrounding the long, ten and one-half feet high, oval mound (Lewis, Lewis, and Sullivan, 1995). The mound began as two small platforms that later were covered to form one mound on which was placed a large, circular building of wall trench construction. After a period of disuse, work on the mound resumed with

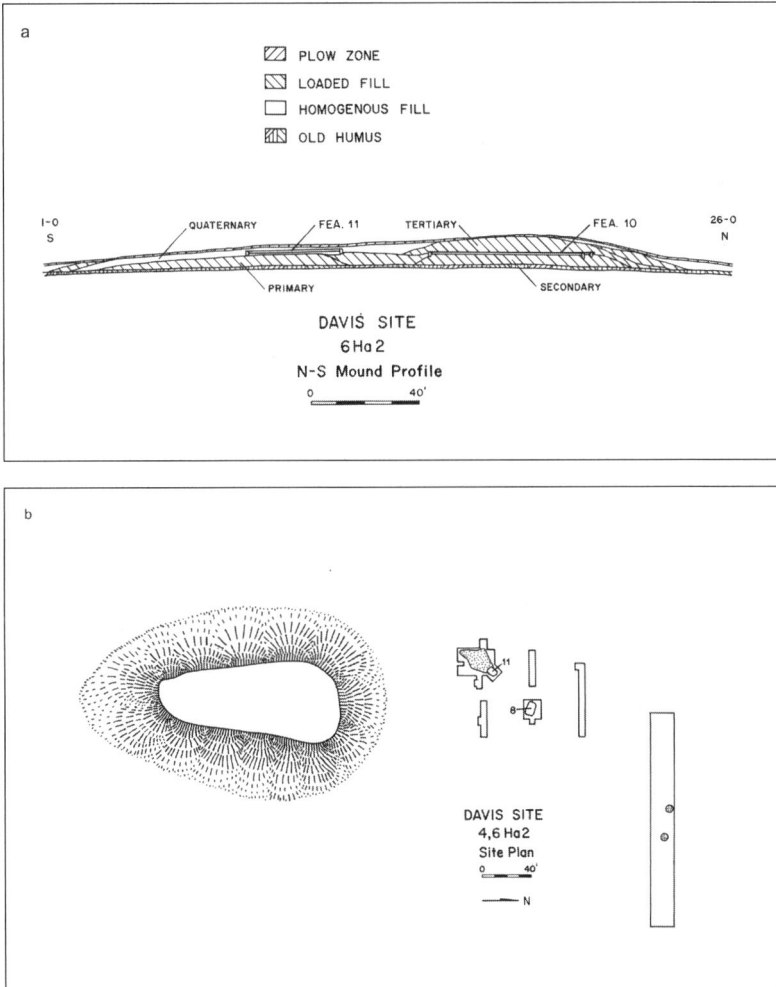

Fig. 7.1. The Davis site (40HA2): (a) mound profile, (b) site plan. Stippled area around structure II is midden deposit. (Lewis, Lewis, and Sullivan 1995, figs. 25.5 and 25.3. Used with permission from the University of Tennessee Press.)

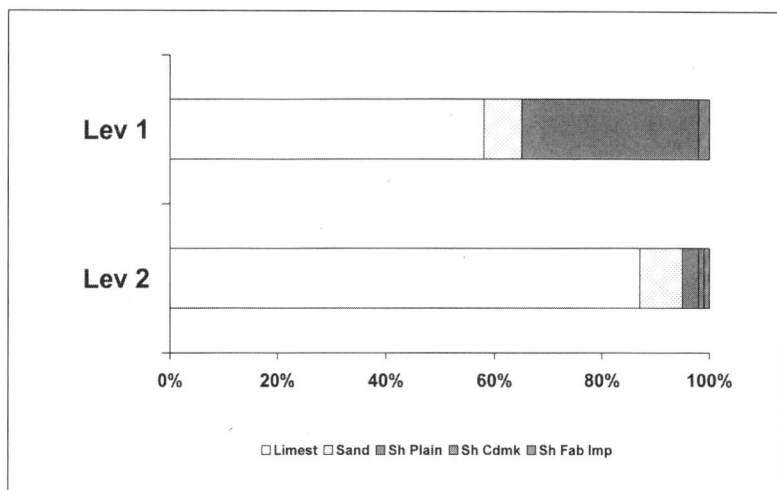

Fig. 7.2. Surface treatments on the rim sherds from the Davis site mound. Level 1 is the uppermost "tertiary" and "quarternary" fills (Fig. 7.1a). Level 2 is the lower "primary" and "secondary" platforms.

the addition of three summits, each topped by one or two rectangular buildings, all with small wall posts, but some with wall trenches and others without. Though the vast majority of the pottery from Davis is of limestone-tempered Woodland types, the shell-tempered ceramics are characteristic of an early Mississippian assemblage: mostly plain, with some fabric impressing and cordmarking. Figure 7.2 shows the distribution of surface treatments on the rim sherds from the mound. No burials definitely could be associated with the mound; several appear to be intrusive. No shell gorgets were found at the site.

The Hixon site mound dates to the thirteenth and early fourteenth centuries (Table 7.2), supported by a date of cal A.D. 1235 (intercept) for Mound Stage B (Sullivan 2001:4, 2007:94–99). This site also included one platform mound (Figures 7.3a and b), about 12 ft high, and little evidence of a village (Lewis, Lewis, and Sullivan 1995). The mound showed numerous construction stages, and several large, wall-trench style buildings existed at the mound location before mound building actually began. Several other wall-trench buildings (designated Level C) were constructed on top of these without markedly adding any elevation. Wall-trench structures predominated in the several summits of mound Stage B. Then, after a period of disuse, mound building resumed with single-post structures built on the new summits of Stage A. The pottery in the Hixon mound also shows a marked change from Stage B to Stage A, as shown in Figure 7.4. Dallas Decorated sherds appear as a significant part of the assemblage (10 percent) in Level A but are completely absent in Levels B and C and below the mound. Hiwassee Island Red-Filmed and Red-on-Buff are most prevalent in Level B. The Hixon mound is well known for the SECC items it contains, such as a monolithic axe, copper headdresses and ornaments, conch vessels, and its sequence of engraved shell gorgets (Sullivan 2001, 2007). Burials with these items occurred throughout the mound, but the most elaborate were in Mound Stage B. The gorgets in the Hixon mound include turkey cock, spider, human

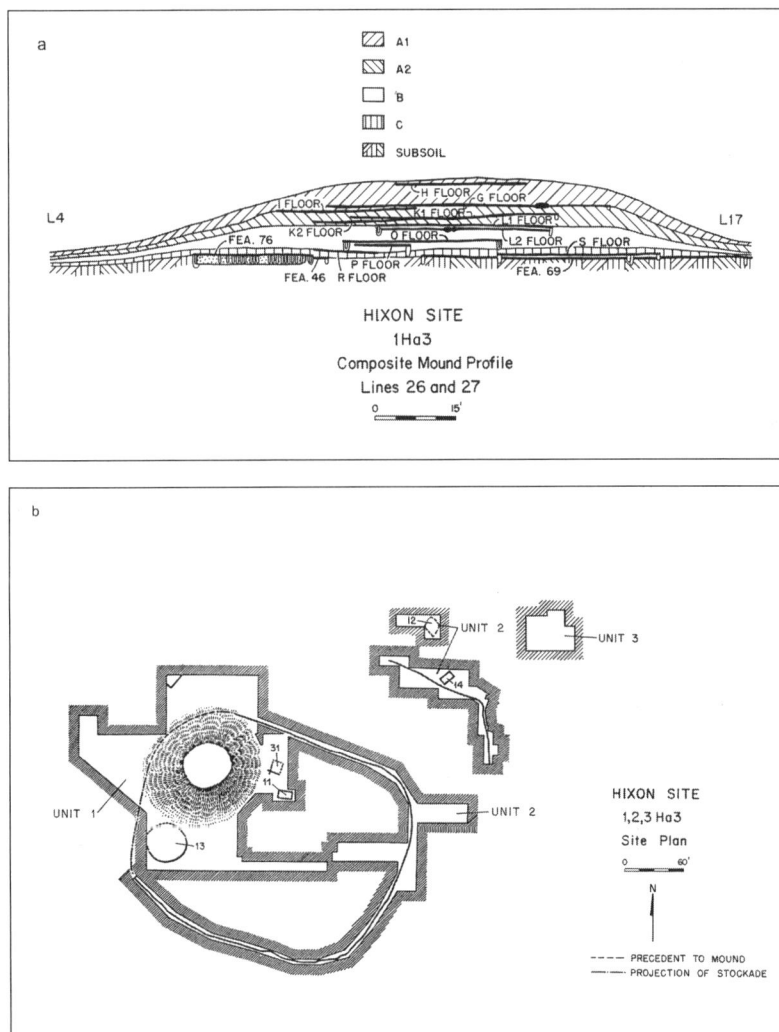

Fig. 7.3. The Hixon site (40HA3): (a) mound profile, (b) site plan. (Lewis, Lewis, and Sullivan 1995, figs. 24.6 and 24.3. Used with permission from the University of Tennessee Press.)

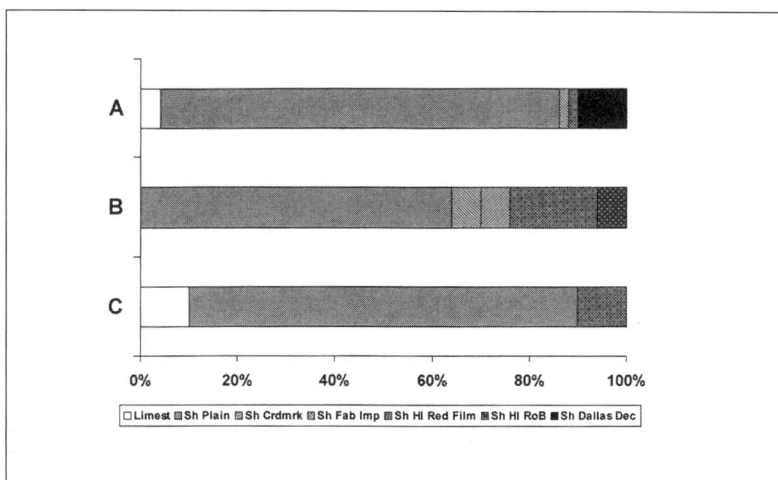

Fig. 7.4. Surface treatments on the rim sherds from the Hixon site mound.

figural ("Big Toco"), and cross and circle motifs. One triskele motif gorget was found in mound Level A2. Muller (1997:373) would place all of these except the triskele in the mid-thirteenth century. He (Muller 1997:371) cites a mid-fifteenth-century date for scalloped triskeles, but the triskele from the Hixon mound is not scalloped, possibly indicating an earlier date given its positioning below several of the other gorget styles.

The Dallas site dates to the late fourteenth and early fifteenth centuries. This palisaded village with a single mound burned shortly after A.D. 1400 (Table 7.2), as evidenced by radiocarbon dates of cal A.D. 1405 (intercept) and cal 1410 (intercept). These dates derive from the burned superstructure from a village dwelling and a wooden burial cover, both associated with the later village midden (Lewis, Lewis, and Sullivan 1995; Sullivan 2001, 2007:99–103). The low mound originally included four levels, but only two survived with intact building patterns (Figure 7.5a). All structures at the Dallas site were of single-post, large-log construction (Figure 7.5b). The ceramic assemblage is relatively uniform from two midden levels recognized at the site, as shown in Figure 7.6 (the mound is contemporary with the upper level). Dallas Decorated sherds are well represented. Burials at the Dallas site occur in both the mound and in and around village structures. Several burials had associated engraved shell gorgets. The gorgets from the Dallas site sequence include circular cross and triskele styles similar to those in the top of the Hixon mound (but the Dallas site triskeles are scalloped) as well as different, later styles

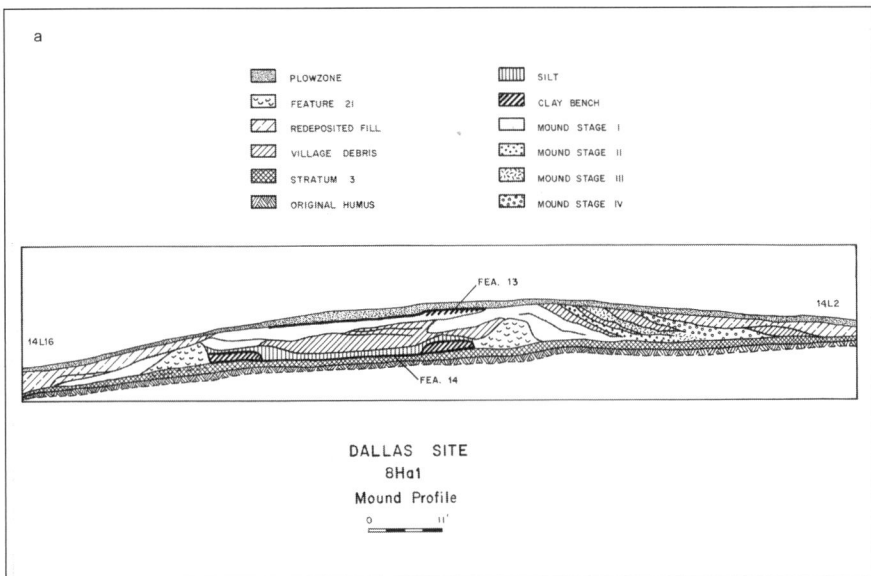

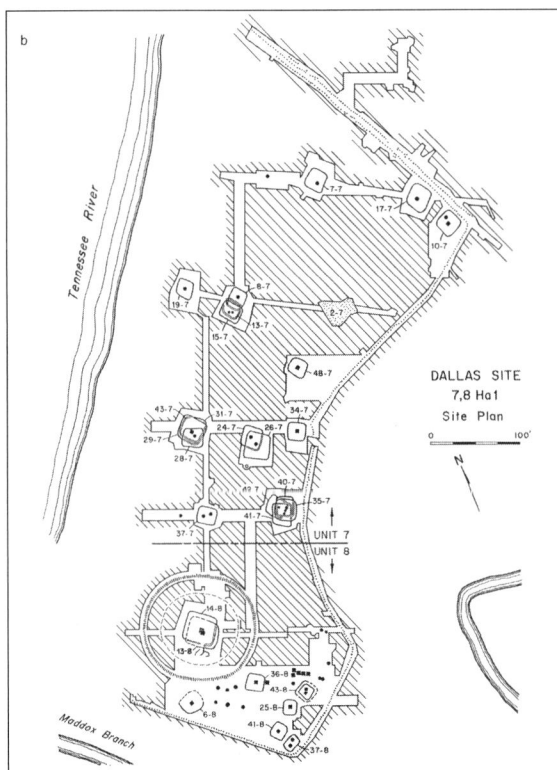

Fig. 7.5. The Dallas site (40HA1): (a) mound profile, (b) site plan. Solid-colored squares and circles are clay hearths. (Lewis, Lewis, and Sullivan 1995, figs. 23.6 and 23.3. Used with permission from the University of Tennessee Press).

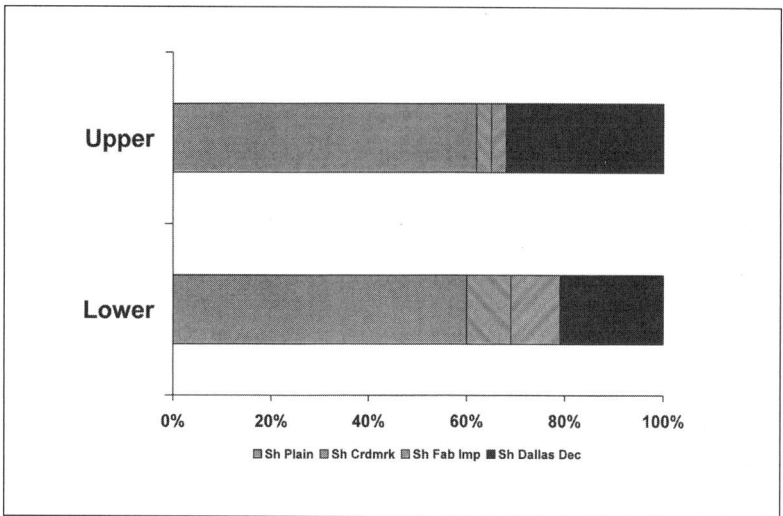

Fig. 7.6. Surface treatments on the rim sherds from the Dallas site midden.

including the "spaghetti men" and fenestrated rattlesnake ("Lick Creek") motifs (Sullivan 2007). Muller (1997:374) places the various rattlesnake styles from the mid–fifteenth century on to the protohistoric period. This dating appears to be somewhat late for the Dallas site fenestrated rattlesnake gorget, given the two early-fifteenth-century dates from the same stratigraphic level.

These three sites thus span and illustrate changes in architecture, pottery, gorget styles, and mortuary practices from the twelfth to the early fifteenth centuries—a period that encompasses the changes from the Hiwassee Island to Dallas phases, as currently defined. With this set of comparative data, it is possible to turn to the Hiwassee Island mound sequence to evaluate its relationship with these trends.

Stratigraphic Sequence of the Hiwassee Island Mound

Before construction of the Hiwassee Island mound began, several large wall-trench buildings occupied the mound location (Figure 7.7a). These were replaced by more wall-trench structures and two small pyramidal mounds, designated Mound Level G (Figure 7.7b). The next level, F, was a single summit that is described as "well-weathered" (Lewis and Kneberg 1946:31). It supported two large, rectangular wall-trench buildings (Figure 7.7c). This architectural sequence is similar to that of the Davis site mound, with its two small pyramids in the initial mound

Table 7.2: Radiocarbon Dates from Chickamauga Basin Sites

Site	Provenience/ Material	Lab Number	Conventional Age	Cal. Date Range (2σ)[a]	Probability (2σ)	Intercept	δ^{13}C
Davis	Md. Fea. 14[b] Wood charcoal	B-127866	900 ± 50 BP	A.D. 1020-1250	95.0%	A.D. 1160	-23.4
Hiwassee Island	Md. Level E-1[d] Bone	B-181800	810 ± 40 BP	A.D. 1170-1280	95.0%	A.D. 1235	-20.5
Hixon	Md. Floor O[c] Wood	B-128375	810 ± 50 BP	A.D. 1155-1285	95.0%	A.D. 1235	-25.0
Dallas	Village Strat. 2[e] Wood	B-128660	560 ± 30 BP	A.D. 1300-1370 A.D. 1380-1430	49.7% 45.7%	A.D. 1405	-22.7
Dallas	Fea. 4[f] Wood charcoal	B-127867	540 ± 60 BP	A.D. 1300-1450	95.0%	A.D. 1410	-28.6

Notes

[a]Stuiver et al., 1998. [b]Dendro, Sample 35; Feature 14, clay-lined hearth just above primary mound. [c]Burial 1HA49 cover.
[d]Bone awl, floor of Building 42. [e]Dendro, Sample 72c; Burial 8HA118 cover. [f]Dendro, Sample 44; part of Feature 7, a burned structure.

phase, followed by a single summit. But at Davis the single summit first supported a large, circular wall-trench building, then two rectangular wall-trench buildings. A circular building, but with small, single posts, first appears in the next level of the Hiwassee Island mound, Level E-2 (Figure 7.7d). The subsequent summit, Level E-1, is quite similar to E-2, with the exception of this building (Figure 7.7e). Both summits had areas of differing heights and supported multiple buildings, most of which were of wall-trench construction. These levels also are the first to include significant percentages of both Hiwassee Island Red-filmed and Hiwassee Island Red-on-Buff pottery (Figure 7.8).[1] The surface of Level E-1 was quite weathered, an observation that Lewis and Kneberg (1946:32) interpret as evidence that this summit "had been in use for a considerable period." A radiocarbon assay on a bone awl from the floor of Building 42 on the summit of Level E-1 (Table 7.2) yielded an early-thirteenth-century date, cal A.D. 1235 (intercept).

Level D is where Lewis and Kneberg placed the split between the Hiwassee Island and Dallas components. The architecture continues mainly to be of wall-trench construction, with multiple buildings on the mound summit, but a much thicker (2 to 7 ft) mantle of earth was added to the mound than was the case for earlier levels (Figure 7.7f). Other changes at Level D are a burial included near the mound's northwest edge and the appearance of Dallas Decorated sherds in the mound fill. Level C is similar to Level D, but the buildings on the summit included large rotundas (Figure 7.7g). Level B is not actually a new construction phase, but instead represents an area of about two feet of fill that was added to the western end of the mound summit (Figure 7.7h). One single-post structure was built after a series of wall-trench buildings occupied this filled area.

Level A is the only mound stage to include only single-post style buildings (Figure 7.7h), and there is evidence that at least some of the buildings on this level burned. There is more than four times the amount of Dallas Decorated pottery in this level as compared with any of the preceding levels (Figure 7.8),[1] and four burials were in pits originating in Level A. None of these burials or the one in Level D was associated with any artifacts of note. The top of the mound contained evidence of a historic period occupation, including several intrusive burials with European trade items. No gorgets were recovered from the Hiwassee Island mound. The only gorget styles that occur at the site are the triskele motif (with scallops) and several mask gorgets, all from the village area.

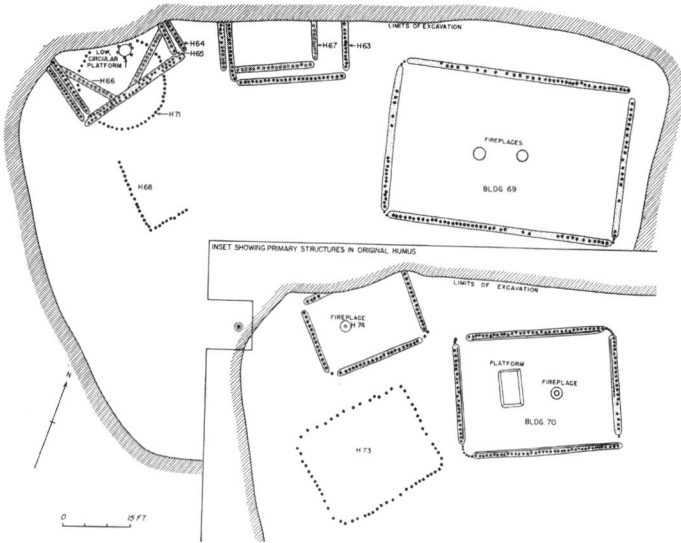

a

LIMITS OF EXCAVATION

LOW,
CIRCULAR
PLATFORM

H64
H65

H66

H67   H63

H71

FIREPLACES

H68

BLDG 69

INSET SHOWING PRIMARY STRUCTURES IN ORIGINAL HUMUS

LIMITS OF EXCAVATION

FIREPLACE
H 74

N

PLATFORM

FIREPLACE

BLDG 70

H 73

0   15 FT.

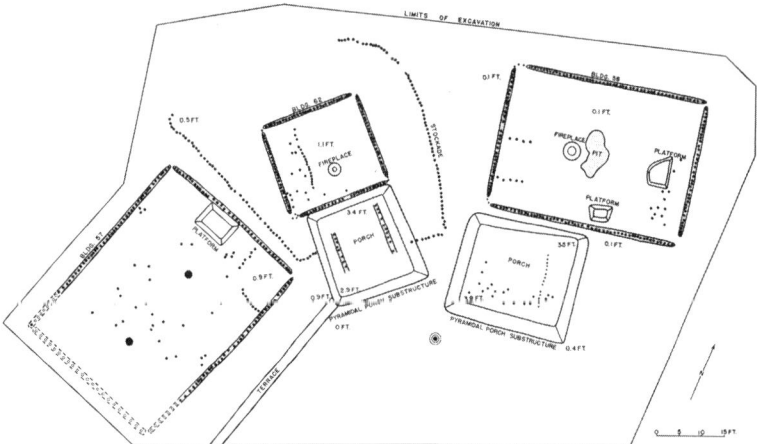

b

LIMITS OF EXCAVATION

0.1 FT.   BLDG 58

0.5 FT.   0.1 FT.

BLDG 62   FIREPLACE   PIT

1.1 FT.   PLATFORM

FIREPLACE

STOCKADE

PLATFORM

BLDG 57

3.4 FT.

PLATFORM   PORCH

0.9 FT.   PORCH   3.8 FT.   0.1 FT.

0.9 FT.   2.9 FT.

PYRAMIDAL PORCH SUBSTRUCTURE

1.8 FT.

0 FT.

TERRACE   PYRAMIDAL PORCH SUBSTRUCTURE 0.4 FT.

0   5   10   15 FT.

c

BLDG. 52

BLDG. 50

BLDG. 51

TEST TRENCH

TEST TRENCH

TEST TRENCH

RAMP

STEPS

4.0 FT.

3.8 FT.

4.5 FT.

3.5 FT.

4.0 FT.

4.7 FT.

4.4 FT.

4.5 FT.

3.3 FT.

0.1 FT.

0.4 FT.

1.2 FT.

0.3 FT.

0.6 FT.

0 FT.

2.1 FT.

3.5 FT.

1.4 FT.

N

0   15 FT.

d

BASAL PERIPHERY OF PHASE E

PERIPHERY OF LEVEL E2

PERIPHERY OF LEVEL E2

TEST TRENCH

TEST TRENCH

TEST TRENCH

BLDG. 48

BLDG. 49

BLDG. 44

FIREPLACE

BLDG. 46

PORCH

PORCH

RAMP

STEPS

TOE HOLDS

3.2 FT.

3.4 FT.

3.7 FT.

4 FT.

5.5 FT.

5.4 FT.

6.3 FT.

6.4 FT.

5.7 FT.

2.3 FT.

3.7 FT.

3.2 FT.

3.8 FT.

8.4 FT.

5.3 FT.

5.4 FT.

6.6 FT.

3.3 FT.

1.3 FT.

0 FT.

0.4 FT.

N

0   15 FT.

e

f

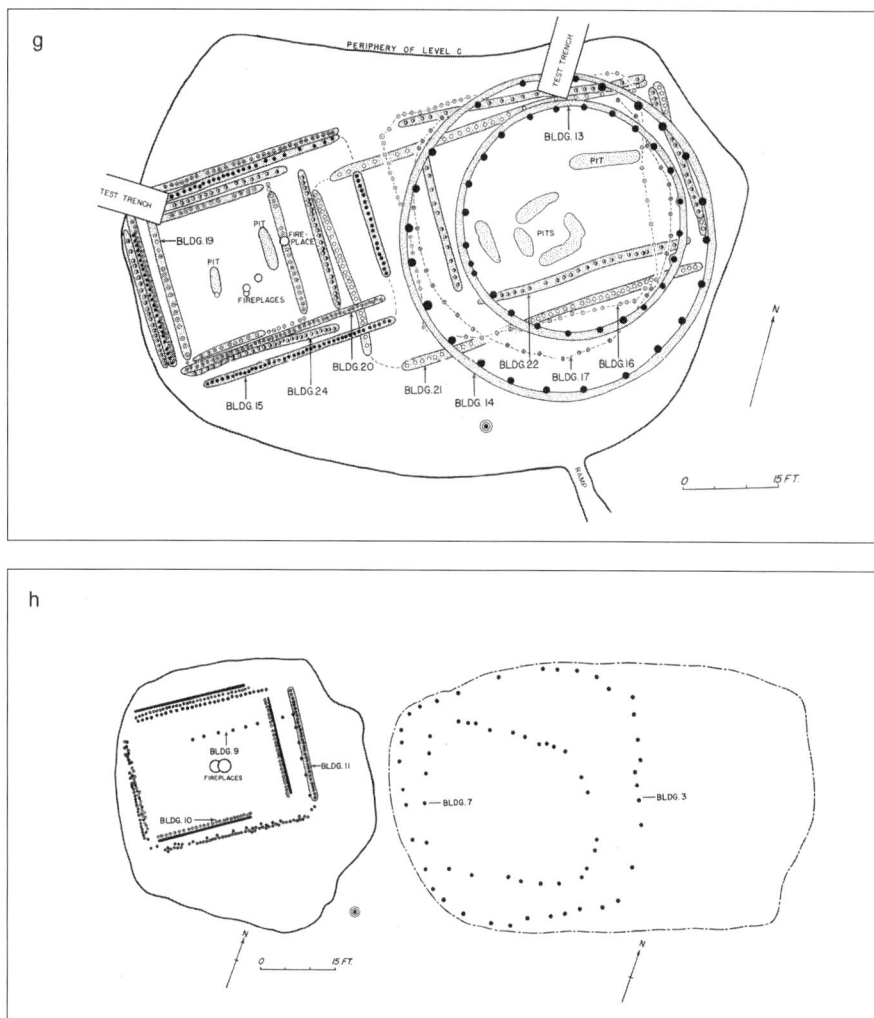

Fig. 7.7. Hiwassee Island site (40MG31) mound sequence: (a) premound, (b) mound Level G, (c) mound Level F, (d) mound Level E-2, (e) mound Level E-1, (f) mound Level D, (g) mound Level C, (h) mound Levels B and A. (Lewis and Kneberg 1946, Plates 13–20. Used with permission from the University of Tennessee Press).

Comparing the Mound Sequences

An initial comparison of the mound sequences is simplest with a limited set of variables. These allow a rough correlation across the sites. I chose several variables typically used to segregate earlier versus later Mississippian components in the Upper Tennessee Valley: architecture—predominately wall trench (early) versus predominately single post (late);

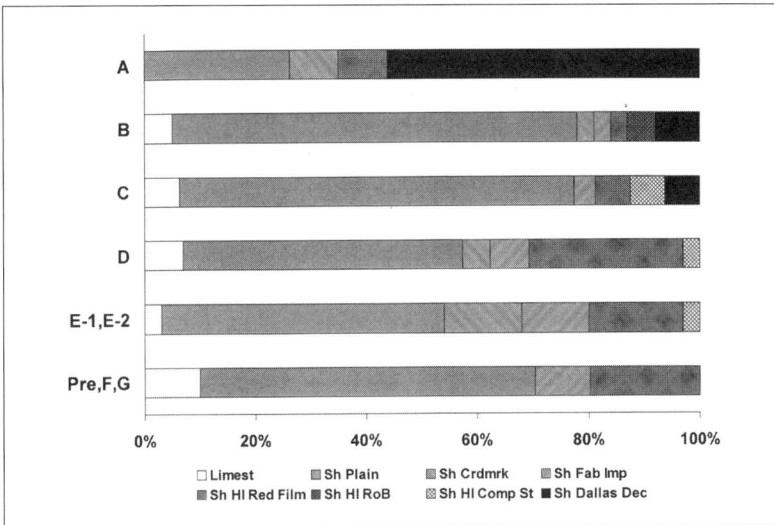

Fig. 7.8. Surface treatments on the rim sherds from the Hiwassee Island mound.

inclusive burials—absent (early) or present (late); and two pottery variables—significant amounts (defined here as 10 or more percent of the rim sherds in a mound stage) of Hiwassee Island Red-filmed pottery (earlier) versus little or none (later); and large versus small amounts versus no Dallas Decorated pottery, the hallmark of the Dallas phase, as represented by the rims. Large amounts are defined here as 20 percent or more of the rim assemblage for a given mound phase, while small is 10 percent or less. Figure 7.9a shows the variables by mound stage for each site, and Figure 7.9b is a rough ordering set against the dates for Davis mound Stage 2, Hixon mound Stage B and Hiwassee Island Mound Level E-1,[2] and the upper midden level at the Dallas site. The figure also indicates the breaks in the mound sequences that the excavators noted as weathered surfaces or periods of abandonment.

We can now fine tune the sequencing by adding additional information about the pottery and the engraved shell gorgets. These reveal two problem areas in the sequencing. The first is that Hixon mound Stage A fits best between Hiwassee Island Levels A and B/C. Both mounds have relatively small amounts of Dallas Decorated pottery at these stages, but the Hiwassee Island mound has wall-trench structures, and those at Hixon are single post. The second problem area is the congruence of Hixon Stage B with Hiwassee Island Levels D and E-1/2. The absolute date from near the base of Hixon Stage B is contemporary with the summit of Hiwassee Island Level E-1 (the uppermost E level). There are

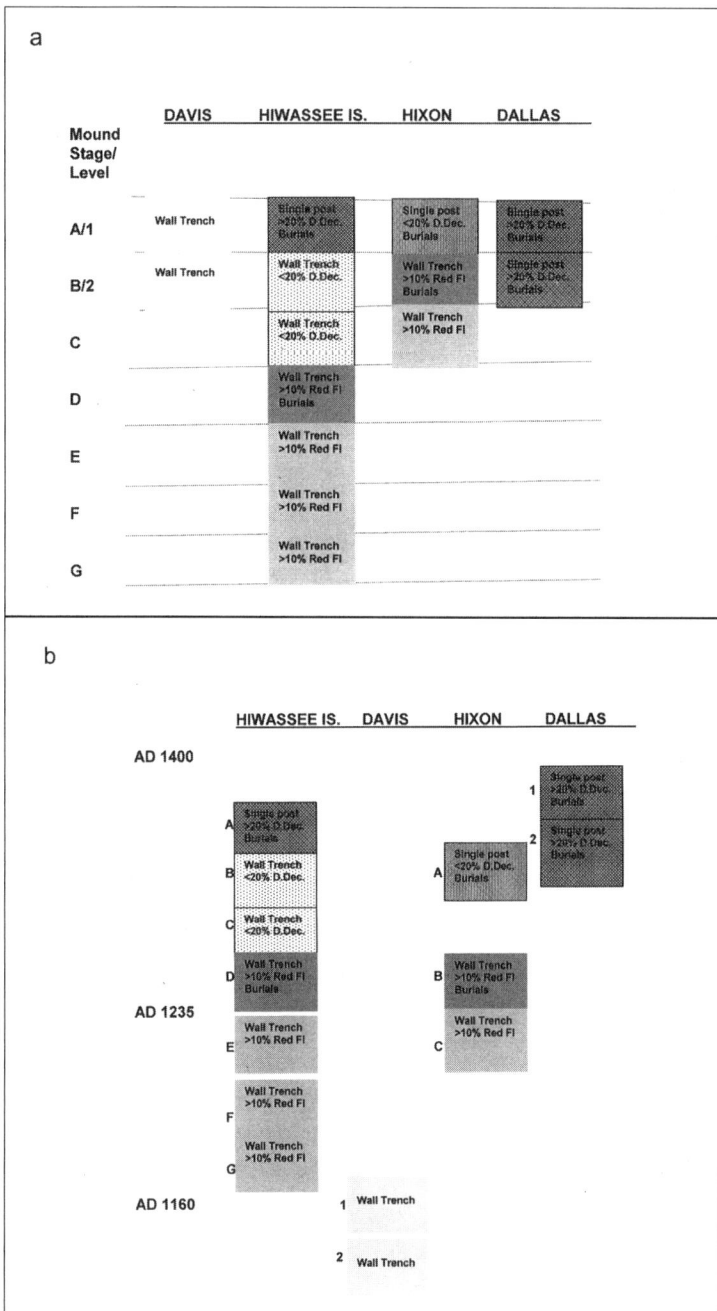

Fig. 7.9. (a) Rough comparison of the Davis, Hixon, Dallas, and Hiwassee Island mound sequences, (b) adjusted arrangement of the mound sequence comparison.

no burials in the Hiwassee Island mound until Level D, but there are numerous burials in Hixon Stage B. No Dallas Decorated sherds appear in the rim sherds from Level D of the Hiwassee Island mound, but these body sherds do occur in small amounts in this level, while there are none in Hixon Stage B. Hixon Stage B appears to fit best between Hiwassee Island Levels D and E.

The gorgets from the sites provide some additional insights to these problem areas. Most of the gorgets in the Hixon sequence are from Mound Stage B. The varieties of gorgets in this part of the mound, including turkey cocks, human figural, and spiders, all are well correlated with the mid–thirteenth century (Muller 1997:373). There are no examples of these types of gorgets from the Hiwassee Island site at all. The engraved shell gorgets found at Hiwassee Island represent only two styles: the scalloped triskele and mask types, and all were with village burials. Triskele gorgets appear with burials in Stage A, the upper part, of the Hixon mound (but as noted above, this one is not scalloped) and with burials found throughout the late-fourteenth/early-fifteenth-century Dallas site midden. Mound Level A at Hiwassee Island is the only mound stage with architecture and pottery that compare favorably with a fourteenth-century or later Dallas component similar to the dated sites. Moving down the mound, Hiwassee Island Levels B/C and D with their wall-trench structures and Dallas Decorated sherds must be earlier than Hixon Stage A, but later than Hixon Stage B. These Hiwassee Island levels must date approximately to the late thirteenth and early fourteenth centuries, when the Hixon mound was abandoned.

On the other hand, Hixon Stage B has no real correlates in the Hiwassee Island sequence. There are no burials below Hiwassee Level D, nor has the suite of SECC objects, including the engraved gorgets, so prevalent in the Hixon mound in Stage B, been found anywhere at Hiwassee Island. A clue to this dilemma is the weathered surface of Hiwassee mound Level E-1. If the Hiwassee mound was not in use for a period of time during the mid–thirteenth century, the sequence falls into place. The elaborate mound summit elevations of Hiwassee Levels E-1 and E-2 date to the late twelfth up to the mid–thirteenth centuries, given the absolute date from Level E-1. This temporal context likely was before the apex of use of the Hixon mound. In essence, the early- to mid-thirteenth-century dating for Level E-1 at the Hiwassee Island mound marks the end of (and a hiatus in) its Hiwassee Island–phase use, while the same time frame marks the beginning of the most intensive and elaborate use of the Hixon mound. Below the E-1 and E-2 levels, the Hiwassee Island

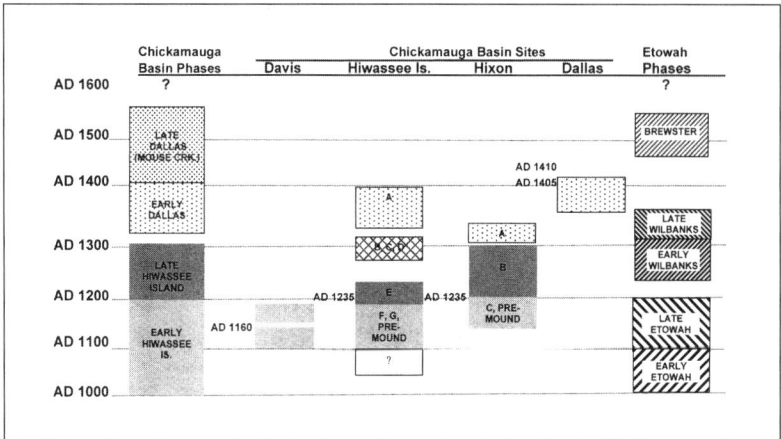

Fig. 7.10. Chronological sequence for Chickamauga basin sites compared with the sequence at the Etowah site.

mound Levels F and G, as well as the premound buildings, appear similar to the Davis site and the lowest level and premound stages at Hixon.

The designs on complicated stamped pottery found at the sites are another line of evidence that supports this interpretation of the dating of the Hiwassee Island and Hixon mounds. Complicated stamped pottery recovered from the Hiwassee Island site is decorated with nested diamond motifs. Although this pottery is found throughout the mound (Lewis and Kneberg 1946:Table 19), only Levels C, D, and E contained rims (Figure 7.8). The designs correspond to those of the late Etowah phase (A.D. 1100–1200) in northern Georgia (personal communication, David Hally, Marvin Smith, and Mark Williams 2003; also see King 2003:30–31; Hally and Langford 1988). Complicated stamped pottery recovered from the Hixon site is decorated with concentric circles and figure eights. Most is grit-tempered, with a few shell-tempered sherds. This pottery dates to the Savannah Period (A.D. 1200–1375) in northern Georgia (King 2003:30–31; Hally and Langford 1988). Lewis and Kneberg incorrectly identified this pottery as Overhill Cherokee pottery (Lewis, Lewis, and Sullivan 1995:Table 24.5).

Results and Implications of the Comparison

Figure 7.10 is an adjusted arrangement of the comparative graph in Figure 7.9b, set against regional chronologies. The revised interpretation of the Hiwassee Island mound sequence suggests several new insights to regional prehistory, as well as offers solutions to some long-standing puzzles about the site itself. First, Hiwassee Island no longer is anomalous when we recognize that there are substantial gaps in the mound sequence. One of the most interesting aspects of the revised sequence is the truncation of the Hiwassee Island phase, as currently defined, at the Hiwassee Island site itself. As represented in the Hiwassee Island mound sequence, the Hiwassee Island phase is confined to the twelfth century and the first part of the thirteenth. The predominant use of wall-trench structures, and a lack of inclusive burials, suggesting use of Hamilton burial mounds at this time, characterizes this period. It also predates characteristic SECC items, such as copper headdresses and ornaments, and marine shell vessels and gorgets, which later become regular features of mound assemblages. And these levels were constructed well before the appearance of Dallas Decorated pottery.

In contrast, the Hixon site, with its impressive array of SECC materials, appears to represent the thirteenth century in the Chickamauga Basin better than any other site in the comparison, including Hiwassee Island. The Hixon mound, as compared with the Davis mound and the earlier, lower levels of the Hiwassee Island mound, suggests dramatic changes during the thirteenth century, the late Hiwassee Island phase, in the Chickamauga Basin. The shift in mortuary practices, from use of Hamilton burial mounds to interments in platform mounds, the marked increase in objects with SECC motifs and in Hiwassee Island Red Filmed and Red-on-Buff pottery, and the wall-trench architecture all predate Dallas Decorated pottery.

Another mystery solved by the reinterpreted sequence for the Hiwassee Island mound is the incongruence of the cooccurring wall-trench structures and Dallas Decorated pottery in a mound that for years has been interpreted as a "classic" example of Dallas "culture." The cooccurrence of the relatively earlier architecture with small amounts of the later pottery makes sense if mound Levels B, C, and D date to the late thirteenth and early fourteenth centuries—the arbitrary division between the Hiwassee Island and the Dallas phases. These levels are well positioned to date to this time as they underlie mound Level A and lie above mound Level E-1 and the subsequent mid–thirteenth century hiatus in use. Level A is the only level in the Hiwassee Island mound that compares favorably with the architecture, pottery, and mortuary practices of Dallas components that date to fourteenth and fifteenth centuries, as exemplified by the Dallas site. The scalloped triskele gorgets in the village deposits also are congruent with the Level A components. The material culture changes represented in Levels B, C, and D of the

Hiwassee Island mound require more scrutiny and consideration of how such changes may fit into a larger regional picture.

The Thirteenth Century in the Chickamauga Basin

A bisection of the three-century long Hiwassee Island phase adds resolution to our understanding of change during the Mississippian period in the Chickamauga Basin as well as the larger region. Based on the data from the Chickamauga sites, there was only modest and continuous change during the twelfth-century, early Hiwassee Island phase from what had transpired in the tenth- and eleventh–century Martin Farm Phase. Platform mound construction became more elaborate, including multiple summits with multiple buildings, shell tempering became almost exclusive in pottery, Hamilton mounds were used for burial, and subsistence practices emphasized a diversity of local flora and fauna as well as increasing use of maize, and likely related population growth. Motifs on complicated stamped pottery from this time suggest interactions with groups in what is now northern Georgia.

In contrast, based on the Hixon site, the thirteenth century was a time of marked change, characterized by a shift from use of Hamilton burial mounds to interments in platform mounds; a marked increase in objects with SECC motifs, including engraved shell gorgets, monolithic axes, and copper ornaments and headdresses; absence of Dallas Decorated pottery and a marked increase in Hiwassee Island Red Filmed and Red-on-Buff sherds; probable predominance of wall trench architecture; and the possibility of a dispersed settlement pattern with ceremonial "precincts," such as Hixon, that lacked a nucleated village around the mound. Although evidence of two post and trench-construction palisades was found at Hixon, one was an early feature that predated part of the mound and only a small portion of the other was investigated about 100 ft away. Four small, rectangular structures (<300 ft^2) and one small, circular structure were the only buildings found at the site other than those in or under the mound.

The nature of interregional relationships at this time is intriguing and suggests probable intensified relationships with other regions, as evidenced by trade items (especially marine shell) and iconography. The presence at Hixon of complicated stamped pottery identical to that dating to the thirteenth century in northern Georgia also adds support for interaction between these two areas. Trade in marine shell is evidenced by tens of thousands of shell beads in necklaces, bracelets, and leg bands associated with mound burials. King (2003:123–125) suggests that Hixon was on an exchange corridor for SECC items that connected the Tennessee Valley and Florida, and that included the Etowah site in

Georgia as well as the Citico site (40HA65), the only other investigated site in the Chickamauga Basin that may well have a thirteenth-century occupation of note. Citico has produced a wealth of SECC objects, but we know almost nothing about the site plan (Hatch 1976).

The contemporaneity of Hixon with the Wilbanks phases at the Etowah site suggests that the changes at Hixon were related to developments at Etowah during this time. The mortuary practices in the Hixon mound are reminiscent of those at Etowah Mound C and suggest a shift in patterns of social and political leadership. A change in Hixon Mound Stage B (Floors P and O) from single, preeminent adult female burials to pairs of preeminent burials consisting of an adult male and female (Stage B, Floor L, and Stage A, Floors K and I) may well document a new political order (Sullivan and Humpf 2001; Hatch 1974). Use of the Hixon mound appears to have fizzled out, rather than a dramatic ending such as the sacking of Mound C at Etowah (King 2003:78–81; Brain and Phillips 1996). Use of the Hixon mound may have ceased before Etowah was attacked, but use of the Hiwassee Island mound resumed and continued for some years after Hixon collapsed, as evidenced by the amounts of Dallas Decorated pottery in Hiwassee Island Mound A.

The changes of the succeeding, fourteenth-century Dallas phase were again quite dramatic: architectural styles shifted to exclusively large-log, single-post structures; new pottery styles appeared including new decorative techniques such as incising, strap handles, and effigy motifs (Dallas Decorated); mounds became less elaborate with single summits supporting single large buildings; nucleated and palisaded villages surrounded the mounds; and burials in and around village houses as well as in platform mounds. Burning of the Dallas site at the turn of the fifteenth century ended the use sequence for these sites until the historic period, when Native American burials again were interred in the Hiwassee Island mound (see Mann 2005) and infant burials from white settlers were interred in the Hixon mound.

These new time constructs allow us to place the Hiwassee Island and nearby sites into a dynamic landscape. The patterns of use and disuse of mound centers in the Chickamauga Basin show numerous early, small mound centers, followed by consolidation at fewer centers, subsequent reuse of some older mounds, and, finally, large, new villages with small mounds. There are other sites yet to be added to this scenario.

Though coarse-grained, this comparative analysis nonetheless demonstrates that it is not only possible but essential to use older collections, even with their limitations, to reevaluate "passed-down wisdom" and to unravel problems. Armed with more and better information than was available to the original investigators, new investigations can lead to new and refined interpretations. Quite simply, the reason a site now is considered a "classic" is because its original interpretation was highly influential. Making changes to those influential interpretations can only lead to significant reinterpretations with far-reaching implications. Perhaps eminent mound sites should even be routinely reevaluated every few decades. Such a "maintenance program" likely would improve our interpretations as much as new, major excavations.

Acknowledgments

Thanks to Sissel Schroeder who invited me to participate in a symposium entitled "Emblems of American Archaeology's Past: Eminent Mound Sites of the Eastern Woodlands Revisited" at the sixty-eighth annual meeting of the Society for American Archaeology in Milwaukee in 2003. An earlier version of this paper was presented there. The Hiwassee Island site collections, as well as those from other sites in the Chickamauga Basin, are curated by the Frank H. McClung Museum at the University of Tennessee.

Notes

1. Figure 7.8 differs somewhat from Lewis and Kneberg's (1946: 101) Table 19 because only rim sherds that currently exist in the collections at the Frank H. McClung Museum were counted, rather than the total sherd counts. The existing rims were used to make the Hiwassee Island chart comparable with those constructed for the Davis, Hixon, and Dallas sites.

2. The calibrated intercept dates for both of these mound layers are the same, A.D. 1235.

References Cited

ANDERSON, DAVID G.

1994a   *The Savannah River Chiefdoms: Political Change in the Late Prehistoric Southeast.* University of Alabama Press, Tuscaloosa.

1994b   Factional Competition and the Political Evolution of Mississippian Chiefdoms in the Southeastern United States. In *Factional Competition in the New World,* edited by Elizabeth M. Brumfiel and John W. Fox, pp. 61–76. Cambridge University Press, Cambridge.

BRAIN, JEFFREY P., AND PHILLIP PHILLIPS

1996   *Shell Gorgets: Styles of the Late Prehistoric and Protohistoric Southeast.* Peabody Museum of Archaeology and Ethnology, Harvard University, Cambridge, MA.

FAIRBANKS, CHARLES H.
1970   What Do We Know Now That We Did Not Know in 1938? *Southeastern Archaeological Conference Bulletin* 13:40–45.

FAULKNER, CHARLES
1967   Tennessee Radiocarbon Dates. *Tennessee Anthropologist* 23:12–30.
1972   The Mississippian-Woodland Transition in the Eastern Tennessee Valley. *Southeastern Archaeological Conference Bulletin* 15:38–45.

HALLY, DAVID J.
1996   Platform-Mound Construction and the Instability of Mississippian Chiefdoms In *Political Structure and Change in the Prehistoric Southeastern United States,* edited by J.F. Scarry, pp. 92–127. The Ripley P. Bullen Series, Florida Museum of Natural History, University Press of Florida, Gainesville.

HALLY, DAVID J., AND JAMES B. LANGFORD, JR.
1988   *Mississippi Period Archaeology of the Georgia Valley and Ridge Province.* Report No. 25 University of Georgia, Laboratory of Archaeology Series, Athens.

HALLY, DAVID J., MARVIN T. SMITH, AND JAMES B. LANGFORD, JR.
1990   The Archaeological Reality of de Soto's Coosa. In *Columbian Consequences II: Archaeological and Historical Perspectives on the Spanish Borderlands East,* edited by David H. Thomas, pp.121–138. Smithsonian Institution Press, Washington, DC.

HATCH, JAMES W.
1974   Social Dimensions of Dallas Mortuary Practices. M.A. thesis, The Pennsylvania State University, University.
1976   The Citico site: A Synthesis. *Tennessee Anthropologist* 1:74–103.

HUDSON, CHARLES M., MARVIN T. SMITH, DAVID J. HALLY, RICHARD POLHEMUS, AND CHESTER DEPRATTER
1985   Coosa: A Chiefdom in the Sixteenth-century Southeastern United States. *American Antiquity* 50:723–737.

JENNINGS, JESSE
1994   *Accidental Archaeologist: Memoirs of Jesse D. Jennings.* University of Utah Press, Salt Lake City.

KIMBALL, LARRY R. (EDITOR)
1985   *The 1977 Archaeological Survey: An Overall Assessment of the Archaeological Resources of the Tellico Reservoir.* Report of Investigations No. 40. Tellico Archaeological Survey Report No. 1, Department of Anthropology, University of Tennessee, Knoxville.

KING, ADAM
2001   Long-term Histories of Mississippian Centers: The Development Sequence of Etowah and Its Comparison to Moundville and Cahokia. *Southeastern Archaeology* 20(1):1–17.

2003   *Etowah: The Political History of a Chiefdom Capital.* The
        University of Alabama Press, Tuscaloosa.
2007   Mound C and the Southeastern Ceremonial Complex in the
        History of the Etowah Site. In *Southeastern Ceremonial Complex:
        Chronology, Content, and Context,* edited by Adam King, pp.
        107–133. University of Alabama Press, Tuscaloosa.

LEWIS, THOMAS M. N.
1935   The Lure of Prehistoric Tennessee. *Journal of the Tennessee
        Academy of Science* 10(3):153–159.
1937   Annotations Pertaining to Prehistoric Research in Tennessee.
        University of Tennessee Record, University of Tennessee Press,
        Knoxville.

LEWIS, THOMAS M. N., AND MADELINE KNEBERG
1946   *Hiwassee Island: An Archaeological Account of Four Tennessee
        Indian Peoples.* University of Tennessee Press, Knoxville.

LEWIS, THOMAS M. N., MADELINE KNEBERG LEWIS, AND LYNNE P.
SULLIVAN (COMPILER AND EDITOR)
1995   *The Prehistory of the Chickamauga Basin in Tennessee,* 2 vols.
        University of Tennessee Press, Knoxville.

MANN, ROB
2005   Intruding on the Past: The Reuse of Ancient Earthen Mounds by
        Native Americans. *Southeastern Archaeology* 24(1):1–10.

MULLER, JON
1997   *Mississippian Political Economy.* Plenum Press, NY.

SCHROEDL, GERALD F.
1973   Radiocarbon Dates from Three Burial Mounds at the McDonald
        Site in East Tennessee. *Tennessee Archaeologist* 29:3–11.
1978   *Excavations of the Leuty and McDonald Site Mounds.* Report of
        Investigations No. 22, Department of Anthropology, University of
        Tennessee, Knoxville.

SCHROEDL, GERALD F., C. CLIFFORD BOYD, JR., AND R. P. STEPHEN
DAVIS, JR.
1990   Explaining Mississippian Origins in East Tennessee. In *The
        Mississippian Emergence,* edited by B. D. Smith, pp. 175–196.
        Smithsonian Institution Press, Washington, DC.

SCHROEDL, GERALD F., R. P. STEPHEN DAVIS, JR., AND C. CLIFFORD
BOYD, JR.
1985   *Archaeological Contexts and Assemblages at Martin Farm.* Report
        of Investigations No. 39, Department of Anthropology, University of
        Tennessee, Knoxville.

SMITH, MARVIN T.
2000   Coosa: The Rise and Fall of a Southeastern Mississippian Chiefdom. University Press of Florida, Gainesville.

STUIVER, MINZE, PAULA J. REIMER, EDOUARD BARD, J. WARREN BECK, G. S. BURR, KONRAD A. HUGHEN, BERND KROMER, GERRY MCCORMAC, JOHANNES VAN DER PLICHT, AND MARCO SPURK
1998   INTCAL98 Radiocarbon Age Calibration, 24,000–0 cal BP. Radiocarbon 40(3): 1041–1083.

SULLIVAN, LYNNE P.
1999   Madeline D. Kneberg Lewis: Leading Lady of Tennessee Archaeology. In Grit-Tempered: Early Women Archaeologists in the Southeastern United States, edited by Nancy M. White, L. P. Sullivan, and Rochelle Marrinan, pp. 57–91. Florida Museum of Natural History, Ripley P. Bullen Series, University Press of Florida, Gainesville.

2001   Dates for Shell Gorgets and the Southeastern Ceremonial Complex in the Chickamauga Basin of Southeastern Tennessee. Research Notes, No. 19. Frank H. McClung Museum, University of Tennessee, Knoxville.

2007   Dating the Southeastern Ceremonial Complex in Eastern Tennessee. In Southeastern Ceremonial Complex: Chronology, Content, Context, edited by Adam King, pp. 88–106. University of Alabama Press, Tuscaloosa.

SULLIVAN, LYNNE P., AND DOROTHY HUMPF
2001   Realm to Realm: A Comparison of Etowah and Mississippian Eastern Tennessee. Paper presented in the symposium "The Lost Realm of Itaba," organized by Adam King. 66th Annual Meeting of the Society for American Archaeology, New Orleans.

TAYLOR, WALTER W.
1948   A Study of Archeology. Originally published as Memoir 69, American Anthropologist 50(3), pt. 2. Reprinted by the Center for Archaeological Investigations, with foreword by Patty Jo Watson, Southern Illinois University, Carbondale, 1983.

WILLEY, GORDON R., AND JEREMY SABLOFF
1977   A History of American Archaeology, 3rd edition. W. H. Freeman, San Francisco, 1993.

WILLIAMS, MARK, AND GARY SHAPIRO (EDITORS)
1990   Lamar Archaeology: Mississippian Chiefdoms in the Deep South. University of Alabama Press, Tuscaloosa.

PART IV
CURRENT RESEARCH ENDEAVORS IN THE VALLEY

8
Prehistoric Cave Art Sites and TVA: An Update on Painted Bluff, 1st, and 18th Unnamed Caves

Jan F. Simek, Sarah A. Blankenship, and Alan Cressler

THE TENNESSEE VALLEY AUTHORITY (TVA) has long been a vital steward of archaeological resources in the Tennessee River Valley, both in the early days of river control and in today's era of power generation, flood control, and resource management. The current archaeologists of TVA, led at the time of this writing by J. Bennett Graham, are among the very best and most dedicated archaeological resource managers in the country. Ever since our senior author, Jan F. Simek, began working with TVA some years ago, it has been clear that a primary focus of TVA archaeology is to protect and preserve the record, not simply to ensure compliance with the law. In this the TVA has been one of the strongest stewards of the archaeological record in the public sector.

Our involvement with TVA archaeology and our work, more generally, in the study of cave art in North America are closely linked. In 1993 TVA approached Simek about a survey project on a large TVA reservoir near Knoxville. While the Southeast was not his area of expertise, there were students in the Department of Anthropology at the University of Tennessee who were interested in working on the area, so Simek took on the project with senior graduate students as lead personnel. Field crews were instructed routinely to look in caves, as Charles H. Faulkner of the University had completed his studies of the prehistoric cave art in Mud

Glyph Cave a short decade before (Faulkner, Deane, and Earnest, Jr., 1984; Faulkner 1986; Faulkner 1988), and this TVA project was to be carried out not far from that important site. In 1994 a mud-glyph art site was discovered, one we came to designate as "1st Unnamed Cave" (Simek et al. 1997). Thus TVA began its management of prehistoric cave art. Since the discovery of 1st Unnamed Cave, a large number of new cave-art sites have been discovered (more than 60 cave-art sites are now known in the Southeast) and a number that were shown to Faulkner based on his work at Mud Glyph Cave have been revisited and analyzed. Two cave sites lie on TVA-managed lands, and we have had the opportunity to undertake extensive studies of both as part of TVA's inventory assessments and their effort to develop management strategies for archaeological resources. One site is 1st Unnamed Cave, which has entailed an ongoing and ever-more-complicated documentation effort since its discovery (Simek et al. 1997; Simek, Frankenberg, and Faulkner 2001; Faulkner and Simek 1996a, 1996b, 2001). The other site is one we refer to as "18th Unnamed Cave," a discovery made by avocational cavers in north Alabama and the subject of a documentation and protection project that the University of Tennessee undertook in 1998, partly under contract, partly in collaboration with TVA. Both of these examples exhibit the complexity and beauty of southeastern prehistoric cave art and warrant description on that level alone.

In addition to cave art, TVA has for many years managed a number of open-air prehistoric rock-art sites along the shores of the Tennessee River and its tributaries. These open-air sites, which include painted pictographs and engraved petroglyphs, are quite variable, comprising in some cases a few small figures and in others an elaborate array of images (Cambron and Waters 1959; Hensen and Martz 1979; Hensen 1996). Perhaps the most extensive of these open-air localities is "Painted Bluff" in northern Alabama. First reported in the 1960s, the site has seen numerous episodes of documentation by TVA-sponsored archaeologists as part of management activities. Despite its great artistic import, however, Painted Bluff has never received the attention it deserves as a rock-art locality; it has been our great fortune over the past few years to be able to undertake detailed work at the site with significant TVA logistical and financial support. In our estimation Painted Bluff is one of the most impressive and important rock-art sites in the Southeast.

In all of these cases, TVA not only inventoried the sites but also protected them, and these bluffs and caves exemplify the important role TVA continues to play in conserving the prehistoric record of ancient southeastern cultures. Brief descriptions of our TVA-sponsored research at all three sites follows, as well as a history of discovery and work at the sites, the prehistoric art they contain, their archaeological context, and measures TVA has taken to protect these valuable prehistoric resources. The TVA helps maintain our cultural and natural heritage in the region, including the variability and beauty of prehistoric rock art in the Tennessee River Valley.

1st Unnamed Cave, Tennessee

In 1993 TVA sponsored an inventory survey of a large dam reservation near Knoxville, Tennessee, and during that survey, Todd Ahlman, then a graduate student at the University of Tennessee, Knoxville, and his field crew discovered prehistoric mud-glyph art in a small subterranean stream passage now called "1st Unnamed Cave" (Simek et al. 1997; Simek 1996; Faulkner and Simek 1996a; Simek, Frankenberg, and Faulkner 2001). The contract for that survey was signed with the University of Tennessee, and the survey was carried out by the Department of Anthropology at the Knoxville campus. This was not the first coverage of the reservoir. The university had undertaken previous investigations for TVA on the property and had located a number of archaeological sites in the area. The mouth of 1st Unnamed Cave had been discovered in the earlier survey, but it had not been entered to look for archaeological contents. Thus the archaeological import of 1st Unnamed Cave was not recognized until 1994, when Ahlman and his crew explored the main passage of the cave, discovered some of the mud glyphs the cave contains, and excavated a shovel test pit in the vestibule to determine if stratified archaeological deposits were present in the entrance sediments. Since that time, we have visited the cave frequently, examining and documenting the mud glyph assemblage, mapping the cave and the glyph distribution, excavating the vestibule sediments, which are eroding at a rapid rate, studying the preservation environment of the cave, and installing a large protective gate in the entrance. There have been several interim reports on the cave (Faulkner and Simek 1996a; Simek et al. 1997), but the ongoing work has caused a continual reevaluation of our view of the cave and its assemblages. Thus this chapter reflects our current understanding, one that may not change too much as we prepare a final monograph publication on the site.

1st Unnamed Cave is located on the south side of the Tennessee River. A single central passageway extends several hundred meters into the Knox limestone formation, a member of the Mississippian group, from the cave mouth. Lateral galleries join the central one at several points along its length, with a shallow stream flowing out of one of these toward the cave entrance. About halfway into the cave, an intermittent sump suggests an underwater connection with lower karst features that are inaccessible today. The stream's seasonal flow surges have eroded the floor of the cave, and over the years there has been frequent and sometimes dramatic remodeling of the alluvium on the cave floor, with braided stream deposits and significant particle sorting characteristic of the depositional events. At least until the present day, interior fluvial activity has not obviously damaged the mud glyphs on the cave walls and ceilings. It now seems likely that the assemblage that exists today closely mirrors what was produced in the past.

The initial report on 1st Unnamed Cave, in a 1997 *Southeastern Archaeology* paper (Simek et al. 1997), documented chronological evidence of two kinds from the cave. A small series of ceramic sherds from shovel test pits at the cave mouth indicated Late Woodland and Late Mississippian occupations in the vestibule. More extensive excavations in the mouth have supported that finding. In 1997 a single C^{14} age determination from river cane torch charcoal inside the cave calibrated to between 1480 and 1680 A.D. Now three C^{14} ages from the interior passages (Table 8.1) corroborate the Late Mississippian age of the site.

The 1997 report documents some 42 mud glyphs scattered through the cave, and these were organized into four discrete areas within the cave (see Simek et al. 1997), referred to as Groups 1–4. There were differences in the disposition of glyphs depending on the group concerned: Group 1 glyphs, closest to the cave opening, were only on the ceiling; Groups 2 and 3 were positioned only on the south wall of the cave; Group 4 images were located on both walls of the cave. From this it seemed likely that there was organization and content not only in the individual images that showed pictures of serpents, birds, turtles, humans, and so on, but

Table 8.1: Radiocarbon Age Determinations from Sites Described in Text		
Site	Age	Calibrated Date
1st Unnamed Cave, TN	380 + 50	A.D. 1430–1640
	260 + 50	A.D. 1480–1680
	120 + 50	A.D. 1660–1950
18th Unnamed Cave, AL	800 + 60	A.D. 1155–1295
Painted Bluff, AL	570 + 40	A.D. 1300–1440

also in the composition of the assemblage through the cave itself. A similar observation was also made a decade earlier by Faulkner (Faulkner 1986) for the nearby Mud Glyph Cave. This implies that 1st Unnamed Cave was decorated at a single time according to a plan and that the symbolic content of the art was embedded both in single images and in the assemblage as a whole. Interpretation was problematic at best and, frankly, still is.

Since 1997 exploration and mapping of 1st Unnamed Cave has continued, and the number of glyphs, as well as their complexity and disposition, has changed with the augmentation of the assemblage. Today there are 63 glyphs in the recorded inventory. Though there were four spatial groups defined in 1997, there are eight defined today. Some of the glyphs are isolates, which explains their absence from earlier examinations. Some new groups are complex, but located in areas not examined closely before. Some are very difficult to see and require perfect conditions of surface humidity or particular light sources to detect. All of this to say that documenting a southeastern cave art site is a complicated business, requiring concerted and repeated efforts over time and varied conditions to be considered complete.

A number of new individual glyphs have changed our view of both the nature and the scale of drawings in 1st Unnamed Cave. Dominant among the new images are meandering lines, and short, isolated line segments (both impossible to interpret in representational terms), along with identifiable serpent effigies. To be classified as a serpent, a glyph must have a long bending or coiling body. Serpents usually have a well-defined head that differs from the body in form or production so as to set it apart clearly as a different element of the picture. In several cases images classified as serpents have strange characteristics that are not usually associated with snakes, such as wings and horns. Wings can serve to define the heads of serpents. Several of the newly identified serpent effigies are actually reidentified images that had been interpreted differently before. One of these is a "woodpecker" glyph carved with a single sharp line; originally this was interpreted as an avian image positioned close to a panel of meandering lines, but closer examination has revealed that the body of the bird connects to long meanders that form a serpentine body (Figure 8.1). Now there are no avian images catalogued from 1st Unnamed Cave, an important fact given the frequency of birds in other southeastern cave art sites.

Another serpent image is the largest one known from a southeastern cave, at over 5 m in overall length. This image is positioned directly

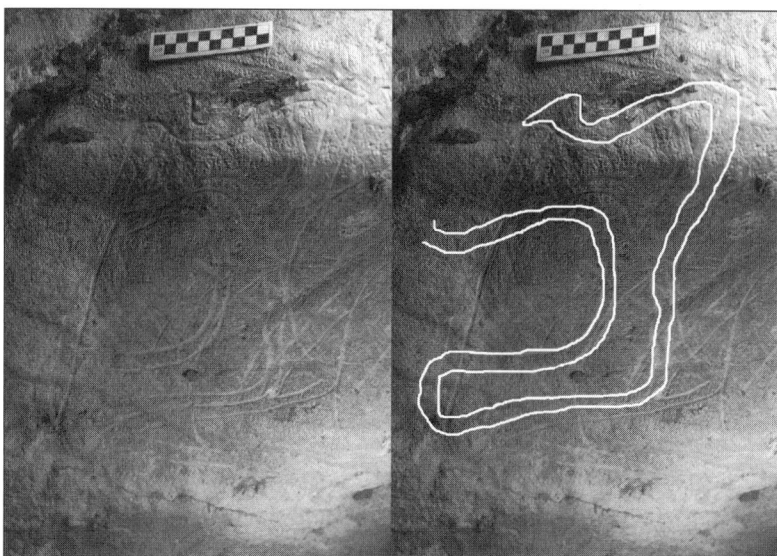

Fig. 8.1. Serpent mud glyph from 1st Unnamed Cave, Tennessee.

above the present stream on a very low section of the main passage ceiling, and the tail of the serpent surrounds a natural hole in the cave ceiling as if to emerge from that hole. This impressive glyph, too large and low to be photographed in its entirety, indicates that glyphs may have been located above the streambed itself, and, with rising and falling water levels, there may have been some erosion of prehistoric art in the past. Perhaps most important, we now know that serpents are by far

Table 8.2: Number of Glyphs by Subject Category in 1st Unnamed Cave	
Image Subject	**Number**
Anthropomorph	3
Barred X	3
Crosshatching	5
Lines	10
Meander	22
Ogee	4
Filled oval	4
Serpent	10
Spider/strider	1
X	1

the most common representation in the cave, with 10 examples, making 1st Unnamed Cave rather distinctive in terms of content (Table 8.2).

There are also new aspects of composition in the cave. Two of the eight glyph groups we now recognize are located on the ceiling of the cave inside side passages leading from the cave's main axial passageway. In both cases individual glyphs are grouped into panels of images close to the junction of the side gallery with the main passage. One of these is the first glyph group encountered navigating the cave; the fact that is it composed of serpent effigies and meandering lines alters our view of the composition of the cave, which was originally thought to begin with an abstract image of a bird/human. The first group is also within sight of the cave mouth, and thus the array does not begin in the cave's dark zone, something made much of in the first publications. At the same time, we have found glyphs on the ceiling of the old Group 3, where it was previously thought only the walls were used, and glyphs are disposed on both walls in some areas where previously they were found only on one side of the passage. Thus the 1997 description and interpretations of 1st Unnamed Cave's glyph distribution have been revised based on recent work, and more detailed information will be forthcoming.

18th Unnamed Cave, Alabama

The second TVA cave we will discuss was discovered in 1991, when avocational cavers Bill Torode and Joe Skipworth, associated with the Huntsville Grotto of the National Speleological Society, noticed engravings on the ceiling and walls of a narrow karst passage on the north shore of a TVA reservoir in northeast Alabama. In 1996 they alerted Jean Allan, an archaeologist with the U.S. Forest Service in Bankhead National Forest near Jasper, Alabama, who initiated a study of the cave. According to Allan, the engraved glyphs were prehistoric, probably Mississippian given the subject matter (turkeys, serpents, metamorphic creatures). She gave the cave the pseudonym "Turkey Cave" in order to discuss it in professional circles without using its common name.

In April 1998 a member of the UTK Cave Archaeology Research Team, Alan Cressler of the U.S. Geological Survey, visited the cave to examine the glyphs. He confirmed the richness and variety of the art assemblage in the cave, characterizing the site as one of the most important for prehistoric cave art in the Southeast and noting that the cave lies on TVA land. Moreover, he cited the special vulnerability of the cave to unauthorized visitation and possible vandalism, because of its proximity to a well-frequented roadway. In consultation with TVA archaeologists, the UTK Cave Archaeology unit returned to the site, designated "18th Unnamed Cave" in our regional naming system, to assess its contents and conservation. That visit resulted in a contract to document the cave. On December 12–13, 1998, Simek, Cressler, Jay Franklin, Nicholas Herrmann, and Sherry Turner-Herrmann mapped, recorded, and photographed the cave's prehistoric art.

18th Unnamed Cave is a short, sinuous crawlway passage, only ca 200 m in length, with a very low ceiling and two small entrances. The cave entrances are both low on a hillside and are in view of a road passing through TVA property that skirts the north side of a creek. Inside the cave's dark zone, we define six linearly distributed glyph areas between the two entrances, differentiated by topographic variations in the cave. After a 29 m flat stomach crawl that passes into the true dark zone, the cave opens into a single wide room divided by three bedrock columns into two areas, which we call the "alcove" to the north of the columns and the "main" passage to the south; in both these areas one can comfortably sit or kneel, but not stand. In the alcove are the first glyphs on this side of the cave passageway. After the alcove rejoins the main passage, a very low, 15 m–long crawlway is the third glyph area we define; this passage is never more than 60 cm high and must be traversed body flat on the floor. Beyond the crawl, a 2 m–high area is encountered, the only area in the cave where a person can stand upright today. Historical period excavation of the floor sediments, probably for mining saltpeter, may have altered the standing area's topography after prehistoric cave use had ceased. Directly connected to the standing area is an inner chamber, roughly circular with a 1.5 m–high ceiling formed by a small dome. This inner chamber gives way to an eastern flat crawl passage, making up fully half of the cave's interior length, leading out to the second entrance. On the walls and low ceilings of the cave through all of these areas are numerous prehistoric petroglyphs, including fish, birds, serpents, stars, transforming creatures, and enigmatic signs. Among these are some of the most detailed and well-executed glyphs known from prehistoric southeastern cave sites.

18th Unnamed Cave contains at least five charcoal pictographs and 122 prehistoric petroglyphs, images engraved into the limestone bedrock in which the cave was formed. There were probably more of these petroglyphs at one time, but some have been obliterated by historical "tally marks," notation scratches made by saltpeter miners as they counted their extracted sediment volumes during excavations. In some cases tally

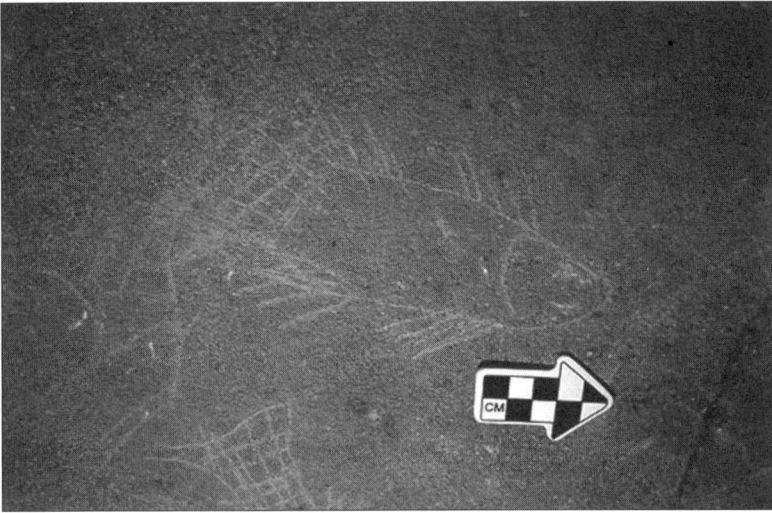

Fig. 8.2. Petroglyph engraving of the most common representational image, one of 22 fish effigies from 18th Unnamed Cave, Alabama.

Fig. 8.3. Petroglyphs of animals that are rarely depicted in cave art from 18th Unnamed Cave, Alabama: (a) a bird effigy, probably a great blue heron (Ardea herodias) which is still common in the area today, (b) a paddlefish (Polyodon spathula), once a common species in the region but rare today in the Tennessee River.

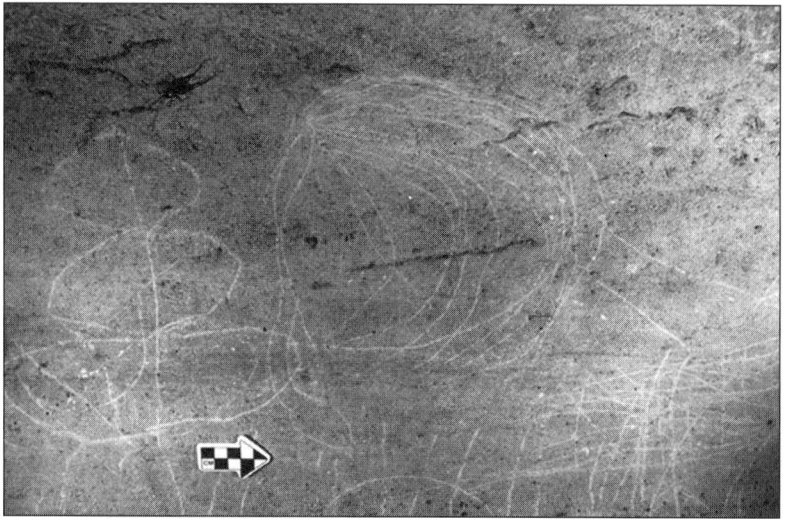

Fig. 8.4. Petroglyph from 18th Unnamed Cave in Alabama showing a turkey (with a striped body and two long legs with three-toed feet, seen on the right) transforming into a serpent (on the left). Note the giant rattle at the left and the triangular serpent head indicating a venomous species, almost certainly the eastern diamondback rattlesnake (Crotalus adamanteus).

marks, which are always linear signs, often in groups of five, may be confused with what we call "line" glyphs; we have been conservative in identifying prehistoric glyphs, however, and believe that all of the 122 glyphs composing our inventory were produced by prehistoric Native Americans.

We distinguish 10 different subjects among the glyphs (Table 8.3). First among these are various geometric forms (boxes, chevrons, circles, lines, and enigmatic signs), for a total of 45 images. The five pictographs identified in the cave, all from deep in the interior crawl passage, are of these geometric forms. The second type of glyph, with a dozen examples, may represent celestial signs: the sun and stars. (It is possible that the "stars" may represent animal tracks). The vast majority of glyphs in the cave are representational images of animals, including 22 fish (Figure 8.2), 10 garfish, 20 turkeys, and five owls. Paddlefish, a heron, and an insect are rare animal effigies (Figure 8.3). A small (four examples) but impressive group of glyphs represents transformational creatures: fish turning into turkeys and a turkey/serpent image (Figure 8.4). In their detail and accuracy, the glyphs from 18th Unnamed Cave are among the most impressive from any southeastern prehistoric site.

All glyphs in 18th Unnamed Cave were mapped and a distribution plan of the images was produced. Clearly the great majority of glyphs

Table 8.3: Number of Glyphs by Subject Category in 18th Unnamed Cave	
Image Subject	Number
Geometric	45
Celestial	12
Fish	22
Gar	10
Turkeys	20
Owls	5
Paddlefish	2
Heron	1
Insect	1
Transforms	4

are located in the western half of the cave, in the alcove (10 glyphs), the main passage (22), the west crawlway (22), the standing area (41), and the inner chamber (14). Only a few glyphs (13) are scattered through the eastern crawl passage. Moreover, glyphs of particular subject matter tend to occur in certain parts of the cave: turkeys in the main passage, fish in the western crawl, a variety of rare forms in the standing chamber, and turkeys in the inner area. This evident composition is one of the more interesting aspects of 18th Unnamed Cave, and it will be the subject of more detailed analysis to come (Simek and Cressler 2008). What is clear is that organization of glyphs occurs on a cavewide scale, suggesting a grammar or principles guiding the decoration of this cave.

There is little or no prehistoric archaeological material evident on the cave floor, perhaps caused by alteration of the floor resulting from historic saltpeter mining. No ceramics or worked lithics were observed that might aid in chronological placement of the art. An isolated human phalanx was discovered and left in place in the alcove; as the piece was at some distance from the cave mouth and not likely to have arrived at its location by erosion from the exterior, it is possible that 18th Unnamed Cave saw use as a mortuary cave. A single piece of burned mammal bone was encountered at a different place in the main passage, and it appeared prehistoric based on weathering and condition. That bone was submitted to Beta Analytic Inc. for radiocarbon age determination using funds provided by the National Geographic Society. An age of 800 ± 60 years B.P. was obtained by AMS counting; this age calibrates to A.D. 1250, well within the Mississippian Period in this area of the Tennessee Valley

(Table 8.1). While there is no certain correlation between the glyphs and the bone used for age determination, the date does accord well with the subject matter depicted in the cave art. Thus a Mississippian ascription for the art is not unreasonable.

18th Unnamed Cave contains a rich and varied assemblage of dark-zone cave art possibly dating to the Mississippian Period. The cave art is detailed, finely executed, and variable in subject matter. Individual glyphs are differentially distributed through the cave, suggesting compo-sition in realizing the prehistoric artwork. Because of all of these factors and because the glyph assemblage itself is one of the largest and best preserved of all presently known in the Southeast, 18th Unnamed Cave warranted permanent protection. This was especially important given the open nature of the entrances and the cave's proximity to a modern, heavily used roadway.

It is in the protection of these cave-art sites, once they were discovered and their significance recognized, that the Tennessee Valley Authority has excelled. The first cave to be protected was 18th Unnamed Cave. Immediately after the visit in 1998, its importance was communicated to TVA archaeologists; they initiated a program for the site's assessment and protection. First our inventory project was completed. Then biol-ogy personnel from TVA inspected the site to be sure that there were no endangered bat populations using the cave for habitat; once it was clear that there was no need for a gate adapted to the needs of migratory bats, Michael Sears, Alan Cressler, and Jan Simek brought steel and welding gear to the site to gate the two entrances against unauthorized access. One entrance is larger and better concealed from view, and a function-ing gate now protects it with a hidden lock box into that entrance. This allows access to the cave for necessary monitoring and research but protects the site from encroachment. The other opening, lower on the hillside and easily viewed from the nearby roadway, was closed without access by welding up a heavy steel grate pinned to the rock outcrop. Sears designed and built both of the barriers, and he deserves special mention for his skill and innovation in construction. As might be expected, TVA bore all costs of protecting 18th Unnamed Cave through gate construc-tion. But we believe that their unflinching resolve and speed in protecting this important site have been especially laudable. Today the cave remains closed and is monitored periodically by TVA police on the reservation.

Gating 1st Unnamed Cave came later, partly because of our ongo-ing work in the site and partly because of its remote location. However, when it was suggested to TVA in 1999 that gating was necessary because of apparent incursions including some new graffiti, they moved quickly to send Sears to the cave. While there is only a single opening to 1st Unnamed Cave, it is much larger than any of the 18th Unnamed Cave entrances, and the remote location required more complex logistics. A barge with a generator, welding machine, and long wires was needed, and significant quantities of steel had to be transported to the site. Because endangered bat species did use 1st Unnamed Cave as a migration roost, Sears designed a gate in accordance with Bat Conservation International standards for airflow maintenance and accessibility. This required 6-inch angle iron of considerable weight, and equipment had to be capable of working with heavy stock. The result was a remarkable gate that has not disturbed the bats at all and that has withstood years of assault by river surge and unauthorized visitation. Again TVA's stewardship of this site has extended as far as required to ensure conservation and protection of this important and fragile archaeological resource.

Painted Bluff, Alabama

In 1959 James W. Cambron and Spencer A. Waters published a paper in the *Journal of Alabama Archaeology*, describing a variety of open-air rock art sites along the main reaches of the Tennessee River (Cambron and Waters 1959). Among these were some of the earliest known rock-art sites in the region: Paint Rock, North Carolina, for example, that had been referenced by scholars such as Garrick Mallery (1893) in the nineteenth century. Cambron and Waters also described new sites that had not been previously discussed in the archaeological literature. Among the latter was a group of hematite pictographs on a massive limestone cliff face in Marshall County, Alabama, which they called "Painted Bluff." According to Cambron and Waters, the prehistoric artwork at Painted Bluff comprised pictographs at two elevation levels. On a high ledge ("three hundred feet up this sheer bluff") were six solid circles and one ring, all less than 10 inches in diameter (Cambron and Waters 1959:41 43). At the time of their recording, there was already substantial graffiti at this high ledge that may have obscured other ancient pictographs. On a lower ledge, some 5 meters above the base of the cliff, they noted, "other paintings, one a bird and the other small circles connected by lines." They cite the presence of other images at this lower ledge, "which appear to be very recent" (ibid.). Cambron and Waters show a very crude sketch of the red dots (1959:42), but their description and analysis of Painted Bluff goes no further than to catalog its existence in the context of their regional survey. A decade later, noted Alabama rock art specialist B. Bart Hensen visited Painted Bluff and took numerous photographs of the cliff paintings (Hensen and Martz 1979); these photos, most unpublished, show a surprisingly extensive array of complex pictographs, including geometrics, avian figures, anthropomorphs, and serpent images, scattered along the lower levels of the bluffs in much greater numbers than reported by Cambron and Waters (Hensen, personal communication 2004).

In 2000, as part of an opportunistic survey for the Wheeler Reservoir Lands Plan undertaken for TVA and directed by Scott Shaw, the Office of Archaeological Services at the University of Alabama visited Painted Bluff and generated state site file numbers for the bluff art site itself and for a small cave site associated with the bluff (Shaw 2000). Both sites are within TVA Wheeler Tract 198, an 8.5 ha tract on the right riverbank near river mile 345. The Painted Bluff site was assigned site number 1Ms394, but it was not described except to note the presence of "Woodland motifs" in the artwork. The small cave, recorded for the first time by Shaw and his crew, was given number 1Ms427 and was located some "30m (vertical) below the pictographs" (147). Looting in the cave was noted, but its cultural content was not described.

In 2003 TRC/Garrow, Inc. (TRC) revisited the area as part of another cultural resources assessment under contract to the TVA (Price 2003). The goal of this survey was to aid TVA in its Section 110 compliance, i.e., identification of sites warranting inclusion in the National Register of Historic Places (NRHP), and TRC was specifically charged to visit 1Ms394 and 1Ms427 to assess their NRHP eligibility. At 1Ms394 they "documented several rock paintings" (108), including a number that were more elaborate than the red dots originally illustrated by Cambron and Waters, although the TRC report argues (without explanation) that only some of the pictographs, specifically those in red, are prehistoric. They also located a small cave at the same cliff level as the pictographs "4m high and 2m wide and extending approximately 8m deep" (109), in which they found little archaeological material. They identified this as 1Ms427. Because of contextual considerations, TRC recommended both sites as eligible for inclusion in the NRHP.

In late May of 2004, a group of archaeologists from the University of Tennessee visited Painted Bluff with TVA permission, after Cressler sent Simek photographs of some of the pictographs he had seen during a casual visit to the site. It was clear from these that the site is very complex and elaborate, with the probability of polychrome paintings and stratigraphic superposition of prehistoric images in various locations along the cliff face. This was confirmed during the May trip, when more than 50 individual images were observed, including human effigies (Figure 8.5), animal figures, serpents, birds (Figure 8.6), fish (Figure 8.7), ovals, circles, and a variety of other geometric and abstract pictographs. Subsequent documentation visits, under a research contract between the University of Tennessee and TVA, have increased the catalog of individual glyphs to more than 80 (Table 8.4). Fine engravings were found in several places in association with the paintings. Stratigraphic layering of pictures was confirmed in at least one location, and polychrome paintings were recorded, comprising red, yellow, and orange hematite, that must have been produced as single images (Figure 8.8). A precarious visit to the upper ledge (Figure 8.9) showed that the array of red circles depicted originally by Cambron and Waters was actually found high on the bluff, and it may be that those early observers approached the site from a farm on top of the cliff and never descended to the lower ledges far down on the river where the majority of the complex pictures are located. (Their willingness to attend the upper ledges without the service of modern technical climbing gear is impressive.) Technical execution of the paintings is exemplary, and the site contains some of the most beautiful prehistoric art known in any southeastern site. Subject matter resembles many other prehistoric art sites known in Tennessee

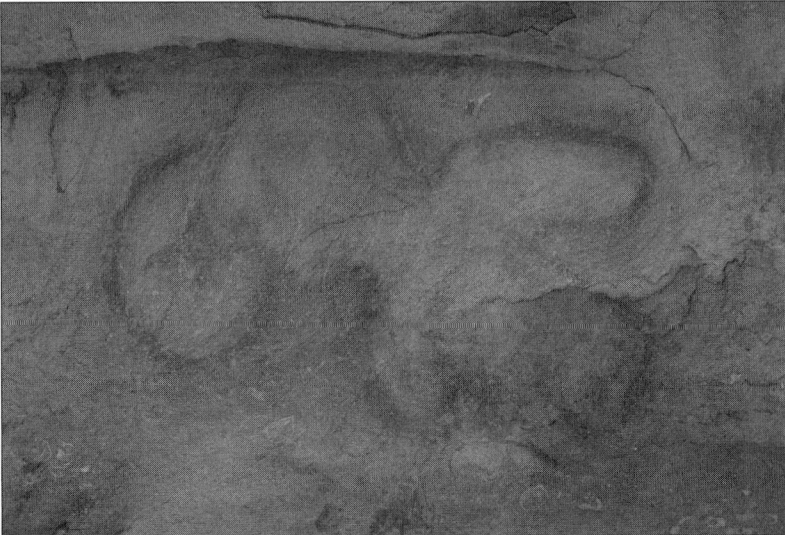

Fig. 8.5. Anthropomorphic pictograph shows a human face in profile from Painted Bluff, Alabama.

Fig. 8.6. Pictograph of a bird, possibly a heron (see fig. 8.3) from Painted Bluff, Alabama.

Fig. 8.7. Fish pictograph from Painted Bluff, Alabama. The presence of barbells near the head suggests a catfish.

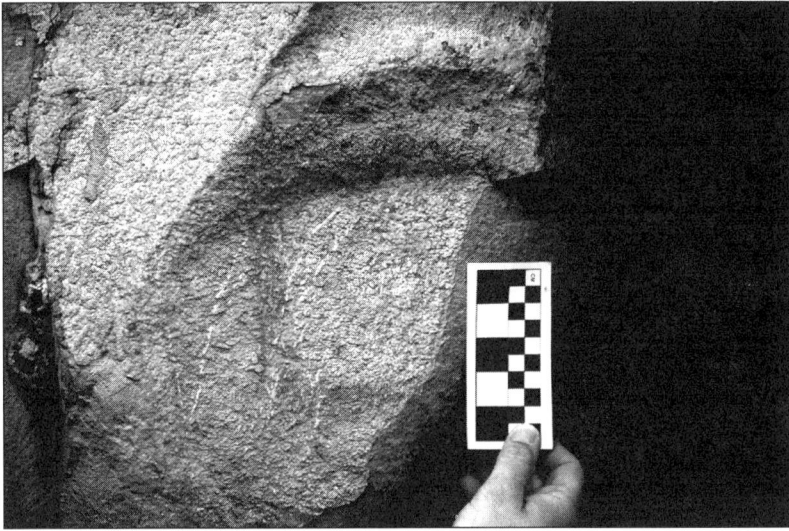

Fig. 8.8. Concentric circles painted in red and yellow ocre from Painted Bluff, Alabama.

Fig. 8.9. Location of pictographs on uppermost ledges at Painted Bluff, Alabama.

Table 8.4: Number of Glyphs by Subject Category at Painted Bluff	
Image Subject	Number
Circles	30
Lines	13
Boxes	3
Animals	3
Birds	4
Fish	3
Anthropomorphs	8
Mace	2
Unique Forms	15

and Alabama, and certain themes are reminiscent of typical Southeast Ceremonial Complex iconography. By its complexity and sophistication, Painted Bluff is one of, if not the most significant open-air rock art occurrence in the southeastern United States.

Surface collected materials from the Painted Bluff site include one burned river cane torch fragment (*Arundinaria gigantea*), which was recovered from the base of the cliff in a very dry location. This artifact was submitted to Beta Analytic for radiocarbon age determination. An AMS counted age of 570 ± 40 was obtained, which calibrates to about A.D. 1400. This age is in agreement with the iconography of the pictographs. An interesting observation is that the torch fragment was used, suggesting at least some visitation at Painted Bluff at night, whether in relation to the bluff paintings or simply using the platform as a trail at the base of the cliff. Myer (Myer 1928) notes a number of Indian trails that approach the river from the north in this area.

Site 1Ms427 (the cave) was also visited in May 2004 by the University of Tennessee team. The actual site is not the one illustrated in the TRC report but in fact a much deeper cave feature located 30m below the pictograph lower ledge (as originally and accurately described by Shaw for the OAS). The cave has been extensively looted, but there are still human bones, chert, and mica sheets scattered across and within the sediments in the cave's interior passages. These characteristics are consistent with Copena burial caverns, which were found in this area of Alabama (Walthall and DeJarnette 1974). The cave is itself quite significant, whether it relates to the exterior artwork or not, and deserves protection in its own right. Again, TVA wasted no time in constructing a gate to protect the cave once it knew of the contents, and today it has a stout steel closure with a hidden lock box protecting the cave's record. It should be noted that it is this cave, not the one located by TRC in their 2003 survey, which warrants inclusion in the NRHP.

The Tennessee Valley Authority cultural resources program has been instrumental in advancing current research on prehistoric bluff and cave art in the Southeast. The current team in particular has unfailingly provided material support to the discovery and analysis of sites on properties it manages, and it has been quick to protect sites with the necessary resources when protection is demanded. It has been one of the great pleasures of our research focus to be able to work with the TVA. We thank them for the opportunity to celebrate their 75 years of archaeology with them in this volume.

Acknowledgments

The authors wish to thank Charles H. Faulkner, Jay Franklin, J. Bennett Graham, Nick Herrmann, Dan Olinger, Erin E. Pritchard, Sarah Sherwood, Tim Smith, Sherry Turner-Hermann, and Richard Yarnell, who have all lent advice and assistance in the task of identifying and documenting these cave-art sites. Todd M. Ahlman discovered and worked extensively with us on 1st Unnamed Cave, the first cave-art site discovered on TVA land; we consider him a close colleague in the work described here. The National Science Foundation, the Dogwood City Grotto, SERA, the Lucille S. Thompson Family Foundation, the National Geographic Society, the Tennessee Valley Authority, the Tennessee Historical Commission, and the University of Tennessee, Knoxville, SARIF Fund all contributed funding for the work described here.

References Cited

Cambron, J. W., and S. A. Waters
1959   Petroglyphs and Pictographs in the Tennessee Valley and Surrounding Areas. *Journal of Alabama Archaeology* 5(1):26–51.

Faulkner, Charles H. (editor)
1986   *The Prehistoric Native American Art of Mud Glyph Cave.* University of Tennessee Press, Knoxville.

Faulkner, Charles H.
1988   A Study of Seven Southeastern Glyph Caves. *North American Archaeologist* 9(3):223–246.

FAULKNER, CHARLES H., B. DEANE, AND H. H. EARNEST, JR.
1984   A Mississippian Period Ritual Cave in Tennessee. *American Antiquity* 49(2):350–361.

FAULKNER, CHARLES H., AND JAN F. SIMEK
1996a   1st Unnamed Cave: A Mississippian Period Cave Art Site in East Tennessee, USA. *Antiquity* 70(270):774–84.
1996b   Mud Glyphs: Recently Discovered Cave Art in Eastern North America. *International Newsletter on Rock Art* 15:8–13.
2001   Variability in the Production and Preservation of Prehistoric Mud Glyphs in Southeastern Caves. In *Fleeting Identities: Perishable Material Culture in Archaeological Research*, edited by P. B. Drooker, pp. 335–356. Southern Illinois University Press, Carbondale.

HENSEN, B. BART
1996   Rock Art Distribution in North Alabama as a Function of Motif Style. In *Rock Art of the Eastern Woodlands*, edited by C. H. Faulkner, pp. 119–126. American Rock Art Research Association, San Miguel, CA.

HENSEN, B. BART, AND J. MARTZ
1979   *Alabama's Aboriginal Rock Art*. Alabama Historical Commission, Montgomery, AL.

MALLERY, GARRICK
1893   Picture Writing of the American Indian. In *10th Annual Report of the Bureau of American Ethnology*, pp. 4–822. Government Printing Office, Washington, DC.

MYER, WILLIAM E.
1928   Indian Trails of the Southeast. In *42nd Annual Report of the U.S. Bureau of American Ethnology*, pp. 727–857. Government Printing Office, Washington, DC.

PRICE, G. D.
2003   *Archaeological Survey along the Flint River and Paint Rock River Portions of the Wheeler Reservoir, Morgan and Madison Counties, Alabama*. Tennessee Valley Authority, Knoxville, TN. TRC/Garrow, Inc., pp. 103–114. Atlanta, GA.

SHAW, SCOTT
2000   *Cultural Resources in the Wheeler Reservoir*. Tennessee Valley Authority, Knoxville, TN. Office of Archaeological Services, University of Alabama, p. 147. Tuscaloosa, AL.

SIMEK, JAN F.
1996   1st Unnamed Cave: CSA Cooperative Research on a New "Mud Glyph" Cave in East Tennessee. *Journal of the Cumberland Spelean Association* 3(1):12–23.

SIMEK, JAN F., AND ALAN CRESSLER

2008   On the Backs of Serpents: Prehistoric Cave Art in the Southeastern
         Woodlands. In *Cave Archaeology of the Eastern Woodlands: Papers
         in Honor of Patty Jo Watson*, edited by David H. Dye, pp. 169–192.
         University of Tennessee Press, Knoxville.

SIMEK, JAN F., C. H. FAULKNER, S. R. FRANKENBERG, W. E. KLIPPEL,
T. M. AHLMAN, N. P. HERRMANN, S. C. SHERWOOD, R. B. WALKER,
W. M. WRIGHT, AND R. YARNELL

1997   A Preliminary Report on the Archaeology of a New Mississippian
         Cave Art Site in East Tennessee. *Southeastern Archaeology*
         16(1):51–73.

SIMEK, JAN F., S. R. FRANKENBERG, AND C. H. FAULKNER

2001   Toward an Understanding of Southeastern Prehistoric Cave Art.
         In *Archaeology of the Appalachian Highlands*, edited by Lynne P.
         Sullivan and Susan C. Prezanno, pp. 49–64. University of Tennessee
         Press, Knoxville.

WALTHALL, JOHN A., AND DAVID L. DEJARNETTE

1974   Copena Burial Caves. *Journal of Alabama Archaeology* 20(1):1–62.

9
The Dust Cave Archaeological Project, Lauderdale County, Alabama

Boyce N. Driskell

DISCOVERED AS THE RESULT of TVA's commitment to survey and appraisal of cultural resources on its lands, Dust Cave is a small, unimposing grotto in the limestone bluffs forming the north rim of TVA's Pickwick Lake near Florence, Alabama (Figure 9.1). Initially investigated in the summer of 1989, Dust Cave was explored by an archaeological team under my direction from the University of Alabama in fulfillment of a contract with TVA to assess potential cultural resources in local caves. Later, TVA and other agencies provided support to continue research at Dust Cave in light of the importance of the deposits and ongoing threats to their integrity (Goldman-Finn 1994; Sherwood 1997; Walker et al. 2001; Sherwood et al. 2004).

The project's origins date back to an earlier summer project in 1984 in which archaeologist Charles Hubbert tested the talus of Smith Bottom Cave (1Lu498), along the same bluff line, with the assistance of staff and high school students of the Alabama Museum of Natural History's Summer Expedition program (Cobb 1987; Cobb, Driskell, and Meeks 1995). Intrigued by the concentrations of animal bone revealed in deposits of Smith Bottom Cave, Carey Oakley, founder and long time director of the Office of Archaeological Research at the University of Alabama, recruited Sue Scott, then a Ph.D. candidate, to direct in the summer of 1987 a field school for undergraduate students that was

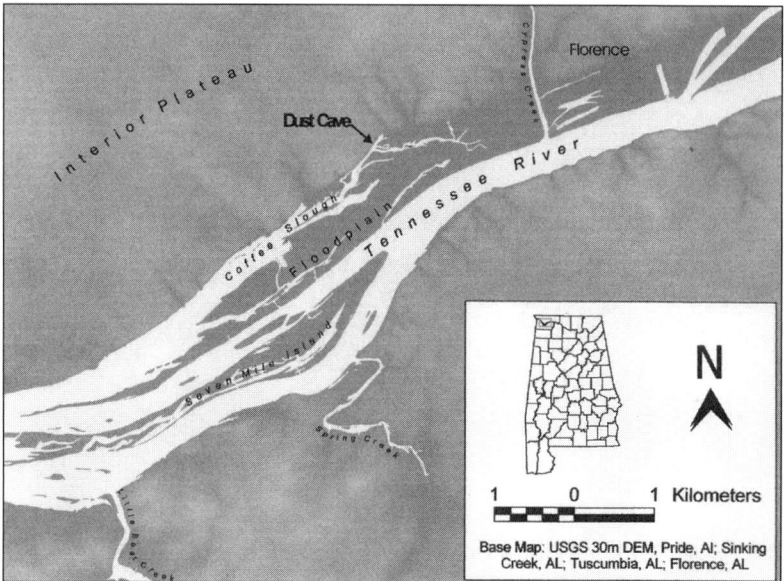

Fig. 9.1. Location of Dust Cave. (This digital elevation model is modified from Sherwood et al. 2004: Figure 1).

jointly sponsored by the University of North Alabama in Florence. This author assumed charge of the field school in the summer of 1988 and work continued at Smith Bottom Cave through the summer of 1989.

Because of the interest generated by the Smith Bottom investigations and his own long time interest in the natural and cultural history of the area, Richard M. Cobb, a local educator and amateur speleologist, submitted to the author a report on about two dozen local caves which might have some archaeological potential (Cobb 1987; Cobb, Driskell, and Meeks 1995). Cobb's 1987 report, which includes scaled maps and summaries of archaeological materials observed, made it quite clear that cave localities had not been systematically investigated in earlier archaeological surveys including an on-going TVA site survey and assessment (Meyer 1995) conducted by the University of Alabama in which above pool, open-air sites in Pickwick Lake were found or revisited and further investigated. This oversight led to TVA sponsorship of a cave-testing program in the summers of 1988 and 1989.

As an initial step in the project, Michael B. Collins of the Texas Archaeological Research Laboratory was asked to evaluate the potential of each of Cobb's caves to contain intact, buried archaeological deposits. Collins's (1995) report that resulted from his visit to each of the caves with Cobb in 1987, recommended testing of 20 of the caves in the area.

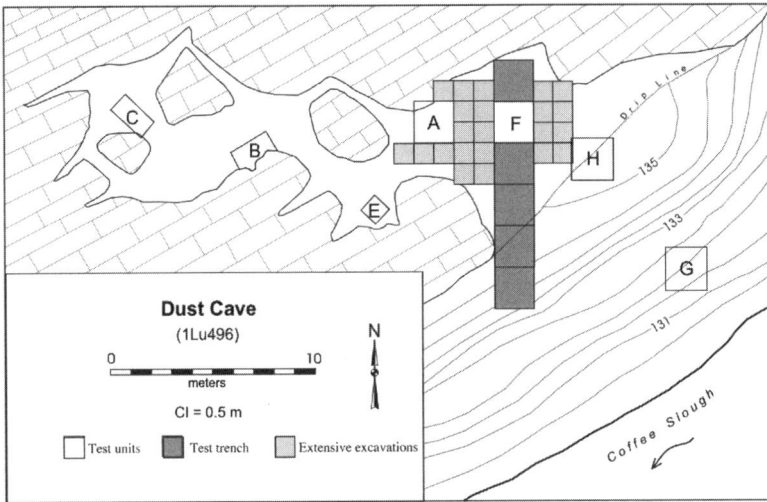

Fig. 9.2. Plan map of Dust Cave illustrating placement of excavations (modified from Sherwood et al. 2004, fig. 2).

Begun in 1988 in conjunction with the field school at Smith Bottom Cave, small crews under Cobb's field direction ventured into each of these caves to excavate small test pits into cave deposits (Cobb, Driskell, and Meeks 1995). The program continued during the summer of 1989, when Dust Cave was one of several caves slated for testing.

Two small (30 by 30 cm) test pits (A and D) were excavated into the deposits within the entrance chamber. Test Pit D was later subsumed within Test Unit F. Another test pit (E) was placed in the passageway to the second chamber, and two test pits (B and C) were excavated within the second chamber (Figure 9.2). Literally at arm's length in the restricted exposure of Test Unit D, near the entrance to the cave, the telltale scraping of trowel on flint alerted us to the possible presence of archaeological deposits in the cave, quickly confirmed by darker, organic fill and recovery of flakes. Soon after, human remains were discovered in Test Unit A, placed toward the rear wall of the entrance chamber. This unit was enlarged to a 1 by 1 meter square, and later to a 2 by 2 meter square. Returning in the summer of 1990, bedrock within the entrance chamber of the cave was eventually reached at a depth of 4.92 meters below datum in Test Unit F, a 2 by 2 meter square subsuming the original Test Unit D. Test Unit H was excavated in the zone between the entrance chamber and the exterior talus slope, and Test Unit G was excavated into

Fig. 9.3. View of a profile in the entrance showing the stratigraphic complexity of the deposits in Dust Cave.

the talus slope several meters in front of the cave mouth. No cultural material was encountered in Test Unit G, but, nearer the cave entrance, Test Unit H produced an artifact array and stratigraphic sequence similar to test units within the entrance chamber. Microstratigraphy seen in the probes within the cave, however, was not preserved in Test Unit H.

The fieldwork at Dust Cave continued for 12 summers. The summers of 1990 to 1994 were devoted to initial testing. During this period field methods were refined and adapted to the specific characteristics of the archaeological deposits. Excavation by arbitrary level, employed in early test excavations, was replaced by attempts to define and excavate by natural or stratigraphic units with arbitrary subdivisions to maintain discrete small provenience units. Also, initial small volume sampling for flotation/fine screening was increased to include flotation/fine screening of about 10 percent of the excavated matrix by volume (Goldman-Finn and Driskell 1994). Test excavations revealed amazingly well preserved archaeological deposits extending to almost 5 meters below the cave's present floor (Driskell 1994, 1996, 1998; Goldman-Finn and Meeks 1995). These deposits were stratified and laden with fragile organic remains (Figure 9.3) including animal bone, charred plant remains, and large quantities of ash and charcoal (Driskell and Goldberg 1994; 1995a, 1995b). Protected within the relatively dry cave environment for thousands of years, these deposits are now threatened by capillary action of heightened ground water levels occasioned by impoundment of Pickwick Lake (Sherwood et al. 2004; Driskell 1999, 2001).

Completion of the test pits and a 2-meter-wide trench (1989 to 1994) extending from outside the cave mouth to the back wall (Sherwood et al. 2004) revealed a nearly horizontal suite of organic laden strata representing occupations from the middle to late Paleoindian through middle Archaic periods (10,650–3,600 calibrated B.C.). Because of the threat to the fragile organic contents of the deposits, test excavations were followed by full-scale excavation (1996–2000, 2002) of a large portion of the deposits within the entrance chamber. Flotation was increased to include all feature fill and about 25 percent of the excavated matrix. Later, in 1999–2002, flotation volumes were decreased as areas were considered to be well represented. Most of the deposits within the entrance chamber have now been excavated, and the project has been disbanded. Plans are being formulated for long-term stabilization of remaining deposits.

Fieldwork at Dust Cave was conducted by students and staff of our summer field schools; a group of professional collaborators contributed to a multidisciplinary research perspective, and graduate research was organized and coordinated to investigate important research issues relevant to the cave, its deposits, and its ancient inhabitants. The Dust Cave Archaeological Project will be remembered for several reasons.

First, because of the rare occurrence, remarkable preservation, and great antiquity of the cave's deposits, archaeological data have figured importantly in reinterpretations of the lifeways of Late Pleistocene and early Holocene hunter-gatherers of the middle Tennessee Valley. Although excavations at Dust Cave are finished, the collections will continue to inform understanding of these lifeways for many years to come.

Second, Dust Cave has served as a training ground for some of the newest generation of archaeologists and thus has tested the mettle of students, staff, and collaborators alike. A camaraderie born in the shared sense of commitment to an important endeavor and tempered in the summer heat and humidity of a north Alabama swamp, Dust Cavers feel a particular sense of nostalgia as we embellish our adventures at the cave, remember fond and miserable moments in camp, and share fraternity with those before and after us.

Third, Dust Cave provided opportunities to inform and engage the public with participation from teachers, students, and avocational archaeologists. Several formal training opportunities were offered during summers at Dust Cave.

Research

Rod Riley, past associate director of the University of Alabama Computer Center and currently employed by IBM Corp., served as manager of the computerized database and related field and laboratory computer-based activities. The university's Seebeck Computer Center provided additional technical assistance as needed. Riley and several colleagues from the University of Alabama provided computer equipment necessary to construct a computer network linking the cave, camp, and a van truck that served as a climate-controlled computer room where servers were located (Figure 9.4). IBM Corporation donated 15 laptops that were used in the field by students and staff in the research.

A relational database, constructed in IBM's Universal Database, was designed by this team to organize and manage different categories of data from the project (Riley 2001). Using location in three-dimensional space as the principal key, the team members experimented with various ways to record and organize attributes related to stratigraphic placement and categories of recovered material culture (Sherwood and Riley 1998). An electronic version of our level (provenience) form was developed in 1999 and used experimentally in the summer of 2000. Riley later used technology developed at Dust Cave to develop the relational database for the Townsend Project, a large archaeological project resulting from widening of Highway 321 in Tuckaleechee Cove in eastern Tennessee.

Dust Cave has served as a laboratory for experimentation with innovative ways to generate data on the cave's prehistoric occupants from the sedimentary record. Techniques include characterization of depositional history (Goldberg and Sherwood 1994; Sherwood 1999a, 1999b, 2001a, 2001b), examination of the magnetic characteristics of the sediments (Gose 2000; Collins, Gose, and Shaw 1994), analysis of structural characteristics of sediments (Sherwood 2001a; Homsey

Fig. 9.4. A computer network linking the cave, camp, and server truck. The lucky few performed their duties in the air-conditioned environs of the server truck.

2004), and consideration of contents and chemical signatures of features (Homsey 2000, 2003a, 2003b; Homsey and Capo 2002, 2005).

The depositional history and nature of deposits at Dust Cave are reasonably well known because of these efforts. Initially Paul Goldberg advised the field team concerning designation of major suites of deposits (major lithostratigraphic units), subdivisions including recognizable strata of substantial lateral extent, and tertiary units within these that are depositional units of limited areal extent. Units were generally recorded in an alphanumeric system where major suites were designated with upper case letters (A through Y); subdivisions were designated with numbers, and tertiary units were identified with lowercase letters. These designations were made based on macroscopic examination of *in situ* deposits. Micromorphological analyses supplemented field inspections and observations (Goldberg and Sherwood 1994; Sherwood 2001a). The complexity of the stratigraphy is suggested in the illustration of the east profile of the entrance trench (Figure 9.5).

Michael B. Collins (Collins 1995; Collins, Gose, and Shaw 1994; Collins, Goldberg, and Gose 1995, Sherwood 2001a) concluded that degradation of the deposits from higher ground water levels occasioned by impoundment of Pickwick Lake is but the latest of a long history

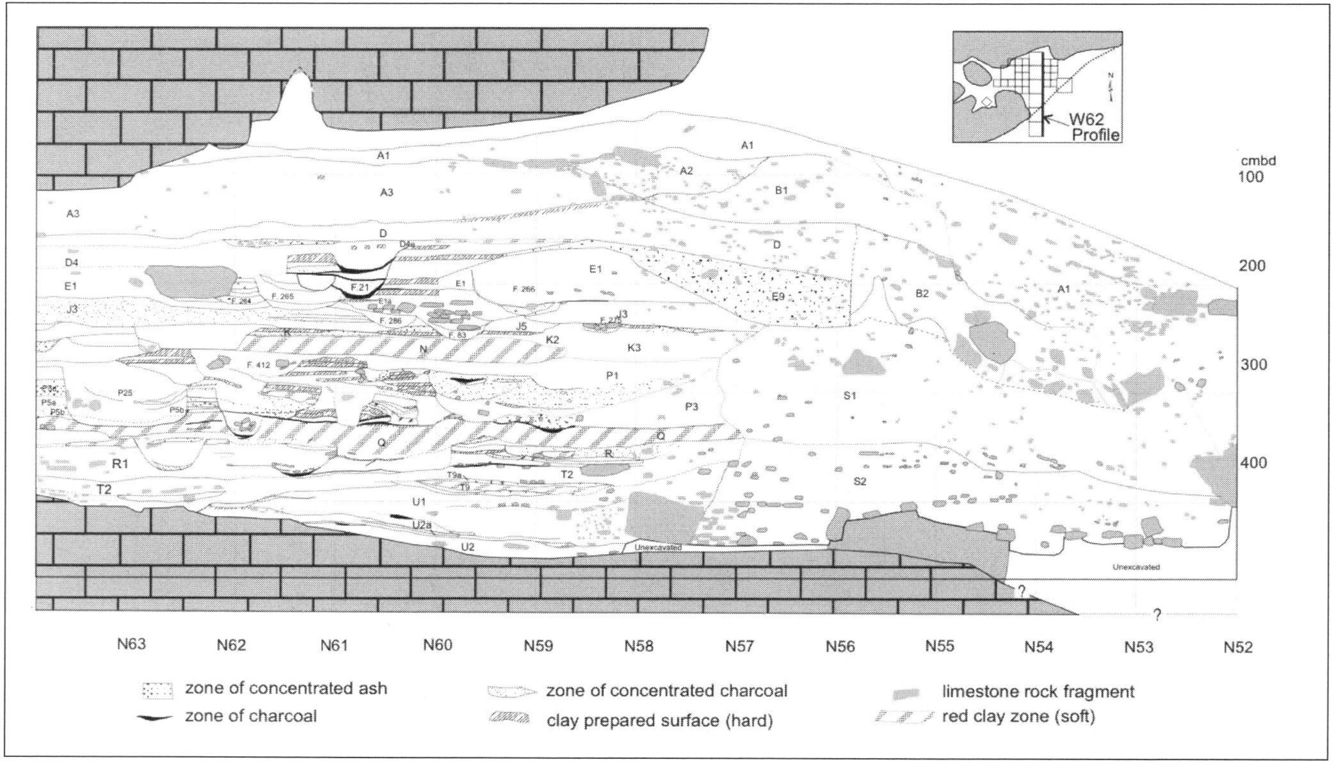

Fig. 9.5. Stratigraphy revealed in the entrance trench at Dust Cave.

of geophysical changes within the cave. Dust Cave was choked with Tennessee River alluvium in the Late Pleistocene. In fact Collins and his colleagues postulate that the cave was buried several meters beneath the floodplain about 17,000 to 15,000 years ago. By 13,000 years ago, downcutting of the river and concomitant lowering of the water table created outflow pressures within the cave that scoured and removed alluvium exposing the cave entrance, entrance chamber and passages near the entrance. After the water table dropped below the cave floor, the cave once again began accumulation of sediments.

The earliest new sediments were from flooding of the Tennessee River; later sediments were primarily derived from colluvial movement from the talus, which itself continued to accumulate soil and rock falling from the top of the bluff (Sherwood 2001a; Collins, Gose, and Shaw 1994; Goldberg and Sherwood 1994, Sherwood et al. 2004). Informed by 43 14C dates and numerous thin section samples from cave deposits, Sarah Sherwood reconstructed the major aspects of the cave's depositional history, beginning with initial human use about 10,650 calibrated radiocarbon years B.C. (Sherwood 2001a; Sherwood et al. 2004). Humans altered and augmented the natural depositional process in various ways. About 3,600 calibrated radiocarbon years B.C., headroom became so restrictive that the cave was finally abandoned. Additional detritus from bluffline and cave roof accumulated on the talus and cave floor concealing the archaeological record until recent investigations.

Our work at Dust Cave contributes substantially to an enhanced precision of regional chronology during the Late Pleistocene and early to middle Holocene. Sherwood et al. (2004) summarize the material culture, stratigraphy, and radiocarbon dates supporting the temporal placement of five superimposed, remarkably discrete prehistoric archaeological components:

Quad/Beaver Lake/Dalton	10,650 to 9,200 calibrated B.C.
Early Side Notched	10,000 to 9,000 calibrated B.C.
Kirk Stemmed	8,200 to 5,800 calibrated B.C.
Eva/Morrow Mountain	6,400 to 4,000 calibrated B.C.
Benton	4,500 to 3,600 calibrated B.C.

Homsey's research (2000, 2003a, 2003b; Homsey and Capo 2002, 2006) has focused on the function and organization of features at the cave with investigations ranging from structural analysis to chemical signatures. Red clay surfaces are an intriguing feature within the Dust Cave deposits that seem to date from earliest to latest use of the cave. These features have been investigated by Sherwood and Goldberg (2001) and later by Homsey (2004). Freeman (2003) reported basketry-impressed surfaces of some of these features. Sherwood and Chapman (2005) conclude that these prepared and fired clay surfaces are common features of eastern U.S. prehistoric sites but have not been very widely recognized. Function of these features remains a question, but perhaps they were used for roasting or drying foods, as early as the Late Pleistocene.

Dust Cave is remarkable for preservation of organic remains (Walker et al. 1999). The archaeological deposits throughout the sequence contain ash and charcoal in thin strata (even microstrata), discrete lenses, and dispersed within the general matrix. Bone preservation is excellent because of the protected environment of the cave. Human burials from Dust Cave, dating primarily to the middle Archaic period, have been analyzed by Hogue (1994) and Davis (2004).

Because of remarkable preservational factors, subsistence studies have been a prominent aspect of inquiry (Walker 1998, 2003; Driskell and Walker 2001; Detwiler, Walker, and Meeks 1998; Driskell 2000a; Walker 2002; Hollenbach 2005b; Driskell, Meeks, and Sherwood 2005). Fragile animal bone and charred plant remains are present. These include small mammal and fish bones, fish scales (Grover 1993, 1994; Walker 1995, 1996, 1997, 1998, 2000a, 2000b, 2001; Walker and Richardson 1999), small seeds and other botanical remains (Gardner 1994; Detwiler 2000, 2001, 2003; Hollenbach 2004a, 2004b, 2005a), articulated dog remains (Morey 1994; 2005; Walker, Morey, and Relethford 2005), and fresh water mussels (Parmalee 1994). Phytoliths are present (Kooeyman 2001) but not yet examined in detail. Initial examination of a sample of animal bone from the cave was conducted by Jennifer Grover (1994); later, more substantial analyses by Renee B. Walker (1997, 1998) confirmed preliminary findings of large quantities of small animal bone, with few examples of large mammal remains including few elements from white tail deer. These data suggest that birds, particularly aquatic waterfowl and other aquatic species, were very important to the earliest, Late Pleistocene inhabitants of the cave (Figure 9.6). Interestingly, a cache of goose humeri was recovered from an early context at Dust Cave (Walker and Parmalee 2004).

These results challenged the common notion that these earliest inhabitants (Paleoindians) in the southeast were organized in highly mobile, small hunting bands depending on large animals, even sometimes now extinct megafauna such as mammoths and mastodons, for the main source of food. This theory rested mostly on evidence from western sites where megafaunal remains have been more reliably associated with

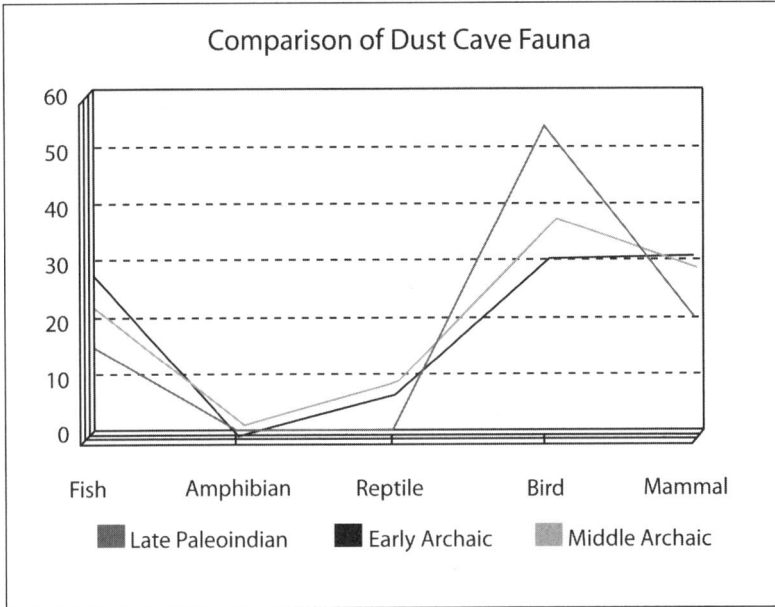

Fig. 9.6. Faunal remains from Dust Cave suggesting that small animals (fish and avifauna) were an important food resource of early hunter-gatherers in the mid-South.

Paleoindian hunters and from open-air sites in the Southeast where faunal remains are primarily bones of large mammals, the most durable of faunal remains. Although the Dust Cave fauna clearly represent a more reliable sampling of animal exploitation because of its preservational qualities, Dust Cave may have been a special function site whose refuse was not a very good indicator of the overall subsistence economy of these early peoples. Hollenbach's (2005b) dissertation research resolved this question.

Hollenbach (2005a, 2005b) examined plant macrofossils from Dust Cave and compared these data to plant use at several other early, sheltered sites (LaGrange, Rollins, and Stanfield-Worley shelters) in the region. She found that subsistence activities in the region changed little during the time from late Paleoindian to Early Archaic (Hollenbach 2005c, 2006, 2007). By calculating costs of procurement and seasonality of availability of resources (plant and animal) represented in the archaeological collections of these sites, she then modeled annual subsistence/settlement patterning for late Paleoindian and Early Archaic foragers of the region. Her research suggests that foragers of the area exploited upland nut mast and nearby animal/floral resources in fall, seeds in early winter, floodplain resources including aquatic resources in the winter and spring, and fruits in the summer. Her findings strongly support the notion that subsistence and settlement were organized around collectables. Women, children, and the elderly most likely formed the principal labor force to exploit these resources. Hunting activities were probably embedded in the collecting cycle, and not the reverse. Hollenbach points out that prey animals were often attracted to the same plant resources (young shoots, mature seeds, nut mast) as their human predators. Her interpretations are consistent with other recent research concerning the organization of North American foragers (Walker and Driskell 2007).

Our research has suggested that population densities, and perhaps population concentrations, changed through the first seven millennia of human habitation in this area (highland rim) of the middle Tennessee Valley (Meeks 2001; Driskell, Meeks, and Sherwood 2005). Climate change during the Late Pleistocene is punctuated by the Younger-Dryas, a cold period in which Quad peoples and some Dalton peoples of the highland rim maintained a foraging lifeway similar to their predecessors in spite of the harsher climatic conditions and its impact on floral and faunal resources. Unless strictly an artifact of archaeological visibility, Quad peoples reoccupied sites more often and exhibited preferences for upland habitats, particularly sinks. As might be expected, population density increased in the Highland Rim with milder climatic conditions of the Holocene.

Generally, in the temperate south, artifacts of perishable materials are poorly preserved. At Dust Cave, however, textile impressions in prepared clay surfaces (Sherwood and Chapman 2005; Freeman 2003) testify to the presence of a fiber industry (Quad through Early Side Notched). Baskets, bags, lines, nets, and the like were probably an important part of subsistence technology from the earliest times, providing various con-tainers, cordage, and matting. Bone tools, particularly awls, pins, and needles are prominent in the material inventory of Dust Cave (Quad through Early Side Notched). A bone fishhook found at Dust Cave testi-fies to line fishing early (9,000 RYBP) in the Archaic Stage (Goldman-Finn and Walker 1994:113). As noted above, the prepared clay surfaces, first recognized in the Quad component, but present throughout the sequence at Dust Cave, could have functioned as heated cooking surfaces to dry nut meats, roast other plant materials, or possibly cook fish (Sherwood and Chapman 2005; Pike, Hollenbach, and Homsey 2005).

Many of the chipped stone artifacts found in the region are made of Ft. Payne chert (Johnson and Meeks 1994), a locally available chert of very high quality. Bifaces dominate the stone-tool inventory throughout (Meeks 1993, 1994, 1995, 1996, 1998, 1999, 2000), providing preforms for formal tools and an abundance of flakes for expedient tools (Randall 1999). In a coexisting technology, blades struck from prepared blade cores are prevalent in the earlier part of the sequence but precipitously disappear by the end of the Dalton horizon (Randall 2001; Driskell, Meeks, and Sherwood 2005). Other shaped unifaces, such as teardrop and side scrapers, are more prominently represented in the earlier part of the sequence as well, but diminish gradually in proportion to bifacial tools during subsequent Archaic periods. Although the roles of formal unifaces are poorly understood, functions associated with these artifacts may have been increasingly filled by bifacial tools or expedient tools made on flakes.

Some technofunctional studies of the Dust Cave lithic assemblage have been attempted (Randall 2002, 2003). Meeks (Walker et al. 2001:184–189) examined 31 artifacts for indications of use. His results suggest that butchering, hide working, and bone working were the most common activities. Unifacial end and side scrapers (N=7) analyzed for usewear were primarily used to scrape hide, although one exhibited use on hard material. Of four thinned bifaces examined for microwear, two were used as butchering tools, and a hafted "drill" was actually used as a leather or hide perforator. Four of the five blades inspected by Meeks functioned as knives used in butchering activities. Finally, a crude biface was used to adze or plane wood.

Most of the chipped stone assemblage from Dust Cave has not been analyzed in detail but a new dissertation project at the University of Tennessee designed by Katherine E. McMillan (2005) plans to examine the Dust Cave lithic assemblage in order to reconstruct the organization of technology from late Paleoindian to middle Archaic periods and to investigate the reasons for changes in the tecnhnology. It is hoped that this future research will reveal the meaning of perceived changes in the "hunting kit" from late Paleoindian to middle Archaic times in the middle Tennessee Valley. What are the primary roles of prominent tool types? Are other bifacial or flake tools substituted for the distinctive unifacial tools from the earliest deposits? Do changes in the tool kit reflect fundamental changes in hunting techniques or subsistence strategies?

Training

An undergraduate archaeological field school was organized for each of the 12 summers of field investigations at Dust Cave (Driskell 2000b). In total these field schools have attracted well over 100 students from more than two dozen universities and colleges within the United States.

Table 9.1 (placed at the end of this chapter after the references) presents a list of people who worked at the cave; the list was developed from field notes in the project files.

From the beginning the project was organized around a summer field school for undergraduates. Project staff developed an experiential and didactic program that challenged students with an intensive exposure to archaeology. Lecture series in special analysis topics such as chipped stone technology, geoarchaeology, botanical analysis, and zooarchaeology supplemented closely supervised fieldwork experiences within the cave (Walker, Driskell, and Sherwood 2006). Because of challenges presented by the deep and complex stratigraphy, students were exposed to aspects of archaeological method and techniques that are difficult to demonstrate in other archaeological settings. During the later field seasons, undergraduate students also conducted and reported research, either as individuals or as small groups, supervised by field school staff.

Graduate students served as field school supervisors, and most pursued research topics that led to research papers, published articles, theses, or dissertations. Scott Shaw, Jennifer Grover, Nurit Goldman-Finn; Renee B. Walker, Scott C. Meeks, and Kandace D. Hollenbach served as senior graduate assistants during the course of the project. Two former graduate assistants, Renee B. Walker and Sarah C. Sherwood, organized their own field schools from Skidmore College and Middle Tennessee State University, respectively, at Dust Cave during 2002.

Professional collaborators enriched the field school experience with lectures and personal interaction with the students. Of particular note are the contributions of Paul Parmalee, Michael B. Collins, Paul Goldberg, Rod Riley, and Danny Reese. Beth Justice, Susan Driskell, Steve Tillman, Klete Rooney, and Sharon Freeman served as cooks and camp managers over the years.

Outreach

The project has also contributed to public education and K–12 instruction. Over the years the project has accepted numerous adult volunteers who contribute labor in exchange for experiential learning. Several adult volunteers are long-standing and regular participants returning to help out each summer. Of particular note, Joe Copeland, an economics professor (retired) at the University of North Alabama in Florence, and his wife, Nancy Copeland, have been stalwart workers, supporters, and friends to the project (Figure 9.7).

Fig. 9.7. Volunteers were a valuable asset at Dust Cave. Joe Copeland (left) and Nancy Copeland (far right) donated many hours of labor to the Dust Cave Project each summer.

Additionally, the project has hosted several teachers and school groups. The project sponsored a three-day Project Archaeology workshop for teachers in the summer of 1998, five workshops were offered in the summer of 1999, and two additional workshops were offered for the summer of 2000. My wife, Susan Driskell, a retired school teacher, cotaught these workshops with me. The 1999 and 2000 workshops were cosponsored by a grant from the Alabama Humanities Foundation.

Several summer enrichment groups visited the cave, and children and teachers benefited directly from the research and findings at Dust Cave through *Discovering Archaeology in Alabama,* a supplement to the Bureau of Land Management's Project Archaeology lesson plans that Susan and I coauthored. Written at the elementary level, this volume incorporates the setting and some of the findings from Dust Cave to create a story of the lifeways of prehistoric peoples of Alabama.

Acknowledgments

The project has been funded through research grants from the University of Alabama, the National Geographic Society, the Alabama Historical Commission, the Tennessee Valley Authority, the National Science Foundation, and IBM Corporation. Additional student support has been provided by IBM, Energen, and several private donors. Carey Oakley, director emeritus of the Office of Archaeological Research at the University of Alabama, and Bennett Graham, former manager of the Cultural Resources Section at TVA, have supported the project from inception to conclusion. Many others, mostly named above or in Table 1, have assisted to get the job done at Dust Cave. The Alabama Humanities

Foundation generously supported five Project Archaeology teacher's workshops in conjunction with Dust Cave in 1999 and two workshops in 2000. Our sincere thanks go to these organizations and individuals.

References Cited

COBB, RICHARD M.

1987   *A Speleoarchaeological Reconnaissance of the Pickwick Basin in Colbert and Lauderdale Counties in Alabama.* Report submitted to the Office of Archaeological Research, University of Alabama.

COBB, RICHARD M., BOYCE N. DRISKELL, AND SCOTT C. MEEKS

1995   Speleoarchaeological Reconnaissance and Test Excavations in the Pickwick Basin. In *Cultural Resources in the Pickwick Reservoir,* edited by Catherine C. Meyer. University of Alabama, Tuscaloosa, Division of Archaeology, Report of Investigations 75:219–261.

COLLINS, MICHAEL B.

1995   Observations on the Geomorphology of Ten Cave/Rockshelter Localities in the Pickwick Basin of Colbert and Lauderdale Counties, Alabama. In *Cultural Resources in the Pickwick Reservoir,* edited by Catherine C. Meyer. University of Alabama, Tuscaloosa, Division of Archaeology, Report of Investigations 75:351–376.

COLLINS, MICHAEL B., PAUL GOLDBERG, AND WULF A. GOSE

1995   Geoarchaeology in the Middle Tennessee Valley in Northern Alabama. Paper read at the annual meeting of the Geological Society of America, Lincoln, Nebraska.

COLLINS, MICHAEL B., WULF A. GOSE, AND SCOTT SHAW

1994   Preliminary Geomorphological Findings at Dust and Nearby Caves. *Journal of Alabama Archaeology* 40:34–55.

DAVIS, VALERIE SUZANNE

2004   A Study of Stress Indicators as Evidence for Possible Differential Treatment of Males and Females at Dust Cave (1LU496), Alabama. Master's thesis, Department of Sociology, Anthropology, and Social Work, Mississippi State University.

DETWILER, KANDACE

2000   Gathering in the Late Paleoindian: Botanical Remains from Dust Cave, Alabama. Paper read at symposium entitled "Mice to Mammoths: Studies in Paleoindian Subsistence Strategies," 57th annual meeting of the Society for American Archaeology, Philadelphia.

2001   Plant Use during the Late Paleoindian/Early Archaic Transition at Dust Cave. Paper read at for the symposium "To Change or Not to Change: The Late Paleoindian and Early side-Notched Transition at Dust Cave," organized by Asa Randall and Kandace Detwiler, 58th annual meeting of the Southeastern Archaeological Conference, Chattanooga.

2003　Nuts and More Nuts: Plant Use in the Middle Archaic at Dust Cave, Alabama. Paper read at the 60th Annual Southeastern Archaeological Conference, Charlotte, North Carolina.

DETWILER, KANDACE, RENEE WALKER, AND SCOTT C. MEEKS

1998　Berries, Bones and Blades: Reconstructing Late Paleoindian Subsistence at Dust Cave, Alabama. Paper read at the 55th annual Southeastern Archaeological Conference, Greenville, South Carolina.

DRISKELL, BOYCE N.

1994　Stratigraphy and Chronology at Dust Cave. *Journal of Alabama Archaeology* 40:17–34.

1996　Stratified Late Pleistocene and Early Holocene Deposits at Dust Cave, Northwest Alabama. In *The Paleoindian and Early Archaic Southeast,* edited by David Anderson and Kenneth Sassaman, pp. 315–330. University of Alabama Press, Tuscaloosa.

1998　Dust Cave. In *Archaeology of Prehistoric Native America: An Encyclopedia,* edited by Guy Gibbon, pp. 224–226. Garland Publishing, Inc., New York.

1999　Prehistoric Utilization of Caves and Shelters in Alabama. In the symposium entitled "Karst in Alabama," a session in the annual meeting of the Alabama Academy of Science, Athens College.

2000a　Discussant remarks in the symposium "Mice to Mammoths: Studies in Paleoindian Subsistence Strategies," 65th annual meeting of the Society for American Archaeology, Philadelphia.

2000b　The University of Alabama Archaeological Field School at Dust Cave, Northwest Alabama. Read in "Field Schools for the Next Millennium: Mixing Student Training, Research, and Public Education," symposium at the annual meeting of the Society for American Archaeology, Philadelphia.

2001a　Late Paleoindian and Archaic Research at Dust Cave, Northwest Alabama. Paper presented at the annual meeting of the Southeastern Archaeological Conference, Chattanooga.

2001b　Field Investigations at Dust Cave, Northwest Alabama, 1989–2000. Paper prepared for the symposium "To Change or Not to Change: The Late Paleoindian and Early Side-Notched Transition at Dust Cave," organized by Asa Randall and Kandace Detwiler, 58th annual meeting of the Southeastern Archaeological Conference, Chattanooga.

DRISKELL, BOYCE N., AND PAUL GOLDBERG

1994　*Archaeological Field Investigation at Dust Cave, Northwest Alabama.* Final Report (Grant # 5023–93) to the National Geographic Society, Washington, DC.

1995a　The Geoarchaeology of Dust Cave. Paper read at the 60th annual meeting of the Society for American Archaeology, Minneapolis.

1995b   *Continued Archaeological Investigations at Dust Cave and Related Sites in Northwest Alabama.* Preliminary report (grant # 5260–94) to the National Geographic Society, Washington, DC.

DRISKELL, BOYCE N., SCOTT C. MEEKS, AND SARAH S. SHERWOOD
2005   The Transition from Paleoindian to Archaic in the Middle Tennessee Valley. Read at the symposium "From Paleoindian to Archaic—Views on a Transition," Britt Bousman and Bradley Vierra, organizers. 70th annual meeting of the society for American Archaeology, Salt Lake City.

DRISKELL, BOYCE N., AND RENEE WALKER
2001   Late Paleoindian Subsistence at Dust Cave, Northwest Alabama. In *On Being First: Cultural Innovation and Environmental Consequences of First Peopling,* 31st Annual Chacmool Conference Proceedings, Jason Gillespie, Susan Tupakka, and Christy de Mille, eds., pp. 409–425. University of Calgary, Alberta, Canada.

FREEMAN, SHARON
2003   Prepared Surfaces: A First Impression. Paper presented at the 60th annual meeting of the Southeastern Archaeology Conference, Charlotte, NC, November 12–15.

GARDNER, PAUL
1994   Carbonized Plant Remains from Dust Cave. *Journal of Alabama Archaeology* 40:189–207.

GOLDBERG, PAUL, AND SARAH SHERWOOD
1994   Micromorphology of Dust Cave Sediments: Some Preliminary Results. *Journal of Alabama Archaeology* 40:56–64.

GOLDMAN-FINN, NURIT
1994   Dust Cave in Regional Context. *Journal of Alabama Archaeology* 40:208–226.

GOLDMAN-FINN, NURIT, AND BOYCE N. DRISKELL
1994   Introduction to Archaeological Research at Dust Cave. *Journal of Alabama Archaeology* 40:1–16.

GOLDMAN-FINN, NURIT, AND SCOTT C. MEEKS
1995   Dust Cave (1Lu496): An Overview of the 1989 to 1994 Field Seasons. Paper presented at the 72nd annual meeting of the Alabama Academy of Science, Birmingham.

GOLDMAN-FINN, NURIT, AND RENEE B. WALKER
1994   The Dust Cave Bone Tool Assemblage. *Journal of Alabama Archaeology* 40:104–113.

GOSE, WULF A.
2000   Palaeomagnetic Studies of Burned Rocks. *Journal of Archaeological Science* 27:409–421.

GROVER, JENNIFER
1993   Middle Holocene Adaptations as Seen from the Analysis of
        Faunal Remains from Dust Cave. Paper prepared for symposium
        "Preliminary Archaeological Investigations at Dust Cave, Northwest
        Alabama," 50th annual Southeastern Archaeological Conference,
        Raleigh, N.C., November 1993.
1994   Faunal Remains from Dust Cave. *Journal of Alabama Archaeology*
        40:114–131.
HOGUE, S. HOMES
1994   Human Skeletal Remains from Dust Cave. *Journal of Alabama
        Archaeology* 40:170–188.
HOLLENBACH, KANDACE D.
2004a   Gathering Implications: Late Paleoindian and Early Archaic Plant
        Use in Northwest Alabama. Paper presented at the 69th annual
        meeting of the Society for American Archaeology, Montreal.
2004b   Gathering and Mobility Decisions in the Late Paleoindian and Early
        Archaic Periods, Northwest Alabama. Paper presented at the 61st
        Annual Southeastern Archaeology Conference, St. Louis.
2005a   Beyond Nuts and Fruits: Late Paleoindian and Early Archaic Plant
        Use in Northwest Alabama. Paper presented at the 70th annual
        meeting of the Society for American Archaeology, Salt Lake City.
2005b   Gathering in the Late Paleoindian and Early Archaic Periods in the
        Middle Tennessee River Valley, Northwest Alabama. Ph.D. disserta-
        tion, Department of Anthropology, University of North Carolina,
        Chapel Hill.
2005c   Modeling Resource Procurement of Southeastern Hunter-Gatherers:
        A View from Northwest Alabama. Paper presented at the 62nd
        Annual Southeastern Archaeology Conference, Columbia, South
        Carolina.
2006   Modeling Resource Procurement of Late Paleoindian Hunter-
        Gatherers: A View from Northwest Alabama. Paper presented at the
        71st annual meeting of the Society of American Archaeology, San
        Juan, Puerto Rico.
2007   Gathering in the Late Paleoindian: Archaeobotanical Remains from
        Dust Cave, Alabama. In *Foragers of the Terminal Pleistocene in
        North America*, edited by Renee B. Walker and Boyce N. Driskell,
        pp. 132–147. University of Nebraska Press, Lincoln.
HOMSEY, LARA K.
2000   Feature Variability in the Early Archaic and Late Paleoindian
        Components at Dust Cave. Paper prepared for the symposium
        "To Change or Not to Change: The Late Paleoindian and Early
        side-Notched Transition at Dust Cave," organized by Asa Randall
        and Kandace Detwiler, 58th annual meeting of the Southeastern
        Archaeological Conference, Chattanooga.

2003a   Feature Variability in the Early and Middle Archaic Components at Dust Cave, Al. Paper presented at the 60th annual meeting of the Southeastern Archaeological Conference, Charlotte, NC, November 12–15.

2003b   The Spatial Organization of the Late Paleoindian through Middle Archaic Occupation at Dust Cave, Al. Paper presented at the 68th annual meeting of the Society for American Archaeology, Milwaukee, WI, April 9–13.

2004   The Form, Function and Organization of Anthropogenic Deposits at Dust Cave, Alabama. Ph.D. dissertation, Department of Anthropology, University of Pittsburgh.

HOMSEY, LARA K., AND ROSEMARY C. CAPO

2002   Geochemical Identification of Feature Function and Activity Areas at a Late Paleoindian through Middle Archaic Archaeological Site: Dust Cave, Al. *2002 Geological Society of America Abstracts with Programs*, p. 51–5.

2006   Integrating Geochemistry and Micromorphology to Interpret Feature Use at Dust Cave, a Paleoindian through Middle Archaic Site in Northwest Alabama. *Geoarchaeology* 21:237–269.

JOHNSON, HUNTER, AND SCOTT C. MEEKS

1994   Source Areas and Prehistoric Use of Fort Payne Chert. *Journal of Alabama Archaeology* 40:65–76.

KOOYMAN, BRIAN P.

2001   Letter report dated March 19, 2001, concerning presence and nature of phytolyths in two soil samples (1989.51.585 and 1989.51.564) from Dust Cave. In project files, archaeological collections of the Alabama Museum of Natural History, Tuscaloosa.

MCMILLAN, KATHERINE E.

2005   Archaeological Investigations at Dust Cave, Alabama: Past Research and Future Directions. Final paper for Anthropology 563, Lithic Technology.

MEEKS, SCOTT C.

1993   Lithic Technology at the Dust Cave Site: An Interpretation of Early and Middle Archaic Chipped Stone Tools. Paper presented at the symposium "Preliminary Archaeological Investigations at Dust Cave, Northwest Alabama," 50th annual Southeastern Archaeological Conference, Raleigh, North Carolina.

1994   Lithic Artifacts from Dust Cave. *Journal of Alabama Archaeology* 40:77–103.

1995   The Function of Stone Tools in Prehistoric Exchange Systems: A Look at Benton Interaction in the Mid-South. Invited paper for symposium "The Archaeology of Exchange in the Midsouth." 16th annual meeting of the Midsouth Archaeological Conference, Jackson, MS.

1996   The Organization of Late Middle Archaic Lithic Technology at Dust Cave, Northwest Alabama. Paper presented at the 53rd annual Southeastern Archaeological Conference, Birmingham.

1998   Projectile Point Form and Function: A View from the Terminal Middle Archaic Period in the Midsouth. M.A. thesis, Department of Anthropology, University of Alabama, Tuscaloosa.

1999   The Function of Stone Tools in Prehistoric Exchange Systems: A Look at Benton Interaction in the Mid-South. In *Raw Materials and Exchange in the Mid-South*, edited by Evan Peacock and Samuel O. Brookes, pp 29–43. Archaeological Report 29, Mississippi Department of Archives and History, Jackson.

2000   *The Use and Function of Late Middle Archaic Projectile Points in the Midsouth.* University of Alabama Office of Archaeological Services, Report of Investigations 77. Moundville, Alabama.

2001   Wandering around Dust Cave: An Overview of Late Paleoindian and Early Archaic Settlement Patterns in the Middle Tennessee River Valley. Paper prepared for the symposium "To Change or Not to Change: The Late Paleoindian and Early Side-Notched Transition at Dust Cave," organized by Asa Randall and Kandace Detwiler, 58th annual meeting of the Southeastern Archaeological Conference, Chattanooga.

MEYER, CATHERINE C. (EDITOR)
1995   *Cultural Resources in the Pickwick Reservoir.* University of Alabama, Division of Archaeology, Report of Investigations 75, Tuscaloosa.

MOREY, DARCY F.
1994   *Canis* Remains from Dust Cave. *Journal of Alabama Archaeology* 40:160–169.

PARMALEE, PAUL
1994   Freshwater Mussels from Dust and Smith Bottom Caves, Alabama. *Journal of Alabama Archaeology* 40:132–159.

PIKE, META, KANDACE D. HOLLENBACH, AND LARA K. HOMSEY
2005   *Changes in Plant Use and Associated Plant Processing Technologies at Dust Cave, Al.* Poster presented at the 70th annual meeting of the Society for American Archaeology: Salt Lake City, March 30–April 3.

RANDALL, ASA
1999   Analysis of Paleoindian and Early Archaic Debitage from Dust Cave, Alabama. Paper submitted for partial fulfillment of the B.A. in Archaeological Studies with Distinction, Department of Archaeology, Boston University.

2001   Untangling Late Paleoindian and Early Side-Notched Stone Tool Assemblages at Dust Cave. Paper prepared for the symposium

"To Change or Not to Change: The Late Paleoindian and Early Side-Notched Transition at Dust Cave," organized by Asa Randall and Kandace Detwiler, 58th annual meeting of the Southeastern Archaeological Conference, Chattanooga.

2002   Technofunctional Variation in Early Side-Notched Hafted Bifaces: A View from the Middle Tennessee River Valley in Northwest Alabama. M.A. thesis, Department of Anthropology, University of Florida.

2003   Archaic Technological Practice at Dust Cave, Alabama. Paper prepared for the symposium "The Early and Middle Archaic at Dust Cave, Alabama," organized by Kandace Detwiler and Asa Randall, 58th annual meeting of the Southeastern Archaeological Conference, Chattanooga.

RILEY, ROD

2001   The Three C's of Database Usage at Dust Cave. Paper prepared for the symposium "To Change or Not to Change: The Late Paleoindian and Early Side-Notched Transition at Dust Cave," organized by Asa Randall and Kandace Detwiler, 58th annual meeting of the Southeastern Archaeological Conference, Chattanooga.

SHERWOOD, SARAH C.

1997   The Dust Cave Project, Alabama. *Newsletter of the Archaeological Geology Division, The Geological Society of America* 20(1):10–12.

1999a   The Geoarchaeology of Dust Cave: The Depositional History of a Late Paleoindian through Middle Archaic Site in the Middle Tennessee River Valley. Ph.D. dissertation proposal, Department of Anthropology, University of Tennessee, Knoxville.

1999b   The Geoarchaeology of Dust Cave in the Context of the Middle Tennessee River Valley. Paper presented at symposium "The Geoarchaeology of Big Rivers," the 64th annual meeting of the Society for American Archaeology, Chicago.

2001a   The Geoarchaeology of Dust Cave: A Late Paleoindian through Middle Archaic site in the Western Middle Tennessee River Valley. Ph.D. dissertation, Department of Anthropology, University of Tennessee, Knoxville.

2001b   The Geoarchaeology of the Late Pleistocene through Early Holocene at Dust Cave. Paper prepared for the symposium "To Change or Not to Change: The Late Paleoindian and Early Side-Notched Transition at Dust Cave," organized by Asa Randall and Kandace Detwiler, 58th annual meeting of the Southeastern Archaeological Conference, Chattanooga.

SHERWOOD, SARAH C., AND JEFFERSON CHAPMAN

2005   Identification and Potential Significance of Early Holocene Prepared Clay Surfaces: Examples from Dust Cave and Icehouse Bottom. *Southeastern Archaeology* 24(1):70–82.

SHERWOOD, SARAH C., BOYCE N. DRISKELL, ASA RANDALL, AND
SCOTT C. MEEKS
2004   Chronology and Stratigraphy at Dust Cave, Alabama. *American
Antiquity* 69(3): 533–554.

SHERWOOD, SARAH C., AND PAUL GOLDBERG
2001   Recognition and Organization of Burned Surfaces at Dust Cave:
A Microstratigraphic Approach. Paper presented at symposium
"Multi-occupations and Complex Depositions: Archaeology
in Three Dimensions," 66th annual meeting of the Society for
American Archaeology, New Orleans

SHERWOOD, SARAH C., AND ROD RILEY
1998   Geoarchaeological Structure and Interim Management of the Dust
Cave Relational Database. Paper presented at the 55th annual
meeting of the Southeastern Archaeological Conference, Greenville,
South Carolina.

WALKER, RENEE B.
1995   A Comparison of Late Paleoindian, Early Archaic and Middle
Archaic Faunal Remains from Dust Cave (1Lu496), Alabama. Paper
presented at the annual meeting of the Southeastern Archaeological
Conference, Knoxville, Tennessee.

1996   Faunal Remains from Dust Cave (1Lu496): Changes in Subsistence
from Paleoindian through Archaic Occupations. Paper presented at
the 61st annual meeting of the Society for American Archaeology,
New Orleans.

1997   Late Paleoindian Faunal Remains from Dust Cave, Alabama.
Current Research in the Pleistocene 14:85–87.

1998   *The Late Paleoindian through Middle Archaic Faunal Evidence
from Dust Cave, Alabama.* Ph.D. dissertation, Department of
Anthropology, University of Tennessee, Knoxville.

2000a   *Subsistence Strategies at Dust Cave: Changes from the Late
Paleoindian through Middle Archaic Occupations.* University of
Alabama Office of Archaeological Services, Tuscaloosa, Report of
Investigations 78.

2000b   Hunting in the Late Paleoindian: Faunal Remains from Dust Cave,
Alabama. Symposium entitled "Mice to Mammoths: Studies in
Paleoindian Subsistence Strategies," 65th annual meeting of the
Society for American Archaeology, Philadelphia.

2001   Refining Our Understanding of Subsistence Strategies at Dust Cave:
An Analysis of a Recently Excavated Paleoindian Faunal Sample.
Paper prepared for the symposium "To Change or Not to Change:
The Late Paleoindian and Early Side-Notched Transition at Dust
Cave," organized by Asa Randall and Kandace Detwiler, 58th
annual meeting of the Southeastern Archaeological Conference,
Chattanooga.

2002   Early Holocene Ecological Adaptations in North Alabama. In *Culture, Environment, and Conservation in the Appalachian South,* edited by Benita J. Howell, pp. 21–41. University of Illinois Press, Urbana.

2003   Transitions in Animal Use from the Early to Middle Archaic at Dust Cave, Alabama. Paper presented at the 60th annual meeting of the Southeastern Archaeology Conference, Charlotte, NC.

2005   The Role of Domestic Dogs during the Archaic Period in the Southeast and Midwest. Paper presented at the 62nd annual meeting of the Southeastern Archaeology Conference, Columbia, SC.

WALKER, RENEE B., KANDACE DETWILER, SCOTT C. MEEKS, AND BOYCE N. DRISKELL

2001   Berries, Bones, and Blades: Reconstructing Late Paleoindian Subsistence Economy at Dust Cave, Alabama. *Midcontinental Journal of Archaeology* 26(2):169–198.

WALKER, RENEE B., AND BOYCE DRISKELL (EDITORS)

2007   *Foragers of the Terminal Pleistocene in North America.* University of Nebraska Press, Lincoln.

WALKER, RENEE B., BOYCE N. DRISKELL, AND SARAH C. SHERWOOD

2006   The Dust Cave Archaeological Project: Investigating Paleoindian and Archaic Lifeways in Southeastern North America. Case study in *Seeking Our Past: An Introduction to North American Archaeology,* edited by Sarah W. Neusius and G. Timothy Gross, student CD, section D-5, pp. 83–94. Oxford University Press, Oxford and New York.

WALKER, RENEE B., BOYCE DRISKELL, SARAH SHERWOOD, SCOTT C. MEEKS, AND KANDACE R. DETWILER

1999   Recent Investigations at Dust Cave: A Late Paleoindian through Middle Archaic Site in Northwest Alabama. Paper presented at the 64th annual meeting of the Society for American Archaeology, Chicago.

WALKER, RENEE B., DARCY F. MOREY, AND JOHN H. RELETHFORD

2005   Early and Mid-Holocene Dogs in Southeastern North America: Examples from Dust Cave. *Southeastern Archaeology* 24(1): 83–92.

WALKER, RENEE B., AND PAUL W. PARMALEE

2004   A Noteworthy Cache of *Branta canadensis* at Dust Cave, Northwestern Alabama. *Journal of Alabama Archaeology* 50(1):18–35.

WALKER, RENEE B., AND N. L. RICHARDSON

1999   A Consideration of Taphonomic Factors Affecting the Faunal Assemblage from Dust Cave. Paper presented at the 56th annual meeting of the Southeastern Archaeological Conference, Pensacola.

Table 9.1: Staff, Student, and Volunteer Participants at Dust Cave

Participant	Season/s	Role/s	Affiliation
Adams, Luana-lei	1998	student	Indiana University
Anderson, David	1993-2002	volunteer, collaborator	NPS; University of Tennessee
Anderson, Matthew C.	1999	student	University of Arkansas Fayetteville
Arnold, Kim	1997	student	Southern Methodist University
Autry, Mark	1990	student	University of Alabama
Avsharian, Barbara	1994	volunteer	Opelika, Alabama
Baggett, Klint	1998	student	University of Alabama
Barnes, Nancy	1989	student, staff	University of Alabama
Bivrton, Jackie	1990	student	University of North Alabama
Blair, Fuller	1994	volunteer	Mobile, Alabama
Blurton, Jackie	1991	student	volunteer
Borden, Faye	1992	student	University of North Alabama
Bowers, Lauren	2002	student	Middle Tennessee State University
Boyer, David	2000	student	University of Memphis
Bradley, Debra	1999	student	University of Washington
Brecht, Tatiana	1992	student	UNC Chapel Hill
Briggs, Melissa	1994	student	Samford University
Brock, Daniel	2002	student	Middle Tennessee State University
Brown, J. Emmett	1993	student	University of Alabama Birmingham
Byers, Pam	2002	student	Middle Tennessee State University
Cahoon, John	1991	student	University of North Alabama
Cahoon, Kathy	1989	student	University of North Alabama
Cannon, Roy Gregory	2002	student	Middle Tennessee State University
Carbonie, George	1990	student	University of Alabama
Carr, Katherine	1997	volunteer	Sweet Briar College
Carroll, Sue	1996	student	University of Michigan

Table 9.1 (continued): Staff, Student, and Volunteer Participants at Dust Cave			
Participant	Season/s	Role/s	Affiliation
Clark, Stacey	1998	student	College of the Mainland
Cobb, Daniel	1994	volunteer	Birmingham, Alabama
Cobb, Donna K.	1993	student	University of Alabama Birmingham
Cobb, Richard	1989	staff	Florence City Schools
Cobb, Vincent	1990	student	University of North Alabama
Collins, Michael	1989-2002	collaborator	University of Texas Austin
Compton, Cecil	1994	volunteer	Orange Beach, Alabama
Copeland, Abby	2002	student	Skidmore College
Copeland, Joe	1989-2002	student, volunteer	University of North Alabama
Copeland, Nancy	1989-2002	volunteer	Florence, Alabama
Cox, Elizabeth	1989	student	University of Alabama
Daniel, Jerry	1991	student	University of North Alabama
Davis, Angela	1996-1997	student	University of Alabama
Davis, Valerie S.	2004	student	Mississippi State University
De La Rosa, Paul Edward	2000	student	University of Texas Austin
Decker, Michael	1998	student	University of Tennessee Knoxville
DeGomez, Marie	1998-1999	student, staff	Boston University
DeWitt, Theresa	1992	student	University of Florida
Donley, Colleen	1998	student	Stanford University
Driskell, Boyce	1989-2002	director	University of Ala; University of Tenn
Driskell, Nathan	2002	volunteer	Tuscaloosa, Alabama
Driskell, Susan	1990-2000	volunteer, staff	Tuscaloosa County Schools
Easter, Nancy	1991	student	University of North Alabama
Eastman, Nancy	1991	volunteer	University of North Alabama
Ellis, Jane Matthews	1991-94	student, volunteer	University of Georgia
Ernsberger, Jr., Jerry	1994	student	University of Alabama Tuscaloosa

Estes, Myron	1991-1992	student	University of North Alabama
Flemming, Tracy	1998	student	Morehouse College
Francis, Bobby	1999	student	Florida State University
Franklin, Ronald	2000	student	Tennessee Tech University
Frederick, Jan	1989	student	University of North Alabama
Freeman, Sharon	1999-2002	student, staff	University of Alabama
George, Randy	1997-1998	volunteer	Birmingham, Alabama
Gifford, Kathy	2002	student	Middle Tennessee State University
Gill, Sarah Amanda	1993	student	University of Alabama Tuscaloosa
Goldberg, Paul	1992-2002	collaborator	Boston University
Goldman-Finn, Nurit	1992, 1993	staff	University of Michigan
Goodmaster, Christopher	2002	student	Middle Tennessee State University
Grimes, Burley	2002	student	Middle Tennessee State University
Grover, Jennifer	1990-1991	staff	University of Alabama
Guidry, Hannah	2002	student	Middle Tennessee State University
Hack, Steven R.	1989	student	University of Alabama Tuscaloosa
Hall, Malcolm	1992	student	University of North Alabama
Hammer, Daniel S.	1999-2000	student	Ohio State University
Hand, John	1994	volunteer	Auburn, Alabama
Hand, Roberta	1994	volunteer	Auburn, Alabama
Harkins, Kelly (Fife)	2002	student	Skidmore College
Henderlight, Joshua C.	1999	student	University of Tennessee Knoxville
Henderson, Karen	1994	student	University of Central Florida
Hendrickson, Chris	1998	student	Ohio State University
Hiestand, Del	1992	student	University of Alabama Birmingham
Hogan, Chris	2002	student	Middle Tennessee State University
Hollenbach, Kandace Detwiler	1997-2002	student, staff	Washington University; UNC Chapel Hill

Table 9.1 (continued): Staff, Student, and Volunteer Participants at Dust Cave

Participant	Season/s	Role/s	Affiliation
Homsey, Lara	1996-2002	student, staff	Shippensburg University; U Pittsburgh
Houston, Jeff	1994	student	University of Alabama
Jeffery, Mark	1997	student	Lane College
Johnson, Hunter	1992	student	University of North Alabama
Jolly, A. F.	1994	volunteer	Rolla, Missouri
Jolly, Chris	1994	volunteer	Rolla, Missouri
Jones, Bobby	2000	volunteer	Moundville, Alabama
Jones, Kari	1997, 1999	student, staff	University of Illinois Urbana
Jones, Steve	1996-1998	staff	University of Alabama
Justice, Beth	1989-1994	volunteer, staff	Huntsville, Alabama
Karle, Isabel	1994	volunteer	Germany
Lamanna, Andy	1994	student	University of Alabama Tuscaloosa
Lauderdale, Ester	1994	volunteer	Tuscumbia, Alabama
League, Carrie	1996	student	Judson College
Lerner, Adrienne	1998	student	Oglethorpe University
Lewis, Chris	1994	volunteer	Evans, Georgia
Lewis, Gary	1994	volunteer	Evans, Georgia
Lieb, Brad	1997	student	Mississippi State University
Livingood, Patrick	1994	volunteer	University of North Carolina, Chapel hill
Livingood, Peggy	1997	volunteer	Murfreesboro, Tennessee
Livingood, Suzanne	1997	volunteer	Murfreesboro, Tennessee
Lobezoo, Jeremy	1993	student	University of Michigan
Lowery, Grady	2002	student	Middle Tennessee State University
Lydick, Christopher M.	1999	student	Florida State University
Madden, Molley	1994	volunteer	Ozark, Alabama
Mastranunzio, Stephen A.	1999	student	Skidmore College
McCanless, Carol	1993-1996	volunteer	Oxford, Georgia
McCray, Tim	1998-2000	volunteer	Moundville, Alabama

McDonald, Larry	1999	student	University of Alabama
McElwain, Kim	1989	student	University of North Alabama
McGhee, John	2002	student	Middle Tennessee State University
McLendon, John	1996	volunteer	Brentwood, Tennessee
Meadows, John	1996	staff	University of Sheffield, U.K.
Meeks, Scott	1991-1998	student, staff	Tulane University; University of Alabama
Miller, Jessica	1998	student	Mississippi State University
Miller, Michael	1997	student	Wabash College
Much, Bryan	1999	student	Shippensburg University
Mukhtar, Zubaidah	1990	student	University of Alabama Tuscaloosa
Mullen, Dianne	1994	volunteer	Auburn, Alabama
Mullen, Gary	1994	volunteer	Auburn, Alabama
Mustafa, Mentor	1999	student	Boston University
Neutzling, Kim	1993-1994	student	Ohio State University
Olsen, Nancy	1996	volunteer	Athens, Alabama
Overbey, Winifred	1989	student	University of North Alabama
Owens, Faith L.	1999	student	University of Alabama Tuscaloosa
Paddock, Chris	1996	student	Shippensburg University
Parmalee, Paul	1989-2002	collaborator	University of Tennessee Knoxville
Parrott, Colby	2002	student	Middle Tennessee State University
Pieroni, Amy	1989	student	University of North Alabama
Pike, Meta	2002	staff	University of Tennessee Knoxville
Pritchard, Erin	1996	student	University of Tennessee Knoxville
Pryor, David	1997	volunteer	Dothan, Alabama
Randall, Asa	1997-2002	student, staff	Boston University
Reese, Danny	1996-2000	volunteer	University of Alabama
Reese, Margaret Allen	1993	student	University of Mississippi

Participant	Season/s	Role/s	Affiliation
Rice, Stuart	1994	student	University of North Alabama
Richardson, Nicholas	1997-2000	student, staff	University of Washington
Riley, Rod	1993-2002	collaborator	University of Alabama; IBM
Rivers, Teresa	1992	student	University of North Alabama
Rodgers, Shannon	1991	student	University of Alabama Tuscaloosa
Rooney, Clete	1997-1998	staff	University of Alabama
Roskowski, Laura Ann	1999	student	Michigan State University
Ryba, Beth	1991	staff	University of Alabama Tuscaloosa
Savage, Helen	1989	student	University of Alabama Tuscaloosa
Saxon, Ashley	1991	student	University of Alabama Tuscaloosa
Scott, Robert B.	1989	student	University of North Alabama
Shaw, Jeff	1994	volunteer	Cuba, Alabama
Shaw, Scott	1989-1992	student, staff	University of North Ala; University of Ala
Shaw, Wes	1999	student	University of Alabama
Sherrod, Joseph	1994	volunteer	Mobile, Alabama
Sherwood, Sarah	1996-2002	staff	University of Tennessee Knoxville
Silcox, Paige	2002	student	Middle Tennessee State University
Simmons, Chad	2002	student	College of Charleston
Skipper, Tara	1993	student	Southern Methodist University
Smith, Anthony	1998	student	University of Tennessee Knoxville
Smith, Brian	1992	student	University of Alabama Tuscaloosa
Snyder, Asa T.	2002	student	Skidmore College
Spry, Marla Jo	1989	volunteer	University of Alabama
Szatkowski, Tammy	1993	student	University of Michigan

Table 9.1 (continued): Staff, Student, and Volunteer Participants at Dust Cave

Terziogh, Murat	2002	student	Skidmore College
Thompson, Leigh	1994	student	University of North Alabama
Thurlow, George	1996	volunteer	Huntsville, Alabama
Tice, Doug	1998	student	Mississippi State University
Tillman, Steve	1992-1994	staff	University of Alabama employee
Townsend, Dalgliesha L.	1997	student	Stillman College
Trachenberg, Sam	1997	staff	Tulane University
Van Valkenburg	1994	volunteer	Orange Beach, Alabama
Wachowiak, Paula	1997	student	SUNY Buffalo
Walker, Jimmy	1991	student	University of North Alabama
Walker, Renee	1994-2002	student, staff	University of Tennessee Knoxville
Walker, Sarah	1994	volunteer	Eclectic, Alabama
Wallinger, Jon	1994	student	Pennsylvania State University
Webb, Peter	1994	student	University of New Orleans
Webb, Steve	1992	student	University of North Alabama
Weeks, William Rex	1994	student	University of Tennessee Knoxville
Winchester, Margaret S.	2002	student	Skidmore College
Windham, Rachel Jeannine	2000	student	University of Alabama Tuscaloosa
Wisenbaker, Joshua	1997	student	Alabama State University
Wood, Linda	1994	volunteer	Guntersville, Alabama
Zivin, Casey	2002	student	Skidmore College

PART V
TVA AND FUTURE STEWARDSHIP IN THE TENNESSEE RIVER VALLEY

10
Understanding Cultural Pattern and Process in the Tennessee River Valley: The Role of Cultural Resources Management Investigations in Archaeological Research

Scott C. Meeks

SINCE THE IMPLEMENTATION of federal legislations enacted in the 1960s and 1970s—National Historic Preservation Act (1966), National Environmental Policy Act (1969), and the Archaeological and Historic Preservation Act (1974)—cultural resources management (CRM) investigations of Tennessee Valley Authority (TVA) properties have provided the archaeological community with a wealth of information for understanding 14,000 years of Native American occupation in the Tennessee River Valley.[1] To appreciate fully the extent that CRM has played in the understanding of cultural pattern and process in the Tennessee Valley region, it is important to consider the magnitude of the work that has been conducted as part of federally mandated compliance work. To date more than 800 archaeological reports have been produced stemming from CRM work on TVA properties with the number of investigations increasing incrementally over the past three decades (Figure 10.1). These reports vary greatly in both scope and content, differences largely resulting from the scale of the investigations. Reports range from surveys of small land parcels to large-scale reservoir surveys, from small testing projects to large-scale mitigations. The amount of archaeological research also varies in space, with some reservoirs (e.g., Chickamauga, Pickwick, Normandy, Tellico) receiving extensive investigations, including testing and large-scale excavations, while other reservoirs (e.g., Chatuge, Ocoee, Nottley, Watauga) have only begun to be investigated, with little work beyond the level of survey. Despite the varying scopes of these studies, there is a common thread that unites them all—they tell us something about the archaeology of the Tennessee Valley region. This is, of course, a truism, but it highlights the fact that archaeological investigations are not conducted in a vacuum. When considered in totality, the varying CRM investigations conducted within TVA properties provide a large corpus of data to further our understanding of Native American cultural pattern and process in the region, including culture history, settlement and subsistence practices, technological organization, and social organization.

Given the large volume of archaeological literature, the vast spatial coverage of TVA properties, and the great time depth of Native American occupation in the region, it is beyond the scope of this chapter to exhaustively discuss many of the important works that have been generated over the past three decades or to adequately consider the many spatiotemporal shifts in the archaeological record associated with varying trajectories of cultural process. Rather, a major premise of this chapter is to demonstrate the importance of examining the archaeological record of TVA properties at a broad regional scale that allows cultural patterning to be understood within the broader context of cultural process. To achieve this goal, this chapter presents two case studies employing archaeological data contained in reports generated by CRM investigations related to TVA

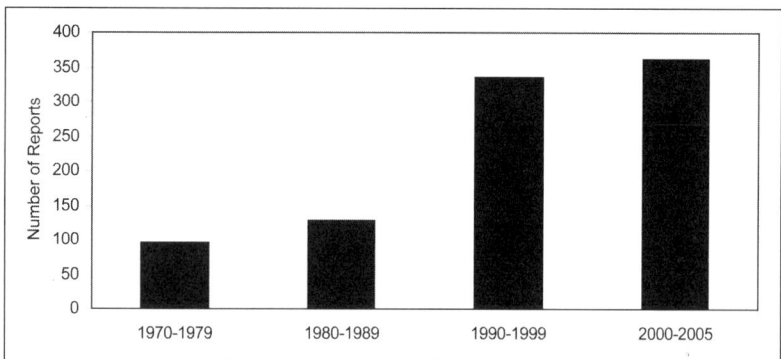

Fig. 10.1. Number of Cultural Resources Management reports by decade associated with investigations of Tennessee Valley Authority properties.

undertakings to explore trends relating to Native American occupation of the region. The first case study examines broad demographic trends in the Tennessee River Valley inferred from spatiotemporal shifts reflected in the distribution of archaeological sites. The second case study is more specific, focusing on the distribution of Mississippian and Protohistoric sites in the valley and considering the distribution of these sites within the context of a changing sociopolitical landscape. Having illustrated the utility of examining the archaeological record of TVA properties from a regional perspective, it is worthwhile to explore the future role that CRM will play in our further understanding of cultural pattern and process in the Tennessee River Valley and how such work can be formulated to explore questions germane to archaeological research.

Regional Analysis and Cultural Patterning: Native American Demographic Trends

The importance of employing regional analysis for identifying patterning in the archaeological record is not a novel idea (e.g., Anderson 1991a; Ammerman 1981; Johnson 1977; Sassaman and Anderson 1996; Struever 1971), and numerous examples of such an approach in the southeastern United States illustrate the interpretive power of broad analyses and overviews (e.g., Anderson 1991a, 1991b, 1995, 1996a; Anderson, Ledbetter, and O'Steen 1990; Gilliam 1995; Kowalewski 1995; Milner, Anderson, and Smith 2001; Rafferty 2002). Factors influencing the regional distribution and abundance of Native American populations in the Tennessee River Valley (as well as outside of the valley) were wide-ranging in scope, including variations in physiography, climate, resource structure and availability, and intensity of social interaction.

To understand how such factors influenced the distribution and abundance of Native American populations across the landscape in both time and space requires the adoption of a regional analytical framework. To this end, three decades of CRM investigations of TVA-owned properties provide an excellent opportunity to examine demographic trends associated with 14,000 years of Native American occupation throughout the Tennessee River Valley.

Data Compilation and Potential Biases

Understanding the archaeological record at a regional level requires at a minimum the spatiotemporal distribution of archaeological sites across the landscape. Presently there are more than 11,000 archaeological sites recorded within the bounds of TVA reservoir systems. The total number of recorded sites within the bounds of TVA reservations includes sites recorded prior to the implementation of federal legislation enacted in the 1960s and 1970s, the vast majority of which were recorded during federally sponsored archaeology in the 1930s and 1940s. Although many of these earlier recorded sites are now permanently inundated, sites occurring above reservoir pool levels and sites exposed during periods of winter low pool have been reinvestigated as part of TVA's efforts to identify and evaluate archaeological resources for management purposes and stewardship. Using information provided in large-scale surveys of TVA reservoirs (Figure 10.2), data was collected for a total of 8,631 sites of which 7,150 contain evidence of Native American occupation(s). Of these 7,150 sites, a total of 6,243 cultural affiliations could be assigned to broad temporal periods spanning Paleoindian through Historic Native American occupation of TVA properties.[2] These data are presented in Table 10.1 by subregion and reservoir along with numbers of total sites, total Native American sites (including sites designated as unknown aboriginal), and the number of specific temporal periods.

The subregions employed in this study are based on hydrological units as defined by the U.S. Geological Survey with a subregion including "the area drained by a river system, a reach of a river and its tributaries in that reach, a closed basin(s), or a group of streams forming a coastal drainage area" (Seaber, Kapinos, and Knapp 1987:3). The four subregion units are used in this study as a means of collapsing the various reservoir data into broad, yet spatially meaningful, units to make comparison of site data across the Tennessee River Valley more manageable. These subregion units are not meant to imply cultural geography "realized" by Native American inhabitants of the region. It also important to note that the numbers presented in Table 10.1 for each specific temporal period represent total number of sites and not the total number of components for a given period. During the data compilation, it was realized that some reports presented total number of components for a given period while others presented only total number of sites for a given period. In those cases where total number of components was presented, it was possible based on information provided in the reports to determine the total number of sites for a given period. In some cases, however, the necessary data (i.e., description of diagnostic materials) were not presented to allow the total number of components for a given reservoir to be determined, so all reservoir site data were based on total number of sites for a given period to normalize the data across reservoirs (e.g.,

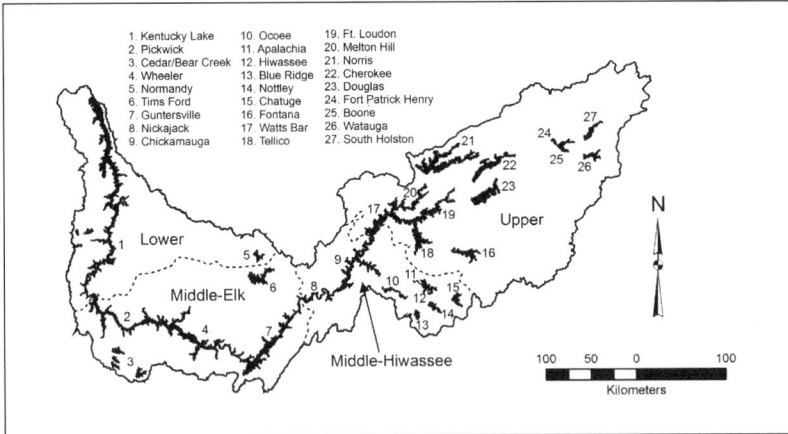

Fig. 10.2. Map of the Tennessee River Valley illustrating the locations of the reservoirs examined in this study and the boundaries of the four subregions.

a site that had three Early Archaic components identified [Early Side Notched, Corner Notched, and Bifurcate] was treated as a single Early Archaic site).

Before discussing demographic trends reflected in the archaeological record of TVA properties, it is first necessary to consider potential biases of the site database employed in this study. The foundation of identifying meaningful trends of archaeological site distribution, both spatially and temporally, is the archaeological site database. However, the utility of site databases for such investigation varies widely in terms of the range and quality of data for several reasons, including variations in the comprehensiveness and intensity of survey in a region (this problem is particularly acute across TVA reservoirs, as both the total areas investigated and the levels of investigations vary among the reservoirs); incomplete and/or unreliable information for particular sites; varying methods of investigation; component definition and intensity; and the fact that the archaeological record is more a reflection of archaeological investigations and less a record of aboriginal land use. Despite these problems, the position taken here is that the site database (a total of 6,234 specific Native American temporal periods with adequate spatial coverage at the subregion level) used in this study is robust enough to obviate these concerns, allowing general trends of aboriginal site frequencies and distribution in both time and space to be investigated.

In addition to considering the potential biases inherent in large site databases, it is also necessary to consider the temporal resolution and chronological control employed in this study. Considering the geographical

Table 10.1: Absolute Frequency of Native American Sites on Tennessee Valley Authority Properties by Subregion and Reservoir

Sub-Region	Reservoir	Total Sites	Native American Sites[1]	Paleo-indian	Early Archaic	Middle Archaic	Late Archaic	Early Woodland	Middle Woodland	Late Woodland	Mississippian	Proto-historic	Historic
Lower	Kentucky[2]	1019	751	11	31	55	99	54	92	60	40	0	0
	Normandy[3]	172	172	11	55	42	59	53	51	20	6	0	0
	Total	1191	923	22	86	97	158	107	143	80	46	0	0
Middle-Elk	Bear/Cedar Creek[4]	615	561	6	23	48	59	28	55	51	9	0	0
	Pickwick[5]	888	820	37	58	58	160	53	94	122	103	0	4
	Wheeler[6]	853	805	25	85	81	186	60	91	127	77	0	1
	Tims Ford[7]	82	64	1	13	5	4	5	5	2	0	0	0
	Guntersville[8]	683	589	3	19	48	74	65	59	112	51	9	4
	Total	3121	2839	72	198	240	483	211	304	414	240	9	9
Middle-Hiwassee	Nickajack[9]	98	61	0	4	5	12	4	13	13	12	6	9
	Chicka-mauga[10]	522	487	9	64	59	118	78	83	59	79	11	18
	Ocoee[11]	20	17	0	1	3	3	0	2	1	1	1	0
	Apalachia[12]	16	11	0	1	0	1	0	2	0	0	1	1
	Hiwassee[13]	253	222	1	12	40	35	14	37	14	26	0	57
	Blue Ridge[14]	84	84	2	10	32	11	5	5	3	6	0	2
	Nottely[15]	157	153	1	10	11	19	8	12	10	9	0	4

Chatuge[16]	218	172	0	9	7	20	10	2	9	27	0	22
Total	1368	1207	13	111	157	219	119	156	109	160	18	113
Upper	Watts Bar[17]	504	288	5	30	11	35	50	81	60	64	4	2
Melton Hill[18]	98	72	0	4	5	6	6	16	7	21	0	0
Tellico[19]	883	777	19	173	140	125	60	112	40	171	3	35
Ft. Loudon[20]	24	21	0	5	1	4	2	3	2	4	2	0
Norris[21]	459	270	2	30	22	26	15	20	17	19	0	0
Douglas[22]	105	79	0	7	1	4	15	13	5	4	4	0
Cherokee[23]	578	404	5	58	34	73	39	41	40	51	0	3
Fort Patrick Henry[24]	65	60	0	9	4	21	19	23	6	12	0	0
Boone[25]	53	43	0	0	0	0	0	0	0	0	0	0
Watauga[26]	112	111	1	14	15	39	22	16	14	22	13	0
South Holston[27]	49	46	0	5	4	5	2	3	3	2	0	0
Fontana[28]	21	10	0	2	4	3	2	3	1	1	0	3
Total	2951	2181	32	337	241	341	232	331	195	371	26	43
Grand Total	8631	7150	139	732	735	1201	669	934	798	817	53	165

[1]Includes sites with unknown Native American occupations; [2]Kerr 1996; [3]Faulkner and McCollough 1973; Prescott 1978; [4]Hendryx 1999, Lafferty and Solis 1980, McNutt and Weaver 1985; [5]Meyer 1995, Pietak et al. 2002; [6]Price 2002, 2003, Shaw 2000; [7]DuVall 1998, Lawrence 2000, Wampler et al. 2002; [8]Solis and Futato 1987; [9]Driskell and Mistovich 1990; [10]Benthall 1995, Elliot 1993, Staynard 1997; [11]Ahlman 2002; [12]Riggs et al. 1995; [13]Riggs and Kimball 1996; [14]Riggs and Kimball 2005; [15]Adams 1999; [16]Ahlman et al. 2000, Cannon 1986; [17]Herrmann and Frakenberg 2000; [18]Davis 1990, Frankenberg and Ahlman 2000; [19]Gage 2005a; [20]Gage 2005b, Pietak and Holland 1997, 1999; [21]Stanyard and Holland 2004; [22]Herrmann and Frakenberg 2000; [23]Frankenberg et al. 2000, Gage 2005; [24]Polhemus 2000; [25]McNutt et al. 1997, Pietak and Holland 1998a; [26]Boyd 1986; [27]Pietak and Holland 1998b; [28]Shumate et al. 1999.

coverage of the Tennessee River Valley, it is not surprising that the cultural-historical frameworks applied to Native American manifestations vary across the region. Some areas have received intensive investigation and accordingly have much tighter temporal sequences derived from both stratigraphic excavations and radiometric dates (e.g., Bear/Cedar Creek, Normandy, Pickwick, Tellico), while the study of other areas (e.g., Apalachia, Chatuge, Nottely, Ocoee) employs chronologies extrapolated from other regions. In order to normalize the data from a chronological standpoint, all components used in this analysis were placed into a *generalized* cultural-historical framework for the Tennessee River Valley (Table 10.2). Although this chronology may conflict with specific cultural-historical frameworks for a given reservoir, the differences are considered minor and do not greatly undermine the temporal resolution at the regional scale of analysis.

Table 10.2: General, Cultural, and Chronological Framework for Native American Occupation in the Tennessee Valley Region

Period	Uncalibrated Conventional	Calibrated Conventional[1]	Calibrated Radiocarbon[1]
Historic	A.D. 1650–1840	cal A.D. 1650–1840	300–110 cal BP
Protohistoric	A.D. 1500–1650	cal A.D. 1500–1650	450–300 cal BP
Mississippian	A.D. 900–1500	cal A.D. 1000–1500	950–450 cal BP
Late Woodland	A.D. 600–900	cal A.D. 650–1000	1300–950 cal BP
Middle Woodland	200 B.C.–A.D. 600	300 cal B.C.–cal A.D. 650	2250–1300 cal BP
Early Woodland	1000–200 B.C.	1200–300 cal B.C.	3150–2250 cal BP
Late Archaic	3000–1000 B.C.	3700–1200 cal B.C.	5650–3150 cal BP
Middle Archaic	6000–3000 B.C.	6900–3700 cal B.C.	8850–5650 cal BP
Early Archaic	8000–6000 B.C.	9450–6900 cal B.C.	11,400–8850 cal BP
Paleoindian	9500–8000 B.C.	11,450–9450 cal B.C.	13,400–11,400 cal BP

Note [1]Approximate calibrated ranges using the CALIB v5.0 program (Stuiver and Birks 1993) and the INTCAL98 dataset (Stuiver et al. 1998).

Inferring Native American Demographic Trends

Both synchronic and diachronic shifts in site frequency across the landscape are key aspects in understanding prehistoric land-use patterns, reflecting broad demographic trends and/or the amount of activity within a region during a particular time span. Inferring spatiotemporal demographic trends using the number of archaeological sites must be scrutinized, however, as the frequency of sites is a problematic gauge with regard to land-use patterns. A larger number of sites at a particular time may indicate that there was a larger population or that more activity (i.e., increased land use) transpired during that period. Alternatively, it might indicate that a steady or even a diminishing population was more dispersed across the landscape and may be reflective of settlement reorganization. Despite these problems, the use of a large number of sites covering a vast geographical region should provide baseline data for understanding broad demographic trends in the archaeological record. In the ensuing analysis, the demographic trends are examined only with respect to the Tennessee Valley as a whole and the four subregions with no reference made to the specific reservoirs. While such an approach undoubtedly masks intra-subregional variation (which is important), the goal of this analysis is to examine demographic trends at the regional level.

In order to account for varying durations of time periods, the data were standardized by dividing the total number of sites of a given period by 100-year increments relative to their estimated time range (Figure 10.3). Considering demographic trends within the Tennessee River Valley as a whole, the frequency of sites through time indicates a general increase in the number of sites over the course of prehistory. Such a time-transgressive increase is not unexpected if we assume a general increase in Native American populations prior to European contact. The minor drop witnessed between the Early Archaic and Middle Archaic periods is likely related to a shift in settlement organization and not an actual population decrease; such a trend has been identified across the southeastern United States (Anderson 1996). Following this slight drop, there appears to be a steady growth in populations beginning in the Late Archaic period and continuing into the Middle Woodland period. This is followed by a rather dramatic rise in the number of sites per century between Middle Woodland and Late Woodland. Such a dramatic increase in the number of sites per century can be assumed, at least in part, to be reflective of increasing populations. This trend continues relatively

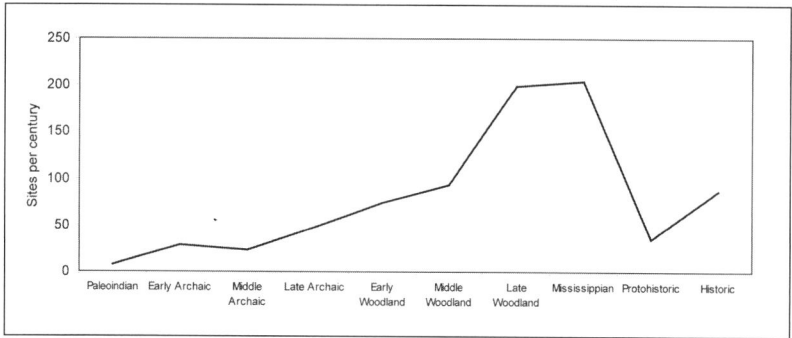

Fig. 10.3. Frequency of sites per century by cultural period. Note the number of sites per century for each period based on approximate calibrated date ranges.

unchanged into the Mississippian period. Equally impressive as the dramatic increase in population during late prehistory is the apparent collapse in population during the Protohistoric period. Such a drop in the frequency of sites is not unexpected during the Protohistoric period given the problems wrought by disease and conflict characteristic of post-contact times following the arrival of the Spanish into portions of the interior southeastern United States in the 1540s (e.g., Smith 1994). Following this decline, there is an apparent rebound in population with Historic Native American occupation in the Tennessee Valley.

If these regional demographic trends are examined at the subregion level, then patterns emerge that are somewhat at odds with the large-scale patterning witnessed across the entire Tennessee Valley (Figure 10.4). It should be stressed that the numbers of sites per century for each subregion illustrated in Figure 10.4 are not directly comparable given differences in total number of reservoirs within each subregion (i.e., 2 reservoirs in the lower subregion versus 12 in the upper subregion) and differences in levels of investigation within each reservoir; however, the general time-transgressive trends in each subregion can be compared. Overall, the four subregions have similar population trends prior to the Late Woodland period with only minor variation. Beginning with the Late Woodland, there appear to be regional differences in the distributions of populations across the Tennessee Valley. The lower and middle-Elk subregions tend to have peaks in population during the Late Woodland period. The middle-Hiwassee and upper subregions have peak populations occurring during the Mississippian period. The distribution of the number of Protohistoric period sites per century also

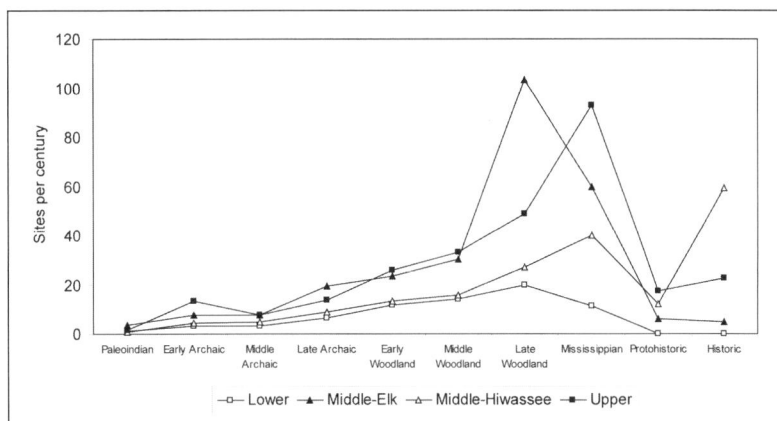

Fig. 10.4. Frequency of sites per century by cultural period. Note the number of sites per century for each period based on approximate calibrated date ranges.

exhibits some subregional variation with no sites in the lower subregion and low populations (relative to the preceding Mississippian period) in the middle-Elk, middle-Hiwassee, and upper subregions. Following this general downturn in demographic structure, there appear to be returns in population during the subsequent Historic period in both the middle-Hiwassee and upper subregions (largely associated with the filling in of previously vacated areas by the Overhill Cherokee [Smith 1994]), but the lower and middle-Elk subregions appear to remain relatively unoccupied during this period.

In summary, demographic trends across the Tennessee River Valley indicate a gradual population increase over most of prehistory with noticeable peaks and valleys in populations during late prehistory and extending into historic times. Given the coarse-grained nature of the site data employed in this analysis, it is impossible to account for other possible factors (such as changes in settlement, subsistence, technology, social interaction, and climate) that undoubtedly influenced the patterns noted. However, the demographic trends inferred from the above analysis do suggest that late prehistoric and early contact period populations more than likely were rising and falling across the Tennessee River Valley at varying times and places. In an attempt to provide some explanation for the patterning witnessed in the archaeological record, it is necessary to examine the distributions of Mississippian and Protohistoric sites across the valley and consider these distributions within the context of a changing sociopolitical landscape.

Regional Analysis and Cultural Process: Late Prehistoric Abandonment and the "Vacant Quarter" Hypothesis

The idea that prehistoric chiefdoms in the southeastern United States underwent periods of emergence, expansion, collapse, and reemergence has received much attention in the archaeological literature regarding the nature of Mississippian sociopolitical organization (e.g., Anderson 1990, 1994, 1996b; Cobb and King 2005; Hally and Rudolph 1986; Steponaitis 1978; Williams and Shapiro 1996). An extreme case of Mississippian collapse is the apparent abandonment of large portions of the midcontinental United States in the period A.D. 1450–1550 (Figure 10.5).[3] Termed the "Vacant Quarter" by Stephen Williams (1983, 1990, 2001), this large-scale (panregional) abandonment was centered on portions of the Mississippi, Ohio, Tennessee, and Cumberland river valleys and characterized by a marked decline in sociopolitical structure. Importantly, the Vacant Quarter hypothesis did not propose a complete depopulation of the region. Rather, it highlighted the apparent cessation in major mound-building efforts and the demise of ceremonial centers in the region. As Williams (1990:173) noted: "Population relocation rather than wholesale decimation is posited as part of a likely explanation. The term 'vacant' is used; however, it should not be understood to suggest that the area was completely devoid of use by Native American peoples who hunted there and made use of other resources as well."

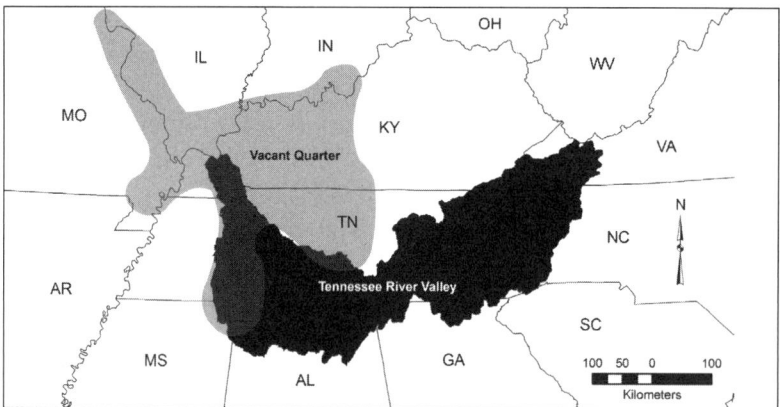

Fig. 10.5. Location of the Vacant Quarter in relation to the Tennessee River Valley (adapted from Williams 1990, fig. 9-1).

Although there has been some objection to the reality of such a vacant quarter (e.g., Lewis 1986, 1990), a growing body of research in the region has provided support for Williams's Vacant Quarter hypothesis (e.g., Anderson 1991a; Cobb and Butler 2002; Milner, Anderson, and Smith 2001; Mainfort 2001; Morse and Morse 1983; Smith 1992). Despite the growing support for the Vacant Quarter hypothesis, the archaeological reality of such in the Tennessee River Valley has remained largely untested by researchers. The Tennessee River Valley is central to exploring the Vacant Quarter hypothesis not only because the lower valley represents the southern terminus of the Vacant Quarter but also because the valley as a whole represents a unique opportunity to examine the late prehistoric sociopolitical landscape at a regional level.

The demographic trends presented earlier indicated that late prehistoric and early contact period populations were waxing and waning across the Tennessee River Valley at varying times and places. If abandonment occurred within the lower Tennessee River Valley ca. A.D. 1450–1550 as suggested by the Vacant Quarter hypothesis, then it would be expected that the number of Mississippian sites should be less frequent in the lower Tennessee Valley compared to other parts of the valley (assuming a constant rate of occupation thru time in other subregions) and that the number of Protohistoric sites in the lower Tennessee River Valley should be lower (or nonexistent) compared to other parts of the valley. To explore these expectations, the data presented earlier in Table 10.1 were combined with information contained in the Alabama and Tennessee state site files for the Tennessee River Valley, thereby providing a larger database from which to examine demographic trends (Table 10.3).[4]

In order to make the data presented in Table 10.3 comparable across the four subregions (accounting for differences in subregion size and

Table 10.3.: Absolute frequency of sites by sub-region and cultural period[1]				
Sub Region	Late Woodland	Mississippian	Protohistoric	Historic
Lower	152	150	0	1
Middle-Elk	426	278	19	17
Middle-Hiwassee	142	206	20	91
Upper	238	443	23	86
Total	958	1077	62	195

[1]Data based on table 10.1 and the Alabama and Tennessee state site files.

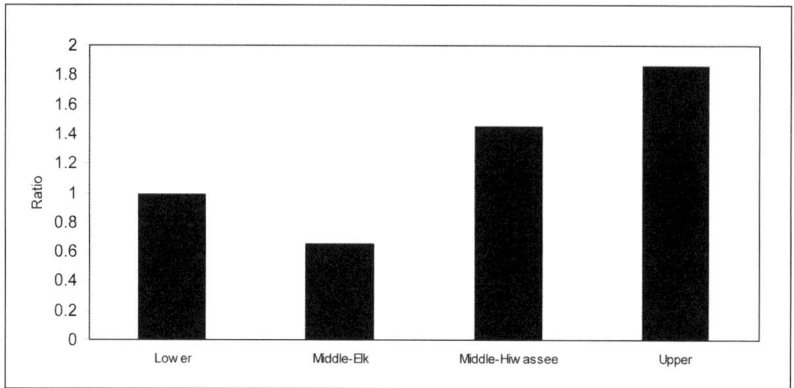

Fig. 10.6. Comparison of Mississippian:Late Woodland site ratios by subregion in the Tennessee River Valley.

varying levels of investigation), the data were normalized by using the ratio of Mississippian to Late Woodland sites as a proxy for occupational intensity. As figure 10.6 illustrates, sites in the middle-Hiwassee and upper subregions of the Tennessee Valley have much higher Mississippian:Late Woodland ratios compared to sites in the lower and middle-Elk subregions, suggesting a major shift in the spatial distribution of sites across the landscape and presumably in occupational intensity. What is more, these ratios correspond to the spatial distribution of Protohistoric sites in the Tennessee Valley, which are largely confined to the middle-Hiwassee and upper subregions of the valley (Figure 10.7). Those few sites that do occur in the middle-Elk subregion are restricted to the extreme eastern portion of the area. Taken together, the differences in Mississippian:Late Woodland ratios and the spatial distribution of Protohistoric sites provide support for shifts in the demographic structure of Mississippian and Protohistoric populations across the Tennessee River Valley with later Mississippian and Protohistoric populations being largely restricted to the eastern portion of the valley (i.e., areas outside the Vacant Quarter).

With evidence supporting an apparent abandonment (or relocation of populations) of the lower and western portions of the Tennessee River Valley, the question to be addressed is one of when this occurred. The timing of this abandonment can be explored by examining the frequency of radiocarbon dates (107 dates from 36 sites) throughout the Tennessee River Valley (Figure 10.8). All conventional radiocarbon dates were calibrated employing the CALIB v5.0 program (Stuiver and Birks 1993) and the INTCAL98 dataset (Stuiver et al. 1998). In order to provide single calendar dates for estimating half-century distributions

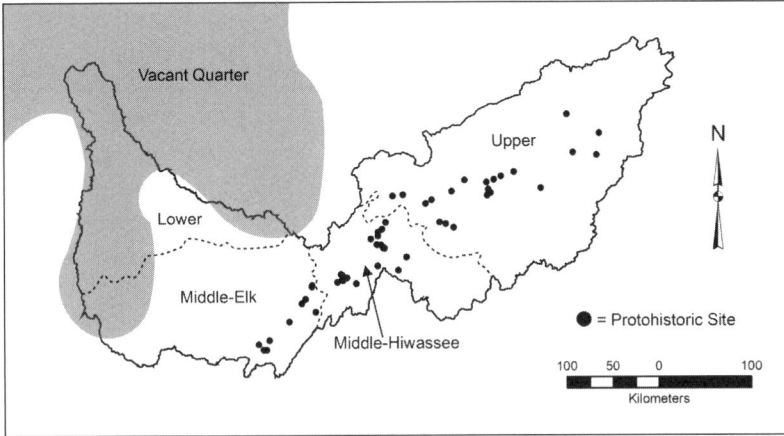

Fig. 10.7. Spatial distribution of Protohistoric sites in the Tennessee River Valley in relation to the southern extent of the Vacant Quarter.

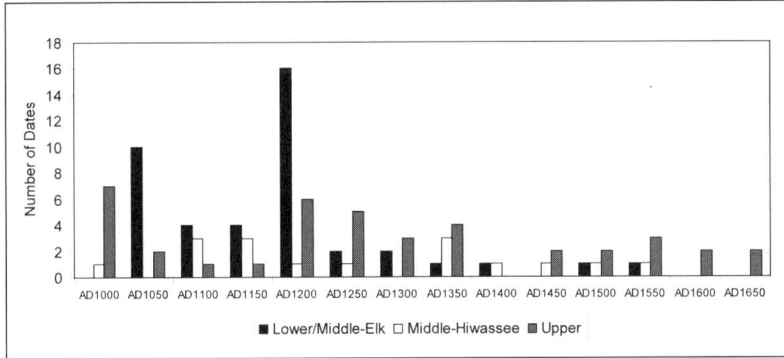

Fig. 10.8. Number of radiocarbon dates (calibrated) by half century and subregion in the Tennessee River Valley.

for Mississippian and Protohistoric dates, it was necessary to acquire a fixed date based on the calibrated age ranges. This was accomplished by deriving a fixed date using the weighted mean of the calibration probability distribution (at two sigma [95.4%]) as defined by the CALIB v5.0 program (sensu Telford et al. 2004). The lower and middle-Elk subregions were collapsed, given the low number of dates from sites in the middle-Elk.

Inspection of the dates by 50-year intervals indicates that the majority of dates (N=42; 93 percent) in the lower and middle-Elk subregions predate A.D. 1400. In contrast, sites in both the middle-Hiwassee and upper subregions have much higher frequencies of dates post-A.D. 1400, including dates extending into the sixteenth and seventeenth centuries A.D. Based on the spatiotemporal distributions of sites and radiocarbon dates, the Vacant Quarter does appear to be an archaeological reality in both the lower and western-middle Tennessee River Valley with abandonment occurring by approximately A.D. 1400. This region, once the domain of complex chiefdoms such as Shiloh, became a political backwater with little evidence that sustained populations remained in the region post-A.D. 1400. The timing of the apparent abandonment of the lower and western-middle Tennessee River Valley corresponds closely with the abandonment times for the lower Ohio River Valley (Cobb and Butler 2002), the central Mississippi River Valley (Morse and Morse 1983), and the middle Cumberland River Valley (Smith 1992), suggesting that the Vacant Quarter was a synchronic phenomenon across the region (Meeks 2006).[5] Interesting to note, the demise of political power in the lower and western-middle Tennessee Valley corresponds to the apparent rise of political power in the eastern-middle and upper valley and the subsequent ascension of the Coosa chiefdom throughout eastern Tennessee, northeastern Alabama, and northwestern Georgia during the fifteenth, sixteenth, and seventeenth centuries A.D. (Hally 1994; Smith 2001).

Why the Vacant Quarter underwent population relocation and sociopolitical change remains elusive, and adequate examination of possible explanations is beyond the scope of this chapter, but reasons posited for abandonment range from environmental deterioration associated with the onset of the Little Ice Age, subsistence stress, pandemics associated with European contact, social strife, and chiefly cycling (e.g., Anderson 1991a; Cobb and Butler 2002; Mainfort 2001; Meeks 2006; Meeks and Anderson 2006; Williams 1990). What this analysis can offer is to illustrate that, at least in the lower and western portions of the Tennessee Valley, the timing of this apparent abandonment by Mississippian peoples by approximately A.D. 1400 precludes the effects of disease as an explanation (although disease does appear to have affected Protohistoric populations in the eastern valley post-A.D. 1540). Additionally, the cessation in major mound-building efforts and the demise of ceremonial centers in the region by the mid-1300s (e.g., Shiloh in the Lower Tennessee Valley [Anderson and Cornelison 2005]; Mound Bottom in the Middle Cumberland Valley [Smith 1992]; and Kincaid in the Lower Ohio Valley [Butler 1991]) suggest that Mississippian chiefdoms in the region were well within a period of collapse between A.D. 1350 to 1400. Why chiefdoms collapse is elaborate and multivariate and is not attributable

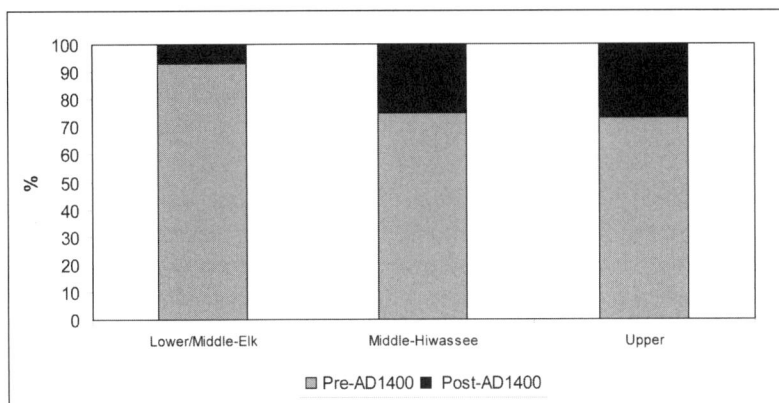

Fig. 10.9. Cumulative percentages of pre-A.D. 1400 (A.D. 1000–1400) and post-A.D. 1400 (1400–1650) radiocarbon dates by subregion in the Tennessee River Valley.

to a single cause but rather a host of interrelated factors (see Anderson 1994 for an in-depth discussion of possible causes). If, however, environmental deterioration (which could result in crop failure and loss of surplus foodstuffs), political instability, and social strife were occurring in the lower and western-middle Tennessee Valley during the mid-1300s, then it is probably not coincidental that the apparent abandonment of the region by Mississippian peoples corresponds to the termination of mound construction and the demise of major ceremonial centers.

The Future Role of CRM in Archaeological Research

This very broad synthesis of archaeological data (site distribution) resulting from CRM investigations of TVA-related projects (largely survey oriented) spanning the past three decades illustrates the important role that CRM has played in our understanding of the Native American occupation in the Tennessee River Valley. The regional analysis presented here would not have been possible without the large corpus of data that has been generated from CRM investigations of TVA properties. This illustrates the value of the archaeological data contained in these reports for advancing scientific research at the regional level and how such data must be understood within the broader context of the archaeological record of the southeastern United States. Unfortunately, the examination of regional patterns in the archaeological record is rarely studied within the context of CRM. This shortfall has been noted by Sassaman and Anderson: "The cultural resource management 'revolution' led to a marked expansion in the field and in the quantities of data collected and reports produced yet almost paradoxically forced archaeologists to work within limited, imposed spatial boundaries and under tight constraints of time and money. The combination of these recent trends has, unfortunately, all but eliminated large-scale comparative studies of prehistory" (1996:216).

The basis of CRM, specifically with regard to TVA properties in recent years, is the identification and evaluation of archaeological resources for management purposes and stewardship (see Pritchard, this volume). This is not a problem in itself, as the many CRM projects conducted within the bounds of TVA properties has the positive effect of building an impressive archaeological database (at least in terms of identifying archaeological sites across the landscape). However, such an approach often relegates large bodies of archaeological data to the backwaters of gray literature that rarely see the light of day after the review process is completed. What are needed are regional overviews to incorporate the large corpus of CRM site-specific and local data within the broader context of the regional archaeological record.

The title of this paper suggests that CRM investigations should promote archaeological research. This is true to some degree, as all archaeology, be it contract-based or grant-funded research, must be directed to forming a better understanding of the past. And in this it can be said that all archaeology is cultural resources management. Given that federal agencies, state and local governments, and private companies have become the principal funding of archaeology, CRM will continue to produce the bulk of the archaeological information gathered from TVA properties. As such, it burdens CRM with the responsibility of conducting investigations that both satisfy the compliance requirements of the various federal legislations and provide data that is usable for archaeological research. With the increasingly prominent role of CRM as the primary means of gathering archaeological data, it should be noted that there are necessary steps in CRM investigations to further both stewardship and archaeological research of TVA properties: standardized field procedures, quality control of information, incorporation of existing archaeological data, and publication of data beyond "gray" literature. The above comments are not intended to be critical of CRM investigations. Rather, they are meant to provide stimulus for future investigations as CRM will continue to play an important role in our understanding of cultural pattern and process in the Tennessee River Valley.

Notes

1. Although not the focus of this chapter, the contributions of investigations conducted prior to the 1960s are important to our understanding of cultural pattern and process in the region; specifically of interest is the New Deal archaeology sponsored by TVA, the Works Progress Administration, Civil Works Administration, Civilian Conservation Corps, and the Federal Emergency Relief Administration (Haag 1985; Lyon 1982). These include surveys and site excavations in Kentucky Lake (Webb and Funkhouser 1932), Chickamauga basin (Lewis, Lewis, and Sullivan 1995), Guntersville basin (Webb and Wilder 1951), Norris basin (Webb 1938), Pickwick basin (Webb and DeJarnette 1942), and Wheeler basin (Webb 1939).

2. The Gulf Formational Stage, as defined by Walthall and Jenkins (1976), is not employed in this analysis since this stage is not recognized across the entirety of the study area. The stage is traditionally divided into early, middle, and late periods; the latter two periods are represented in the lower Kentucky Lake reservoir and throughout the middle Tennessee Valley, specifically in Bear/Cedar Creek, Pickwick, Wheeler, and Guntersville, although the distributions of both Middle and Late Gulf Formational wares are rare in the upper Wheeler basin and Guntersville basin (Futato 1998; Meeks 2000:26–27). Middle Gulf Formational pottery (fiber-tempered Wheeler wares) is poorly dated for the Tennessee Valley although a review of dates possibly associated with Wheeler wares in the region suggests a date range of 3600–3000 cal B.P. (3400–2900 R.C.B.P.) (Futato 1998). This date range is in large part synchronic with the estimated range of Wheeler wares (3400–2600 cal B.P. [3200–2500 R.C.B.P.]) to the south in the Tombigbee drainage (Jenkins and Meyer 1998). Sites listed as Middle Gulf Formational were included with Late Archaic sites during data compilation given their contemporaneity with various Late Archaic hafted biface types (e.g., Little Bear Creek, Flint Creek, and Wade) in the region (Futato 1983). Late Gulf Formational pottery (sand-tempered Alexander wares) in the Tennessee Valley has an estimated date range of 2900–2400 cal B.P. (2800–2400 R.C.B.P. [Futato 1998]) and is generally coeval with other Early Woodland pottery in the region, including Colbert I pottery (2750–2350 cal B.P. [2600–2300 R.C.B.P.]; Futato 1998) in northeastern Alabama, Watts Bar pottery (3000–2250 cal B.P. [2900–2200 R.C.B.P.]; Kimball 1985) in eastern Tennessee, and Swannanoa pottery (2750–2250 cal B.P. [2600–2200 R.C.B.P.]; Wetmore 2002:254) pottery in northern Georgia and western North Carolina. Sites listed as Late Gulf Formational were included with Early Woodland sites during this analysis.

3. It appears that abandonment of the Vacant Quarter occurred during the period A.D. 1350–1400, about a century earlier than initially proposed.

4. Site file data for Alabama (Alabama State Site File, Moundville) and Tennessee (Tennessee Division of Archaeology, Nashville) encompassing the entirety of the Tennessee River Valley in both states were used to increase the total number of sites for the analysis and to include those areas outside the reservoirs, thereby providing information on sites in upland localities not routinely investigated during surveys of TVA reservoirs. Portions of the Tennessee River Valley in Georgia, Kentucky, North Carolina, Mississippi, and Virginia, representing 28 percent (approximately 29,860 km²) of the total area of the valley, were not included in the site database expansion because of the absence of state site file data at the time of this writing.

5. Meeks's (2006) analysis of 414 radiocarbon dates ranging between A.D. 1200 to A.D. 1650 from regions both within (n=171) and immediately adjacent to (n=243) the Vacant Quarter demonstrated that those regions within the Vacant Quarter contained radiocarbon dates that largely fell prior to A.D. 1400 with only 18 percent of dates occurring after A.D. 1400. In contrast, those regions immediately adjacent to the Vacant Quarter contained radiocarbon dates that spanned the period A.D. 1200–1650, suggesting that occupation outside the Vacant Quarter was relatively uninterrupted.

References Cited

ADAMS, NATALIE P.
1997   Archaeological Survey of Approximately 59 Linear Miles of the Nottely Reservoir Shoreline Management Zone, Union County, Georgia. New South Associates, Technical Report 505, Stone Mountain, GA.
1999   Archaeological Survey of the Chatuge Reservoir Shoreline Management Zone and 603 Acres of Public Lands, Towns County Georgia and Clay County, North Carolina. New South Associates, Technical Report 504, Stone Mountain, GA.

AHLMAN, TODD M.
2002   Archaeological Identification Survey of the Ocoee No. 1 (Parksville) Reservoir, Polk County, Tennessee. Louis Berger Group, Richmond, VA.

AHLMAN, TODD M., SUSAN R. FRANKENBERG, AND NICHOLAS P. HERRMANN
2000   Archaeological Reconnaissance Survey of the Tennessee Valley Authority Lands on the Watts Bar Reservoir. Department of Anthropology, University of Tennessee, Knoxville.

AMMERMAN, ALBERT J.
1981   Surveys and Archaeological Research. Annual Review of Anthropology 10:63–88.

ANDERSON, DAVID G.
1990   Stability and Change in Chiefdom-Level Societies: An Examination of Mississippian Political Evolution on the South Atlantic Slope. In *Lamar Archaeology: Mississippian Chiefdoms in the Deep South*, edited by Mark Williams and Gary Shapiro, pp. 187–213. University of Alabama Press, Tuscaloosa.

1991a   Examining Prehistoric Settlement Distribution in Eastern North America. *Archaeology of Eastern North America* 19:1–22.

1991b   The Bifurcate Tradition in the South Atlantic Region. *Journal of Middle Atlantic Archaeology* 7:91–106.

1995   Paleoindian Interaction Networks in the Eastern Woodlands. In *Native American Interaction: Multiscalar Analyses and Interpretations in the Eastern Woodlands*, edited by Michael S. Nassaney and Kenneth E. Sassaman, pp. 1–26. University of Tennessee Press, Knoxville.

1994   *The Savannah River Chiefdoms: Political Change in the Late Prehistoric Southeast*. University of Alabama Press, Tuscaloosa.

1996a   Approaches to Modeling Regional Settlement in the Archaic Period Southeast. In *Archaeology of the Mid-Holocene Southeast*, edited by Kenneth E. Sassaman and David G. Anderson, pp. 157–176. University Press of Florida, Gainesville.

1996b   Fluctuations between Simple and Complex Chiefdoms: Cycling in the Late Prehistoric Southeast. In *Political Structure and Change in the Prehistoric Southeastern United States*, edited by John F. Scarry, pp. 231–252. Ripley P. Bullen Series, Museum of Natural History, University Press of Florida, Gainesville.

ANDERSON, DAVID G., R. JERALD LEDBETTER, AND LISA D. O'STEEN
1990   *Paleoindian Period Archaeology of Georgia*. Georgia Archaeological Research Design Paper 6. Laboratory of Archaeology Series Report 28. University of Georgia, Athens.

ANDERSON, DAVID G., AND JOHN E. CORNELISON, JR.
2005   Revealing Mound A: Research Results and Future Directions. Paper presented in the symposium "Revealing Mound A, Shiloh, Tennessee: Research Results of the 1999–2004 Field Program," organized by David G. Anderson, John E. Cornelison, Jr., and Sarah C. Sherwood, 62nd annual meeting of the Southeastern Archaeological Conference, Columbia, SC.

BENTHALL, JOSEPH L.
1995   *An Archaeological Reconnaissance of Portions of the Hiwassee and Ocoee Rivers in Polk, Bradley, and McMinn Counties, Tennessee, 1985–1986*. Tennessee Department of Environment and Conservation, Division of Archaeology, Report of Investigations no. 12, Nashville.

BOYD, C. CLIFFORD, JR.
1986   *Archaeological Investigations in the Watauga Reservoir, Carter and Johnson Counties, Tennessee.* University of Tennessee, Department of Anthropology Report of Investigations no. 44, Knoxville. Tennessee Valley Authority, Publications in Anthropology no. 46, Norris.

BUTLER, BRIAN M.
1991   Kincaid Revisited: The Mississippian Sequence in the Lower Ohio Valley. In *Cahokia and the Hinterlands,* edited by Thomas E. Emerson and R. Barry Lewis, pp. 264–273. University of Illinois Press, Urbana.

CANNON, KENNETH P.
1986   *An Assessment of the Archaeological Resources of the Watts Bar Reservoir, East Tennessee.* Department of Anthropology, University of Tennessee.

COBB, CHARLES R. AND BRIAN M. BUTLER
2002   The Vacant Quarter Revisited: Late Mississippian Abandonment of the Lower Ohio Valley. *American Antiquity* 6:625–641.

COBB, CHARLES R., AND ADAM KING
2005   Re-Inventing Mississippian Tradition at Etowah, Georgia. *Journal of Archaeological Method and Theory* 12:167–192.

DAVIS, R. P. STEPHEN, JR.
1990   *Aboriginal Settlement Patterns in the Tennessee River Valley.* Department of Anthropology, Report of Investigations no. 50, University of Tennessee, Knoxville. Tennessee Valley Authority, Publications in Anthropology no. 54, Norris, TN.

DRISKELL, BOYCE N., AND TIM S. MISTOVICH
1990   *Cultural Resource Investigations in the Nickajack Reservoir Area, Marion County, Tennessee.* Office of Archaeological Research, University of Alabama, Tuscaloosa.

DUVALL, GLYN D.
1998   *Phase I Archaeological Survey of Approximately 1300 Acres within Tims Ford Reservoir, Franklin and Moore Counties, Tennessee.* DuVall and Associates, Franklin, TN.

ELLIOT, DANIEL T.
1993   *Chickamauga Reservoir Archaeological Site Inventory: Results of Survey from 1987 to 1993, Draft Report.* Garrow and Associates, Atlanta.

FAULKNER, CHARLES H., AND C. R. McCOLLOUGH
1973   *Introductory Report of the Normandy Reservoir Salvage Project: Environmental Setting, Typology, and Survey.* Normandy Archaeological Project, vol. 1. Report of Investigations no. 11, Department of Anthropology, University of Tennessee, Knoxville.

Frankenberg, Susan R., Nicholas P. Herrmann, and Todd M. Ahlman

2000   *Archaeological Reconnaissance Survey of Tennessee Valley Authority Lands on the Cherokee Reservoir.* Department of Anthropology, University of Tennessee, Knoxville.

Futato, Eugene M.

1983   *Archaeological Investigations in the Cedar Creek and Upper Bear Creek Reservoirs.* University of Alabama, Office of Archaeological Services, Report of Investigations 29.

1998   Ceramic Complexes of the Tennessee River Drainage, Alabama. *Journal of Alabama Archaeology* 44:208–241.

Gage, Matthew D.

2005a   *Archaeological Inventory of 30.9 Miles of Shoreline along Wheeler, Guntersville, Fort Loudon, and Norris Reservoirs in Alabama and Tennessee.* Archaeological Research Laboratory, Department of Anthropology, University of Tennessee, Knoxville.

2005b   *Archaeological Site Identification and Erosion Monitoring for the TVA Reservoir Operations Study: The 2005 Field Seasons on Portions of Cherokee, Norris, Pickwick, and Wheeler Reservoirs.* Archaeological Research Laboratory, Department of Anthropology, University of Tennessee, Knoxville.

Gilliam, Christopher J.

1995   Paleoindian Settlement in the Mississippi Valley of Arkansas. M.A. thesis, Department of Anthropology, University of Arkansas, Fayetteville.

Haag, William G.

1985   Federal Aid to Archaeology in the Southeast, 1933–1942. *American Antiquity* 50:272–280.

Hally, David J., and James L. Rudolph

1986   *Mississippi Period Archaeology of the Georgia Piedmont.* University of Georgia Laboratory of Archaeology Series Report no. 24. Athens.

1994   The Chiefdom of Coosa. In *The Forgotten Centuries: Indians and Europeans in the American South 1521–1704,* edited by Charles Hudson and Carmen Chaves Tesser, pp. 227–253. University of Georgia Press, Athens.

Hendryx, Greg S.

1999   *An Intensive Above Pool Archaeological Survey within the Upper Bear and Big Bear Creek Reservoirs.* Office of Archaeological Services, University of Alabama, Tuscaloosa.

Herrmann, Nicholas P., and Susan R. Frakenberg

2000   *Archaeological Reconnaissance Survey of Tennessee Valley Authority Lands on the Melton Hill Reservoir.* Department of Anthropology, University of Tennessee, Knoxville.

JENKINS, NED J., AND CATHERINE C. MEYER
1998   Ceramics of the Tombigbee-Black Warrior River Valleys. *Journal of Alabama Archaeology* 44:188–207.

JOHNSON, GREGORY A.
1977   Aspects of Regional Analysis in Archaeology. *Annual Review of Anthropology* 6:479–508.

KERR, JONATHAN P.
1996   *Archaeological Survey of Kentucky Lake, Western Tennessee and Kentucky*, vols. 1–3. Cultural Resources Analysts, Lexington.

KIMBALL, LARRY R. (EDITOR)
1985   *The 1977 Archaeological Survey: An Overall Assessment of the Archaeological Resources of Tellico Reservoir*. Report of Investigations 40, Department of Anthropology, University of Tennessee, and TVA Publications in Anthropology 39, Knoxville.

KOWALEWSKI, STEPHEN A.
1995   Large-Scale Ecology on Aboriginal Eastern North America. In *Native American Interaction: Multiscalar Analyses and Interpretations in the Eastern Woodlands,* edited by Michael S. Nassaney and Kenneth E. Sassaman, pp. 147–173. University of Tennessee Press, Knoxville.

LAFFERTY, ROBERT H., III, AND CARLOS SOLIS
1980   *The Cedar Creek Above Pool Survey in Franklin County, Alabama.* Office of Archaeological Research, Report of Investigations 16, University of Alabama, Tuscaloosa.

LAWRENCE, WILLIAM L.
2000   *An Archaeological Survey of 45 Land Parcels at Tims Ford Reservoir, Franklin County, Tennessee.* Tennessee Division of Archaeology, Nashville.

LEWIS, R. BARRY
1990   The Late Prehistory of the Ohio-Mississippi Rivers Confluence Region, Kentucky and Missouri. In *Towns and Temples along the Mississippi,* edited by David H. Dye and Cheryl A. Cox, pp. 38–58. University of Alabama Press, Tuscaloosa.

LEWIS, R. BARRY (EDITOR)
1986   *Mississippian Towns of the Western Kentucky Border: The Adams, Wickliffe, and Sassafras Ridge Sites.* Kentucky Heritage Council, Frankfort.

LEWIS, THOMAS M. N., MADELINE KNEBERG LEWIS, AND LYNNE P. SULLIVAN (COMPILER AND EDITOR)
1995   *The Prehistory of the Chickamauga Basin in Tennessee,* 2 vols. University of Tennessee Press, Knoxville.

Lyon, Edwin A.
1982   New Deal Archaeology in the Southeast: WPA, TVA, NPS, 1934–1942. Ph.D. dissertation, Department of History, Louisiana State University.

Mainfort, Robert C.
2001   The Late Prehistoric and Protohistoric Periods in the Central Mississippi Valley. *In Societies in Eclipse: Archaeology of the Eastern Woodlands Indians, A.D. 1400–1700*, edited by David S. Brose and Robert C. Mainfort, Jr., pp. 173–190. Smithsonian Institution Press, Washington, DC.

McNutt, Charles H., and Guy G. Weaver
1985   *An Above Pool Survey of Cultural Resources within the Little Bear Creek Reservoir Area, Franklin County, Alabama.* Anthropological Research Center, Occasional Papers no. 13, Memphis State University, Memphis, TN.

McNutt, Charles H., Jr., Tracy Millis, and Bruce Idol
1997   *Phase I Archaeological Survey of 565 Acres of TVA Fee Lands Above NSP on Boone Lake, Washington and Sullivan Counties, Tennessee.* TRC Garrow and Associates, Memphis.

Meeks, Scott C.
2000   Prehistory of the Wheeler Basin Area. In *Cultural Resources in the Wheeler Basin*, by Scott Shaw, pp. 9–35. University of Alabama, Office of Archaeological Services, Report of Investigations 79.

2006   Drought, Subsistence Stress, and Political Instability: Late Prehistoric Abandonment in the Tennessee River Valley. Paper presented at the 2006 Southeastern Archaeological Conference, symposium entitled "Southeastern Historical Ecology and Landscapes," Little Rock, AR.

Meeks, Scott C., and David G. Anderson
2006   The Vacant Quarter Hypothesis: Changing Late Prehistoric Political Landscapes in the Tennessee River Valley from a Paleoecological Perspective. Invited paper presented at the 19th Biennial Meeting of the American Quaternary Association entitled "Ocean/Atmosphere Interactions and Continental Consequences: Environmental Forecasting from the Quaternary Sciences," Bozeman, MT.

Meyer, Catherine C.
1995   *Cultural Resources in the Pickwick Reservoir.* Division of Archaeology, Report of Investigations 15, University of Alabama, Tuscaloosa.

Milner, George R., David G. Anderson, and Marvin T. Smith
2001   The Distribution of Eastern Woodlands Peoples at the Prehistoric and Historic Interface. In *Societies in Eclipse: Archaeology of the Eastern Woodlands Indians, A.D. 1400–1700*, edited by David S.

Brose and Robert C. Mainfort, Jr., pp. 9–18. Smithsonian Institution Press, Washington, DC.

MORSE, DAN F., AND PHYLLIS A. MORSE

1983   *Archaeology of the Central Mississippi Valley.* Academic Press, New York.

PIETAK, LYNN MARIE, AND JEFFERY L. HOLLAND

1997   *Phase I Archaeological Survey of Norris Lake, Anderson, Campbell, Claiborne, Grainger, and Union Counties, Tennessee.* TRC Garrow and Associates, Atlanta.

1998a   *Phase I Archaeological Survey of Boone Lake, Sullivan and Washington Counties, Tennessee.* TRC Garrow and Associates, Atlanta.

1998b   *Phase I Archaeological Survey of South Holston Lake, Sullivan County Tennessee and Washington County, Virginia.* TRC Garrow and Associates, Atlanta.

1999   *Phase I Archaeological Survey of Norris Lake, Anderson, Campbell, Claiborne, Grainger, and Union Counties, Tennessee.* TRC, Atlanta.

PIETAK, LYNN MARIE, AARON DETER-WOLF, RUTH NICHOLS, JIM D'ANGELO, AND KRISTIN WILSON

2002   *Cultural Resources Survey for the Muscle Shoals Reservation, Lauderdale and Colbert Counties, Alabama.* TRC, Atlanta.

POLHEMUS, RICHARD R.

2000   *Archaeological Survey of the Fort Patrick Henry Reservoir, Sullivan County, Tennessee.* Polhemus Archaeological Consulting, Sevierville, Tennessee.

PRESCOTT, WILLIAM D.

1978   An Analysis of Surface Survey Data from the Normandy Reservoir. M.A. thesis, University of Tennessee, Knoxville.

PRICE, GEORGE D.

2002   *Archaeological Survey along the Flint Creek Portion of the Wheeler Reservoir, Morgan County, Alabama.* TRC, Atlanta.

2003   *Archaeological Survey along the Flint River and Paint Rock River Portions of the Wheeler Reservoir, Morgan and Madison Counties, Alabama.* TRC, Atlanta.

RAFFERTY, JANET

2002   Woodland Period Settlement Patterning in the Northern Gulf Coastal Plain of Alabama, Mississippi, and Tennessee. In *The Woodland Southeast,* edited by David G. Anderson and Robert C. Mainfort, Jr., pp. 204–227. University of Alabama Press, Tuscaloosa.

RIGGS, BRETT H., M. SCOTT SHUMATE, AND PATTI EVANS-SHUMATE

1995   *An Archaeological Reconnaissance of Apalachia Reservoir, Cherokee County, North Carolina.* Blue Ridge Cultural Resources, Boone, NC.

RIGGS, BRETT H. AND LARRY R. KIMBALL
1996   *An Archaeological Survey of Hiwassee Reservoir, Cherokee County,*
        North Carolina. Appalachian State University Laboratories of
        Archaeological Science, Department of Anthropology, Appalachian
        State University, Boone, NC.
2005   *An Archaeological Survey of Blue Ridge Reservoir, Fannin*
        County, Georgia. Appalachian State University Laboratories of
        Archaeological Science, Department of Anthropology, Appalachian
        State University, Boone, NC.

SASSAMAN, KENNETH E. AND DAVID G. ANDERSON
1996   The Need for a Regional Perspective. In *The Paleoindian and Early*
        Archaic Southeast, edited by David G. Anderson and Kenneth E.
        Sassaman, pp. 215–221. University of Alabama Press, Tuscaloosa.

SEABER, PAUL R., F. PAUL KAPINOS, AND GEORGE L. KNAPP
1987   Hydrologic Unit Maps: U.S. Geological Survey Water-Supply Paper
        2294.

SHAW, SCOTT
2000   *Cultural Resources in the Wheeler Reservoir.* Office of Archae-
        ological Services, Report of Investigations 79, University of Ala-
        bama, Tuscaloosa.

SHUMATE, M. SCOTT, PATTI EVANS-SHUMATE, AND BRETT H. RIGGS
1999   *An Archaeological Reconnaissance Survey of Selected Tracts within*
        Fontana Reservoir, Swain County, North Carolina. Blue Ridge
        Cultural Resources, Boone, NC.

SMITH, KEVIN E.
1992   The Middle Cumberland Region: Mississippian Archaeology
        in North-Central Tennessee. Ph.D. dissertation, Department of
        Anthropology, Vanderbilt University.

SMITH, MARVIN T.
1994   Aboriginal Depopulation in the Postcontact Southeast. In *The*
        Forgotten Centuries: Indians and Europeans in the American South
        1521–1704, edited by Charles Hudson and Carmen Chaves Tesser,
        pp. 257–275. University of Georgia Press, Athens.
2001   The Rise and Fall of Coosa, A.D. 1350–1700. In *Societies in Eclipse:*
        Archaeology of the Eastern Woodlands Indians, A.D. 1400–1700,
        edited by David S. Brose and Robert C. Mainfort, Jr., pp. 143–155.
        Smithsonian Institution Press, Washington, DC.

STAYNARD, WILLIAM F.
1997   *Chickamauga Reservoir Shoreline Cultural Resources Survey: 1996*
        and 1997 Field Seasons and Phase I Cultural Resources Survey
        of the Proposed Cherokee Memorial Park at Blythes Ferry, Meigs
        County, Tennessee. Garrow and Associates, Atlanta.

STANYARD, WILLIAM F. AND JEFFREY L. HOLLAND
2004   *Phase I Archaeological Investigations on TVA Fee-Owned Land at Douglas Lake in Cocke, Hamblen, Jefferson, and Sevier Counties, Tennessee.* TRC, Atlanta.

STEPONAITIS, VINCAS P.
1978   Locational Theory and Complex Chiefdoms: A Mississippian Example. In *Mississippian Settlement Patterns,* edited by Bruce D. Smith, pp. 417–453. Academic Press, New York.

STRUEVER, STUART
1971   Comments on Archaeological Data Requirements and Research Strategy. *American Antiquity* 36(1):9–19.

STUIVER, MINZE, PAULA REIMER, EDOUARD BARD, J. WARREN BECK, G. S. BURR, KONRAD A. HUGHEN, BERNARD KROMER, GERRY MCCORMAC, JOHANNES VAN DER PLICHT, AND MARCO SPURK
1998   INTCAL98 Radiocarbon Age Calibration, 24,000 cal BP. *Radiocarbon* 40:1041–1083.

STUIVER, MINZE, AND PAULA J. BIRKS
1993   Extended 14C Data Base and Revised CALIB 3.0 14C Age Calibration Program. *Radiocarbon* 35:215–230.

TELFORD, R. J., E. HEEGAARD, AND H. J. B. BIRKS
2004   The Intercept Is a Poor Estimate of a Calibrated Radiocarbon Age. *Holocene* 14:296–298.

WALTHALL, JOHN A., AND NED. J. JENKINS
1976   The Gulf Formational Stage in Southeastern Prehistory. *Southeastern Archaeological Conference Bulletin* 19:43–49.

WAMPLER, MARC E., AARON DETER-WOLF, JEFF HOLLAND, AND LARRY MCKEE
2002   *Phase I Archaeological Survey of Tennessee Valley Authority Property (ca. 1500 Acres) along Tims Ford Reservoir, Franklin County, Tennessee.* TRC, Nashville.

WEBB, WILLIAM S.
1938   *An Archaeological Survey of Norris Basin in Eastern Tennessee.* Bureau of American Ethnology 118. Washington, DC.
1939   *An Archaeological Survey of Wheeler Basin on the Tennessee River in Northern Alabama.* Bureau of American Ethnology 122. Washington, DC.

WEBB, WILLIAM S., AND W. D. FUNKHOUSER
1932   *Archaeological Survey of Kentucky.* University of Kentucky Reports in Anthropology 2. Lexington.

WEBB, WILLIAM S., AND DAVID L. DEJARNETTE
1942   *An Archaeological Survey in Pickwick Basin in the Adjacent Portions of the States Alabama, Mississippi, and Tennessee.* Bureau of American Ethnology 129. Washington, DC.

Webb, William S., and Charles G. Wilder
1951   *An Archaeological Survey of Guntersville Basin on the Tennessee River in Northern Alabama.* University of Kentucky Press, Lexington.

Wetmore, Ruth
2002   The Woodland Period in the Appalachian Summit of Western North Carolina and the Ridge and Valley Province of Eastern Tennessee. In *The Woodland Southeast,* edited by David G. Anderson and Robert C. Mainfort, Jr., pp. 249–269. University of Alabama Press, Tuscaloosa.

Williams, Mark, and Gary Shapiro
1996   Mississippian Political Dynamics in the Oconee Valley, Georgia. *In Political Structure and Change in the Prehistoric Southeastern United States,* edited by John F. Scarry, pp. 128–149. Ripley P. Bullen Series, Museum of Natural History, University Press of Florida, Gainesville.

Williams, Stephen
1983   Some Ruminations on the Current Strategy of Archaeology in the Southeast. *Southeastern Archaeological Conference Bulletin* 21:72–81.

1990   The Vacant Quarter and Other Late Events in the Lower Valley. In *Towns and Temples along the Mississippi,* edited by David H. Dye and Cheryl A. Cox, pp. 170–180. University of Alabama Press, Tuscaloosa.

2001   The Vacant Quarter Hypothesis and the Yazoo Delta. In *Societies in Eclipse: Archaeology of the Eastern Woodlands Indians,* A.D. *1400–1700,* edited by David S. Brose and Robert C. Mainfort, Jr., pp. 191–203. Smithsonian Institution Press, Washington.

11
The Future of Archaeology and Stewardship at TVA

Erin E. Pritchard

As AN AGENCY, TVA has experienced many highs and lows, and as a result it is difficult to predict what direction it is headed as it enters into its seventy-fifth year of operation. As the nation's largest public power company, TVA's goals are to support sustainable economic development, supply affordable, reliable power, and manage a thriving river system. Within this mission lies an important strategic objective to improve the quality of life in the Tennessee Valley through integrated management of the river system and environmental stewardship.

Environmental stewardship requires TVA to balance the competing uses and needs of the valley's natural and cultural resources while meeting the goals that define its role in the Tennessee Valley. This balance has become a challenge to the agency as TVA has not received federal appropriated funds since 1999 and is dependant on ratepayer dollars to fund all of its programs including land management responsibilities. Despite this funding change, TVA continues to maintain a strong commitment to the environment.

History of Archaeological Stewardship at TVA

Early in its history, TVA garnered a reputation as an archaeological steward. Because of the pioneering efforts of archaeologists William S. Webb and David DeJarnette, TVA began this stewardship by participating in several large-scale archaeological excavations prior to the construction of its earliest dams. Archaeological projects took place

within the Norris, Wheeler, Pickwick, Guntersville, Hiwassee, Chickamauga, Gilbertsville (later renamed Kentucky), and Watts Bar Basins,
were completed without any federal requirements, and were supported
fully by the TVA Board of Directors. Archaeological excavations that
took place during this time focused on larger, more highly visible sites
such as mound and village sites.

As cited in Olinger's chapter (this volume), archaeological efforts
dwindled in the 1940s when TVA directed its attention toward the
national war effort. As a result few archaeological excavations took
place under the auspices of TVA until the 1960s. Following the passage
of the Reservoir Salvage Act (1960) and the National Historic Preservation Act in 1966 (NHPA), TVA once again began to consider the effects
of its undertakings on archaeological resources. TVA hired its first full-
time archaeologist, J. Bennett Graham, in 1974. Graham's responsibilities included the management of several million-dollar contracts that
were currently being conducted through the agency. A majority of these
projects are outlined in Olinger's chapter (this volume). TVA oversaw a
number of large-scale excavations in the 1970s and 80s and supported
the academic community through the publication of numerous volumes
related to these projects. More than 40 research volumes were published
during this time.

In 1983 TVA initiated an experimental archaeological site stabilization program in partnership with the University of Mississippi (Thorne
1983; Fay 1986). The experimental program, titled "Preservation Is a
Use," examined various forms of shoreline stabilization and their potential effects to the sensitive archaeological deposits being exposed along
the banks. Several techniques were applied and monitored over a period
of several years. In addition to stabilization techniques, the project also
included experiments regarding archaeological warning signs and an
interpretative center/park created at a threatened site. Many of the stabilization techniques proved effective, as well as the posting of signs and
use of interpretive material. These efforts were somewhat innovative for
the time, given that most archaeologists were focusing their attention on
archaeological data recovery then site preservation. Those interested in
site protection were focusing attention on sites being damaged from vandalism, rather than those being affected by natural forces such as erosion.
However, the agency was beginning to see a shift away from extensive
excavation projects as a result of fewer large-scale federal undertakings,
and efforts shifted to protection of the remaining archaeological sites
under its management. The project generally proved successful. TVA con-

tinues to post signs at heavily visited sites to warn visitors of the legal ramifications for illegal excavation.

Though large-scale projects have been reduced since the 1980s, the agency continues to be involved in a number of activities that affect archaeological resources. TVA maintains a core staff of five archaeologists, a historian, and an archaeological technician. This staff reviews a number of different federal projects each year, as well as a great volume of requests for permits. As required by Section 26a of the TVA Act (U.S. Congress 1933), every facility, structure, or other construction that may impede navigation, flood control, or public lands requires a permit from TVA. In addition to permitting, TVA reviews requests for use of TVA land, activities on TVA's nuclear, fossil, or power transmission properties, construction of power transmission lines, and economic development projects. Cultural resources staff review over 1,500 projects each year.

Current Archaeological Stewardship Efforts

As required under the implementing regulations for the NHPA, the Archaeological Resources Protection Act (ARPA), and the Native American Graves Protection and Repatriation Act (NAGPRA), TVA is responsible for all historic properties within its domain and those affected by its actions. Historic properties are defined as any prehistoric or historic district, site, building, structure, or object included in or eligible for inclusion in the National Register of Historic Places.

Within this domain TVA manages more than 293,000 acres of land above pool level, 600,000 acres of inundated land, and nearly 11,000 miles of shoreline in the Tennessee Valley. TVA has records of approximately 11,000 archaeological sites and other historic properties within the Tennessee Valley with an average of 2,800 acres being surveyed each year.

The Tennessee Valley boasts some of the most significant archaeological sites in the Southeast. Archaeological research conducted during prereservoir surveys greatly influenced the understanding of cultural history in this region. While many sites, such as the Jonathan Creek site (see Schroeder, this volume) and Hiwassee Island (see Sullivan, this volume) have been extensively excavated, many significant archaeological deposits from these and other sites remain and are monitored and managed through TVA's cultural resources program.

As with many federal agencies that cover a large area, TVA, with limited cultural resources staff, faces a number of different challenges to its archaeological resources. Among the most damaging are erosion, which is caused by reservoir level fluctuation and heavy boat traffic, and the illegal excavation of archaeological sites, a process referred to as "looting" by professional archaeologists. The effects of erosion and looting go hand in hand in that one typically intensifies the other. Where extensive erosion occurs along the shoreline of an archaeological site, significant deposits, artifacts, and often burials are exposed, increasing the potential for looting to occur.

Where looters have significantly removed portions of a shoreline bank, erosion is likely to increase because soils are broken up and exposed. Looting will often undercut the bank and affect the stability of vegetation. Once vegetation is removed or depleted, soil erosion occurs at a rapid rate. Types of looting that occur on TVA lands include surface collection along the shoreline and bank gouging, as well as above pool excavation of sites.

Illegal excavation is one of the most significant causes of destruction of archaeological sites in the United States. The value of artifacts on the black market continues to grow as resources become scarce. Price guides used by collectors indicate that complete projectile points can sell from between one and 18,000 dollars (Overstreet 2005). With the popularity of online auctions, the illegal trade of artifacts has only expanded (Chippendale and Gill 2001). A search for arrowheads on eBay produced as many as 2,000 items. The fact that one is unable to determine the authenticity of these items does not appear to have affected the market for this venue. Trade of antiquities also thrives in low-tech venues such as antique stores and flea markets as well as on the black market. The increasing value of these resources only intensifies the problem of the criminal activity involved in their acquisition. The blame lies not only with the looters, but with the dealers and the investors as well.

One of the most effective strategies for curbing erosion and illegal looting is site stabilization of the affected shoreline banks. In the late 1990s, TVA renewed its commitment to archaeological site protection and now designates a specific dollar amount to stabilization each year. TVA's primary method for stabilization is through the placement of hard armor riprap over filter fabric. The rock is placed on the bank by barge, and no bank shaping is conducted in order to protect all remaining portions of the site. Since 1998 TVA protected approximately 120 archaeological sites, including more than 17 miles of shoreline. Most of these sites are situated within a shoreline setting and were being adversely effected by both erosion and looting. The agency will evaluate more than 1,000 sites over the next several years in terms of their eligibility status and the severity in which they are being threatened. This procedure has also been used in emergency situations to stabilize prehistoric burials that have been exposed through erosion and extensively affected by looting activities.

In addition to its stabilization efforts, TVA maintains a federally trained police force with jurisdiction over all TVA facilities, nuclear plants, fossil plants, and dam reservations. These officers are given ARPA training and have apprehended many looters in the valley. In 2006 TVA Cultural Resources staff hired two investigative officers who devote 100 percent of their time to ARPA investigations. These officers have participated in undercover operations and surveillance in order to catch illegal looters in the act. TVA management has committed several hundred thousand dollars toward this program, and it is anticipated that this will be an effective strategy to reduce illegal excavation on TVA-managed lands. This program is in its initial stages; however, it has already resulted in two convictions and has a number of cases pending that are expected to go forward through the criminal court system.

Toward Better Compliance: Innovative Stewardship versus Forced Compliance

Although TVA's stabilization and police efforts have been strong, it has become increasingly obvious to many in the archaeological community that a greater effort must be exerted to share archaeological data with the public (Little 2002; Knudson 2000; Pokotylo and Mason 2000; Smardz and Smith 2000; Fagan 1993).

Very little archaeological research is published in a format for public consumption. It is imperative that archaeologists use more popular media to reach the public audience. The laws protecting archaeological resources guide a majority of archaeological research being conducted in the United States. These laws are founded on the premise that archaeological preservation is in the public interest. Therefore archaeologists in academic, government, and private business settings are charged with the responsibility of sharing archaeology with the public. In the last several decades, there have been many archaeologists who have encouraged, supported, and preached the growing importance of public education (Little 2002; Knudson 2000; Pokotylo and Mason 2000; Smardz and Smith 2000; Fagan 1993).

Those familiar with governmental archaeology programs understand how easy it is to get caught up in regulation responsibilities and to forget what it means to be an archaeologist. Compliance responsibilities can be overwhelming, and all the paperwork that ensues can be draining. Government archaeologists are often criticized by our academic colleagues for abandoning *true* archaeology.

But all archaeologists must also ask themselves whether or not they are making a difference in the preservation of these resources. Sites are being lost on a daily basis through vandalism, at a rate much faster than sites are being excavated scientifically. A significant amount of archaeological research conducted in the United States is related either to some federal undertaking or to resources maintained by the federal government. Archaeologists from academic and nonacademic and professional and nonprofessional communities must work together to preserve these resources. It is important to appreciate the diverse interests in these resources and draw from the strengths of each of these groups.

What must be understood is that compliance is stewardship and stewardship is compliance. Compliance laws were designed to promote stewardship, and our efforts should be in developing ways to improve our process of compliance so that it serves the interest of stewardship of archaeological resources—which is our ultimate responsibility. As a step toward better stewardship, the TVA cultural resources staff developed a plan to increase public awareness of the importance of archaeological resources within the Tennessee Valley. The idea behind this project is that TVA can rely on those who use TVA-managed lands on a daily basis to help protect cultural resources. As a steward of public land, TVA is influenced by public opinion. For example, in TVA's recent Reservoir Operations Study (TVA 2004), community respondents ranked resource protection and recreation higher than power production in their preference for where management priorities should lie.

TVA initiated these efforts through a program that was generated as a result of the events on 11 September 2001. This program, called LakeWatch, is a partnership of citizens, business owners, boaters, and reservoir users who work in cooperation with TVA police and watershed teams and other law enforcement agencies (TVA 2006a). The goal of LakeWatch is to reduce criminal activity on TVA reservoirs. The program has since increased to include boating safety, water quality, and illegal archaeological looting on TVA-managed land.

Inspired by the LakeWatch mission and the idea of having the public be the eyes and ears on the water, cultural resources staff named its site stewardship program "A Thousand Eyes." A Thousand Eyes is built on the premise that preservation is in the public interest. Archaeological resources on public lands are the property of the United States government and therefore belong to the people. Our mission is to promote stewardship through public awareness and interaction. By working together with the community and sharing our wealth of knowledge, the program can increase the public's appreciation for our nation's heritage.

TVA's public outreach efforts include presenting material to groups that have an interest on TVA reservations or undertakings. By coordinating stewardship efforts with projects, TVA is beginning to improve their compliance process. Current TVA projects are evaluated for the potential to include programs to increase public awareness. Other activities include presentations to local historical groups, scouting events, as well as environmental conservation efforts with high school groups within the Valley. Through increased public involvement, TVA archaeologists can share what they know and appreciate about archaeological resources and encourage this interest in others. To this end, TVA cultural resources staff completed a Web site in 2003 (TVA 2007). This site links off the official TVA Web page and has useful information about TVA archaeology, history, historic structures, and the responsibilities of the cultural resources staff.

The Future of Archaeological Stewardship at TVA

The future of TVA will likely be as unique as its past. Lack of federal funding make its stewardship efforts dependent on its management and board decisions concerning environmental stewardship. Current practices mandate environmental stewardship as one of the fundamental goals of the agency.

Most recently the agency was the subject of much controversy surrounding its decision to sell public land for private residential development, which caused the public to question TVA's land stewardship and resource protection policy. In 2006, when TVA's governance structure changed from a three-member full-time board of directors to a nine-member part-time board, special task committees were formed. One group, the Community Relations Committee, listened to public concerns regarding the agency's current land managing policies and initiated a moratorium on disposals and other transactions involving public lands managed by TVA while policy and public land interests were evaluated through an intensive examination process. In November 2006, the TVA Board of Directors voted 8–1 to establish a land policy guiding management of federal land under the stewardship of TVA. This policy stated that the agency would no longer sell public land for residential development but would continue with the intended mission of economic development and recreation of the Tennessee Valley.

Archaeological stewardship at TVA has changed over the years as the agency has faced many challenges. With the addition of two ARPA officers and with the amount of archaeological site stabilization being conducted each year and the development of a site stewardship program, it is anticipated that TVA will see a decrease in the destruction of archaeological sites on TVA lands. With continued management support, these programs can have a significant impact on the protection and preservation of sites and ultimately the culture history of the Tennessee Valley.

References Cited

ARIZONA SITE STEWARD PROGRAM
2006   Arizona Site Steward Program. Electronic document, http://www. pr.state.az.us/partnerships/shpo/sitestew.html (accessed June 10, 2008).

CALIFORNIA ARCHAEOLOGICAL SITE STEWARDSHIP PROGRAM
2006   Help Protect the Past. Electronic document, http://www.cassp.org/ (accessed July 3, 2006).

FAGAN, BRIAN M.
1993   The Arrogant Archaeologist. *Archaeology* 46(6):14–16.

FAY, PATRICIA M.
1987   Archaeological Site Stabilization in the Tennessee River Valley Phase III. Tennessee Valley Authority Publications in Anthropology no. 49; Archaeological Papers of the Center for Archaeological Research no. 7, University of Mississippi, University, Mississippi.

JAMESON, J. H., JR. (EDITOR)
1997   *Presenting Archaeology to the Public: Digging for Truths.* AltaMira Press, Walnut Creek, CA.

KNUDSON, RUTHANN
2000   The Archaeological Public Trust in Context. In *Protecting the Past.* Edited by George S. Smith and John E. Ehrenhard. Electronic document, http://www.cr.nps.gov/seac/protecting/index.htm (accessed 3 July 2006).

LITTLE, BARBARA J.
2002   *Public Benefits of Archaeology.* University Press of Florida, Gainesville.

OVERSTREET, ROBERT M.
2005   *Overstreet Identification and Price Guide to Indian Arrowheads.* Gemstone Publishing, New York.

POKOTYLO, DAVID L., AND ANDREW R. MASON
2000   Public Attitudes towards Archaeological Resources and Their
        Management. In *Protecting the Past*. Edited by George S. Smith and
        John E. Ehrenhard. Electronic document, http://www.cr.nps.gov/
        seac/protecting/index.htm (accessed 3 July 2006).

SMARDZ, KAROLYN, AND SHELLY J. SMITH
2000   *The Archaeology Education Handbook: Sharing the Past with Kids*.
        AltaMira Press, Walnut Creek, California.

TENNESSEE VALLEY AUTHORITY
2004   Tennessee Valley Authority Reservoir Operations Study. Final
        Programmatic Environmental Impact Statement. Completed in co-
        operation with the U. S. Army Corps of Engineers and U.S. Fish and
        Wildlife Service.

2006a   Cultural Resources. Electronic document, http://www.tva.gov/river/
        landandshore/culturalresources/index.htm (accessed July 3, 2006).

2006b   Lake Watch Electronic Document, http://www.tva.gov/abouttva/
        tvap/lakewatch.htm (accessed July 3, 2006).

THORNE, ROBERT M.
1985   Preservation Is a Use: Archaeological Site Stabilization, an
        Experimental Program in the Tennessee River Valley. Tennessee
        Valley Authority Publications in Anthropology Number 40;
        Archaeological Papers of the Center for Archaeological Research
        Number 5, University of Mississippi, University, Mississippi.

U.S. CONGRESS
1933   Tennessee Valley Authority Act of 1933, as amended. 16 USC
        Section 831, 831c, 831d-831h-1, 831i-831ed.

UTAH SITE STEWARDSHIP PROGRAM
2006   Site Stewardship Program. Electronic Document, http://history.utah.
        gov/archaeology/public_archaeology/stewardshipproject.html (ac-
        cessed May 7, 2008).

Appendix
Archaeological Site Reports Conducted as a Result of TVA's Environmental Compliance and Stewardship

Scott C. Meeks

THIS APPENDIX INCLUDES REFERENCES for TVA-related projects on or adjacent to its 35 managed reservoirs. While not all-inclusive of TVA-related projects, it largely encompasses those site reports associated with TVA reservoir properties and the immediate watersheds. Other reports relating to the agency's transmission line operations, off-reservoir fossil plants, and other TVA-related projects not on or adjacent to the reservoir properties are not included in this appendix. It is estimated that this table includes approximately two-thirds of the documents housed in the TVA Cultural Resources Library.

Date	Title	Author(s)
1946	Hiwassee Island: An Archaeological Account of four Tennessee Indian Peoples	Thomas M. N. Lewis and Madeline Kneberg
1971	An Archaeological Survey of the Proposed Normandy Reservoir Interim Report	Charles Faulkner
1971	An Early History of the Bear Creek Watershed Area of Northwest Alabama, With Emphasis on the Overton Farm	James Norwood
1971	Archaeological Investigations in the Bear Creek Watershed	Jerry J. Nielsen

Date	Title	Author(s)
1971	An Archaeological Survey of the Proposed Yellow Creek Port and Harbor and Associated Railway Spur and Industrial Parks	Richard Marshall
1971	Archaeological Survey of Proposed Yellow Creek Port and Harbor and Associated Railway Spur and Industrial Parks	Richard Marshall
1972	Intensive Survey of the Bear Creek Watershed	Carey B. Oakley
1972	Archaeological Survey of Poor Valley Reservoir in Proposed Walters State Park	Charles Faulkner
1972	Archaeology Impact-Rieves Bend Site, Maury County, Tennessee	David R. Evans
1972	Preliminary Survey of the Widow's Creek Power Plant Area, AL	Frank Calabrese and Victor Hood
1972	Archaeological Reconnaissance and Test Excavations in the Clinch River Liquid Metal Fast Breeder Reactor Plant Site Area	Gerald Schroedl
1972	Archaeological Survey of Tims Ford Lake Shoreline	John C. Coverdale
1972	Archaeological Investigations in Portions of Tishomingo County, MS	Sheila Lewis and Barry Lewis
1973	An Appraisal of the Prehistoric Population Expansion and Settlement Patterns of the Bear Creek Watershed	Boyce N. Driskell
1973	Appraisal of the Prehistoric Population and Settlement Patterns of the Bear Creek Watershed	Boyce N. Driskell
1973	Introductory Report of the Normandy Reservoir Salvage Project: Environmental Setting, Typology, and Survey	Charles Faulkner and Major C. R. McCollough
1973	The Spring Creek Site, Perry County, Tennessee: Report of the 1972–1973 Excavations	Drexel A. Peterson
1973	Icehouse Bottom Site 40MR23	Jefferson Chapman
1973	Archaeological Survey of the Upper Elk River Basin	Kenneth D. Hasty
1973	Archaeological Survey of the Phipps Bend Plant Site on the Holston River near Surgoinsville, Hawkins County, Tennessee	Major C. R. McCollough
1973	Archaeological Survey of the Richland Creek Flood Study Area at Dayton, Rhea County, Tennessee	Major C. R. McCullough
1973	Archaeological Survey of the Duck River Area Downstream From the Normandy Dam	Robert Gordon

1973	Duck River Project: Normandy and Columbia Reservoirs Planning Report No. 65-100-1	Tennessee Valley Authority Cultural Resource Program
1973	Archaeological and Historical Survey of the Watts Bar Steam Plant Fly Ash Disposal Pond Extension	Walter J. Burnett and John C. Coverdale
1974	Reports in Anthropology #1: Summary Field Report: The Nowlin II Site, 40Cf35	Bennie C. Keel
1974	Remote Sensing of Archaeological Sites in the Tellico Reservoir/Tellico Blockhouse Historic Site Stabilization	Danny E. Olinger and Richard Polhemus
1974	Archaeological Investigations of the Satillo, Tennessee Generating Plant Site	Drexel A. Peterson
1974	University of Tennessee at Chattanooga Widows Creek Archaeological Project Interim Report	Frank Calabrese
1974	Historic Sites Reconnaissance in the CRBRP Area	Gerald Schroedl
1974	Test Excavations at Site 40RE129 in the Clinch River Breeder Reactor Area (CRBRP)	Gerald Schroedl
1974	Archaeological Survey of the Proposed Johnson Waterfowl Management Area 26 Acre Pond	James H. Polhemus
1974	Preliminary Report on the Archaeological Investigations at the Rose Island Site 40MR44	Jefferson Chapman
1974	Report on Old Bellefonte: Historical Site in Northern Alabama	Roger C. Nance and Beverly E. Bastian
1974	Tellico Blockhouse	Richard Polhemus
1974	Tellico Blockhouse Historic Site Stabilization	Richard Polhemus
1975	Reports in Anthropology, #2: Summary Field Report of the Wiser-Stephens 1 Site, 40CF81	Bennie C. Keel and R. P. Stephen Davis
1975	Archaeological Investigations in the Little Bear Creek Reservoir	Carey B. Oakley and Eugene M. Futato
1975	A Comprehensive Research Design for Archaeological Investigations in the Tellico Reservoir—1975 to 1980	Gerald Schroedl, Jefferson Chapman, and Richard Polhemus
1975	Rose Island Site	Jefferson Chapman
1975	Synthesis and Interpretation of the Hamilton Mortuary Patterns in East Tennessee	Patricia E. Cole
1975	Intensive Archaeological Reconnaissance South Chickamauga Creek Drainage Area Contract 37A, 44, 45, 47, 47A, 50A, and 54	Raymond Evans and Jane L. Brown
1975	Prehistoric Unionacean (Freshwater Mussel) Utilization at the Widows Creek Site (1JA305)	Robert E. Warren

Date	Title	Author(s)
1975	The Davis-Noe Site, 40RE137, Oliver Springs, Tennessee: Surface Collection Analysis	Victor Hood
1975	Archaeological Investigations of the Proposed Recreation Easement on Jonathan Creek Embayment East of Hwy 68 in Marshall County, Kentucky	William P. McHugh
1976	Final Report on the 1972–73 Archaeological Site Reconnaissance in the Proposed TVA Columbia Reservoir, Maury and Marshall Co's., Tennessee	D. Bruce Dickson
1976	Phase II Intensive Survey of Phipps Bend Generating Plant Site, Hawkins County, Tennessee	J. Bennett Graham and Lawrence S. Alexander
1976	Archaeological Excavations and Survey at the Proposed Yellow Creek Power Plant Tishomingo County, Mississippi	Betty Broyles
1976	Archaeological Mitigation of the Bear Creek Watershed Project, Northwest Alabama	Carey B. Oakley
1976	Interim Report Concerning the Intensive Survey and Testing of the Upper Bear Creek Reservoir	Carey B. Oakley
1976	Normandy Archaeological Project Report, Vol. 3	Charles Faulkner and Major C. R. McCullough
1976	Excavations at 40RH6 Watts Bar Area, Rhea County, Tennessee	Frank Calabrese
1976	Cultural Resource Reconnaissance of the Proposed Westmoreland Power Plant Located in the Tennessee River Valley of Northern Alabama	John W. Cottier and Randy L. Cottier
1976	Archaeological Survey of Coal Loading and Barge Terminal, Guntersville Reservoir, Marion County, Tennessee	James H. Polhemus
1976	Excavation of a Dallas Component Mound, Anderson County, Tennessee	Michael J. O'Brien
1976	Normandy Traditional Architecture and Material Folk Culture Patterns	Norbert F. Reidl, Donold B. Ball, and Anthony P. Cavender
1976	Archaeological Mitigation of the Phipps Bend Generating Plant Site, Hawkins County, Tennessee	OAR, University of Alabama
1976	Miscellaneous Papers and Reports on Yellow Creek	Robert Thorne et al.
1977	Phase II Intensive Survey and Testing of the Proposed Tenna-Tech Industrial Site in Rhea County, Tennessee	Douglas Prescott

1977	Cultural Resources Survey: Colewell Land Exchange, Nottely Lake, Union County, Georgia	Ernie Seckinger Jr.
1977	Bellefonte Site (1JA300)	Eugene Futato
1977	A Phase I Cultural Resources Reconnaissance of four Proposed Recreation Areas Adjacent to Upper Bear Creek Reservoir in Franklin, Marion and Winston Counties, AL	Lawrence S. Alexander and Bennett Graham
1977	Phase I Cultural Resource Reconnaissance of Four Proposed Recreation Areas Adjacent to Upper Bear Creek Reservoir in Franklin, Marion, and Winston Co's., Alabama	Lawrence S. Alexander and Bennett Graham
1977	An Archaeological Reconnaissance of the Potential TVA Reynolds Creek Pumped Storage Site, Reynolds and Big Brush Creeks Sequatchie, TN	Major C. R. McCollough
1977	Phase I Archaeological Survey of Rorex Creek Pumped Storage Site, Reynolds and Big Brush Creeks, Sequatchie County, Tennessee	Major C. R. McCullough
1977	Archaeological Investigations of the Tellico Blockhouse Site: Federal and Military Trade Complex	Richard Polhemus
1977	Intensive Archaeological Survey and Testing at the Proposed Yellow Creek Power Plant Site Tishomingo County, Mississippi	Robert Thorne, Betty Broyles, and Jay Johnson
1978	Archaeological Survey of Access Roads, Railroad, and Discharge Line Yellow Creek Generating Plant Site Tishomingo County, Mississippi	Betty Broyles
1978	Archaeological Survey of the Northeast Mississippi Demonstration Project Tishomingo County, Mississippi	Betty Broyles
1978	Archaeological Survey of TVA Experimental Village Tishomingo County, Mississippi	Betty Broyles
1978	Normandy Archaeological Project Report, Vol. 5	Charles Faulkner and Major C. R. McCullough
1978	Normandy Archaeological Project Report, Vol. 6	Charles Faulkner and Major C. R. McCullough
1978	Archaeological Reconnaissance of a 40 Acre Tract of Land in Muscle Shoals, Alabama	Charles M. Hubbert
1978	Report of a Survey for Prehistoric, Architectural, and Historic Resources in the Pickwick Reservation Near Counce, Tennessee	Charles McNutt
1978	Patrick Site: Tellico Reservoir	Gerald Schroedl
1978	Excavation of the Leuty and McDonald Site Mounds	Gerald Schroedl and M. Wright

Date	Title	Author(s)
1978	Bacon Farm Site and a Buried Site Reconnaissance	Jefferson Chapman
1978	Archaeological Testing of Sites 40SL8 and 40SL9 for the Proposed State Route 137 Over the Long Island of the Holston River	Neil D. Robinson
1978	Analysis of Surface Survey Data From the Normandy Reservoir	William D. Prescott
1979	American Indian Burials Excavated in the Tellico Reservoir Pool Area and an Estimate of the Burial Remains	Gerald Schroedl
1979	40SL29: Information Gained from a Shallow Disturbed Site in Upper East Tennessee	Harry M. Piper and Jacquelyn G. Piper
1979	Cultural Resources of the Tellico Project (Draft Report)	Interagency Archaeological Services–Atlanta
1979	1978 Archaeological Investigations at the Citico Site (40MR7)	Jefferson Chapman
1979	Howard and Calloway Island Sites	Jefferson Chapman
1979	A Summary Report of Probabilistic Sampling of Select Excavated Sites in Tellico Reservoir, 1979	Larry Kimball
1979	Phase I Cultural Resource Reconnaissance of the Mallard–Fox Creek Property for Industrial Development	Lawrence S. Alexander
1979	Phase I Cultural Reconnaissance of Selected Areas of Redstone Arsenal, Madison County, Alabama	Lawrence S. Alexander
1979	Archaeological Survey and Testing of the TVA Watts Bar Waste Heat Park, Brief Preliminary Report	Quentin R. Bass
1979	A Summary Report of Probabilistic "Non-Site" Sampling in Tellico Reservoir, 1979	R. P. Stephen Davis Jr.
1979	An Archaeological Reconnaissance and Assessment of the Proposed Longview Subdivision Relocation by TVA: Benton and Marshall County, KY	William O. Autry Jr.
1980	Historic Cherokee Faunal Remains from Citico (40MR7) Monroe County, Tennessee	Arthur Bogan
1980	Overview of Archaeological Sites in the Pickwick Basin, With Certain Observations on Site Locations and Suggestions for Management of the Resources	Charles M. Hubbert
1980	Archeological Survey of Proposed Ash Pond Area for John Sevier Steam Plant	James H. Polhemus and Richard Polhemus

1980	Cultural Resources Investigations at Redstone Arsenal Madison County, Alabama (Vol. 2)	Prentice M. Thomas, ed.
1980	Cultural Resources Investigations at Redstone Arsenal Madison County, Alabama (Vol. 3)	Prentice M. Thomas, ed.
1980	Cultural Resources Investigations at Redstone Arsenal Madison County, Alabama (Vol. I)	Prentice M. Thomas, ed.
1980	Archaeological Survey and Testing of the TVA Watts Bar Waste Heat Park, Final Report	Quentin R. Bass
1980	A Preliminary Report of Probabilistic and Nonprobabilistic Archaeological Sampling in Industrial Area II Tellico Reservoir, Tennessee	R. P. Stephen Davis Jr.
1980	Archaeological Survey of Lower Duck and Middle Cumberland Rivers in Middle Tennessee	Robert Jolley
1980	An Archaeological Survey of the Lower Duck and Middle Cumberland Rivers in Middle Tennessee	Robert Jolley
1980	Cedar Creek Above Pool Survey in Franklin County, Alabama	Robert Lafferty and Carlos Solis
1980	Lithic Analysis of Ten Features at Citico (40MR7)	Wayne D. Roberts
1981	Excavations at Tomotley, 1973–74, and the Tuskegee Area: Two Reports	Alfred K. Guthe and Marian Bistlion
1981	Archaeological Survey and Evaluation for the Shawnee 200 MW AFBC Plant, McCraken County, Kentucky	Brian M. Butler
1981	Reconnaissance and Testing Near 40MI70, Guntersville Lake, Marion County, Tennessee	Charles M. Hubbert
1981	Taking a Look at Poteete Creek: An Archaeologists' First Glance at the Appalachian Summit	Charles M. Hubbert
1981	John Sevier Steam Plant	Daniel Schaffer
1981	Designing and Testing a Model of Raw Material Variability for the Central Duck River Basin, TN	Daniel Amick
1981	Murphy Hill Site: The Structural Study of a Copena Mound and Comparative Review of the Copena Burial Complex	Gloria G. Cole
1981	Bacon Bend and Iddins Site: The Late Archaic Period in the Lower Tennessee River Valley	Jefferson Chapman

Date	Title	Author(s)
1981	Lithic Procurement and Utilization Trajectories: Archaeological Survey and Excavations, Yellow Creek Nuclear Power Plant Site Tishomingo County, Mississippi, Vol. II	Jodi Johnson
1981	A Cultural Resources Survey and Evaluation of the Tennessee Synfuels Associates Site, Oak Ridge Reservation Roane County, Tennessee	Major C. R. McCollough
1981	Icehouse Bottom Site 1977 Excavations	Patricia A. Cridlebaugh
1981	Phipps Bend Archaeological Project	Robert Lafferty
1981	Lithic Procurement and Utilization Trajectories: Archaeological Survey and Excavations, Yellow Creek Nuclear Power Plant Site Tishomingo County, Mississippi, Vol. I	Robert Thorne, Betty Broyles, and Jay Johnson
1981	Preliminary Case Report Columbia Dam and Reservoir, Columbia, Tennessee	Tennessee Valley Authority Cultural Resource Program
1981	Cultural Resource Reconnaissance of the Tennessee National Wildlife Refuge with Archaeology Survey of Selected Areas of Benton, Decatur, Henry, and Humphreys Co's., Tennessee	William O. Autry Jr. and Jane S. Hinshaw
1982	Management Summary of Cultural Resources Located within the Clinch River Breeder Reactor Project Area Roane County, Tennessee	Building Conservation Technology
1982	Normandy Archaeological Project Report, Vol. 7	Charles Faulkner and Major C. R. McCullough
1982	Normandy Archaeological Project Report, Vol. 8	Charles Faulkner and Major C. R. McCullough
1982	Cultural Resource Reconnaissance of the Dry Creek Marina, Tims Ford Lake	Charles M. Hubbert
1982	Buried Component Testing at the Clay Mine Site (40MU347)	Daniel Amick
1982	Interassemblage Raw Material Variability Among Middle and Late Archaic Sites in Southwestern Middle Tennessee	Daniel Amick
1982	The Tellico Archaeological Survey: A Management Summary (Draft)	Jefferson Chapman
1982	Aboriginal and Modern Freshwater Mussel Assemblages (*Petecypoda: Unionidae*) from the Chickamauga Reservoir, Tennessee	Paul Parmalee and Walter Klippel
1982	Archaeological Survey and Assessment of Aboriginal Settlement Within the Lower Tennessee River Valley, Vol. 1	R. P. Stephen Davis, Larry Kimball, and William W. Baden
1982	Archaeological Survey and Assessment of Aboriginal Settlement Within the Lower Tennessee River Valley, Vol. 2	R. P. Stephen Davis, Larry Kimball, and William W. Baden

1982	Archaeological Investigations in the Clinch River Breeder Reactor Project Area 1981–82	Robert Jolley
1982	Archaeological Testing of Historic Sites in the Proposed Columbia Reservoir Middle Tennessee	Robert Jolley
1982	Columbia River Abstracts	Walter Klippel
1982	Paleontology of Cheek Bend Cave: Phase II Report	Walter Klippel and Paul Parmalee
1983	Bibliography for the Tellico Archaeological Project: Compilation of Sources Pertaining to the Archaeology and Ethnography of Lower Little Tennessee River Valley	Brett H. Riggs and Jefferson Chapman
1983	Phase II Archaeological Testing of the Mallard–Fox Creek Property for Industrial Development, Morgan County, Alabama	Carlos Solis
1983	Archaeological Investigations in the Cedar Creek and Upper Bear Creek Reservoirs	Eugene Futato
1983	Archaeological Investigations at the Swan Bay Site (40HY66) Henry County, Tennessee	Guy G. Weaver and Mitchell R. Childress
1983	Historical Site Analysis: 1Mg32 and 1Mg118, Mallard–Fox Creek Industrial Locality Wheeler Reservoir, Morgan County, Alabama	Gary Mills
1983	Ervin: Mid-Holocene Shell Midden on the Duck River, Consideration of Significance and Research Orientation	Jack L. Hofman
1983	Archaeological Investigations at the 18th Century Overhill Cherokee Town of Mialoquo (40MR3) Draft	Kurt C. Russ and Jefferson Chapman
1983	Inventory of Archaeological Resources Around Kentucky Lake in Kentucky	Kenneth Carstens, ed.
1983	A Prehistoric Aboriginal Freshwater Mussel Assemblage from the Duck River in Middle Tennessee	Paul Parmalee and Walter Klippel
1983	Field Investigations in Old Butler, Watauga Reservoir, Johnson County, TN	Richard Polhemus
1983	Archaeological Reconnaissance of TVA Property Scheduled for Development Adjacent to the Yellow Creek Port Facility Tishomingo Co, Mississippi	Robert Thorne
1983	Tomotley: An 18th-Century Cherokee Village	William W. Baden
1984	Columbia Project Lithic Analysis: Chert Resource Survey, Buried Holocene Terrace Site Testing, and Evaluation of Lithic Procurement	Daniel Amick
1984	Final Report on Archaeology Test Excavations at Cave Spring: Buried Eva Site Component on the Duck River . . . Middle Tennessee	Jack L. Hofman

Date	Title	Author(s)
1984	Native American History and Prehistory in the Lower Tennessee River Valley: The Results of the Tellico Archaeological Project	Jefferson Chapman
1984	Archaeological Investigations at the 18th Century Overhill Cherokee Town of Mialoquo	Kurt C. Russ and Jefferson Chapman
1984	Investigations in the Center of Hampton Place at Chattanooga	Major C. R. McCullough, Quentin R. Bass
1984	An Archaeological Reconnaissance and Evaluation of the Proposed Wastewater Treatment Plant Site, City of Cleveland, Tennessee and Supplementary Report	Robert A. Pace
1984	Underwater Archaeology and Historical Investigations at Johnsonville, Tennessee Civil War Shipwreck Site, Kentucky Reservoir	Tennessee Valley Authority Cultural Resources Program
1984	A Cultural Resources Survey of the Proposed Pellissippi Parkway Extension, Knox and Blount Counties, Tennessee	Wayne Roberts and Charles Faulkner
1985	Above-Pool Survey of Cultural Resources Within the Little Bear Creek Reservoir Area, Franklin County, Alabama	Charles McNutt and Guy G. Weaver
1985	Archaeological Contexts and Assemblages at Martin Farm	Gerald Schroedl, R. P. Stephen Davis, and Charles C. Boyd
1985	1977 Archaeological Survey: An Overall Assessment of the Archaeological Resources of Tellico Reservoir	Larry Kimball, ed.
1985	Carden Farm Archaeological Survey	Michael Morris
1985	A Probabilistic Sample Reconnaissance of TVA Lands Around Kentucky Lake. TVA Contract #TV62216A	R. Diess and Pamela A. Schenian
1985	Fort Southwest Point Archaeological Project: Interim Report	Samuel Smith
1986	Material Chronology at 40MU430: Stratified Rockshelter in Middle Tennessee	Charles L. Hall
1986	Archaeological Investigations in the Watauga Reservoir, Carter and Johnson Co's., Tennessee	Charles C. Boyd, ed.
1986	Survey Assessment of Extant Data Pertaining to Prehistoric Cultural Resources of the Chickamauga Reservoir	Donna C. Boyd
1986	Overhill Cherokee Archaeology at Chota-Tanassee	Gerald Schroedl, ed.
1986	Cultural Resource Surveys of Deaverstown Tract and Chapman Ford Road, Union County, Georgia	Jack T. Wynn
1986	Assessment of the Archaeological Resources of the Watts Bar Reservoir, East Tennessee	Ken P. Cannon

1986	Late Mississippian Village: Community and Society of the Mouse Creek Phase in SE Tennessee	Lynne P. Sullivan
1986	The Chickamauga Reservoir Area: The Two Souths	Michael J. McDonald, William B. Wheeler, and Sarah Weeks
1986	Tellico Duck Pond Archaeological Project: An Example in Cooperative Mitigation	Norman D. Jefferson
1987	Archaeological Inventory of TVA Lands in Nickajack Reservoir: Preliminary Summary	Boyce N. Driskell
1987	Middle and Late Woodland Settlements in Middle Duck River Drainage, Maury County, Tennessee	Charles H. Bentz
1987	Phase I Investigation of Archaeological Resources Within Kentucky Reservoir Tract #XGIR-13PT on the Sledd Embayment in Marshall County, Kentucky	Calvert McIlhaney
1987	Cultural Resource Investigations in the Guntersville Reservoir Area, Marshall and Jackson Counties, Alabama and Marion County, Tennessee	Carlos Solis and Eugene M. Futato
1987	Lithic Raw Material Variability in the Central Duck River Basin: Reflections of Middle and Late Archaic Organizational Strategies	Daniel Amick
1987	Archaeological Data Recovery Plan for Sites 1MA50 and 1MA141, Madison County, Alabama	James Knight
1987	Sample Inventory of the Widows Creek Collection	Laura A. Compton and Robin L. Smith
1987	Archaeological Survey of Portions of the Chickamauga Reservoir, Tennessee: Management Summary (Draft)	Marvin Smith
1987	Speleoarchaeological Reconnaissance of the Pickwick Basin in Colbert and Lauderdale Co's., Alabama	Richard Cobb
1987	Speleoarchaeological Reconnaissance of the Pickwick Basin in Colbert and Lauderdale Counties of Alabama	Richard Cobb
1988	Historical Archaeological Investigations in Cedar Creek Reservoir, Franklin County, Alabama	Beverly E. Bastian
1988	Unmodified Vertebrate Faunal Remains from Stratified Archaic Deposits at the Hayes Site, Middle Tennessee	Darcy Morey
1988	Ervin: Mid-Holocene Shell Midden on the Duck River in the Nashville Basin of Tennessee	Jack L. Hofman
1988	Archaeological Inventory of Selected TVA Lands Within the West Sandy Creek Dewatering Area, Henry County, Tennessee	John C. Phillips

Date	Title	Author(s)
1988	Archaeological Inventory of TVA Lands at Bear Creek and Upper Bear Creek Reservoirs	John C. Phillips
1988	Cultural Resources Surveys on the Brasstown Ranger District, FY 88, Towns and Union Co's., Georgia	Jack T. Wynn
1988	Archaeological Survey of Portions of the Chickamauga Reservoir, Tennessee 1987–1988	Marvin Smith
1988	Observations on the Geomorphology of Ten Cave/Rockshelter Localities in the Pickwick Basin of Colbert and Lauderdale Counties, Alabama, June 1988	Michael Collins
1988	Snodgrass Small Mound and Middle Tennessee Prehistory, Draft	Richard Krause
1988	Snodgrass Small Mound and Middle Tennessee Valley Prehistory	Richard Krause
1988	Reported Paleontological Sites Within the Wilson Dam Reservation in Colbert County, Alabama	Richard Cobb
1988	Reconnaissance Survey of Archaeological Resources Within the Proposed International Technology, Inc. Development Area in the Clinch River Industrial Park, Roane County, Tennessee	William B. Turner
1989	An Archaeological Reconnaissance at a Proposed Development Near Nickajack Dam, Marion County, Tennessee	Charles M. Hubbert
1989	Historical Investigations in the Pickwick Lake Region	David C. Weaver
1989	Archaeological Research at 40RE107, 40RE108, and 40RE124	Gerald Schroedl
1989	A Final Report on Phase I Archaeological Investigations at the CASP Site (40FR177) within the Proposed Location of the Center for Advance Space Propulsion, University of Tennessee Space Institute Research Park, Franklin County, Tennessee	James E. Myster
1989	Ross's Landing at Chattanooga: A Cultural Resource History of the Chattanooga Waterfront	R. Bruce Council
1989	Cultural Resource Survey of the Proposed Location of Weyerhaeuser Wood Chipping and Barge Loading Facility on the Tennessee River at River Mile 138.0R in Perry County, Tennessee	Richard D. Taylor, Robert C. Lightfoot, and Andrew Schenker

1989	Archaeological Survey of the Kimberly-Clark Industrial Location Project Loudon County, Tennessee (Phase II)	Richard Polhemus
1989	Archaeological Survey of the Kimberly-Clark Industrial Location Project, Loudon County, Tennessee (Phase I)	Richard Polhemus
1989	Toqua Site: Late Mississippian Dallas Town, Vols. I and II	Richard Polhemus
1990	Cultural Resources Investigations in the Nickajack Reservoir Area, Marion County, Tennessee	Boyce N. Driskell, Tim S. Mistovich, and Eugene M. Futato
1990	Cultural Resources Survey of the Proposed Donghae Wood Chipping Facility, Jackson County, Alabama	Carey B. Oakley
1990	Historical Investigations in the Wheeler Reservoir Region	David C. Weaver
1990	An Archaeological and Historical Overview of Portions of Matlock Bend, Loudon County, Tennessee	Glyn D. DuVall
1990	Cultural Resources Survey of a Portion of the Fulton Industrial Park	James R. Atkinson
1990	The Kimberly-Clark Site (40LD208) and Site 40LD207	Jefferson Chapman
1990	Cultural Resource Reconnaissance of the O'Neal Harbor Area in Florence, Alabama	John Hollis
1990	Archaeological Survey of the Council Fire Department Tract, Hamilton County, Tennessee and Catoosa County, Georgia	Mitchell R. Childress and Patrick H. Garrow
1990	Survey Report of Archaeological Resources in Portions of the Chickamauga Reservoir 1987, 1988, and 1989 Field Seasons	Marvin Smith
1990	Aboriginal Settlement Patterns in the Little Tennessee River Valley	R. P. Stephen Davis Jr.
1990	Phase II Archaeological Survey of the Carden Farm Site (40AN44), Anderson County, Tennessee	Richard Polhemus
1990	Human Skeletal Remains From the Vicinity of Nickajack Dam, Marion County, Tennessee	Stephen P. Langdon
1990	Cultural Resources Survey for the Proposed Chambers Creek Timber Sale	William H. Radisch et al.
1991	Preliminary Appraisal of Vertebrate Faunal Collections from the Widow's Creek Site, 1JA305, Jackson County, AL	Darcy Morey
1991	Archaeological Faunal Assemblage from Smith-Bottom Cave, Lauderdale County, Alabama	Lynn M. Snyder and Paul W. Parmalee

Date	Title	Author(s)
1991	Archaeological Reconnaissance of a Proposed Chipping and Barge Loading Facility at New Hope, Marion County, Tennessee	Lawrence S. Alexander
1991	Phase II Archaeological Testing of Sites 40MI94 and 40MI212, New Hope, Marion County, Tennessee	Lawrence S. Alexander
1991	Organization and Lithic Analysis: Prehistoric Hunter-Gatherer Occupation of the Hayes Site (40ML139)	Patti Carr
1991	Freshwater Mussels as Paleoenvironmental Indicators: Quantitative Approach to Assemblage Analysis	Robert E. Warren
1991	Phase I Reconnaissance Report: South Holston Dam and Osceola Island Development Area	Susan C. Andrews et al.
1992	Phase I Investigation of Archaeological Resources along the Bristol, Virginia Utilities Beaver Creek Interceptor Extension in Washington County, Virginia	Calvert McIlhany
1992	A Phase I Investigation of Archaeological Resources along the Bristol Virginia Utilities Beaver Creek Interceptor Extension in Washington County, Virginia	Calvert McIlhany
1992	Supplement to Phase II Testing of the Proposed South Holston Weir Recreation Area, Sullivan County, Tennessee	Danny E. Olinger
1992	A Cultural Resources Reconnaissance of Selected Tracts Owned by TVA in Jackson County	DuVall and Associates
1992	Preliminary Results of Phase II Testing of the Biedleman Site, Sullivan County, Tennessee	DuVall and Associates
1992	Archaeological Reconnaissance of Selected Areas of the Skyline Wildlife Management Area, Jackson County, Alabama	Elizabeth A. Ryba
1992	Paleoethnobotany of the Hayes and Ervin Sites: Pursuing the Beginnings of Plant Domestication and Food Production in Eastern North America	Gary Crites
1992	Archaeological Reconnaissance of Approximately 25 Acres of the Proposed Sandpiper Development, Roane County, Tennessee	Glyn D. DuVall
1992	Cultural Resources Survey of a Proposed Educational Building South of Hamilton, Marion County, Alabama	Jeffery M. Meyer
1992	Phase III Archaeological Investigations of the Sellers Site (31CY42), Chatuge Dam Infusion Weir, Clay County, North Carolina	Joel D. Gunn
1992	Rose Island Revisited: The Detection of Early Archaic Site Structure Using Grid Count Data	Larry Kimball

1992	Phase II Testing of the Biedleman Site (40SL69), Sullivan County, Tennessee	A. Merrill Dicks and Glyn DuVall
1992	Cultural Resource Investigation for the Rat Branch Boat Launch, Watauga Ranger District, Cherokee National Forest, Carter County, Tennessee	Norman D. Jefferson
1992	Phase II Archaeological Testing of Specific Site and Proposed Disturbance Areas Within Matlock Bend, Loudon County, Tennessee	Patricia Anderson and Glyn D. DuVall
1992	Phase I Investigations at the Watts Bar Dam and Lock, Meigs County, Tennessee	Patrick H. Garrow
1992	Analysis of the Debitage at the Hayes Site (40MU139): Examining Prehistoric Hunter-Gatherer Mobility	Patti Carr
1992	Phase I Investigations at the Chickamauga Dam , Hamilton County, Tennessee	Robert J. Fryman
1992	Cultural Resources Reconnaissance: Approximately 30 Acres located on Matlock Bend, Loudon County, Tennessee	Richard D. Taylor
1992	Archaeological Reconnaissance of the Toccoa River Regulation Dam Project. Fannin County, Georgia	Robert A. Pace and Glyn D. DuVall
1992	Archaeological Survey and Investigation of the Proposed Sink Mountain Recreation Area, Watauga Ranger District, Cherokee National Forest, Johnson City, Tennessee	Thomas Whyte
1992	Appendix Part I-III Management Summary of Archaeological Investigations in the Proposed Columbia Reservoir Area of Middle Tennessee (1978–1986)	Walter Klippel
1993	A Phase I Archaeological Reconnaissance Survey of a Proposed Lake Access Ramp, Kentucky Lake, Marshall County, Kentucky	A. Merrill Dicks
1993	Archaeological Investigation of Site 40PK388 Proposed Ocoee River 1996 Olympic Whitewater Venue Site, Polk County, Tennessee	A. Merrill Dicks
1993	Chickamauga Reservoir Archaeological Site Inventory: Results of Survey from 1987 to 1993, Volume I (DRAFT)	Daniel T. Elliott
1993	Chickamauga Reservoir Archaeological Site Inventory: Results of Survey from 1987 to 1993, Volume II (DRAFT)	Daniel T. Elliott
1993	A Cultural Resources Survey of Proposed Ground Surface Repair Locations at the Turkey Bay Off Highway Vehicle Recreational Area at LBL, Trigg County, KY, with Accompanying Cultural Resource Management Recommendations	Hugh Curry
1993	Archaeological Research at 31CY78, Clay County, North Carolina	Jane L. Brown and Anne F. Roger

Date	Title	Author(s)
1993	Phase I Archaeological Investigations of the Chatuge Woods Public Use Area, Towns County, Georgia	Joel D. Gunn
1993	Phase I Archaeological Investigations of the Brake Property and Shelin Site (31CY44), Clay County, North Carolina	Joel D. Gunn and Thomas G. Lilly
1993	Preliminary Survey of the Florence Wagon Works Site, Lauderdale County, Alabama	Joel H. Watkins
1993	Early Archaic Settlement and Technology Lessons from Tellico	Larry Kimball
1993	Phase I and II Archaeological Investigations Along State Route 30 Bridge and Approaches Over Tennessee River, Rhea and Meigs County, Tennessee	Mitchell R. Childress
1993	Preliminary Report State Route 30 Bridge, Tennessee River, Additional Archaeological Investigations on Hunter's Bend, Meigs County, Tennessee: Phase II Testings at 40MG7, and Survey of a Wetland Mitigation Area on McK	Mitchell R. Childress
1993	Phase I Cultural Resources Survey of Tract N-877, Wayah Ranger District, Nantahala National Forest, Swain County, North Carolina	Paul A. Webb, Thomas G. Lilly, and Kathy J. Wilson
1993	Archaeological Reconnaissance of the Blue Ridge Hydro Plant Upgrade, Fannin County, Georgia	Robert A. Pace
1993	Cultural Resources Assessment of the Tennessee Valley and Lauderdale Co's., Alabama	Scott Shaw
1994	Cultural Resources in the Pickwick Reservoir, Draft	Catherine C. Meyer
1994	A Phase I Investigation of Archaeological Resources for a Proposed Engineering Services Maintenance Base on the Boone Dam Reservation in Sullivan County, Tennessee	Calvert McIlhany
1994	A Phase I Reconnaissance Level Cultural Resource Survey of Borrow Area A within the South Holston Dam Reservation in Sullivan County, Tennessee	Calvert McIlhany
1994	Phase I Archaeological Survey of a 1.4 ha (3.1acre) TVA Lot in Grand Rivers. Livingston County, Kentucky	Charles Stout
1994	Phase I Archaeological Survey on the Pine Lake Shoreline, Henderson County, Tennessee	Gerald P. Smith
1994	Muscle Shoals Reservation Historical Overview, Colbert County, Alabama	Gene Ford

1994	Archaeological Phase I Pedestrian Survey of the Proposed Jackson County Water Authority Project, Jackson County, Alabama	Harry O. Holstein and Curtis E. Hill
1994	Phase I Archaeological Reconnaissance Survey for Cultural Resources in the Proposed State Route 32 Realignment Right-of-Way, Claiborne and Grainger Counties, Tennessee	Joanne M. Juchniewicz and Richard Alvey
1994	Cultural Resource Survey of a Proposed Borrow Pit Located in Marshall County, Alabama	Joel H. Watkins
1994	Data Recovery at the Ditto Landing Site, Madison County, Alabama	Joseph T. Betterman III
1994	Archaeological Survey Within the Hiwasee River Valley: US-64 in Murphy to East of North Carolina 141, Cherokee County, North Carolina	Lawrence E. Abbot
1994	A Phase I Archaeological Reconnaissance of the Chickamauga Lock Replacement Bank Modification Hamilton County, Tennessee	Lawrence S. Alexander
1994	Phase I Archaeological Reconnaissance of the East Ridge Flood Control Project on Spring Creek Hamilton County, Tennessee	Lawrence S. Alexander
1994	Red Fox Mound: an analysis of the pottery and stone	Orval E. Shinn
1994	Organization of North American Prehistoric Chipped Stone Tool Technologies	Patti Carr
1994	Archaeological Survey to Provide Additional Data for Management Purposes: Tellico Reservoir	Richard Polhemus
1994	Bushell Island and Mainland Village Archaeology Survey to Provide Additional Data for Management Purposes, Tellico Reservoir	Richard Polhemus
1994	A Phase I Reconnaissance Level Cultural Resources Survey of the Proposed Holston Electric Cooperative 161-kV Substation, Poor Valley Creek Embayment, Cherokee Reservoir, in Hawkins County, Tennessee	Richard Polhemus
1994	A Cultural Resources Assessment of the TVA's Muscle Shoals Reservation, Colbert and Lauderdale Counties, AL	Scott Shaw
1994	A Cultural Resources Survey of the Tennessee Valley Authority's Muscle Shoals Reservation, Colbert and Lauderdale Counties, Alabama	Scott Shaw
1994	Cultural Resources Evaluation of Previously Recorded Sites and Selected Tracts Owned by the Tennessee Valley Authority in Jackson Co, AL	Scott Shaw

Date	Title	Author(s)
1994	Phase I Archaeological Survey of the Proposed Southern Ionics Chemical Plant Tract, Calhoun, McMinn County, Tennessee	Susan R. Frankenberg and Wendy Goodman
1995	Final Report: Continued Archaeological Investigations at Dust Cave and Related Sites in Northwest Alabama	Boyce N. Driskell and Paul S. Goldberg
1995	Archaeological Phase I Survey of the Historic Boring Farmstead Tract, Washington County, Tennessee	Brett H. Riggs
1995	Archeological Reconnaissance of Appalachia Reservoir, Cherokee County, North Carolina	Brett H. Riggs et al.
1995	Aenon Creek Site (40MU493): Late Archaic, Middle Woodland, and Historic Settlement and Subsistence in the Middle Duck River Drainage of Tennessee	Charles H. Bentz, ed.
1995	Cultural Resources in the Pickwick Reservoir	Catherine C. Meyer
1995	Phase I Archaeological Survey of a .8 ha (1.8 acre) TVA Lot on Wildcat Creek in Calloway County, Kentucky	Charles Stout
1995	Phase I Archaeological Survey of a 5 Mile Long Proposed TVA Corridor Near Adamsville in McNairy County, Tennessee	Charles Stout
1995	Phase I Archaeological Survey of a 1.0 ha (2.5 acre) TVA Lot for the Proposed Public Dock on Buckhorn Bay in Marshall County, Kentucky	Charles Stout
1995	Phase I Archaeological Survey of Site 40SW47, Situated at the TVA Cumberland Steam Plant Stewart County, Tennessee	DuVall and Associates
1995	Archaeological Reconnaissance of Portions of the Hiwassee and Ocoee Rivers in Polk, Bradley, and McMinn Co's., Tennessee, 1985–1986	Joe Benthall
1995	Summary on the Status of Archeological Investigations Under the Columbia Archeological Project 1978–1986	Judith Patterson
1995	Phase II Testing at Site 1JA321, Jackson County, Alabama	Joel H. Watkins
1995	Archaeological Survey of a Portion of the Proposed Doublehead Resort and Lodge in Northwest Lawrence County, Alabama	John Hollis
1995	Archival Research, Preliminary Historic Structure Inventory and Limited Archaeology, Northside Waterfront Redevelopment Project Area, Knoxville, Tennessee	Lynn Patrick, Jeffrey L. Holland, and Patrick H. Garrow
1995	Archaeological Evaluation of Site 40CP60, Campbell County, Tennessee	Robert A. Pace

1995	A Cultural Resources Survey of the Proposed Camp Barber Expansion Project Located North of Fishers Hollow on Guntersville Reservoir, Marshall County, Alabama	Scott C. Meeks
1995	Report of Preliminary Archaeological Reconnaissance of the Ijams Nature Center Expansion, Knoxville, Tennessee	Susan R. Frankenberg, Nicholas P. Herrmann, and Todd M. Ahlman
1996	Removal Period Cherokee Household and Communities in Southwestern North Carolina (1835–1838)	Brett H. Riggs
1996	An Archaeological Survey of Hiwassee Reservoir, Cherokee County, North Carolina	Brett H. Riggs and Larry R. Kimball
1996	Archaeological Survey and Testing Along State Route 3 in Loudon County, Tennessee	Charles McNutt
1996	Vertebrate Resource Utilization at the Widows Creek Site (1JA305) Jackson County, Alabama	Darcy Morey
1996	Phase I Archaeological Survey of 250 Acres in Fanning Bend Of Tims Ford Reservoir, Franklin County, Tennessee	DuVall and Associates
1996	Phase I Archaeological Survey of 250 Acres in Fanning Bend of Tims Ford Reservoir, Franklin County, TN	DuVall and Associates
1996	An Evaluation of Previously Recorded and Inventoried Archaeological Sites on the Oak Ridge Reservation, Anderson and Roane Counties, Tennessee	Glyn D. DuVall
1996	Archaeological Evaluation of Approximately 250 Acres Within the Fina Tract, Jackson County, Alabama	Glyn D. DuVall
1996	Phase I Archaeological Overview of the Proposed Southern Natural Gas Company North Alabama Pipeline Project	Goodwin & Associates
1996	An Archaeological Survey of the Proposed TVA Boat Ramp Site, Swain County, North Carolina	Jane L. Brown and Anne F. Rogers
1996	Archaeological Survey of Kentucky Lake, Volumes 1–3	Jonathan P. Kerr
1996	A Phase I Archaeological Survey of a Ten Acre Tract and Adjacent Barrow Pit on the Carden Farm Industrial Park, on the Clinch River, in Clinton, Anderson County, Tennessee	Lawrence S. Alexander
1996	Report of a Phase I Archaeological Survey of a Ten Acre Tract and Adjacent Barrow Pit on the Carden Farm Industrial Park, on the Clinch River, in Clinton, Anderson County, Tennessee	Lawrence S. Alexander

Date	Title	Author(s)
1996	Report of a Phase I Archaeological Survey of an Eighteen Acre Tract on the Carden Farm Industrial Park, on the Clinch River, Melton Hill Reservoir at Clinton, Anderson County, Tennessee	Lawrence S. Alexander
1996	Archaeological Phase I Survey of the Historic Alison/Jennings Farmstead Tract, Sullivan County, Tennessee	M. Scott Shumate
1996	The Economic Influence of Towns on Individual Inhabitants at 40BT70, Louisville, Blount County, Tennessee	Melissa Wilson
1996	Phase I Archaeological Survey of the Proposed Centerville Industrial Park	Patricia Anderson and Glyn D. DuVall
1996	An Archaeological Survey of a Portion of the Proposed Jackson Bend Subdivision, Blount County, Tennessee	Robert A. Pace
1996	Technological Analysis of Modified Bone from the Widows Creek Site (1JA305), Alabama	Sean P. Coughlin
1996	A Cultural Resources Reconnaissance Survey and Records Search of Areas to be Impacted by Hedge Row Clearing and Road Improvements Within the Seven Mile Island Wildlife Management Area Lauderdale County, AL	Scott C. Meeks
1996	Management Summary Archaeological Testing of 1LU342 Lauderdale County, AL	Scott C. Meeks
1996	Phase I Cultural Resources Survey and Phase II Testing of the Cypress Creek Wastewater Plant Expansion Project, Lauderdale County, Alabama	Scott C. Meeks
1996	Cultural Resources in the Wheeler Reservoir (Draft)	Scott Shaw
1996	An Archaeological Reconnaissance Survey of Selected Tracts within Fontana Reservoir, Swain County, North Carolina	Scott Shumate, Patti Shumate, and Brett H. Riggs
1996	Management Summary of the Chickamauga Reservoir Shoreline Archaeological Survey: Summer 1996	William F. Stanyard
1997	Dust Cave Field School, 1997 Season, Project Information	Boyce N. Driskell
1997	Early History of the Bowman House: Results of Limited Archaeological Testing and Archival Research on Site 40LD232, Loudon County, Tennessee	Dean Owens, Susan R. Frankenberg, and Charles Faulkner
1997	Archaeological Survey of Approximately 59 Linear Miles of the Nottely Reservoir Shoreline Management Zone, Union County, GA	Jack W. Joseph and Natalie P. Adams

1997	A Preliminary Report on the Archaeology of a New Mississippian Cave Art Site in East Tennessee	Jan F. Simek et al.
1997	A Cultural Resources Survey for the Proposed Wheeler Dam–Columbia Transmission Line Loop to Dunn Right-of-Way, Lawrence County, Tennessee	John Hollis
1997	Phase I Archaeological Survey of Norris Lake, Anderson, Campbell, Claiborne, Grainger, and Union Counties, Tennessee Volume 1	Lynn M. Pietak and Jeffrey L. Holland
1997	Phase I Archaeological Survey of Norris Lake, Anderson, Campbell, Claiborne, Grainger, and Union Counties, Tennessee Volume 2: Appendices	Lynn M. Pietak and Jeffrey L. Holland
1997	Phase III Archaeological Data Recovery in the Proposed Northside Waterfront Redevelopment Project Area, Trench 1 in Area 2, and Trench 4 in Area 3, Knoxville, Knox County, Tennessee	Lance K. Greene
1997	Archaeological Investigations at Prehistoric Site 40HW69 Hawkins County, Tennessee	M. Scott Shumate, Brett H. Riggs, and Patti Evans-Shumate
1997	Archaeological Survey of Approximately 60 Linear Miles of the Chatuge Reservoir Shoreline Management Zone, Towns County, Georgia and Clay County, North Carolina	Natalie P. Adams
1997	Phase I Cultural Resource Survey of a 16.85 Acre Tract in the Carden Farm Industrial Park, Clinton, Tennessee	Palmetto Research Institute
1997	Phase II Archaeological Testing of Selected Areas of the USG Tract in Bridgeport, Jackson County, Alabama	Patricia Anderson, Deborah Keene, and W. Bozarth
1997	An Archaeological Survey of a Proposed Residential Development on Lyons Bend, Knox County, TN	Robert A. Pace
1997	Archaeological Test Excavations at Lithic Shoals (1LU342): A Multicomponent Site in the Seven Mile Island Wildlife Management Area, Lauderdale County, Alabama	Scott C. Meeks
1997	Management Summary/Research Design Archaeological Testing of Site 1LU356 Lauderdale County, Alabama	Scott C. Meeks
1997	Phase I Archaeological Survey of the Fall Creek Recreation Area, Hamblen County, TN	Todd M. Ahlman, Michael J. Elam, and Susan R. Frankenberg
1998	An Archaeological Reconnaissance of Leuty Island Cemetery, Rhea County, Tennessee	A. Eric Howard

Date	Title	Author(s)
1998	Prehistoric Utilization of Caves and Shelters in Alabama	Boyce N. Driskell
1998	Archaeological Survey of a Proposed Private Boat Ramp on Douglas Lake McGuire Creek Embayment Jefferson County, Tennessee	Danny E. Olinger
1998	Phase II Archaeological Investigation at 40RE415: The Center's Ferry Site	Dean Owens, Susan R. Frankenberg, and Michael Elam
1998	Phase I Archaeological Survey of Approximately 1300 Acres within Tims Ford Reservoir, Franklin and Moore Counties, TN (Draft)	Glyn D. DuVall
1998	Correspondence regarding Southern Natural Gas Company, North Alabama Pipeline Project, Response to Alabama Historical Commission Comments on AHC 98-1354, Phase II Archaeological Testing at Site 1MG74, Morgan County Alabama	Goodwin & Associates
1998	Geomorphological and Archaeological Investigations of the Tennessee River Crossing of the Amended Route of the Proposed Southern Natural Gas Company North Alabama Project	Goodwin & Associates
1998	A Cultural Resources Survey of a Proposed Industrial Development in Colbert County, AL	Greg S. Hendryx
1998	Limited Data Recovery at the Tapscott-Eason Site (1MG774): A 19th–20th Century Homestead in Morgan County AL	Greg S. Hendryx
1998	Archaeological Phase II Testing of the Tapscott-Eason Site (1Mg774), Morgan County, Alabama	Greg S. Hendryx
1998	An Archaeological Pedestrian Phase I Survey of the Proposed Connor's Island Industrial Park Project Marshall County, Alabama	Harry O. Holstein and Curtis E. Hill
1998	Archaeological Survey of 603 Acres Adjacent to Chatuge Reservoir	Jack W. Joseph and Natalie P. Adams
1998	An Archeological Survey of Proposed FY 1999 Timber Harvest and Cultural Resources Assessment of LBL, Lyon and Trigg Counties, KY and Stewart County, TN	James D. Merritt
1998	Phase I Archaeological Survey of South Holston Lake, Sullivan County, Tennessee, and Washington County, Virginia	Lynn M. Pietak and Jeffrey L. Holland
1998	Phase I Archaeological Survey of a Proposed 16 Acre Industrial Development on Moccasin Bend Chattanooga, Hamilton County, TN	Lawrence S. Alexander et al.

1998	A Phase I Cultural Resource Survey of the May Springs Public Access Area Grainger County, Tennessee	Palmetto Research Institute
1998	Archaeological Resources Survey at the Singleton Marineways, Blount County, TN	Robert A. Pace
1998	Archaeological Survey of a Proposed Development Area on Tooles Bend, Knox County, Tennessee	Robert A. Pace
1998	Phase I Archaeological Survey of Boone Lake, Sullivan and Washington Counties, Tennessee	Sullivan and Washington Counties, Tennessee
1998	Phase I Archaeological Survey of a 13.5-Acre Tract, Campbell County, Tennessee	Tasha Benyshek
1998	A Report on Phase II Archaeological Investigations of 40LD179, The Tipton/Dixon House Site, Loudon County, TN	Todd M. Ahlman
1998	Phase I Cultural Resource Survey of the Proposed Cherokee Memorial Park at Blythes Ferry, Meigs County, Tennessee (draft)	William F. Stanyard and Jeffrey L. Holland
1998	Phase I Cultural Resource Survey of the Proposed Cherokee Memorial Park at Blythes Ferry, Meigs County, Tennessee (Final Report)	William F. Stanyard and Jeffrey L. Holland
1998	Phase I Cultural Resource Survey of the Proposed Cherokee Memorial Park at Blythes Ferry, Meigs County, Tennessee	William F. Stanyard and Jeffrey L. Holland
1999	A Phase I Archaeological Survey of the South Chickamauga Creek Greenway Trail Hamilton County, Tennessee	Alexander Archaeological Consultants
1999	Phase I Archaeological Reconnaissance Survey for Cultural Resources of Three Shoreline Development Areas in the Pickwick Reservoir, Hardin County, Tennessee	Andrew P. Bradbury
1999	Phase I Cultural Resources Survey and Assessment of the Proposed Beechview Marina Near Clifton, Wayne County, Tennessee	Brian R. Collins and Guy G. Weaver
1999	Phase I Archaeological Survey of 11.4 Acres in Hawkins County, TN	Brian W. Thomas
1999	Phase I Archaeological Survey at the Southwind Development Adjacent to Kentucky Lake (Tennessee River), Decatur County, Tennessee (draft report)	C. Andrew Buchner
1999	An Archaeological Reconnaissance of Appalachia Reservoir, Cherokee County, North Carolina	Eugene Futato
1999	A Phase I Archaeological Survey of Approximately 11 Miles (17.7 KM) of Tennessee River Shoreline Loudon County, Tennessee	Glyn D. DuVall and Patricia Anderson

Date	Title	Author(s)
1999	A Cultural Resources Survey of the Proposed Cottonport Fish 'n Camp, Meigs County, Tennessee	Greg S. Hendryx
1999	An Intensive Above Pool Archaeological Survey within the Upper Bear and Big Bear Creek Reservoirs	Greg S. Hendryx
1999	Phase I Archaeological Resource Investigations at the Downtown Island Airport, Dickinson Island Knoxville, Tennessee	Joseph Charles
1999	Phase I Archeological Survey of Norris Lake, Anderson, Campbell, Claiborne, Grainger, and Union Counties, Tennessee Volume 1	Lynn M. Pietak, Raymond Ezell, and Jeffrey L. Holland
1999	Phase I Archeological Survey of Norris Lake, Anderson, Campbell, Claiborne, Grainger, and Union Counties, Tennessee Volume 2 (Appendices)	Lynn M. Pietak, Raymond Ezell, and Jeffrey L. Holland
1999	Phase I Archaeological Survey of Norris Lake, Anderson, Campbell, Claiborne, Grainger, and Union Counties, Tennessee	Lynn M. Pietak, Raymond Ezell, and Jeffrey L. Holland
1999	Archaeological Investigations Bridge No. 16 on SR 1309 over Cartoogechaye Creek Mason County, North Carolina	Lance K. Greene et al.
1999	Archaeological Survey of Tellico Industrial Park, Monroe County, TN	Larissa A. Thomas
1999	Archaeological Testing of 40LD116, Loudon County, TN	Larissa A. Thomas
1999	Cultural Resources Assessment: Bridge and Approaches on Savage Garden Road, Over Coal Creek, Log Mile 0.01, Anderson County, Tennessee	Lawrence S. Alexander
1999	A Cultural Resources Reconnaissance Survey of the Proposed Decatur Utilities Limestone County Sewer System, Limestone County, Alabama	Matthew D. Gage
1999	Historic Architectural Resources Survey Report Replace Bridge No. 16 on SR 1309 Over Cartoogechaye Creek Macon County, North Carolina Department of Transportation	Mattson, Alexander & Associates, Inc.
1999	Phase I Archaeological Survey for a 5-acre Tellico West Parcel, Monroe County, TN	Michael J. Wild
1999	Archaeological Survey of the Chatuge Reservoir Shoreline Management Zone and 603 acres of Public Lands, Towns County, Georgia and Clay County, North Carolina	Natalie P. Adams
1999	Phase I Archaeological Survey of the Tennessee Lone Mountain Shores Development, Claiborne County, TN	Patrick H. Garrow

1999	Phase II Archaeological Testing of the Grigsby Bottom Site 40LD132, Loudon County, Tennessee	Patrick H. Garrow
1999	Preliminary Report: Intensive Cultural Resources Survey Proposed Chestnut Ridge Landfill Expansion Site Anderson County, Tennessee	Robert S. Webb
1999	Phase II Archaeological Testing of Site 40HS290 in Humphreys County, Tennessee	Shane A. McCorkle and A. Merrill Dicks
1999	On the Potential of Archaeomagnetic Dating in the Midcontinent Region of North America: Toqua Site Results	Stacey. N. Lengyel, Jeffery. L. Eighmy, and Lynne P. Sullivan
1999	A Cultural Resources Survey of Two Areas Associated with the Yamaha Motor Corporation Research and Development Facility Bridgeport, Jackson County, Alabama	Scott C. Meeks
1999	Management Summary Archaeological Testing of Site 1Ja637 Jackson County, Alabama	Scott C. Meeks
1999	Phase I Survey for Archaeological Resources of a Fort Loudoun Lake Shoreline Area, Knox County, Tennessee	Spence C. Meyers
1999	A Report on Phase I Archaeological Survey of a 30-Acre Tract on the Tellico Reservoir Subject to TWRA Use	Todd M. Ahlman
1999	Intensive Phase I Archaeological Survey of 23.7 Acres Along Proposed Savannah Harbor at Southwest Point on Watts Bar Lake, Kingston, Roane County, TN	Todd M. Ahlman and Susan R. Frankenburg
1999	A Report on Phase III Archaeological Investigations at the Tipton Dixon House Site (40LD179), Loudon County, TN	Todd M. Ahlman, Susan R. Frankenburg, and Erin E. Pritchard
2000	Cultural Resource Survey of a 13-Acre Parcel, Chickamauga Reservation, Hamilton County, Tennessee	Brian W. Thomas
2000	Cultural Resources Survey of the Fred Haley Bankline Riprap Project, Hardin County, Tennessee	Gerald P. Smith
2000	Cultural Resources Survey of the Beechview Development, Wayne County, Tennessee	Gerald P. Smith and John W. Matthews
2000	A Phase I Archaeological Survey of Approximately 6 Acres for the Proposed Relocation of Vulcan's Parsons Quarry Entranceway, Decatur County, Tennessee (negative findings report)	Glyn D. DuVall
2000	Archaeological Evaluation of Directional Bore Locations on the Tennessee River (RM 333.3), Madison and Morgan Counties, Alabama	Glyn D. DuVall

Date	Title	Author(s)
2000	Phase I Archaeological Survey of Approximately 69 Miles of Shoreline, Tims Ford Reservoir, Franklin and Moore Counties, TN	Glyn D. DuVall
2000	A Cultural Resources Survey of a Proposed Approximate 6 Mile Water Line Extending from Cedar Creek Lake to Lake Elliott, Franklin County, Alabama	Joel H. Watkins, Jennifer L. Richardson, and Ellen Mussleman
2000	A Cultural Resources Survey of a Proposed Boat Dock at the Pride Station Boat Ramp, Colbert County, Alabama	Jennifer L Richardson and Joel H. Watkins
2000	Phase I Archaeological Survey of the Proposed Macedonia Industrial Park (Phase III); Roane, Tennessee	J. Scott Jones
2000	Archaeological Reconnaissance Survey and Limited Deep Testing of the Proposed Kingston Fossil Plant Rail Spur Corridor	Jay D. Franklin and Susan R. Frankenberg
2000	Gathering in the Late Paleoindian: Botanical Remains from Dust Cave, Alabama	Kandace Detwiler
2000	Assessment of the Research Potential of Wilson Dam Village Number 2, on the Muscle Shoals Reservation, Colbert County, Alabama	Larissa A. Thomas
2000	Archaeological Survey of a Section of Shoreline along Blue Creek, Humphreys County, Tennessee	Larry McKee
2000	A Phase I Archaeological Survey of a Proposed Water Intake, Pumping Station, and Irrigation Line on Petty Farms, Polk County, Tennessee (draft report)	Lawrence S. Alexander
2000	Cultural Resources Assessment: Bridge and Approaches Over Little Emory River, on Clacks Gap Road, Log Mile 3.80, Roane County, Tennessee	Lawrence S. Alexander and Emily J. Williams
2000	Report of an Intensive Phase I Testing of a 4.8 acre Tract in the Carden Farm Industrial Tract, Anderson County, Tennessee	Lawrence S. Alexander and Jennifer Azzarello
2000	Intensive Phase I Testing of a 4.8 Acre Tract in the Carden Farm Industrial Park, Anderson County, TN	Lawrence S. Alexander and Jennifer Azzarello
2000	Phase II Testing of Archaeological Site 40LD52 in Loudon County, Tennessee	Lawrence S. Alexander, Carl Kuttruff, and Victor Thompson
2000	Phase I Archaeological Survey of Selected Portions Below the 1007 Foot Contour of the Swann-Williams Farm in Douglas Reservoir, Jefferson County, Tennessee	Lee T. Gamble

2000	Archaeological Phase I Survey of the Below Pool Portion of the Proposed Lemmons Branch Boat Ramp, Swain County, North Carolina	M. Scott Shumate
2000	A Cultural Resources Reconnaissance Survey of Two Locations for the Proposed Expansion of the Elliott Branch Recreation Area, Franklin County, Alabama	Matthew D. Gage
2000	A Cultural Resources Reconnaissance Survey of a Proposed Wildlife Habitat Expansion near Fackler, Jackson County, Alabama	Matthew D. Gage
2000	Archaeological Survey of 505 Acres in Lower Watts Bar Management Unit, Watts Bar Reservoir, Meigs and Rhea Counties, Tennessee	Michael J. Wild
2000	Archaeological Survey of the High Erosion Potential Areas Along the Douglas Dam Tailwater on the French Broad River, Sevier and Knox Counties, Tennessee	Nicholas P. Herrmann
2000	Appendices for Archaeological Reconnaissance Survey of Tennessee Valley Authority Lands on the Melton Hill Reservoir	Nicholas P. Herrmann and Susan R. Frankenberg
2000	Archaeological Reconnaissance Survey of Tennessee Valley Authority Lands on the Melton Hill Reservoir	Nicholas P. Herrmann and Susan R. Frankenberg
2000	Archaeological Survey of 174.5 Acres of Pine Beetle Infested Timber Stands on Tellico and Watts Bar Reservoirs, Monroe, Loudon, Rhea and Roane Counties, Tennessee	Raymond Ezell
2000	Archaeological Survey of 245 Acres at Jackson Bend, Loudon County, Tennessee	Raymond Ezell
2000	Phase I Archaeological Survey of Two Alternate Ash Disposal Sites Near the TVA Johnsonville Fossil Plant, Humphreys County, Tennessee	Raymond Ezell
2000	Subsistence Strategies at Dust Cave: Changes from the Late Paleoindian through Middle Archaic Occupations	Renee B. Walker
2000	Archaeological Survey of the Fort Patrick Henry Reservoir, Sullivan County, Tennessee	Richard Polhemus
2000	Phase One Archaeological Survey Wild Pear Shores S/D Douglas Reservoir, Jefferson County, TN	Richard Polhemus
2000	Phase I Archaeological Survey of a Seven Acre Tract (XTFL13) on Ft. Loudon Lake, Blount County, Tennessee	Robert A. Pace
2000	Phase I Cultural Resources Survey and Subsurface Reconnaissance of the McFarland Park Golf Course Project, Florence, Alabama	Sarah Sherwood and Scott C. Meeks

Date	Title	Author(s)
2000	Cultural Resources in the Wheeler Reservoir	Scott Shaw
2000	Appendices for Archaeological Reconnaissance Survey of Tennessee Valley Authority Lands on the Tellico Reservoir	Susan R. Frankenberg and Nicholas P. Hermann
2000	Archaeological Reconnaissance Survey of Tennessee Valley Authority Lands on the Tellico Reservoir	Susan R. Frankenberg and Nicholas P. Herrmann
2000	Archaeological Reconnaissance Survey of Tennessee Valley Authority Lands on the Tellico Reservoir (site Distribution Maps)	Susan R. Frankenberg and Nicholas P. Herrmann
2000	Archaeological Reconnaissance Survey of Tennessee Valley Authority Lands on the Cherokee Reservoir	Susan R. Frankenberg, Nicholas P. Herrmann, and Todd M. Ahlman
2000	Archaeological Reconnaissance Survey of Tennessee Valley Authority Lands on the Watts Bar Reservoir	Todd M. Ahlman, Susan R. Frankenberg, and Nicholas P. Herrmann
2000	A Phase I Archaeological Survey of the Niles Ferry Tract, Monroe County, Tennessee	William F. Stanyard
2000	Archaeological Survey of the Tellico West Industrial Park, Monroe County, Tennessee	William F. Stanyard
2000	An Archaeological Survey of 45 Land Parcels at Tims Ford Reservoir, Franklin County, Tennessee	William L. Lawrence
2001	An Archaeological Survey of Sloan and Rivers Property's Proposed Access Road on Douglas Reservoir in Jefferson County, Tennessee (Draft)	Amy D. Hill and Craig Lee
2001	A Cultural Resources Survey of Approximately 15 Acres of the Rufe Miller Pine Beetle Salvage Tract, Union County, Tennessee	Amy D. Hill and Erin E. Pritchard
2001	Archaeological Survey of the Proposed Town of Spring Hill Raw Water Intake Structure at Duck River Mile 166L, Maury County, Tennessee	Don Merritt
2001	An Archaeological Reconnaissance of the Proposed Low Level Discharge Outlet Construction on Blue Ridge Dam, Fannin and Union Counties, Georgia	Danny E. Olinger and Erin E. Pritchard
2001	An Archaeological Reconnaissance of the Barge Coal Handling Facility, Tennessee River Mile 11, Marshall County, Kentucky	Don Merritt
2001	Archaeological Survey of the Proposed Town of Spring Hill Raw Water Intake Structure at Duck River Mile 166L, Maury County, Tennessee	Don Merritt
2001	Phase I Archaeological Survey for the Poteet Ferry Bridge and Flanary Bridge Projects, Lee County, Virginia	Dwayne W. Pickett

2001	Phase I Archaeological Survey of Proposed Sewer Line in Murphy, Cherokee County, North Carolina	George D. Price
2001	Cultural Resources Survey Santana Dredging Company Gravel Dump Site	Greenhouse Consultants
2001	Phase I Archaeological Survey of the Proposed Macedonia Industrial Park, Tracts 24, 39–42; Roane County, TN	J. Scott Jones
2001	Archaeological and Historical Investigations of Oates Cemetery, Pickwick Lake, Colbert County, Alabama	Jeffrey L. Holland and Michael J. Wild
2001	Archaeological Survey (Phase I) of the Proposed Kingsport Sheeter Plant, Sullivan County, Tennessee	Kathy Manning
2001	Phase I Cultural Resources Survey for the Hall Bend Tract, Tellico Reservation, Loudon County, Tennessee	Lynn M. Pietak George D. Price, Jeffrey L. Holland, and Joseph Tomberlin.
2001	Phase I Archaeological Survey of Campbell County Park in Northeastern Tennessee	Larissa A. Thomas and George D. Price
2001	Phase I Archaeological Survey of 34 Acres on the Yarberry Peninsula, Loudon County, Tennessee	Larissa A. Thomas, Ruth Nichols, and Jeffrey L. Holland
2001	Phase I Archaeological Survey of a Proposed Generator Plant on the TVA Johnsonville Steam Plant Reservation, Humphreys County, Tennessee	Larry McKee
2001	Phase I Archaeological Survey of the Pearcey Property on the Tennessee River in Decatur County, Tennessee	Larry McKee
2001	Technical Proposal to Conduct Phase I Cultural Resources Survey and Monitoring at Selected Exit Pathway Monitoring Well Installation Sites at Redstone Arsenal, Madison County, Alabama	Lawrence S. Alexander
2001	Phase I Archaeological Survey of the Harbor and Boat Docks at the Vineyard Cove Subdivision, River Mile 588.1, Loudon County, Tennessee	Lawrence S. Alexander
2001	Phase II Archaeological Testing of the Bamagas Pipeline Corridor at Site 1LA210 Lawrence County, Alabama	Lawrence S. Alexander
2001	Phase I Archaeological Survey of a 6.25 Acre Tract Adjacent to Mud Creek, Rhea County, Tennessee	Lawrence S. Alexander and Russell Campbell
2001	Phase I Archaeological Survey of a 13 Acre Tract Encompassing the Southlake Park and Campground, Knox County, Tennessee	Marc E. Wampler

Date	Title	Author(s)
2001	A Cultural Resources Reconnaissance Survey of Three Locations for the Proposed Expansion of Browns Ferry Nuclear Power Plant in Limestone Co., Alabama	Matthew D. Gage and Kimberly Rutherford
2001	A Cultural Resources Reconnaissance Survey of Three Locations for the Proposed Expansion of Browns Ferry Nuclear Power Plant in Limestone County, Alabama	Matthew D. Gage and Kimberly Rutherford
2001	Phase I Archaeological Survey of a 60-Acre Tract in Chota Wildlife Refuge, Located on the South Side of Tellico Reservoir, Monroe County, Tennessee	Michael J. Wild
2001	Archaeological Investigations in the Lower French Broad River Valley	Raymond Ezell
2001	Berries, Bones, and Blades: Reconstructing Late Paleoindian Subsistence Economy at Dust Cave, Alabama	Renee B. Walker et al.
2001	Phase II Testing of Ten Archaeological Sites and Five Rockshelters in the Proposed State Route 32 (U.S. route 25E) Right-of-way, from 0.8 km North of Indian Creek to 1.6 km North of the Powell River, Claiborne and Grainger Counties	Richard Alvey and Lance K. Greene
2001	A Phase I Cultural Resources Reconnaissance of a Proposed Land Easement from the Tennessee Valley Authority to the Alabama Department of Conservation and Natural Resources on the Wheeler National Wildlife Refuge, Limestone County, Alabama	Thomas M. Shelby
2001	Archaeological Survey and Deep Testing of the Proposed Kingston Fossil Plant Gas Pipeline	Todd M. Ahlman
2002	Archaeological Testing of Site 1JA186 of the Widows Creek Steam Plant, on the Tennessee River in Jackson County, Alabama	Aaron Deter-Wolfe
2002	Archaeological Testing of Site 40DR12 on the Tennessee River in Decatur County, Tennessee	Aaron Deter-Wolfe
2002	Dust Cave Field School, 2002 Season	Boyce N. Driskell
2002	Phase I Investigation of Two Proposed TVA Projects in Limestone and Colbert Counties, Alabama	Eric Watley
2002	Archaeological Survey Along the Flint Creek Portion of the Wheeler Reservoir, Morgan County, Alabama	George D. Price, William Duckworth, and Jeffrey L. Holland
2002	Cultural Resources Survey of the Hummingbird Lane Development, Hardin County, Tennessee	Gerald P. Smith

2002	Cultural Resources Survey of Proposed Industrial Park, Clay County, North Carolina	Grace F. Keith
2002	Cultural Resources Survey of Proposed Industrial Park, Towns County, Georgia and Clay County, North Carolina	Grace F. Keith
2002	Cultural Resources Survey and Archaeological Testing Clifton Marina Improvements Kentucky Lake, Wayne County, TN	Greenhouse Consultants
2002	Cultural Resources Survey and Archaeological Testing Tennessee River Shoreline Rip-Rap Hamburg Estates Community Outlot Kentucky Lake, Hardin County, Tennessee	Greenhouse Consultants
2002	Phase I Cultural Resources Survey of Four Tracts along Fort Loudoun Lake and the French Broad River in Knox County, Tennessee	James J. D'Angelo
2002	A Cultural Resources Survey of a Proposed Deed Modification Area Located on Lake Guntersville, Marshall County, Alabama	Joel H. Watkins
2002	Archaeological Testing at Sites 1Lu642 and 1Lu644 near Lexington, Lauderdale County, Alabama	Joel H. Watkins
2002	Cultural Resources Survey and Archaeological Testing Tennessee Shoreline Rip-Rap	John Matthews
2002	Phase II Investigations at Two Sites at the Downtown Island Airport, Knox County, Tennessee	Joseph Charles
2002	Phase II Archaeological Testing of a Proposed Shoreline Retaining Wall and River Access Ramp at Tennessee River Mile 511.4L Meigs County, Tennessee	Julie Coco, Max Schneider, and Lawrence S. Alexander
2002	Cultural Resources Survey for the Muscle Shoals Reservation, Lauderdale and Colbert Counties, Alabama, Volume I	Lynn M. Pietak, Aaron Deter-Wolfe, Ruth Nichols, Jim D'Angelo, and Kristin Wilson
2002	Phase I Archaeological Survey of a Proposed Private Boat Ramp on the Tennessee River at Peters Landing in Perry County, Tennessee	Larry McKee
2002	A Phase I Archaeological Survey of a Proposed Spring City Waste Water Pump Station at the Intersection of State Route 68 and New Lake Road in Rhea County, Tennessee	Lawrence S. Alexander and Jennifer Azzarello
2002	Phase II Testing of Sites 40HS4 and 40HS74 and an Intensive Phase I Survey of the Duck River Flood Plain in Conjunction with the Proposed State Route 13 Bridge over the Duck River, Log Mile 7.72, Humphreys County, Tennessee	Lawrence S. Alexander and Richard Walling

Date	Title	Author(s)
2002	A Phase I Archaeological Survey of the 21st Century Chattanooga Waterfront, Hamilton County, Tennessee	Lawrence S. Alexander, R. Bruce Council, and Harry Hays
2002	Phase I Archaeological Survey of Tennessee Valley Authority Property (C.A. 1500 Acres) Along Tims Ford Reservoir, Franklin County, Tennessee	Marc E. Wampler, Aaron Deter-Wolfe, and Larry McKee
2002	Archaeological Survey of a Section of the Paw Paw Creek Drainage in the Roane County Regional Business and Technology Park, Roane County, Tennessee	Matthew Spice and Robert A. Pace
2002	Archaeological Survey of Portions of Melrose Landing Development (Tract No. XCR-188) Rhea County, Tennessee	Matthew Spice, Robert A. Pace, and Wendy Tanner
2002	Archaeological Survey of an Approximately 6-acre Tract, as Part of a Project to Install Ammonia Removal Equipment at Colbert Fossil Plant in Colbert County, Alabama	Michael J. Wild and Jeffrey L. Holland
2002	Phase I Cultural Resources Survey— Short Report of a Proposed TDOT Project in Chattanooga, Tennessee	Phillip Hodge
2002	A Cultural Resource Survey of the Proposed Grant Low-Pressure Sewer System in Marshall County, Alabama	Rebecca K. Turley
2002	Phase I Survey for Archaeological Resources of River Islands Plantation Subdivision in Knox County, Tennessee	Richard Alvey
2002	Archaeological Survey of a 7.5 Acre Tract (Portions of Parcels 17 and 18) Roane County Regional Business and Technology Park Roane County, Tennessee	Robert A. Pace
2002	Archaeological Resources Survey for the Proposed Loudon Utilities Wastewater Treatment Plant Expansion, Loudon County, Tennessee	Thomas G. Whitley
2002	Phase I Archaeological Survey Report for the Sunset Bay Development Eastern Access Road Project in Union County, Tennessee	Thomas Grooms
2002	Phase I Cultural Resource Survey Report for the Sunset Bay Development in Union County, Tennessee	Thomas Grooms
2002	Archaeological Identification Survey of the Ocoee No. 1 (Parksville) Reservoir, Polk County, Tennessee	Todd M. Ahlman
2002	Archaeological Identification Survey of the Ocoee No. 1 (Parksville) Reservoir, Polk County, Tennessee	Todd M. Ahlman

2002	Archaeological Survey of the Ocoee No. 1 Reservoir, Polk County, Tennessee	Todd M. Ahlman and Brad Duplantis
2002	Archaeological Survey of the Proposed Blue Ridge Dam Access Road, Fannin County, Georgia	Todd M. Alhman
2002	Phase I Archaeological Investigations on TVA Fee-Owned Land at Douglas Lake in Cocke, Hamblen, Jefferson, and Sevier Counties, Tennessee	William F. Stanyard and Jeffrey L. Holland
2003	Phase I Archaeological Survey of the Current and Proposed Chester Frost Park Low Pressure Sewer System, Hamilton County, Tennessee	Alexander Archaeological Consultants
2003	Underwater Archaeological Survey and Diver Inspection Chattanooga Waterfront Chattanooga, Tennessee	Andrew D. W. Lydecker
2003	Phase I Archaeological Survey of Lot 59, Tennessee River Mile 190.3, Kentucky Lake, Hardin County, Tennessee (Pittsburgh Landing Quadrangle, Tenn.)	David H. Dye
2003	Archaeological Survey Along the Flint River and Paint Rock River Portions of the Wheeler Reservoir, Morgan and Madison Counties, Alabama	George D. Price
2003	Additional Archaeological Investigations of Trenches on Wright Bluff in Knox County, Tennessee	George D. Price
2003	Cultural Resources Survey, Archaeological Testing and Geomorphic/Geoarchaeological Field Assessment Forrest Crossing Real Estate Development Kentucky Lake, Decatur County, Tennessee	Greenhouse Consultants
2003	Phase I Archaeological Survey of Approximately 325 Acres (43.5 Linear Miles) of Shoreline Along Tellico Reservoir, Adjacent to Three Existing Subdivisions in Monroe and Loudon Counties, Tennessee	James J. D'Angelo
2003	Cultural Resource Survey of Approximately 150 Acres Proposed for a Borrow Pit And Other New Facilities At Colbert Fossil Plant in Colbert County, Alabama	James J. D'Angelo and Todd Cleveland
2003	Phase I Cultural Resources Survey for Proposed Campground and Walking Trail Along the Smoky Branch, on Tellico Reservoir, Monroe County, Tennessee	James J. D'Angelo, Michael D. Wild, and Ted Karpynec
2003	Final Archaeological Data Recovery Report for Bridgeport, Alabama	Jodi Johnson
2003	Phase III Archaeological Investigations at Sites 1JA638, 1JA639, and 1JA624: Bridgeport, Jackson County, Alabama	Jodi Johnson et al.

Date	Title	Author(s)
2003	Cultural Resource Survey of 150 Acres in the Tellico Reservation, Loudon County, Tennessee	Kristin Wilson, Ted Karpynec, and Jeffrey L. Holland
2003	Cultural Resource Survey of Approximately 350 Acres Proposed for Development as Part of the Rarity Pointe Subdivision and Golf Course, Loudon County, Tennessee	Kristin Wilson, Jeffrey L. Holland, and Ted Karpynec
2003	Ross's Landing Wharf Ramp Haer 21st Century Waterfront Chattanooga, TN	Karen L. Serio
2003	Archaeological Survey (Phase I) of a Proposed Retail Development and Wetland Mitigation Area, Midtown, Roane County, Tennessee	Kathy Manning
2003	Archaeological Survey (Phase I) of Proposed Home Building Locations and Borrow Areas off Cottonport Road, Rhea County, Tennessee	Kathy Manning
2003	A Phase I Cultural-Resource Survey For the Proposed Water-Treatment Plant Expansion Project in Jackson County, Alabama	Kenny Pearce and Adrienne Lucas
2003	Phase II Archaeological Testing of the 21st Century Chattanooga Waterfront Project Area South of Riverfront Parkway, Hamilton County, Tennessee	Kristofer M. Beadenkopf
2003	Phase I Archaeological Survey at Gold Point Marina, Chattanooga, Hamilton County, Tennessee	Lawrence S. Alexander
2003	Preliminary Report for the Phase I Archaeological Survey of the proposed Water Haven Development on South Chickamauga Creek	Lawrence S. Alexander
2003	Archaeological Survey, Testing and Monitoring of Seven Groundwater Testing Well Clusters on the Tennessee River Bank, Redstone Arsenal, Madison County, Alabama	Lawrence S. Alexander and Benjamin J. Hoksbergen
2003	Phase I Archaeological Survey of the 21st Century Chattanooga Waterfront Project Area South of the Riverfront Parkway, Hamilton County, Tennessee	Lawrence S. Alexander, R. Bruce Council, and Harry Hays
2003	Phase I Archaeological Survey of the 21st Century Chattanooga Waterfront Project Area North of Riverfront Parkway, Hamilton County, Tennessee	Lawrence S. Alexander, R. Bruce Council, and Harry Hays
2003	Phase I Archaeological Survey of the 21st Century Chattanooga Waterfront Project Area South of Riverfront Parkway, Hamilton County, Tennessee	Lawrence S. Alexander, R. Bruce Council, and Harry Hays

2003	A Phase I Archaeological Reconnaissance Survey of Nine Cabin Site Areas, Tract 156, at White Sulfur Springs on Pickwick Reservoir, Hardin County, Tennessee	Matthew D. Gage
2003	Phase I Survey for Archaeological Resources for Restroom Facilities along the Clinch River North of Norris, Anderson County, Tennessee	Michael G. Angst
2003	Cultural Resource Survey of an Approximately 120-acre Tract for Proposed Storage/Disposal Area Near Kingston Steam Plant in Roane County, Tennessee	Michael J. Wild et al.
2003	Cultural Resources Survey of 41-Acre Tract for Proposed Northshore Campground and Delineation of Vaught Cemetery, Jackson County, Alabama	Michael J. Wild, Ruth Nichols, and Jeffrey L. Holland
2003	Draft Report of Phase I Archaeological Survey for State Route 31 from Old State Route 1 (11W) to Adams Lake, Hawkins County, Tennessee	Paul Avery
2003	Report of Archaeological Monitoring Proposed Turbine Display, Fort Loudon Dam Reservation Loudon County, Tennessee	Paul Avery
2003	Archaeological Resources Survey and Testing of the Little Tennessee River—Cartoogechaye Creek Trunk Sewer Line, Macon County, North Carolina	Ramie Gougeon and Amanda Edge
2003	Mitigation Report for the Buddy Ferrell Bridge Spanning Big Bear Creek on Buddy Durham Road (Co. Road 4) Colbert County, Alabama	Stacey Griffin
2003	Phase I Cultural Resource Assessment Proposed Lindsey Harbor Subdivision Marshall County, Alabama	Terry L. Lolley
2003	Phase I Archaeological Survey and Mechanical Subsurface Reconnaissance of an Area to Be Impacted By Planned Runoff Control Modifications at the Kimberly-Clark Loudon Mill, Site 40LD364, Loudon County, Tennessee	Timothy Smith II and Sarah Sherwood
2003	Cultural Resources Survey of a Proposed Storage/Disposal and Borrow Area on the Clinch River Breeder Reactor Site in Roane County, Tennessee	William F. Stanyard
2003	Cultural Resource Survey of a Proposed Storage/ Disposal and Borrow Area on the Clinch River Breeder Reactor Site in Roane County, Tennessee	William F. Stanyard et al.
2004	21st Century Waterfront Chattanooga, TN: North Shore Cultural Resources Survey	Alexander and Associates

Date	Title	Author(s)
2004	Phase I Archaeological Survey of a Proposed Boat Ramp on Cash Canyon Road Hamilton County, TN	Alexander Archaeological Consultants
2004	Archaeological Resources Survey for the Proposed Campground on Beech Island at the Highway 33 Marina, Norris Reservoir, Union County, Tennessee	Bradley A. Creswell and Gail L. Guymon
2004	Archaeological Survey for the Proposed Edgewater Condominiums Fort Loudoun Reservoir, Knox County, Tennessee	Daniel Marcel and James Kocis
2004	A Report on Phase I Archaeological Survey for the Proposed Golf Course at The University of Tennessee–Knoxville Experiment Station, Knoxville, Tennessee	Daniel Marcel, Sarah Sherwood, and James Kocis
2004	Architectural Assessment for Edgewater Condominiums, Knoxville, Knox County, Tennessee	Gail L. Guymon
2004	Phase II Testing of 1CT523 For the Proposed Polishing Pond at TVA Colbert Steam Plant, Colbert County, Alabama	James J. D'Angelo
2004	Phase II Archaeological Testing of Disturbances Due to Construction of a River Access Ramp and Shoreline Retaining Wall on Site 40Mg210, Meigs County, Tennessee (DRAFT)	Julie Coco, Max Schneider, and Lawrence S. Alexander
2004	Archaeological Monitoring of the Randy Lind Property, Loudon County, Tennessee, TRM 586.1R	Kathy Manning
2004	Phase II Archaeological Evaluation of 40KN276 at the Proposed Edgewater Condominiums, Fort Loudon Reservoir, Knox County, Tennessee	Michael G. Angst and James Kocis
2004	A Cultural Resources Reconnaissance of the Franklin County Water Tank and Distribution Line in Franklin County, Alabama	Myron Estes, Gene Ford, and Matthew D. Gage
2004	Phase I Archaeological Survey of the Montgomery Development at Martin Landing on Kentucky Lake (Tennessee River), Decatur County, Tennessee	Pamamerican Consultants, Inc
2004	A Phase I Archaeological Survey of the Proposed Riverwalk Park Development (Management Area A: Uplands) Along Teaster Lane in Pigeon Forge, Sevier County, Tennessee	DuVall and Associates, Inc.
2004	Phase I Archaeological Survey at the Riverbreeze Estates Development Lots 62 and 63 Adjacent to Kentucky Lake (Tennessee River), Hardin County, Tennessee	Thomas Carty and C. Andrew Buchner

2004	Phase I Archaeological Survey of TVA Tract XRG 176 (1JA577) on the Guntersville Reservoir near Tennessee River Mile 410, Jackson County, Alabama	Todd M. Alhman
2004	Phase I Archaeological Survey and Site Assessment for the Wilson Dam Hydromodernization Project at Pickwick Lake in Colbert and Lauderdale Counties, Alabama	William F. Stanyard
2004	Phase I Cultural Resources Survey and Archaeological Inventory of the Proposed Ditto Landing Phase 2 Bank Stabilization Project, Madison County, Alabama	William P. Athens and David R. George
2005	Phase II Archaeological Testing of Archaeological Sites 1MA141, 1MA285, 1MA1141, and 1MA1142 on Redstone Arsenal Madison County, Alabama	Alexander Archaeological Consultants
2005	Phase II Archaeological Testing On Matlock Bend, Loudon County, Tennessee: Sites 40LD191, 40LD220, and 40LD221	Bernard Slaughter and Shane McCorkle
2005	An Archaeological Survey of Blue Ridge Reservoir, Fannin County, Georgia	Brett H. Riggs and Larry R. Kimball
2005	Phase I Archaeological Survey of the Knoxville Glove Factory Knox County, Tennessee	Christopher Koch
2005	A Report on Phase I Cultural Resources Survey of TVA Tract XTNR-117 on Norris Reservoir, Anderson County, Tennessee	Daniel Marcel and Gail Guymon
2005	Phase I Archaeological Survey of the Proposed Bridge Replacement of the Lamontville Road Bridge Over Agency Creek in Big Spring, Meigs County, Tennessee	Don Merritt
2005	Phase I Archaeological Survey of the Proposed Preston Park Subdivision Knox County, Tennessee	Glyn D. DuVall
2005	Phase I Arch. Survey of An Approx. 105-Acre Tract & 2.6 Miles of Shoreline For Proposed Scrubber Site & Barge Loading Factory for Kingston Steam Plant in Roane County, TN & Phase 1 Arch. Survey of 4-Acre Borrow Area at Bull Run Fossil Plant Anderson County	James J. D'Angelo
2005	A Cultural Resources Survey of the Shoreline Easement for a Residential Development on Goose Pond Island near Scottsboro in Jackson County, Alabama	Joel H. Watkins
2005	Phase I Archaeological Survey of a 50-Acre Project Area on Goose Pond Island, Jackson County, Alabama	Lawrence S. Alexander

Date	Title	Author(s)
2005	Phase I Cultural Resource Survey of the Proposed Chickamauga Dam Lock Replacement at Tennessee River Mile 472, Hamilton County, TN (Draft)	Mary Trudeau
2005	Archaeological Inventory of 30.9 Miles of Shoreline Along Wheeler, Guntersville, Fort Loudoun, and Norris Reservoirs in Alabama and Tennessee	Matthew D. Gage
2005	Cultural Resources Survey of +/- 632 Acres of Cedar Mountain for the Proposed Little Cedar Mountain Development in Marion County, Tennessee	Michael G. Angst
2005	Phase I Archaeological Survey for the Peninsula Subdivision, Campbell County, Tennessee	Michael G. Angst
2005	Phase II Archaeological Evaluation of Sites 40KN45 and 40KN113 for the Proposed Golf Course at the University of Tennessee, Knoxville Experiment Station, Knoxville, Tennessee	Michael G. Angst
2005	Phase I Archaeological Survey for the Emerald Bay RV Resort, Union County, Tennessee	Paul Matchen
2005	Archaeological Assessment of Proposed Dike Rehabilitations, Big Sandy Unit, Tennessee National Wildlife Refuge, Henry County, Tennessee	Richard S. Kanaski
2005	Archaeological Survey of Shoreline Along Koontz Creek Embayment of Douglas Reservoir, Jefferson County, Tennessee	Scott C. Meeks
2005	Archaeological Survey of Tennessee Valley Authority Shoreline Property Along Tims Ford Reservoir Franklin County, Tennessee	Scott C. Meeks
2005	Phase I Investigations of the Proposed Decatur Day Park Improvements, Limestone County, Alabama	Scott C. Meeks
2005	Seven Islands Farm Bank Stabilization Project	William Sharp

Contributors

Todd M. Ahlman is a faculty affiliate in the Department of Anthropology at the University of Montana and an associate archaeologist with Historical Research Associates, Inc. in Missoula, Montana.

Sarah A. Blankenship is a graduate student in the Department of Anthropology at the University of Tennessee, Knoxville.

Alan Cressler is with the United States Geological Survey in Atlanta, Georgia.

Boyce N. Driskell is director of the Archaeological Research Laboratory and research professor in the Department of Anthropology at the University of Tennessee, Knoxville.

Patricia Bernard Ezzell is the historian and Native American liaison with the Tennessee Valley Authority.

Charles H. Faulkner is professor emeritus and Distinguished Professor of Humanities in the Department of Anthropology at the University of Tennessee, Knoxville.

A. Eric Howard is an archaeologist with the Tennessee Valley Authority in Knoxville, Tennessee.

Scott C. Meeks is a doctoral candidate in the Department of Anthropology at the University of Tennessee, Knoxville.

Danny E. Olinger, now retired, was an archaeologist with the Tennessee Valley Authority in Knoxville, Tennessee.

Erin E. Pritchard is an archaeologist with the Tennessee Valley Authority in Knoxville, Tennessee.

GERALD F. SCHROEDL is professor of archaeology in the Department of Anthropology at the University of Tennessee, Knoxville.

SISSEL SCHROEDER is associate professor of anthropology at the University of Wisconsin, Madison.

SARAH C. SHERWOOD is associate director of the Archaeological Research Laboratory and research assistant professor in the Department of Anthropology at the University of Tennessee, Knoxville.

JAN F. SIMEK is Distinguished Professor of Science and professor of anthropology in the Department of Anthropology at the University of Tennessee, Knoxville.

LYNNE P. SULLIVAN is curator of the Frank H. McClung Museum and research associate professor in the Department of Anthropology at the University of Tennessee, Knoxville.

Index

TVA Archaeology was designed and typeset on a Macintosh computer system using InDesign software. The body text is set in 10/13 Sabon and display type is set in Verlag. This book was designed and typeset by Chad Pelton, and manufactured by Thomson-Shore, Inc.